HENRY MOWAT:

VOYAGE OF THE CANCEAUX

1764 – 1776

Andrew J. Wahll

HERITAGE BOOKS, INC.

HENRY MOWAT
VOYAGE OF THE CANCEAUX 1764–1776

Andrew J. Wahll

HERITAGE BOOKS
2019

HERITAGE BOOKS
AN IMPRINT OF HERITAGE BOOKS, INC.

Books, CDs, and more—Worldwide

For our listing of thousands of titles see our website
at
www.HeritageBooks.com

Published 2019 by
HERITAGE BOOKS, INC.
Publishing Division
5810 Ruatan Street
Berwyn Heights, Md. 20740

Heritage Books by the author:

Braddock Road Chronicles, 1755: From the Diaries and Records of Members of the Braddock Expedition and Others Arranged in a Day by Day Chronology

Henry Mowat: Voyage of the Canceaux *1764–1776*
Abridged Logs of H. M. Armed Ship Canceaux

Maxwell's Ranche, Territory of New Mexico

Sabino, Popham Colony (Maine) Reader: 1602–2003

Sea Raptors: Logs of Voyages of Private Armed Vessels, Comet *and* Chasseur, *Commanded by Tom Boyle, 1812–1815*

Westing: Personal Narratives of Life on the Rayado, New Mexico Frontier

International Standard Book Numbers
Paperbound: 978-0-7884-2349-9
Clothbound: 978-0-7884-9180-1

DEDICATION

This book is dedicated with love to Jonathan Andrew Kidd, first grandson born February 15th, 2003, wishing that it sparks his imagination and interest in "good old" American history.

ACKNOWLEDGEMENTS

The compiler would like to thank Grace S. Machemer of Port Clyde, Maine for allowing me to use her microfilm copy of the *Canceaux* logs from the Public Record Office in London. This complete microfilm copy was invaluable in presenting this narrative. Machemer used the microfilm extensively for the preparation of her educational and interesting article entitled "Headquartered at Piscataqua: Samuel Holland's Coastal and Inland Surveys, 1770-1774" published in Historical New Hampshire Vol. 57, Nos. 1 & 2 Spring/Summer 2002.

My transcribing task included making a compact disk (CD) of the Machemer PRO microfilm and while the log was displayed via one computer and monitor, the transcriber sitting at a keyboard typed the log entries into a computer word processing program and which was later printed for review and edit. Knowledge gained in reading the entries was invaluable in transcribing as the same terms, expressions and procedures were encountered over the 12 year record. With time the handwriting of the men keeping the log became familiar to the transcriber speeding up the process considerably. The transcription required the initial five months of my early retirement from National Geographic Maps of the National Geographic Society.

Leslie Wolfinger, Corinne Will and Deborah Riley of Heritage Books, Inc. helped with many aspects in the creation of this book.

Staff of Public Record Office were helpful in all regards and their help is gratefully acknowledged.

Library staff of Maine Historical Society in Portland, Maine were helpful responding to my questions concerning their research collection.

Staff of National Maritime Museum, Greenwich, England were helpful responding to my requests.

Sandra Chin, Permissions Department, W. W. Norton & Company, Inc. responded with the timely permission grant.

CONTENTS

List of Maps Following page 200

List of Illustrations Following page 200

PREFACE

In 1763 with the Treaty of Paris that ended the Seven Years' War (French and Indian War), France ceded to Britain all claim to Acadia, Canada, Cape Breton, and parts of Louisiana. To better utilized the commerce and trade of this new territory, Britain's Lord Commissioners of Trade and Plantations commissioned a great marine atlas of views and charts covering the east coast of North America from the St. Lawrence River southward and westward to the Mississippi River. The Armed Ship *Canceaux* of the Royal Navy was sent in 1764 to begin the coastal survey of the New England and St. Lawrence areas. In 1775 under the gathering storm clouds of the American Revolution, the *Canceaux* was detached from the work of the survey to undertake an expedition along the coast of the District of Maine to assert the authority of the crown using the might of the Royal Navy. The purpose of the expedition was the destruction of rebel coastal ports beginning with Cape Anne. Due to various reasons the expedition ended with the bombardment of the thriving port of Falmouth, District of Maine.

In the Falmouth incident, Lieutenant Henry Mowat was following the orders given him by his superior officer, Admiral Samuel Graves then stationed in Boston. In the intervening 227 years since the incident, Mowat has been cast by some as a villain for his actions as a member of the Royal Navy. He however was obeying the following orders of the Admiralty: "You are hereby required and directed to take the *Symmetry* and *Spitfire* under your Command together with his Majesty's Schooner *Halifax*, and proceed with them as soon as possible to Cape Anne Harbour, that town having fired in the month of August last upon his Majesty's sloop *Falcon*...". The "Voyage of the *Canceaux*" is the journal of proceedings of the ship on that eventful voyage.

The combined ships log is transcribed from the following sources: Public Record Office collection (PRO) ADM 52 1637, ADM 51 3800, ADM 52 1183-4, and ADM 51 4133.

The Public Records Office (PRO) describes the logs as follows: "CAPTAIN'S LOGS (1669-1852) The Captain's logs have been compiled from the master's logs; the Captain added whatever information he thought relevant, or was obliged to give by regulation. In practice this was mainly routine ship board information damage to stores, employment of the ships company, etc, but the logs provide a full picture of the daily routine of a naval vessel under sail".

"MASTER' LOGS (1672-1871) Master's logs record a ship's position, course and weather, and were kept for navigational purposes by the Sailing Master of the ship. They record detail of punishments carried out, employment of hands, and any discrepancies found when opening casks of food or drink so as to make subsequent claims against suppliers. Until the 1850s the Sailing Master was responsible for planning the layout of the log and made sketches and charts of land and harbours which were circulated as navigational aids".

From (PRO) ADM 34/214 we get the *Canceaux's* Ships' Pay Books. From lists therein entitled "Wages & Sea Victualling" we get names of officers and men aboard *Canceaux* as of the 1st of October 1775. From (PRO) ADM 36/9661 we get the Ships' Muster lists that record the presence of every person taken on board the *Canceaux* for the bombardment of Falmouth.

The captain or commander of the *Canceaux,* Henry Mowat, although holding a rank of lieutenant was experienced in seamanship and navigation having passed an exam to get to the rank above midshipman. With the authority of command he was responsible of the ships company and the ship. Without patronage, exemplary record, or good fortune in surviving combat that killed his superiors gaining a captaincy would be difficult and he would remain a lieutenant for a long while.

The sailing master of the *Canceaux* was Wm. Hogg. He was the highest ranking officer holding rank by and from warrant. He was in charge of sailing the ship, working sails, and going into battle his expertise was navigation and marine survey work as recorded in the ships logs and on charts having under him midshipmen and master mates as needed.

In a newspaper article series (Glimpses of the Past) published in the Saint Croix Courier, St. Stephen, NB (January 11, 1894) and authored by J. Vroom we read: "Henry Mowat was born in Scotland in 1734. He was son of Captain Patrick Mowat, of His Majesty's ship *Dolphin.* After an experience at sea of six years he was commissioned as lieutenant of the ship *Baltimore* in 1758.

The certificate of his "passing" by the admiralty records that "He produceth journals kept by himself in the *Chester & Ramilies* (as midshipman), and certificates from Captains Ogle and Hobbs of his Diligence, etc.; he can splice, knot, reef a sail, etc., and is qualified to do the duty of an able Seaman and Midshipman. In 1764, he was promoted to be a commander and served as such aboard the *Canceaux* for twelve years. At the time of the destruction of Falmouth he was forty-one years old. His next vessel the sloop *Albany*, was the flagship of the squadron at Penobscot. After a service of thirty years on our coast, he died of apoplexy (stroke), April 14, 1798, aged sixty-four, on board his ship; the *Assistance*, near Cape Henry. His remains were interred at Hampton, Virginia. He had three brothers in the navy, of whom two were killed in action on the *London*, off St. Domingo, and the other Alexander, died in command of the *Rattlesnake*, in the West Indies, in 1793. He left a son, John Alexander, who entered the Navy in 1804. Although little is known of Capt. Mowat's private character, several incidents concerning him which have been preserved show it in a favorable light. His kindness to many suffering families on the Penobscot is not forgotten; while the letter that accompanied the committal of his son to Mr. Bailey contains sentiments of affection, kindness, and respect, and as the biography of the latter suggests, is not the production of a brutal or ignorant man. In personal appearance Mowat was a little above middle sized, of good form, and with a fresh countenance. One who saw him soon after the siege says he wore a blue coat with lighter blue facings, and has his hair powdered. As a midshipman, a youth served for a while as a volunteer as he prepared for examination between 13 to 20 years of age. Without passing exams or patronage to back him up the midshipman could be in the "gunroom" or midshipman mess for a long time Henry Mowat along with everyone else faced the larger institution of patronage on which advancement was based on who you knew rather than on what you knew. Your patron for a price would support you efforts to get the post or promotion. This might be done for services or financial remuneration or political advantage for family favors. Mowat had the advantage of his father being the Navy. The step from lieutenant to captain was significant and patronage and good fortune were necessary. Lucky was the

lieutenant who found all his superiors killed or disabled in action. Lieutenant Mowat in command of a smaller ship such as the sloop of war *Canceaux* was known as master and commander or a lieutenant in command. Uniforms were new (1748) aboard naval ships and reserved for officers consisting of blue coats with long tails and wide buttoned cuffs, tricorn hat with gold edging and a blue cockade and white knee length trousers. Seniority was shown by the placement of gold coat buttons – three year seniority was shown by the twelve coat buttons arranged by twos on the lapels with a total of 24 buttons. The coat was blue, with blue facings, cuffs and collar. The waist, breeches and hose were white.
While the entire collection of the *Canceaux* logs is available in hand written form, it has been transcribed herewith, and repetitious entries have been abridged for the sake of brevity. These are marked with an asterisk with the period of the abridgement given. "Voyage of *Canceaux*" includes only documents that would be available to officers aboard the *Canceaux* and other English naval forces along the coast of North America. Spellings used are those actually found in the logs. In instances were there is a question as to content or legibility concerns a question mark (?) is shown. The complete collection of *Canceaux* logs in CD format is on file in the Library of Maine Historical Society, Portland, Maine.
The log entries that are included contain detail that is basic to the ship such as resupply, anchorages, movements of ships nearby, smuggling, ship routine including discipline, court martial, weaponry, significant weather events and activities of the surveyors. *Canceaux* a converted merchant vessel formerly named *William*, was taken into naval service for surveying in February 1764 at Quebec and returned to Deptfort, England for refitting. As a sloop of war *Canceaux* was a full rigged ship being smaller than the smallest frigate where speed and shallow draft enabled her to run from larger ships. A sloop of war was, usually armed on a single gun deck and carried anywhere from 14 to 20 six-pounders. The hull plan of the *Canceaux* shows it to be 81 feet long on the main deck and to be 23 feet wide. The plan indicates it had 16 guns on the gun deck. The records of Admiral Graves indicates (see list of ships) that it was armed with 8 guns with a crew of 45 men.

Lines of the *Canceaux* were taken off at Woolrich, England in February 1771.The smaller survey vessels working from *Canceaux* included: *Jupiter, Venus, Surveyor, Spinkes, Polly, Sultana, Diana,* and *Diligence*. The *Canceaux* was a supply vessel (or mother ship) that provided the needed supplies and also a work place where initial drafting and compilation of information from the survey parties was recorded. Each survey party using cutters, pinnaces, and shallops would be assigned a major bay with its river systems and off shore islands. The surveyors traversing the area worked up sketch maps from their initial survey work and then these were taken back into the field for verification and expansion.

For the final draft, a longitude and latitude grid with all inlets and other parts would be joined together. The logs shows survey boats worked from the first "ice-out" in spring to "freeze-up" in the fall. Aboard the *Canceaux* draughtsmen spent the winter drawing the manuscript compilations showing the surveyors bearings and field notes on the emerging charts. When the chart was drawn, a copy was given to a *Canceaux* boat to add soundings as well as location of ledges, wrecks, bottom aspects and currents.

To do the field survey work there were several deputies reporting to Holland: George Sproule, Thomas Wright, James Grant, Thomas Wheeler and Charles Blaskowitz. Each crew according to records of Mowat contained two chain bearers, one man to carry instruments and another two for station colors (this is a flag to mark the survey rods so it could be better seen through a sextant over the long distances off shore), one midshipman, four sailors to man the oars and a local guide. Aboard the *Canceaux* for the surveyors were two cooks (one for officer and one for the men), a medical orderly and guides with local knowledge of the coast.

The logs suggest that life aboard this British man of war were harsh. Some of the statistics from the *Canceaux* with an official crew size of 75 for the thirteen year voyage include the following:

Runaways: 25

Floggings: 37

Execution: 1

Accidental death: 5

The boatswain was responsible for carrying out the commands of the officers and with his hand-picked mates, his orders were carried out and at times discipline was insured with the dreaded cat o' nine tails otherwise known as a "colt" or "starter" which was a short length of rope knotted at the end.

The log does contain provision lists where we see that the men were well fed but without variety having frequent resupply from other larger ships and the shore establishment when accessible. Beer was consumed by the ships company in large amounts reflective mainly of the fact that it was suitable for shipboard storage. The logs suggest the use of leeks and limes as a source for vitamin C (ascorbic acid) to limit the effects of scurvy. The logs also document an outbreak of smallpox aboard the *Halifax* sloop, part of the bombardment flotilla in October 1775.

In 1764 the Armed Ship *Canceaux* began a voyage of 12 years, during which the officers and men performed survey work used in the creation of one of the most important and magnificent coastal marine atlases ever produced covering the northeast coast of North America including New England and Canada along the St. Lawrence River.

Men associated with the survey of the coast of New England are mentioned in the logs by name. Their monumental contribution was surveying 3,000 miles of New England coastline, estuaries, sea bottom, and islands and the preparation for data for atlas plates that were called the Atlantic Neptune. The logs of *Canceaux* include the following names of men contributing to the creation of the Atlantic Neptune:

Mr. Brown, Midshipman
Wm Wright
Lieut. Pringle
Mr. Waits, Midshipman
Commissioner Hanway, Lord Commissioners of Trade and Plant.
Wilm Mouldan
Peter Regiment
Joseph Frederick Wallet DesBarres
Captain Samuel Holland
Mr. Wm Hogg, Ensign
Captain Henry Mowat, Lieutenant

Frederick H Demand
Thomas Walfield
Mr. Sproul, Ensign
Mr. Gusutes
Mr. Chase
Mr. Scurrien
Capt. Harvard
Wm. Duncan Hodge
Mr. Blackowitz
Mr. Georges, Ensign
C. Siamin
Capt. John Knight
Mr. Grant
Mr. Wherterd
James Hingan
Frederick H. Bemand, deputy surveyor

As fate would have it, the *Canceaux* (along with four other vessels) under Admiralty orders carried out the bombardment and subsequent destruction of the thriving seaport of Falmouth, District of Maine that cost the colonies dearly in terms of shipping and commerce. The following record then is a description of that voyage based on the daily logs kept by the commander and the master of the *Canceaux*.

N.A.M. Rodger in his epic work entitled THE WOODEN WORLD An Anatomy of the Georgian Navy comments on many topics that in sum give a detailed description of life aboard the *Canceaux* from 1764 to 1776. The transcriber includes below parts of Rodger's book as they were comprehensive and insightful to me as I worked the logs of the *Cancaux*. Although written reflecting the period of Seven Years War 1755-1763 N.A.M Rodger observes: "I have drawn evidence from, and would apply my conclusions to, the whole period from about 1740 to 1773".

The Sea Service

Afloat:

The most junior commissioned officers were the lieutenants…and the smallest men-of-war of all, the hired cutters and tenders, has as their only sea officers a lieutenant in command. Next after the commissioned officers came the warrant officers, and first those who were included as "sea officers", officers in the loose modern sense, exercising a general authority aboard ship.

The master was the most senior of the warrant officers, and in some respects, including pay, his status was equal to that of the lieutenants. In merchant ships it was, as it is still, the master who holds command, but in the Navy the master was simply the navigator. He plotted the ship's position day by day, with his own instruments and on his own charts. In confined waters he conned (piloted) the ship. It was literally a vital task on which many lives depended, but it was a task for which commissioned officers also were trained and increasingly trained as well as masters or even better. The gunner was another of the warrant sea officers. Unlike the purser he had no pretensions to gentility, though there were exceptions. Gunners were of course responsible for guns and powder, and were unusual in that they owed a dual allegiance. Their accounts were rendered to and their warrants received from the Ordnance Board, an independent department not part of the naval administration or subordinate to the Admiralty. For purposes of discipline and shipboard organization gunners were as much officers of the Navy as any, but administratively their loyalties were divided. Gunners had usually begun their careers as seaman, and in some ships, particularly sloops with few officers, the gunner stood watches.

Very similar in status to the gunner was the boatswain, another warrant officer sea officer who had usually begun as a seaman. The boatswain indeed had a general responsibility for all the "seamanlike" activities in the ship other than handling her, for rigging, sails, ground tackle and all the gear, which went with them. He accounted to the Navy Board for these stores, and like all other sea officers he had to be a man of sufficient education to keep accounts and make reports in writing.

The last of the warrant sea officers was the carpenter, responsible for the maintenance of the hull, masts and spars of the ship. Carpenters were unusual in that they could and often did pass part of their careers in the dockyards and part in the Navy. All standing officers were paid on the books of the dockyard when their ships were out of commission, but carpenters had commonly begun their careers as apprentices in the yards, and not obtained their carpenters' warrants until they were qualified shipwrights of some years standing. The carpenter was a highly skilled man in an essential craft, and though like the boatswain and gunner no gentleman, a good carpenter would enjoy the respect and favor of all sensible captains. In terms of long experience in a complex and demanding job, the carpenter had no rival among the non-seamen aboard.

The final group of a ship's company which had not yet been mentioned was the marines. In previous wars marine regiments of the army had been raised, or ordinary marching regiments sent to sea, but the permanent corps of marines under Admiralty control was first established in 1755, so that during the Seven Years War it was a new force. Every ship except the smallest carried a detachment of marines with their own officer or officers. They were taught to handle a musket, and expected to fight ashore if landing parties were needed, but they were certainly at least as ill-trained as the average British foot-soldier of the day. Although not put in watches, and naturally not seamen, marines were expected to help with the work of the ship when required, usually in pulling and hauling, or walking round the capstan to raise the anchor. No marine could be ordered to work aloft, but they were encouraged to learn seamanship and some left the corps to become able seamen, earning not only higher pay but also a much higher social standing aboard ship.

Shipboard Life

Work and Play

In any case it is proper to describe first the sailors life at sea, for it was this which defined his profession and gave rise to most of its particulars. At sea all men-of-war kept two watches; that is to say that the seamen and landmen, servants and petty officers of each part of ship were divided into two parties, the starboard and larboard watched, and that not less than one whole watch was on deck at all time, night and day. Each watch lasted four hours, except for the two two-hour dog watches between four and eight in the evening, which made the number of watches in the day an odd number and so ensured that the duties of each watch continually varied. The changing of the watch marked the passage of time aboard ship, where no clock would run. A petty officer, usually the quartermaster of the watch, kept a half-hour sandglass; when it turned, he rang the ship's bell, and at eight bells the watch changed. The whole cycle of the sea day, seven watches or twenty-four hours long, began at noon when the officers took their sights and plotted the ship's position, so that the calendar at sea was always twelve hours ahead of that ashore. This was strictly a sea and not a nautical peculiarity; ships in port, freed from the requirements of navigation, reverted to the civil calendar. The 'watch was set' at sea at the start of the first watch at eight in the evening, which was, literally, the moments of 'lights out' when the watch coming off duty went to sleep until midnight. Then the other watch were able to sleep until four when the whole ship's company was roused. At sea all those in watches therefore had only four hours' sleep at most, and were liable to be awoken at any moment if an emergency required the watch below to turn out and bear a hand. The same applied to the idlers or daymen, who normally enjoyed an uninterrupted night's sleep. But were equally liable to be summoned by the pipe for all hands if their strength was required for pulling and hauling. This was quite often necessary in the frigates and sloops where the seamen were a much smaller proportion of the ship's company than in line-of-battle ships. Even in larger and better manned ships, lack of sleep was a constant hardship of the sea life for everyone in watches, mitigated by whatever chances might be snatched of sleeping by day, or the occasional still tropical night when an indulgent officer might let part of the watch sleep on deck.

For the seamen, the actual work of the ship involved much pulling and hauling, for of course all maneuvers depended on manpower. The topmen had to go out on the yards whenever sail was to be made or handed, and worked aloft on all the ceaseless work of maintenance and repair. This was the common occupation of ships' companies during the day when not actually working the ship-the seamen working on the rigging, the carpenter and his crew on the hull and spars, the sailmaker and crew on the sails, and the armourer, who acted as the ship's blacksmith, on ironwork.

Night and day men were posted aloft as lookouts – it was common practice to relieve the man who first sighted something, as a reward, but to continue double time those who allowed something to be seen first from the deck.

Besides the common work of the ship, certain tasks required the united strength of all the seamen if not all hands. Weighing anchor was one; scores or even hundreds of men needed to strain around the capstan for hours to bring in the huge anchors and clumsy hempen cables, and against any considerable wind or tide it was impossible. Hoisting in the longboat, which weighed several tons, likewise called for all the manpower available, and the use of the mainyard as a derrick. Many men-or-war, especially the smaller ones, tended to leave their longboats behind when they cruised in home waters, partly for this reason. In calm weather the small sloops with sweeps and rowing ports could, and sometimes did, row for hours-perhaps the most exhausting of all labour at sea.

The time not occupied in essential work of the ship might be employed in training. With wartime ship's companies containing a large proportion of landmen and ordinary seamen in addition to the usual boys... Formal instruction in seamanship was necessary. The boatswain and his mates could teach the young men such essentials as knotting, and splicing, but much of the work, and especially work aloft, could only be learnt by practice. Admiralty orders of 1758 required landsmen and boys to be exercised aloft daily, the boys on the topgallants and the mizzen topsail, the smallest sails, and the officers were urged to 'endeavor to raise an emulation in them, to outdo those of other ships' This could be done in port, but no amount of sail drill in port was a substitute for the real thing, and 'river discipline' (meaning the best state of training possible before putting to sea) was not to be depended on. For young gentlemen it was considered indispensable to work aloft with the topmen, Some were killed, but the survivors grew up finished seamen, and knew what they were ordering their men to do. To have as a 'sea-daddy" a steady topman…was a great asset to a future officer.

Gun drill was in some way even more important, for there was no natural practice to be had apart from action. Accordingly the Admiralty strongly encouraged flag officers to have their squadrons exercise great guns and small arms as often as possible. The exercises themselves consisted chiefly of going through the drill of loading, running out and firing the guns as quickly and reliability as possible Accuracy at any range was quite outside the capability of the pieces, and there was little attempt at target practice.

In port the work of the ship was generally lighter than at sea. The actual physical labor of fitting the ship for sea; and hoisting in ballast, stores and guns, or conversely stripping a ship to be docked, was considerable, but men could look forward to an unbroken night's sleep, with Sundays and holidays off except in an emergency.

Music and dancing were a part of life in wardroom and mess throughout the Navy. In Boscawen's flagship as they sailed westward across the Atlantic in the mild spring of 1755 the men danced nightly to fiddle, fife, and drum. Even in the rather unlikely situation of a press tender we hear of a mixed set of pressed men, volunteers, press gang and tender's crew dancing on the hatch cover on a sunny summer's day. Some ships had bands of a sort such as horns, flutes, drum fiddle and a Welsh harp.

A less troublesome fashion of the time was backgammon, which officers played a good deal. Officers and men alike fished when they had the chance. Every ship had an outfit of fishing tackle, including hooks and lines for issue to the men. There were occasional boisterous ceremonies particularly on crossing the line, when those who had never crossed paid a forfeit of 'pound and pint' or 'bottle and pound' (a bottle of spirits and a pound of sugar, to make flip) on pain of being ducked from the yardarm.

Perhaps the least noticed of all recreations at sea was reading. How many men would or could read is difficult to say. Many were undoubtedly illiterate, probably more than the average for their class, but there are chance references to men off watch reading in their hammocks, and very likely it was common.

Shipboard Life

Dangers of the Seas

Seafaring was an exceptionally dangerous profession. Men-of-war were certainly safer than merchant ships, for they were larger, better found and better manned, but even the best ships were often at the mercy of wind and current.

All ships had sometimes to trust in their anchors, and very often they had to cut away their masts to reduce the windage aloft. This drastic measure was almost a commonplace (occurance). This was a major cause of the very high consumption of masts and cordage which was one of the most serious limiting factors in naval strategy. Cutting away masts was a desperate and dangerous operation, though not so dangerous as losing them by accident.

Shipboard Life

Violence of the Enemy

Warships were built to fight; though they did so infrequently even in wartime, and fighting was the supreme test of the internal organization of a ship. Each officer and rating was allowed his quarter (his station in action) by a quarter bill posted up in the ship. Quarter bills differed somewhat according to captain's opinions and the size of ships, but in general principles all were much alike. The captain himself commanded from the quarter deck, attended by one or two midshipmen to carry messages. With him were usually the master, one or more mates, and one or more quartermasters at the wheel. The boatswain, his mates and a party of seamen handled sail and repaired damaged rigging. Unless in chase ships often fought under reduced canvas, but it was vital that damaged rigging be knotted or spliced at once because if the ship became unmanageable she would be at the mercy of an enemy still under command. Most of the seamen and landmen manned the guns below, and the lieutenants were also here in charge of one deck or side of a deck each, with the remaining midshipmen and mates under them. The boys were attached to the guns' crews, one or two to each, to fetch powder from the magazines. For safety's sake the guns kept only a small amount of powder, and the cartridges, which were vulnerable to damp, were not filled long in advance. In action therefore the gunner and his mates worked in the handling chamber above the magazine making up cartridges and placing them each in a leather case with a close-fitting lid. These were passed out through double doors hung with wet baize to keep out sparks, and carried by the boys to the guns. An well-organized ship's company would have only the minimum amount of powder in transit from the magazine, on the disengaged side if possible.

The carpenter and his crew attended to damage to the hull, especially to shots 'between wind and water', which had to be plugged promptly before they caused flooding.

Shipboard Life

Hardships and Comforts

They (sailors) slung their hammocks from the beams of the deckhead, which is to say that they lay fore and aft, each hammock with fourteen inches width, according to regulations, which in practice meant twenty-eight inches, since the hammocks were slung starboard and larboard watches alternately, and one watch would always be on deck. In reality the allowance might be more or less than the regulation amount depending on the size and internal arrangements of the ship in proportion to the number of her men. Always the men were crowded, except the petty officers who were allowed more space. By day the hammocks were lashed up into a sausage shape and stowed in the netting troughs which lined each side of the quarter deck and forecastle, and in action protected the men from small arms fire (and flying debris including splinters) somewhat in the manner of sandbags.

The men ate their meals on the gun deck, each mess of six with a table either hinged from the side or slung from the deckhead between the guns. In this deck in fact they passed much of their life on shipboard when not actually working. At sea the gunports, were where less than six feet from the waterline, had to be kept closed, and the only light and air came down the main hatch. Even with the assistance of windsails in fair weather to direct a draught below decks, it must have been close as well as dark, but no doubt it was true then, as it was a century later, that the men 'got all the light and air they had any use for in the fore or main top', and preferred that their messes should be what they called "snug".

One of the worst discomforts at sea was damp. In storms 'the spray of the sea raised by the violence of the wind is dispersed over the whole ship, so that the people breathe, as it were, in water for many weeks together'. If the weather were too severe to light the galley fire there was no means of drying clothes. Since there was often no fresh water to spare to rinse out clothes which had been soaked in salt water, and salt naturally absorbs moisture, seamen's clothes must have been permanently slightly damp. This was unpleasant enough in a warm climate, and there was no means of heating the mess decks. In June 1755, off Cape Breton Island, records indicate the men had chilblains from the cold; in the winter of 1759, with the sea frozen sixty miles offshore, many men in the North American squadron died from frostbite. It was generally reckoned very difficult to keep square-rigged ships at sea in Canadian waters in winter.

The running ropes freeze in the blocks, the sails are stiff like sheets of tin, and the men cannot expose their hands long enough to the cold to do their duty aloft, so that topsails and not easily handled. Even in less extreme conditions, the life of the seamen was always arduous, but it is unusual to find neither officers nor men making much of the weather as a hardship.

What upset the men very much was getting wet on they're hammocks from rain or spray leaking through the deck above. This was not common in line-of-battle ships, but it was a constant Problem in French prizes and in the smaller frigates and sloops. These were much more lightly-built ships …and in a seaway they worked badly, so that the seams opened and leaked.

Since the men berthed on the gun deck, which had to be cleared quickly in the event of action, they could not keep many personal possessions there. Their sea clothes could be bundled up in their hammocks, but those who had sea chests would usually have to stow them on the orlop or in the hold. Not everyone owned a chest, which was a substantial trunk, and implied considerable possessions to put in it, but most regular deep-sea sailors probably had or shared one. In it they kept their clothes, particularly their best shore-going rig, never worn at sea. Though there was no uniform for ratings in the navy, seamen wore extremely distinctive clothes which marked them at once from any other trade. They themselves spoke of their 'short clothes' and the landsman's 'long clothes'. Men ashore wore long coats and waistcoats reaching nearly to the knee, over tight breeches and stockings. Seamen wore short 'bum-freezer' jackets, generally blue, red waistcoats and checked shirts with a scarf or handkerchief loosely knotted round the neck. These clothes were 'short' because they stopped at or just below the waist, leaving no loose skirts to endanger a man working aloft. Instead of breeches they wore a garment then quite unknown to landsmen, unless they happened to have a nautical dictionary to hand: 'Trowsers, a short of loose breeches of canvas worn by common sailors'. For boat work they sometimes wore a canvas 'petticoat' or divided 'petticoat breeches'. These clothes made seamen instantly recognizable, and anyone who adopted them was likely to be taken for one. Except for disguise, seamen scorned to wear landsmen's clothes, and their best clothes were more elaborate and fancy versions of their working rig, with white duck instead of canvas trousers, silver buckles to their shoes, brass buttons on their jackets, colored tape along the seams, and ribbons in their hats.

Victualling and Health

Food

Few things were nearer to the sailor's heart than his stomach. A century after Pepys said it, it was as true as ever that 'Englishmen, and more especially seamen' love their bellies above anything else, and therefore it must always be remembered in the management of the victualling of the Navy that to make any abatement in the quality or agreeableness of the victuals is to discourage and provoke them in the tenderest point, and will sooner render them disgusted with the King's service than any other hardship that can be put upon them'.

The happiness and health of the Navy were greatly dependent on its victualling, and yet of all the administrative difficulties of getting a fleet to sea, This was probably the most intractable. In order to feed men at sea food had to be preserved for months, often for years, but the best methods available of preserving were expensive and unreliable. There were severe limitations on what sorts of foodstuffs could be preserved at all, which posed further problems in an age which was beginning to appreciate the importance of a varied diet, and in particular to understand scurvy as a dietary disease. The actual foods issued by the Victualling Board, in the standard weekly ration, were as follows:

	Bread	Beer	Beef	Pork	Pease	Oatmeal	Butter	Cheese
Sunday	1lb.	1 gal.	-	1 lb.	½ pt.	-	-	-
Monday	1 lb.	1 gal.	-	-	-	1 pt.	2 oz.	4 oz.
Tuesday	1 lb.	1 gal.	2 lbs.	-	-	-	-	-
Wednesday	1 lb.	1 gal.	-	-	½ pt.	1 pt.	2 oz.	4 oz.
Thursday	1 lb.	1 gal.						
Friday	1 lb.	1 gal.			½ pt.	1 pt.	2 oz.	4 oz.
Saturday	1 lb.	1 gal.	2 lbs.	-	-	-	-	-

The bread was in conventional loaves in port, and at sea a sort of biscuit, carefully baked and packed in bags at the Victualling Office on Tower Hill and its branch establishments at Portsmouth and Plymouth. The beef and pork were likewise processed at the Victualling Office, salted and pickled in cask. Casks were also the means of packing all the other commodities, including cheese and butter, which were unusual in not being processed by the government, but supplied by contractors under a six-month warranty. Besides the items specified in the rations, the Board issued flour, suet, raisins, and vinegar, all in cask, some stockfish (dried cod), and oil instead of butter for ships sailing for warm climates.

If when casks were opened aboard ship the contents were found to be decayed a survey had to be held on them by a panel of ship's officers in order that they should be condemned as unfit to eat, and the purser receive credit for them.

The diet supplied by the establishment was plain and very restricted in its range, but it provided more than sufficient calories for hard physical work. All food was cooked in a large "copper" set in a brick hearth, or in more modern ships, in an enclosed iron stove (plans show that *Canceaux* had an iron stove in the fore of the ship which was used for cooking and heating). It was possible to bake or roast on a small scale, for the officers or the sick, but the ship's company as a whole had all their dinners boiled. By the standards of the poor naval food was good and plentiful. To eat meat four days a week was itself a privilege denied a large part of the population, if only because in many parts of the country firing was too expensive for the poor to cook every day. For the same reason many did not eat a lot of vegetables, for most vegetables in common use were roots or green plants like cabbages, which were not eaten raw. The seamen who had a hot dinner daily, with beef and beer, bread and cheese, and sometimes vegetables and fruit, was eating well by his standards, and it seems he knew it, for in an age when seamen could and did complain freely, it is remarkably difficult to find them grumbling about the food .It is sometimes said that seamen were extremely conservative eaters, rejecting any novelty however good for them. Because the connection between scurvy and diet was understood by experienced seamen, if not by the medical world, the Navy went to great expense to provide ships in port and at sea with fresh vegetables, fruit and fresh meat. The livestock so often carried was a part of this effort, and an elaborate logistical organization, extending all over the world, ensured as far as humanly possible that men had to live continually on salt provisions only on long ocean passages. Even frozen beef was supplied to the North American squadron wintering at Halifax. These efforts were successful in reducing scurvy from a permanent disaster, which crippled or destroyed whole squadrons, to a minor irritant of no operational significance. To what extent the seamen appreciated this benefit in their diet is difficult to say, but there is no doubt that its food was one of the attractions of the Navy. Monotonous and basic thought they now seem, the seamen's meals were by his own standards good and plentiful. Even with modern dietary knowledge, it is possible to guess that with a reasonable proportion of fresh provisions the men of the Navy probably ate something nearer a balanced diet than many of their contemporaries ashore.

Victualling and Health
Cleanliness

It was well understood that any serious outbreak of contagious disease afloat required the ship to be stripped and disinfected. There were various ways of doing this, but the method proposed by a conference of captains at Portsmouth in 1758 was as comprehensive as any: the ballast was to be taken out, the hold washed with fresh water and clean ballast put in. With the ship completely battened down and caulked, fires were to be lit in the hold and between decks and trains of gunpowder flashed off several times. Finally the deckhead was to be washed down repeatedly with warm vinegar and smoked with 'pitched loggerheads'. The effect of all this would at least have been to purify the air, and this was the chief object aimed at.

Next after the cleanliness of the ship came the cleanliness of the men, and more particularly of their clothes. Efforts were generally concentrated on clothes because the men's opportunities for washing themselves were limited at sea; there was little fresh water to spare, soap was ineffective in salt water (and an expensive luxury) and there was no suitable place to bathe. Clothes were an easier target, and a more important one, for dirty clothes were rightly suspected to be the bearers of gaol fever and other infections, and were often burnt to destroy them. Admiral Smith's divisional system of 1755 required the men to shift their linen twice a week, and it seems probable that in well-run ships during the war this was the practice as well as weather and circumstances would allow. Washing clothes at sea was not easy; in the absence of soap 'chamberlye' (urine) was used as a detergent, and the clothes rinsed in fresh water if there were enough available.

The Navy's greatest problem was in dealing with new recruits in ragged, dirty and probably infected clothes. There was every reason to wash and reclothe them, and this was often ordered to be done as soon as they were entered on a ship's books, and could have the value of the slops charged to their names.

Manning

Straggling and Desertion

The manning problem had to be addressed in three ways: by finding volunteers, by pressing, and by preventing wastage. In both gains and losses, the men themselves were partly free agents whose wishes affected the Navy's fortunes, and partly the objects of manipulation by others, wither the Navy itself or its rivals for manpower. Many men who had apparently deserted the Service, in the formal sense that they had missed three consecutive weekly musters and been marked "run" on the ship's books, had in reality been kidnapped or lured away when they were not masters of themselves. Nevertheless it seems unlikely that these were more than a minority of those who were made "run". A larger, though still unquantifiable number undoubtedly consisted of people who were legitimately ashore and failed to return for other reasons. All over the world men were ashore in great numbers, on short or long leave, landed as boat's crews, working parties or press gangs, lent in lieu of men pressed out of merchantmen and left to find their own way back to their home port, or sent overland to join a new ship. Apart from a small minority of habitual deserters, impressed smugglers and men awaiting court martial, any man in the Navy could count himself unlucky if he did not at least occasionally get a run ashore, particularly when all ships had to be docked or careened several times a year. There were always many men on leave, and there was usually a small proportion who failed to return and were 'run' on their ships' books. It is easy to assume that these men were 'deserters' in the full sense of the word, men who had deliberately fled the Service intending never to return.

This was not an assumption made by any informed contemporary. Sea officers who were at all careful or language applied the word 'deserter' only to men who had been, or might plausibly have been, accused under the XVth or XVIth Articles of War of deserting the Service. Merely being 'run' on a ship's books was no more than a precondition of being a deserter. Even men who had clearly deserted their ships were not necessarily deserters in this sense, for we shall see that deserting one's ship by no means certainly implied deserting the Service. At the court martial of some men of the Blast bomb vessel in 1760, who had beyond doubt wilfully deserted their ships, one of the accused asked his captain, who had witnessed them pulling away in a boat, "Did you think that we were determined to leave his Majesty's service?' Cautiously the captain replied, 'I cannot tell." He was wise to do so. The term usually employed in the eighteenth century to describe men absent from their duty in culpable, suspicious or simply unexplained circumstances, was "stragglers". This evocative term, vague and comprehensive, covered the multiple of sins, errors and mishaps which might befall seamen shore. Very often men were delayed in return by simple physical causes; by bad roads and bad weather, by illness or accident, by arrest for debt, or simply by death. Men lent in lieu who were longer than expected on passage often found that their tickets of leave had expired before they even landed. All these men were liable to be arrested by soldiers, parish constable or press gangs, all eager for the reward payments on bringing in a straggler.

Besides straggling, there was another category of absence, equally ill-defined and equally common, known as 'rambling'. When ships came into harbour to dock it was virtually impossible to prevent the men going ashore, and captains seldom tried. They put their untrustworthy men aboard another ship and did not worry unduly about the rest.

When the men were needed again, patrols would be sent out for them. It was usually not difficult to find out in which tavern one's shipmates had been drinking and rouse them out.

If seamen did take advantage of their freedom to run away, there were still severe obstacles in their path. Even in landsmen's long clothes they could be recognized from their gait and their weather-beaten complexions. One deserter, confident in his disguise , was alarmed to meet an old woman in the street in the first town he came to who said to him, 'Young man, are you not afraid of the soldiers? In the countryside inland, away from the main roads, a seamen was conspicuous oddity likely to be talked of for miles around. Most absentees did not get so far, and were found easily.

The distinctions between rambling, straggling and desertion were vague, but they could if necessary be specific. At Halifax on 28 May 1758, shortly before sailing to attack Louisbourg crews were warned that 'All seamen taken up by the patrol on being on shore contrary to order, will be paid as stragglers, and the same charged against their wages, and also punished if they other wise misbehave'.

The rewards were fixed at ten shillings for a straggler and thirty for a deserter, defined as anyone more than twenty-four hours overdue, and the latter were threatened with court martial.

Beyond the wide penumbra of ramblers and stragglers, some of whom had been 'run', but hardly any of whom were deserters in the strict acceptance of the word, there was a large number of men who had deliberately left their ships without permission, but not permanently. Men often ran away, generally drunk, and then thought better of it. They ran to visit their families and then returned, and in one case they ran to escape an outbreak of smallpox aboard. Men sometimes ran for a 'run ashore', to take the leave they felt they had been unjustly denied.

There was a large traffic in desertion from one ship to another. Men ran from small ships, especially the cramped and leaky sloops, to the relative comfort and less strenuous work of a ship of the line. Like all the small sloops built in the last peace to prevent smuggling…They are really very bad vessels to cruise all weathers, and so sure as a seaman is trusted on shore from any of them, he runs away.

An officer could be cashiered for receiving a deserter from another ship, but the temptation was not to enquire too closely into the origins of able volunteers was strong, and the captains of sloops often had occasion to complain of their brother officers permitting, or even encouraging this traffic.

APPENDIX I

COMPLEMENT

This table gives the authorized complement of officers, ratings and marines of each rate and size of ship, and from that calculates the percentage which seamen formed of each ship's company, and the ratio of tons to men, and tons to seamen. It will be understood that 'seamen'

				Commissioned Officers		*Warrant Sea Officers*					
Rate	*Guns*	*Complement*	*Tonnage*	*Capt*	*Lieut*	*Mr*	*Bts*	*Gnr*	*Ctr*	*Sgn*	*Prs*
1st	100	880	1800–2090	1	6	1	1	1	1	1	1
1st	90	780	1800	1	6	1	1	1	1	1	1
2nd	90	750–780	1570–1870	1	6	1	1	1	1	1	1
2nd	84	750	1920	1	6	1	1	1	1	1	1
3rd	80	600–700	1350–1980	1	4	1	1	1	1	1	1
3rd	74	600–700	1550–1830	1	4	1	1	1	1	1	1
3rd	70	480–550	1400–1440	1	4	1	1	1	1	1	1
3rd	66	520	1470–1480	1	4	1	1	1	1	1	1
3rd	64	480–520	1220–1400	1	4	1	1	1	1	1	1
4th	60	400–435	1060–1300	1	3	1	1	1	1	1	1
4th	50	300–350	850–1050	1	3	1	1	1	1	1	1
4th	44	250–280	690–850	1	3	1	1	1	1	1	1
5th	38	250	940	1	3	1	1	1	1	1	1
5th	36	240	720–750	1	3	1	1	1	1	1	1
5th	32	220	650–720	1	3	1	1	1	1	1	1
6th	28	200	580–610	1	1	1	1	1	1	1	1
6th	24	160	430–520	1	1	1	1	1	1	1	1
6th	22	160	430–470	1	1	1	1	1	1	1	1
6th	20	160	400–450	1	1	1	1	1	1	1	1
sloop	18	120–130	320–380	1	1	1	1	1	1	1	1
sloop	16	125	310	1	1	1	1	1	1	1	1
sloop	14	110–125	150–190	1	1	1	1	1	1	1	1
sloop	12	80–110	100–220	1	1	1	1	1	1	1	1
sloop	10	100–110	210–230	1	1	1	1	1	1	1	1
sloop	8	80	140	1	—	—	1	1	1	1	—
bomb	8	60	230–310	1	—	—	1	1	1	1	—
fireship	8	45	250–400	1	1	—	1	1	1	1	—
yacht	10	70	230	1	—	—	1	1	1	1	—
yacht	8	40	160–170	1	—	—	1	1	1	1	—

Capt = Captain or Commander; Lieut = Lieutenant; Mr = Master; Bts = Boatswain; Gnr = Gunner; Ctr = Carpenter; Sgn = Surgeon; Prs = Purser.

Note:
Based on records of Admiral Samuel Graves (Graves Conduct, I, 132) entitled "Disposition of the [British] Fleet on the 30th of June 1775" the Armed Ship Canceaux had 6 guns and a complement of 45 men..

included landmen if necessary, and that certain miscellaneous ratings such as barber and midshipman extra were, if borne, subtracted from the total of seamen. The tonnages given are approximate. A few ships, chiefly prizes, did not conform to any of these establishments.

Inferior Warrant Officers							*Petty Officers*						
Ch	*Ck*	*SM*	*SMk*	*Ar*	*SMt*	*MA*	*MM*	*Md*	*CCk*	*QM*	*QMM*	*BM*	*YS*
1	1	—	1	1	5	1	6	24	1	8	6	4	4
1	1	—	1	1	5	1	6	24	1	8	6	4	4
1	1	—	1	1	4	1	4	24	1	8	6	4	4
1	1	—	1	1	4	1	4	24	1	8	6	4	4
1	1	1	1	1	3	1	3	16	1	6	4	2	4
1	1	1	1	1	3	1	3	16	1	6	4	2	4
1	1	1	1	1	3	1	3	16	1	6	4	2	4
1	1	1	1	1	3	1	3	16	1	6	4	2	4
1	1	1	1	1	3	1	3	16	1	6	4	2	4
1	1	1	1	1	2	1	2	10	1	4	4	2	2
1	1	1	1	1	2	1	2	10	1	4	4	2	2
1	1	1	1	1	2	1	2	10	1	4	4	2	2
1	1	1	1	1	2	1	2	6	1	3	3	1	2
1	1	1	1	1	2	1	2	6	1	3	3	1	2
1	1	1	1	1	2	1	2	6	1	3	3	1	2
1	1	—	1	1	1	1	2	4	1	2	2	1	1
1	1	—	1	1	1	1	2	4	1	2	2	1	1
1	1	—	1	1	1	1	2	4	1	2	2	1	1
1	1	—	1	1	1	1	2	4	1	2	2	1	1
—	1	—	1	—	1	—	1	2	1	2	1	1	—
—	1	—	1	—	1	—	1	2	1	2	1	1	—
—	1	—	1	—	1	—	1	2	1	2	1	1	—
—	1	—	1	—	1	—	1	2	1	2	1	1	—
—	1	—	1	—	1	—	1	2	1	2	1	1	—
—	—	—	—	—	—	—	1	1	1	1	—	1	—
—	—	—	—	—	—	—	1	1	1	1	—	1	—
—	—	—	—	1	—	—	1	2	1	2	1	1	—
—	—	—	—	—	—	—	1	1	1	1	1	1	—
—	—	—	—	—	—	—	1	1	1	1	—	1	—

Ch = Chaplain; Ck = Cook; SM = Schoolmaster; SMk = Sailmaker; Ar = Armourer; SMt = Surgeon's Mate; MA = Master at Arms; MM = Master's Mate; Md = Midshipman; CCk = Captain's Clerk; QM = Quartermaster; QMM = Quartermaster's Mate; BM = Boatswain's Mate; YS = Yeoman of the Sheets.

		Petty Officers									Idlers		
Rate	*Guns*	*Cx*	*SMM*	*GM*	*YPR*	*QG*	*CM*	*St*	*Cp*	*Tp*	*SC*	*CC*	*StM*
1st	100	1	1	4	2	25	2	1	2	1	2	12	1
1st	90	1	1	4	2	22	2	1	2	1	2	12	1
2nd	90	1	1	4	2	22	2	1	2	1	2	10	1
2nd	84	1	1	4	2	21	2	1	2	1	2	10	1
3rd	80	1	1	2	2	20	1	1	2	1	2	8	1
3rd	74	1	1	2	2	18	1	1	2	1	2	8	1
3rd	70	1	1	2	2	17	1	1	2	1	2	8	1
3rd	66	1	1	2	2	16	1	1	2	1	2	8	1
3rd	64	1	1	2	2	16	1	1	2	1	2	8	1
4th	60	1	1	1	1	15	1	1	2	1	2	6	1
4th	50	1	1	1	1	12	1	1	2	1	2	6	1
4th	44	1	1	1	1	11	1	1	2	1	2	6	1
5th	38	1	1	1	1	9	1	1	2	1	1	5	—
5th	36	1	1	1	1	9	1	1	2	1	1	5	—
5th	32	1	1	1	1	8	1	1	2	1	1	5	—
6th	28	1	1	1	1	7	1	1	1	1	1	4	—
6th	24	1	1	1	1	6	1	1	1	1	1	4	—
6th	22	1	1	1	1	5	1	1	1	1	1	4	—
6th	20	1	1	1	1	5	1	1	1	1	1	4	—
sloop	18	1	—	1	1	1	1	1	1	—	1	2	—
sloop	16	1	—	1	1	1	1	1	1	—	1	2	—
sloop	14	1	—	1	1	1	1	1	1	—	1	2	—
sloop	12	1	—	1	1	1	1	1	1	—	1	2	—
sloop	10	1	—	1	1	1	1	1	1	—	1	2	—
sloop	8	—	—	1	—	—	1	1	—	—	—	1	—
bomb	8	—	—	1	—	—	1	1	—	—	—	1	—
fireship	8	1	—	1	1	—	1	1	1	—	1	1	—
yacht	10	—	—	1	1	1	1	1	—	—	—	—	—
yacht	8	—	—	1	—	—	1	1	—	—	—	—	—

Cx = Coxswain; SMM = Sailmaker's Mate; GM = Gunner's Mate; YPR = Yeoman of the Powder Room; QG = Quarter Gunner; CM = Carpenter's Mate; St = Steward; Cp = Corporal; Tp = Trumpeter; SC = Sailmaker's Crew; CC = Carpenter's Crew; StM = Steward's Mate.

APPENDIX I

Servants	Widows' Men	Seamen	Tons per Man	Tons per Seaman	Marines						
					Ct	*1L*	*2L*	*Sg*	*Cp*	*Dm*	*Pte*
52	18	569 (65%)	2.0–2.4	3.2–3.7	1	1	1	3	3	2	100
48	16	478 (62%)	2.3	3.8	1	1	1	3	3	2	100
47–48	15–16	455–483 (61–62%)	2.1–2.4	3.4–3.9	1	1	1	3	3	2	100
47	15	466 (62%)	2.6	4.1	1	1	1	3	3	2	90
39–43	12–14	352–446 (59–64%)	2.2–2.8	3.8–4.4	1	1	1	3	2	1	90
39–43	12–14	354–448 (59–64%)	2.6	4.1–4.4	1	1	1	3	2	1	90
34–36	10–11	264–321 (55–59%)	2.7–2.9	4.5–5.3	1	—	1	2	2	1	70
35	10	304 (58%)	2.8	4.8–4.9	1	—	1	2	2	1	70
34–35	10	264–304 (55–58%)	2.5–2.7	4.6	1	—	1	2	2	1	70
30–31	8–9	219–252 (55–58%)	2.6–3.0	4.8–5.2	1	—	1	2	2	1	60
26–28	6–7	137–184 (46–53%)	2.8–3.0	5.7–6.2	—	1	1	2	2	1	50
24–25	5–6	104–132 (42–47%)	2.8–3.0	6.4–6.6	—	1	—	1	2	1	40
24	5	117 (47%)	3.8	8.0	—	1	—	1	2	—	40
23	5	108 (45%)	3.0–3.1	6.7–6.9	—	1	—	1	2		40
22	4	91 (41%)	2.9–3.3	7.1–7.9	—	1	—	1	2	—	40
20	4	91 (45%)	2.9–3.0	6.4–6.7	—	1	—	1	1	—	35
18	3	55 (34%)	2.7–3.2	7.8–9.4	—	1	—	1	1	—	35
18	3	56 (35%)	2.7–2.9	7.7–8.4	—	1	—	1	1	—	35
18	3	56 (35%)	2.5–2.8	7.1–8.0	—	1	—	1	1	—	35
14–15	2–3	47–55 (39–42%)	2.7–2.9	6.8–6.9	—	—	1	1	1	—	25
15	3	50 (40%)	2.5	6.2	—	—	1	1	1	—	25
14–15	2–3	37–50 (34–40%)	1.4–2.3	3.8–4.1	—	—	1	1	1	—	25
13–14	2	36–65 (45–59%)	1.2–2.0	2.7–3.4	—	—	—	—	—	—	—
14	2	55–65 (55–59%)	2.1	3.6–3.8	—	—	—	—	—	—	—
7	2	57 (71%)	1.7	2.5	—	—	—	—	—	—	—
6	1	39 (65%)	3.8–5.2	5.9–7.9	—	—	—	—	—	—	—
7	1	14 (31%)	5.5–8.8	17.9–28.6	—	—	—	—	—	—	—
6	1	48 (69%)	3.3	4.8	—	—	—	—	—	—	—
5	1	22 (55%)	4.0–4.2	7.3–7.7	—	—	—	—	—	—	—

Ct = Captain; 1L = 1st Lieutenant; 2L = 2nd Lieutenant; Sg = Sergeant; Cp = Corporal; Dm = Drummer; Pte = Private

Sources: *Regulations and Instructions*, pp. 146–149; ADM 180/20, p. 219; ADM 2/1152, p. 454.

A Journal of the Proceedings of
His Majesty's Armed Ship
CANCEAUX
by
Lieut. Henry Mowat Commander,
And Ensign William Hogg, Sailing Master
commencing March 1764 and ending April 1776

Mar. 14, 1764 Wednesday
Took command of his Majestys Armed ship *Canceaux* lying at Deptford.

Deptford England 5 miles down the Thames River from central London was a major naval facility being the site for Henry VIII's Royal Naval Dockyard and remained the cradle of the English Navy for over 300 years. It was the base for the most famous English Expeditions, including those lead by Sir Francis Drake, Sir Walter Raleigh and Captain Cook and was the home of the most important naval victualling yard until the 1960s.

Mar. 15, 1764 Thursday
Lying alongside the *Tepouhare* off the Kings yard Deptford.
Mar. 16, 1764 Friday
Lying in the same place
Mar. 17, 1764 Saturday
Transported the ship into Mr. Waits Dock at Deptford
Mar. 18, 1764 Sunday
In Dock Moderate weather all this 24 hours

The Atlantic Neptune was the first great maritime atlas of views and charts covering the east coast of North America from the St. Lawrence River southward to the Mississippi River. The first chart was published in 1774. The Atlantic Neptune has been described as "the most splendid collection of charts, plans, and views ever published. It was executed at the expense of the British government for use by the Royal Navy and no expense appears to have been spared in the execution in order to render it a monument worth of the Nation"
The Neptune was compiled and published for the Royal Navy by Joseph F. W. Des Barres, a Swiss born British subject who

attended the Royal Military College at Woolwich where he learned and carried out surveying tasks.

The Atlantic Neptune that Des Barres compiled is divided into four series: Nova Scotia, New England, the River and Gulf of St. Lawrence, New York southward. Nova Scotia was surveyed by Des Barres and New England and the St. Lawrence were surveyed by Samuel Holland, an engineer of Dutch heritage and veteran of the Seven Years War. Holland became Surveyor General of the Northern District and made his surveys for the Lord Commissioners of Trade and Plantations. The British engineers and surveyors sent to America had been trained in the latest surveying techniques, and were able to make precise measurements of vertical and horizontal angles with the theodolite recently perfected. The accuracy of longitudinal positions had been advanced by the invention of the chronometer in 1730.

** Mar. 19, 1764 to Mar. 28, 1764*

The above entry type that appears throughout this transcription of the logs means that the Logs are abridged for the period of time indicated. In the interest of economy, this was done as the daily shipboard activity described is very short and repetitive and includes only single activity for the entry such as getting provisions on board, cleaning ship, wooding & watering, hearing articles of war, preparing oakum and junk, making points and gaskets, cleaning snow, protecting ship from ice, working on ships boats, caulking, paying seams, painting, sealing and coating yards and masts. Weather comments range from clear weather, light breezes, gales, snow and sleet, freezing weather and hazey/foggy conditions.

Mar. 29, 1764 Thursday
The same weather carpenter employed as before and the painters on board painting the out side of the ship
Mar. 30, 1764 Friday
The weather variable carpenters and painters employed as before.
Mar. 31, 1764 Saturday
The same weather carpenters and painters employed as before Took in iron ballast.
April 1, 1764 Sunday

The weather varied
April 2, 1764 Monday
The weather moderate and fair carried the ship from out the Dock alongside the sheer hulk carpenters and caulkers employed on board, the people Employ in Rigging the lower masts.

The sheer hulk was an old ship hull that was cut down to one or two decks and with masts reinforced and sheer legs equipped with heavy lifting tackle that could lift out or in masts.

April 3, 1764 Tuesday
PM the same weather the latter part cloudy with rain carpenters painters and caulkers Employed as before Employed getting the ballast in.
April 4, 1764 Wednesday
Fresh gales and small rain carpenters and painters and caulkers Employed as before took 30 tons of shingle ballast on board.
April 5, 1764 Thursday
Fresh gales & clear weather carpenters Employd as before.
April 6, 1764 Friday
Moderate and cloudy weather Carpenters Employed as before The ships company employed in setting the lower Riging up.
April 7, 1764 Saturday
Moderate weather carpenter joiner bricklayer and painter Employed, the ships company Employed in filling water casks.
April 8, 1764 Sunday
Fresh breezes and cloudy weather with rain carpenter Employed as before, Ships company getting the topgallants and caps and tops from the yards, and hosing the hold.
April 9, 1764 Monday
Fresh breezes and hazy weather with rain carpenter Employed as before ships company Employed getting the top masts up and stowing the hold.
April 10, 1764 Tuesday
The same weather carpenter Employed as before Ships Company Employed Rigging the topmasts and stowing the hold.
April 11, 1764 Wednesday
Moderate and cloudy weather got the topmasts up and rigged them, carpenter Employed as before.
April 12, 1764 Thursday
Along side the sheer hulk at Deptford
PM calm and cloudy with small rain the latter fresh gales

and squally carpenter Employed as before ships company Employed about the rigging.

April 13, 1764 Friday

Fresh gales and clear weather got the top gallants masts up.

April 14, 1764 Saturday

Moderate and cloudy weather Employed getting the top gallant yards up and catharpening the shrouds carpenter Employed as before.

April 15, 1764 Sunday NW

The same weather Employed in clearing the decks fore and aft.

April 16, 1765 Monday NNE

Moderate and fair weather Employed in setting the lower and topmast rigging up fore and aft Carpenters employed as before, ships draught of water forward 8 : 11; aft 10: 1; diffce1 : 2

April 17, 1764 Tuesday NW

Moderate weather Employed taking on board some of the ending sails bent the fore sails topsails topgallant sails main topmast staysail and mizen Carpenter Employd as before.

April 18, 1764 Wednesday NE

Fresh breezes and cloudy Employed getting Boatswain and Carpenter stores on board, carpenter & Employed as before.

The Boatswain and carpenter were important ratings aboard the Canseaux. The boatswain was responsible for the rigging, sails anchors, cables and boats. With his mates he worked the ship at the order of the officers. His badge of office as the "bosun's pipe" a whistle that he used to give commands – its shrill sound could be heard over the winds at sea. The carpenter was the worker in wood aboard the ship knowledgeable in building and repair of boats and even the ship itself. He reported to the Captain as to condition of hull, masts, yards and decks. He cared for the pumps and water level in the hold making repairs to the ship after battle mainly plugging shot holes.

April 19, 1764 Thursday NNE

PM moderate and cloudy AM fresh breezes Employed in getting the carpenters and Boatswains stores on board received on board a new cutter and pinnace Carpenters & employd as before.
The pinnace is a light boat used as a tender to a larger vessel and a cutter is a ship's boat used for carrying stores or people being single masted fore and aft rigged and sometimes armed. Boats were hoisted in and out by tackle in the yards and stays. Boat types

with various rigs found in New England waters include launch, cutter, whaleboat and jolly boat.
A sloop carried 8 to 20 guns and were ship-rigged and carried guns on one deck. Brig being square rigged hand two masts, brigantinne had square and fore and aft sails and schooners using fore and aft sails were common in New England waters.

April 20, 1764 Friday NE
Moderate and cloudy weather Employd getting stores on board and clearing the Decks fore and aft.
April 21, 1764 Saturday N
Moored with the stream anchor in Gallions
Moderate PM and fair, at 4 PM came on board the Pilot to carry the ship down at 5 do. cast off from the hulk and made sail at 8 anchor'd in Gallions, wear'd out half a cable and moored the stream hawser and cable; people Employd fixing the rigging
April 22, 1764 Sunday N. NE, ESE
Moderate and fair at 5 PM: came alongside a hoy with the guns and gunners stores got all in at 9 do. came along side the sail maker with boatswains and carpenters stores.
April 23, 1764 Monday WNW
Moderate and hazey weather, received on board some Boatswain and carpenters stores.
April 24, 1764 Tuesday WNW
Turning down the river
The same weather Employd as yesterday at 8 AM unmoored and took the stream anchor at 9 do. weighed and got under sail and worked down the river at Noon slight air and clear weather.
April 25, 1764 Wednesday NW, NNW
Sight airs and fair weather at 2 PM anchored in Long Reach, at the Jamehind His Majesty's ship the *Crown* lying there at 5 AM weighed and got under sail at 9 do. anchored at Gravesend. at 11 the Powder came on board in No. 16 ½ Barrels at the same time bent the main sail and small stay sail.
April 26, 1764 Thursday NNW
Dockyard NE and Queensborough
PM moderate & cloudy the latter fresh gales and squally at 3 PM weighed and got under sails at ½ past 9 anchored in 6 fathom water at the Nore the Nore light bore NE 1 mile at 5 AM weighed and got under sail and turned up to Sheerness at 9 anchored off the Dock yards.
April 27, 1764 Friday NNW, WNW

Fresh gales and squaly with rain at Noon weighed and hauled alongside the *Lanceston* the ships company Employd in getting ballast out of her, at 10 PM got down topgallant yards at Noon Commissioner Hanway came from Chatham and paid ships compy two months pay.

The French and Indian War awakened the British government to the need for better maps of its North American empire, and with the advent of peace, a program was undertaken by the Lord Commissioners of Trade and Plantations to undertake surveys and map the entire Eastern seaboard for the development of waterborne trade. To survey the coasts of North America the colonies were divided north and south at the Potomac River and a surveyor general appointed for each district. Wm. Gerard de Brahm for the Southern District. Samuel Holland was Surveyor General for the northern colonies including Prince Edward Island, Cape Breton, and the inhabited parts of Canada and New England, New York and New Jersey. Holland lead a team of six surveyors, 35 assistants, and four local guides. Des Barres prepared the maps for Nova Scotia and parts of New Brunswick and New England as well as Sable Island. The focus of the charts was on coastal waters sand bars and ledge were critical to mariners. Land features were shown as they would be seen by mariners including hills, towns, roads and farm land.

April 28, 1764 Saturday NW, W
Nore light NE 1 mile
Moderate and cloudy weather the ship company Employd as before. At 4 PM the *Chatham Hoy* Wilm: Mouldan master and took away 6 hogsheads full bound, At 8 AM: got on board 19 ton of shingle ballast from the *Lanceston*, at 9 we cast of from her and got under sail at 10 we got up topgallant yards and the purser slops came on board at 11 we anchored with best bower in 3 ½ fathom water.

April 29, 1764 Sunday WSW, Calm, WSW
The first part Moderate and clear the latter fresh gales and cloudy at 6 AM weighed and got under sail at 10 we run thro the narrows at ½ past 10 we shortened and brought too with our head to the southward and took the reefs in the topsails at Noon off. Hargate Town we hoisted in the pinnace.

April 30, 1764 Monday WSW, WNW
Two leagues ? W. B. and Mararet Town

The first part fresh gales the middle moderate and cloudy with rain the latter fresh gales and clear weather at 2 PM we bore away at 3 the North foreland Lighthouse bore NNW 3 miles at 3 anchored in 6 fathom water at 7 weighed and turned into Mararet Road, anchored in 7 fathom water at 3 AM weighed anchor and came to sail at 9 we anchored in the little Dawns. Dawn Castle W b S dist. 3 leagues.

May 1, 1764 Tuesday W, WSW

Sandown Castle NW b W and Deal Town WNW 3 miles

Fresh gales and squaly PM Read the Articles of War and abstract of the new act of Parliament at 4 we weighed anchor and got under sail at 6 we anchored in 6 fathom water with the best bower, received on board fresh beef 244 lb. for the ships company at the same time received on board some carpenters stores from Dale.

In the age of wooden ships the carpenter was a key member of the crew. He must have the skills to build or repair the ship's boats, or the larger ship being responsible for all repairs and knowing the state of the ship at all times including hull, masts, yards and decks. He knew the depth of the water in the hold and the condition of the pumps and most importantly during and after battle he made the needed repair.

May 2, 1764 Wednesday WSW

The same weather the ships companies Employd in setting up the riging fore and aft, at PM His Majestys sloop *Crouser* weighed anchor and sail'd to the westward.

May 3, 1764 Thursday WSW

Fresh gales and cloudy weather Employd in setting up the riging came to anchor here one of His Majestys cutters.

May 4, 1764 Friday WSW, NW

Moderate and fair weather lowered the sails to dry, came to anchor here an East India ship outward bound.

May 5, 1764 Saturday W, WNW

The same weather the ships company Employed filling a lighter with ballast at Noon, warping her on board broke & lost 100 fathom of 1 ½ inch rope several vessels got under way but were obliged to come too again Received onboard 570 lb of fresh beef for the ships company.

May 6, 1764 Sunday SW, WSW

Moderate and fair weather PM came along side a lighter with 14 tons of ballast, Employd getting of it in at 9 AM: came in and anchored here his Majestys ship the *Crown* from the Nore at 11 we sent on shore the lighters.

May 7, 1764 Monday SW, calm, NE

Dover Castle N b E and So. Foreland lighthouse

PM fresh gales and clear weather the middle part calm the latter variable at 8 AM weighed anchor and came to sail as did his Majestys sloop the *Cruiser* with several sails of Merchant vessels, left in the Downes his Majestys ship the *Cruiser* and East India ship outward bound at the same time sent Peter Regiment to Dale to sick quarters.

May 8, 1764 Tuesday W b S, WSW, NNW

Dungines Lighthouse N b E 4 miles

Light air and clear weather Set steering sails at 5 PM saw 6 sail of Dutch East India men at anchor off fair Lighthouse homeward bound hauled down steering sails at 1 AM cloudy weath and small breezes, at 6 tacked, at 8 fresh breezes and cloudy weath

May 9, 1764 Wednesday SW b S, N b W, SW

Beachy Head N b E ½ E 6 0r 7 leagues

Fresh breezes and hazy weather at 5 PM tacked at 6 clear weather at 8 tacked at 10 tacked at 12 light breezes and hazy at 2 AM out 1 reef the topsails, at 8 anchored with the stream anchor and hawser in 23 water.

May 10, 1764 Thursday WNW, W, W b N

Clear weather PM ½ past 4 weighed anchor and came to sail at 6 sett steering sails at 9 took in steering sails at 12 light breezes and cloudy at 3 AM: fresh breezes sounded 25 fathom gray sand at 7 squaly with rain.

May 11, 1764 Friday W b N, NNW, S b E, N b W, WSW

Gilkuker NE & South Sea Castle E b N ½ N dist. 2 miles

Squaly with rain saw the land bearing from south to SW which proved to be Cape Barflour at 6 PM fresh gales and squaly, handed the Main Topsail, at 7 took in 2 and 3 reefs in the fore and Main Topsails, at 10 fresh gales and cloudy. at 12 tacked, and handed fore topsail, at 1 AM wore ship at 4 handed gales at 6 saw the land bearing from N b E to NNW which proved to be the high sand of Pt. Albany at 8 bore away Heverly point bearing NNW dist. 4 miles, at 9 sett F.T: sail at 10 going through the Needles bore south out reefs of the Top sails at 11 Hiss Castle NNW the same weather at 12 anchored at Spithead with the best Bower in 7 fathoms water. Cleared out 2/3 of a cable, S. Sea Castle E b N dist: 2 miles.

May 12, 1764 Saturday W b S, S, S b E

Fresh gales and cloudy Weather at 5 PM veered away and moored with the Hedge, when moored St. Helens S ½ W Gilkecker NW b N found riding here his Majestys sloop *Ferret* with another ship of war.

May 13, 1764 Sunday W
Fresh gales and squaly with rain.

May 14, 1764 Monday WSW
Haylens Hospital W
Hard gales and squaly, people Emplyed variously Received some Boatswains and carpenter stores on board.

May 15, 1764 Tuesday WSW, SW
The same weather at 10 AM lowered down the lower yards and struck Top gallant mast people Employed getting up all the empty beer and water casks out of the hold at Noon moderate - Sailed from hence his Majestys sloop *Sepher.*

May 16, 1764 Wednesday SW, calm
South Sea Castle E b N ½ dist. 2 miles
PM fresh gales and cloudy weather the Middle and latter part Moderate and clear at 5 swayed up the lower yards and got up Top gallant masts AM got up Top gallant yards received some Boatswains and carpenters stores on board at the same time received 5 hogsheads of beer and sent 10 empty casks on shore.

May 17, 1764 Thursday NW
Fair weather PM: unmoored ships and hove short on the best Bower cable, sent on shore to the Hospital William Snow sick furnished Thomas Walden with 12 lashes for drunkeness, Sailed into the Harbor His Majesty's Ship *Ferret*, sent the boats for 11 barrels water.

May 18, 1764 Friday SW
Gilkuker NNW ½ W and St Helen Point south
The same weather People Employed variously at AM weighed and sighted the anchor, at Noon anchored with the best Bower in 7 ½ fathom water, Gilkuker NNW ½ W St. Helens point South got on board 4 barrels water.

May 19, 1764 Saturday WSW
The same weather winds variable sailed from hence several sail of Merchantmen to the Eastward received on board fresh
Beef for the ships company.

May 20, 1764 Sunday SSE, SW, WSW
Read Town SSW ½ mile
Moderate and hazy weather at 2 PM we weighed anchor and came to sail, turning from Spithead towards Cows at 6 we anchored in

10 fathom water with the best Bower, Pude Town bearing SSW dist ½ mile got up the Hammocks and cleaned between decks.

May 21, 1764 Monday SW

W. Cows S b W do. S b E

PM fresh gales and clear weather at ½ past two we weighed and got under sail Employd turning up to Cows at ½ past 5 we anchored in Cows Road with the best Bower in 8 fathoms water AM moored ship with the stream anchor and howser with Cows bearing.

May 22, 1764 Tuesday SW

PM moderate and hazy weather overhauled all the boatswains stores at 9 AM: we fired a gun and made a signal to unmoor ship we took up the stream anchor and hove short up on the best Bower sent the boat for 6 casks water at Noon we weighed and got under sail.

May 23, 1764 Wednesday Calm, W, SW

Hurst Castle WNW, Yarmouth S b W 2 miles

Light breezes and hazey weather at 2 PM anchored with the best Bower 14 fathoms water ¼ mile from the shore, the west point of Cows bearing SSE 1 mile at 4 we weighed anchor and came to sail Employed turning between the white and the main at ½ past of we came too with the best Bower in 5 fathoms water in letting it go broke the chain of the shank painter and lost it overboard Hess Castle NNW Needle point WSW Yarmouth S b W.

May 24, 1764 Thursday SW

Small airs and clear weather the Middle and latter part calm the ship company Employed setting up the Riging fore and aft sent the boat on shore and got 5 barrels water.

May 25, 1764 Friday WSW calm, variable

The same weather People Employed fixing the quarter deck awnings and rattling down the shrouds fore and aft at 6 PM past by His Majestys ship *Montreal* from Naples.

May 26, 1764 Saturday calm, N, NE, E

Island of Alderney SSE 4 leagues the Gasquito S ½ E 3 ½ leagues Calm and clear weather people employed variously at 5 PM light airs from the northward loosed the topsails and fired a gun and made as signal to weigh, at 7 we weighed and got under sail at ½ past 8 the Needles point SSE ¼ of a mile at 4 AM the highland of St. Albans NNE 8 or 9 leagues at 6 several sail in sight at 8 light airs and hazy weather at 9 saw the Island of Aldenney SSW 6 leagues.

May 27, 1764 Sunday N, NW, WNW, W b N

Gasquites SE 4 or 5 leagues
Calm and clear weather PM anchored with the stream anchor and hawser in 35 fathom water at 5 light airs from the NW quarter at 8 weighed and came to sail at 11 sounded 35 fathoms course sand at 2 AM sounded.

May 28, 1764 Monday calm, NW, NNW, NNE
Gasquitos E b S 7 or 8 leagues
Calm and clear weather PM anchored with the stream anchor and hawser in 35 fathoms water at 5 light airs from the NW quarter at 8 weighed and came to sail at 11 sounded AM sounded 38 fathom the same ground at 4 we tacked at 7 we tacked again, at 10 moderate and hazy weather saw several sail of vessels.

May 29, 1764 Tuesday NNW, N, NW
Guernsey East 7 or 8 leagues
PM light airs and hazy weather at 5 variable at 7 we anchored in 27 fathoms water with the best bower to stop tide at 2 AM the same weather we weighed and to sail at 5 clear weather at 10 saw the Island of Guernsey E b S 7 08 leagues.

May 30, 1764 Wednesday N b E, NE, E b N
Lands End N 47:30 E dist. 17 leagues
PM light breezes and weather at 2 we passed three Islands of Guernsey ESE 7 leagues at 7 clear weather and fresh breezes saw 2 sail in the NW quarter at 7 AM saw the land bearing from NW b N to NNE at 9 fresh gales and clear weather at 10 sett steering sails lost sight of the land.

May 31, 1764 Thursday E
Lands End 71 N 56 E dist. 72 leagues
PM fresh breezes and cloudy weather, at 5 squaly took in 1st reefs in the main topsail hauled down the fore topsail at 4 AM sett the fore top sails at 8 the same weather - saw a sail in the NW quarter standing to the northward.

June 1, 1764 Friday E, ESE
Cape Race S 85:25 W dist. 49 leagues
PM fresh gales and clear weather read the Articles of War and abstract of the New Act of Parliament to the ships company, at 7 AM the same weather, people employed in making points and gasketts.

Reading the Articles of war and the Abstract of Parliament was done at least once a month on Sunday with religious observation. Its intent was to inform and remind the ships company what was expected of them. There were 36 articles (18 of which could be

punishable by death), aboard ship they assumed the significance of holy writ being the law aboard His Majesty's Ships.
The Articles of War were originally established in the 1650s and amended in 1749 and in 1757 by an act of Parliament.

June 2, 1764 Saturday E b S
Cape Race S 86:27 W
PM fresh gales and cloudy weather Employed making points at 12 more moderate at 4 AM light breezes and cloudy at 7 out 1 & 2 reef main topsail at 12 light breezes and clear.
June 3, 1764 Sunday E, NW, N
Cape Clear No 53 52 E dist. 120 leagues
PM light breezes and Cloudy at 7 opened cask of Pork No. 2265 contents 216, at 4 AM: the same weather saw a sail in the NW quarter at 7 spoke with her being from Cadiz bound to Guernsey 5 weeks passage.
June 4, 1764 Monday W b N, E b S, SE
Cape Clear N 54:52 E dist. 128 leagues 1 mile
PM calm and clear weather at 7 in first reefs topsails at 4 AM: light airs and cloudy out at 6 first reef of the topsails.
June 5, 1764 Tuesday SSW, S, SW
Cape Clear N. 61:55 E, dist 162 leagues
Fresh gales and clear weather at 9 PM: in first reef mizen topsail at 12 fresh gales and squaly at 5 AM: in first reef fore & main T:sail at 7 moderate and clear at 10 out reefs the topsails at 12 saw a sail in the SW quarter.
June 6, 1764 Wednesday S b W, NW b W, SW, S
PM fresh breezes and cloudy, at 4 in first Reef of the topsails, at 5 fresh breezes and squaly at 6 close reefed both topsails and hauled down mizen topsails, at 9 hard gales and squaly with rain at 10 hauled the mainsail up, run under the foresail and two topsails at 1 AM: more moderate with rain at 2 light breezes and hazy with rain, at 4 fresh gales and squaly, set the mainsail at 10 the same weather with heavy squals hauled up the mainsail and both topsails under the fore sail Main stay sail and mizen.

The upper sails and yards were extremely important in handling the ship and were fragile to the gales that struck them frequently requiring them to be lowered and furled with all possible dispatch. These sails were termed the top hamper in 1791. To handle these sails and spars the best of the ships company was divided into groups and the best of the able seamen were assigned to the three masts as "topmen".

The duty of the topman was to get aloft as soon as possible after ordered to work the upper yards of the masts well above the lower yards. They climbed aloft and lay out on the yards to reef, furl, or loose the sails. Of the topmen of the ship the best of these sailors was called the captain of the top. Topmen had one hand for the ship and the other for themselves.

June 7, 1764 Thursday SW, S b W, N b W, W
Lands End W 79: 34 E dist. 243 leagues
PM hard gales and squaly weather hove too with our head to the northward, at 4 wore ship and lay too with our head to the westward at 8 hard gales and cloudy saw a sail in the SW quarter at 6 AM: the same weather moored ship and lay too with our head to the northward set the topsails and courses, at 9 fresh breezes and cloudy, spoke with a schooner from North Carolina bound to Bristol.

June 8, 1764 Friday W, WSW, SW b W
Lands End N : 46 E dist. 240 leagues
PM fresh breezes and cloudy found the main jeers gone in the nip, slung the main yard and unroofed them at 5 reefed the jeers and swayed the yard up at 2 AM: fresh breezes and cloudy at 6 out 3 reef fore and main topsails, at 12 more moderate and hazey.

June 9, 1764 Saturday W b S, WNW, SSW, S b W
Lands End N 83:40 E dist. 242 leagues
PM light breezes and hazey weather with small rain at 4 out 2d reef topsails, at 5 tacked ship to the westward at 7 light airs and hazy up top gallant yards, at 9 foggy with small rain at 12 AM fresh breezes and hazey.

June 10, 1764 Sunday WSW, W, W b S
Lands End 78:49 E dist. 245 leagues
PM fresh breezes with thick fogs at 3 close reefed the topsails at 3 AM fresh breezes and cloudy out 3d reef the topsails at 8 more moderate and clear out all reefs at 11 in first 2d reefs of the topsails at 12 fresh breezes and cloudy.

June 11, 1764 Monday W, W b S, SW, S b W
Lands End N 80:37 W 249 leagues Fresh breezes and clear weather at 3 tacked ship to the southward at 8 the same weather tacked ship at 12 fresh breezes and cloudy at 3 AM closed reef fore and main topsails handled mizen & topsails at 6 fresh gales and squaly at 8 handed fore and main topsails at 11 the same weather with rain set fore and main topsails.

June 12, 1764 Tuesday W b S, W, S, W b S
Lands End S 89:27 E 256 leagues
PM fresh gales and squaly at 4 handed fore and main topsails at 9 got down topgallant yards, at 11 in clewing up the main topsail split it, unbent it and bent another, at 11 AM more moderate set the close reef topsail, at 6 calm and cloudy with rain at 8 fresh breezes and squaly at 9 took in fore topsail.
June 13, 1764 Wednesday W, NW b N, W, ESE, NNE, NW b N
Lands End 89:54 E dist. 266 leagues PM fresh gales and squaly with rain at 3 handed main topsail, at 4 more moderate with some rain at 5 set the close reefed fore and main topsail, at 3 AM out reefs of the topsails at 4 light breezes with rain, at 5 up topgallant yards, at 12 the sail makers employed making the sails.
June 14, 1764 Thursday NW, NW b W, NW b N, N
Cape Race S 80:59 W dist. 329 leagues
PM light breezes and cloudy, at 4 AM light breezes and clear, at 10 fresh breezes and clear, sail maker Employd mending the sails.

Serving with a warrant, the sail maker was appointed to fill a vacancy and to do a job. He repaired damaged sails and made canvas products such as awnings and replacement sails. He was responsible for spare canvas in the ship's stores which he and his assistants worked with needle, heavy thread and leather palm used to force the needle through layers of heavy canvas.

June 15, 1764 Friday N, N b E, NNE
Cape Race 83:52 W dist. 274 leagues
PM fresh breezes and clear weather, at 11 AM the same weather the sail maker employed in mending the sails.
June 16, 1764 Saturday NNE, NE, N b W
Cape Race 87:07 W 237 leagues 1/3 mile
PM light breezes and clear weather at 6 served the ships company fishing lines and hooks at 9 AM down steering sails, at 11 moderate and cloudy, the sailmaker employed in mending the sails.
June 17, 1764 Sunday N, ENE, S b E, SSW
Cape Race 87:46 W 221 leagues
PM light breezes and calms, at 6 down steering sails the Suns amplitude 20:36 at 7 fresh breezes and cloudy the sail makers employed as before.
June 18, 1764 Monday SSW
Cape Race West 181 leagues
PM fresh breezes and cloudy weather at 7 in first reef fore and

main topsails, at 8 opened a cask of beef at 12 saw a sail in the SW 9 standing to the eastward at 8 AM fresh breezes with rain.

June 19, 1764 Tuesday S b W, WNW, W, SW
Cape Race W 189 leagues
PM fresh breezes and cloudy weather at 8 thick hazy and rain, at 12 light airs and hazy, at 7 AM calm and cloudy at 9 out reef topsails, at 11 tacked ship to the westward.

June 20, 1764 Wednesday NW b N, SSW, SE, ENE, SSE, S
Cape Race N87:47W 172 leagues
PM moderate and cloudy weather with hazy, at 10 close reef topsails at 2 AM light breezes and small rain out reef topsails.

June 21, 1764 Thursday S b E, W b S, NW, NNW, SSE
Cape Race 85 N 22 W 166 leagues
PM moderate and hazy with small rain at 3 down steering sails at 5 tacked ship to the westward at 7 light breezes and cloudy at 1 in first reef topsails at 10 fresh breezes and hazy in 2d Reef topsails, at AM put 2d and 3rd Reef topsails at 10 pleasant breezes and clear, set steering sails fore and aft at 12 in steering sails, the sail maker Employed mending the sails.

June 22, 1764 Friday SW b W, SW, NW b N, N b W, NW, WNW
Cape Race 152 leagues 1/3 m.
PM fresh breezes and clear weather at 2 in first reef the Mizen topsails at 6 squaly with rain, at 10 handed mizen topsails at 11 handed fore & main topsails at 1 AM: handed the courses and hove to under the mizen and foresail at 4 fresh gales squaly with lightening at 5 wore ship the same board fore and mizen tack, at 7 set the topsails at 8 put 2d & 3 reef topsails at 2 reef main top saw a sail in the SW quarter, fired a gun & make a signal to speak to her at 10 moderate and calm, the sail makers finished the main topsail.

June 23, 1764 Saturday SW b W, N, SSW, SW, SW b W
Cape Race dist. 132 leagues 2/3 m.
PM moderate and cloudy weather with rain, at 3 wore ship to the eastward - at 4 fresh breezes and cloudy at 6 saw a sail in the SW qtr. standing to the eastward at 7 in first and 2d reefs fore and main topsails at 8 fresh gales and squaly with rain, at 4 AM handed the mizen topsails, at 5 fresh gales and squaly with thick fog and rain at 7 saw a sail in the SW quarter standing to the Eastward fired a gun and spoke to her bound from N. York to London.

June 24, 1764 Sunday WNW, S, N b E, NE
Cape Race 85:49 128 leagues
PM fresh gales and clear weather, broke the foretop bowling

bridle reeved another and set the topsail, at 4 light breeze and clear at 6 out 2d reef topsail at 7 thick fogg at 4 AM wore ship to the westward out first reef fore and main topsails at 8 cloudy weather set steering sails.

June 25, 1764 Monday S b N, NE, E, NE
Cape Race 101 leagues
PM moderate and cloudy weather at 10 down steering sails at 12 fresh breezes with rain, at 3 AM set steering sails at 10 fresh gales with thick foggs and rain, Employed clearing away to fill salt water in the fore hold.

June 26, 1764 Tuesday NE, ESE, S
Cape Race 8 leagues
PM fresh breezes with haze at 5 saw a sail in the NW quarter standing to the westward, at 7 filled 7 tons of salt water in the fore hold at 2 AM moderate with thick fogg.

June 27, 1764 Wednesday SW b S, W b N, W, W b S
Cape Race dist 80 leagues
PM light breezes and fogg weather at 8 in first & 2d reef mizen topsail at 9 in first & 2d reef fore and main topsails at 11 AM sounded 57 fathom water, broken shells mixed with small stones.

June 28, 1764 Thursday W b S, WSW, NW b N, WSW
Cape Race 66 leagues 2/3 m
PM light breezes with foggs at 2 made sail, out 2d and first reefs mizen, the fore and main topsail, at 5 in first and 2d reefs fore and main topsails, at 7 sounded 45 fathom water, at 10 hove too and sounded 40 fathom sand stones, made sail at 12 the same weather tacked ship at 3 AM fresh breezes and foggy weather, fired 4 guns in the night at 6 hove too and sounded 40 fathoms fine gray sand with black shells, at 11 hove too and sounded 33 fathom the same ground handed topsail and courses and came too with the stream anchor and hawser, Employed in fishing and catched a number of cod made reef and clear, 3 sail in sight.

Most of early navigation was based on the simple activities of time keeping using the sandglass, reel, log chip and the lead. Sounding was a key activity carried out aboard ship by the leadsman giving a description of the bottom immediately below the ship. Since ships sailed the seas the danger of hitting something was the over riding concern of the vessel. Beyond this immediate concern for safety was the basic act of knowing where the vessel was. Sounding did just that by bringing detail of the bottom to the men on deck. Soundings were important to making charts of the shoreline and the survey crews aboard the Canceaux spent most of their time in this endeavor. The lead was a hollow cone filled with tallow so the material on the bottom of the sea would adhere to the lead giving samples of the sea bed. The line was marked at regular intervals with distances that could be easily noted as the line was hauled in all weather conditions. The marking on the line were simple and easily seen in heavy weather: two leather strips for 2 fathoms, three for three fathoms, white duck for five fathoms red bunting for seven and so on.

June 29, 1764 Friday WSW, SW b W, WSW
Cape Race 62 leagues
PM moderate and clear weather at 3 weighed anchor and came to sail at 4 fresh breezes & thick fogg, and wore ship to the northward in 3 reef of the topsail and down topgallant yards at 12 fired 2 guns at 2 AM: sounded 37 fathom water at 4 sounded 44 fathom fine gray sand fired 2 guns, at 6 sounded 40 fathom, at 8 sounded 43 fathom small white sand fired 2 guns, at 9 wore ship and out 2 reef set the main topsail, at 12 sounded 42 fathom small white stones, fresh gales with thick foggs.
June 30, 1764 Saturday W b S, W b N, WSW, W
Cape Race dist 71 leagues 1/3
PM fresh breezes with thick foggs handed mizen topsail at 2 clear reef the fore topsails and handed them at 4 wore the ship to the southward fired 2 guns at 6 set the fore topsail, found the starboard fore futtock shroud gone, set a new fix a new one, at 8 closed reefed the topsails, and reeved at 12 sounded 53 fathoms water gray sand with black stones at 4 AM the same weather sounded 60 fathoms water white sand at 5 set the fore topsails at 8 wore the ship sounded no ground at 70 fathoms set the mizen topsail.
July 1, 1764 Sunday W, W b N, W b S, W
Cape Race 71 leagues
PM fresh breezes with thick foggs Read the Articles of War and abstract of the new act of Parliament to the ships company at 4 moderate and clear put first reefs fore and main topsail, and tacked ship, at 6 tacked ship at 8 tacked ship at 11 handed mizen topsail at 4 AM sounded 35 fathoms small gravel tacked ship, and let the mizen topsail, at 8 saw a large island of ice bearing south 2 leagues, moderate and clear out all reefs, sounded 46 fathom small gravel and glittering stones, at 12 the Island of Ice bearing of E b S 2 leagues sounded 34 fathoms gray sand with broken

shells fresh breezes and clear.

July 2, 1764 Monday NNW, W b S, W, SW

Cape Race 75 leagues

PM fresh breezes and clear weather, made sail at 6 sounded no ground at 120 fathom in first reef topsails at 8 light airs and cloudy at 2 AM sounded no ground at 80 fathom at 3 wore ship at 9 out reefs of the topsails and up topgallant yards saw 3 sail in the NW quarter.

July 3, 1764 Tuesday NW, S, S b E, NW b N, W b S

Island St. Pauls N72 28W dist 125 leagues Cape Raien dist 41 leagues PM fresh breezes and cloudy weather shorten sail sounded 35 fathoms water at 2 made sail and set steering sails at 9 saw 2 sail in SW quarter at 10 fresh gales and squaly with rain down steering sails, at 2 AM in first and 2d reef of the topsails at 4 thick fogg with rain at 7 out 2d reef fore and main topsails at 8 sounded 36 fathom broken shells with brown stones at 10 in 3d reef fore topsail saw a sail in the SW quarter at 12 fresh gales with thick fogs in 3d reef of main topsail.

July 4, 1764 Wednesday W, WNW, N, W, W

Cape Race 43 leagues

PM fresh gales and squaly with thick fogs handed the mizen topsail at 4 tacked ship to the Southward and sounded 40 fathom water, at 8 fresh gales and clear weather at 12 more moderate set mizen topsail, at 4 AM wore ship to the south-ward, brought too and sounded 35 fathom broken shells, saw a sail in the NE quarter, at 7 out 3d and 2d reef topsail and made sail, at 11 sounded 36 fathom shortened sail to fish, light airs clear weather.

July 5, 1764 Thursday SSE, SW b W

Cape Race 24 leagues, Cape Roy 102 leagues, Island of St. Pauls 104 leagues PM light breezes and clear weather, ship head to the southward at 4 set steering sails and made sail at 7 set steering sails at 9 fresh breezes with rain, at 12 close reef the fore topsail 2d reef main topsail, at 9 AM handed mizen topsail, at 4 fresh gales and squaly with rain at 10 sounded 36 fathoms small gravel hard gales and squaly with rain.

July 6, 1764 Friday SW, WNW, NNE, N

Cape Roy dist 105 leagues

PM fresh gales with thick fogs, at 3 handed mizen topsail wore ships and in 3d reef fore and main topsails, at 5 down gallant yards, at 7 hard gales and squaly, with hard claps of thunder and hail, clewed up the fore and main topsails, split the fore topsail unbent him and bent another at 9 split the main topmast stay sail, at

11 under fore sail and main sail at 4 AM more moderate with haze set topsail.

July 7, 1764 Saturday W b S, W, N b W, WSW
Cape Roy 91 leagues.
PM light breezes and clear weather, at 3 out 3d reef topsail at 5 out reefs topsails, at 7 tacked ship, at 4 light breezes and hazy at 8 AM fresh breezes and cloudy, at 9 up top gallant yards.

July 8, 1764 Sunday SW b S, SW, SW b W
Cape Roy
PM fresh breezes and cloudy, at 8 sounded 34 fathom water, at 9 in 2d reef mizen topsail, at 1 AM fresh breezes and squaly with rain, at 2 in 2d reef main topsail at 6 sounded, no ground at 7 at 9 sounded no ground at 120 fathom at 10 out 2d reef topsails.

July 9, 1764 Monday W b S, W b N, NW, NNW
Cape Roy 64 leagues
PM moderate and foggy weather, at 8 tacked ship sounded no ground at 120 fathoms, at 9 fresh breezes and cloudy weather, close reef the topsails and handed the mizen at 10 fresh gales and cloudy with rain handed fore topsail at 10 AM set the fore topsail, at 12 same weather sounded no ground.

July 10, 1764 Tuesday NNW, WNW, W, W b S
Cape Roy 50 leagues
PM light breezes and clear weather sounded 88 fathoms gray sand at 6 tacked ship, at 9 saw two sail to the westward at 11 in first reefs the topsails at 12 fresh breezes and clear, at 7 AM saw a sail in the SW quarter at 9 fresh breezes and cloudy with rain at 10 out first reef topsails.

July 11, 1764 Wednesday WSW, SW b S, NNE, NE, NE b E
Seatara Point dist. 10 leagues
PM fresh breezes with thick fogs, saw the sand bearing from the NE to NW which proved to be the Island of Cape Breton at 7 saw the Island of Porta Nova Bearing ENE 2 miles, down steering sails, spoke a fishing boat belonging to Louisbourg, at 8 lost sight of the land, at 10 fired 2 guns, at 12 sounded 32 fathom rocky ground, fired 2 guns, at 3 sounded 28 fathom the same ground at 4 AM calm, at 7 a small breeze, at 9 saw the land bearing from NW b W to NNW dist 4 or 5 leagues Louisbourg W b N 6 leagues, Seatara NNW ½ N 4 leagues, Movienna NW b N 5 leagues light airs and clear weather.

July 12, 1764 Thursday S b W, S, SSE, W, NW b W
Cape Roy dist. 10 leagues PM light airs and calms with thick fogs, at 2 the north part of Seatara WNW 3 or 4 leagues, and

northernmost land NW 5 or 6 leagues a 5 fresh breezes spoke with a fishing Schooner, at 8 fired a gun, at 2 AM fresh breezes with rain and lightening, at 4 fired a gun, at 7 calm at 8 down steering sails at 9 fresh breezes and foggy fired 2 guns and spoke his Majesty's ship *Senegal* hove too main topsail to the mast in first reef of the topsail fresh breezes with haze.

July 13, 1764 Friday NW, NW b N, WNW, NNW, N

Islands Caisles 5 leagues

PM fresh breezes and fogy, Cape Roy North dist: 7 leagues the extreme of the land from N to E b S dist 5 leagues, saw a sail in the NW quadrant at 5 Cape Roy north 5 or 6 leagues, at 7 hove too main topsail to the mast at 9 made sail at 10 Cape Roy NNE 7 or 8 leagues in first reef fore and main topsail up mizen topsail and down topgallant yards, at 1 AM clear weather at 3 saw a sail to the SE out 2d reef topsails gave chase to her His Majestys Sloop *Senegal* at 5 Cape Roy NE dist 8 leagues Island St. Pauls NW b W 5 leagues Cape North W b N 9 or 10 leagues up topgallant yards out all reefs, tacked ship the *Senegal* and chase out of sight, at 9 Cape North W ½ N 6 or 7 leagues fresh breezes and clear, at 11 AM the Island of St. Pauls W ½ N 4 leagues Cape Moorth ? W b S 8 leagues Cape Roy NE ½ E dist. 12 leagues.

July 14, 1764 Saturday N, WSW, calm, SW b S

Cape Bazoier 32 leagues

PM clear weather and calm at 4 light airs and hazy, Cape North W b S ½ S Island St. Pauls W Cape Roy NE b E, saw a sail in the NW quarter at 6 set steering sails for and aft at 7 the northernmost part of St. Pauls, N b S 6 leagues Took the Suns amplitude N 38 W 30 f at 9 Island St. Pauls SW dist 7 leagues at 10 the No most part of land in sight of Little port, NE b E 11 leagues at 4 AM saw the land bearing SE ½ S at 6 down steering sails at 12 fresh breezes and cloudy.

July 15, 1764 Sunday SW ½ W, SW b S

Cape Rosier 5 or 6 leagues

PM fresh breezes and clear weather, at 7 AM the same weather the land bearing NNW which proved to be the island of Bonadventure at 9 fresh gales in first & 2d reefs of the topsails, at 10 saw 2 sail one in the NE Standing to the Noward and one in the SE standing to the southward, Island of Bonadventure SW Cape Gaspe SW b W Cape Ferson WSW Cape Rosier W b N dist. 5 or 6 leagues.

July 16, 1764 Monday SSW, SW, W b N, SW, NW b W

Point St. Annes 10 leagues

PM fresh gales and clear weather, at 2 spoke the ship *Mary* from

Falmouth bound to Gaspee and Quebec at 6 Point Rosier S b E dist. 9 or 10 leagues Little Fox River SW b S 4 leagues Grandetan Point NW b W 8 leagues, at 7 squaly in the first & 2d reef T:sail at 9 saw a sail in the NE standing to the westward at 10 Grand Etain, S b W 2 leagues Point Magdalin NW b W 4 miles at 12 little N Patty, SSW 3 leagues the point Almadline W b S 4 leagues at 3 AM the river Ss. Magdelion, SW 4 leagues at 8 saw a sail in the NW quarter standing to the southward out 2d & 1st reef topsails at 11 moderate breezes Magdalion River S 3 leagues.

July 17, 1764 Tuesday S, WNW, WSW, W, N b W

Cape Rozier 6 or 7 leagues

PM light breezes at 3 sounded 90 fathoms muddy ground at 5 the River Magdaline SSW 5 leagues fired a gun and made a signal to speak to a schooner at 9 Mount Louis SW b S 5 leagues St. Anne Point W b S 10 leagues at 1 AM fresh breezes and cloudy with lightening in 1 st and 2d reef topsail at 3 set fore & main topsail at 6 down topgallant yards at 8 fresh gales set & at 7 hoist topsails and tacked ship at 10 handed the mizen topsail, hard gales handed fore & mizen topsail hoisted up the & and lay too under the main sail the river Magdalin WSW 8 leagues St. Annes W b S 10 leagues.

July 18, 1764 Wednesday SSW, N b E, NNE, NW b N, SW b W

Cape Rozier 6 or 7 leagues

PM fresh gales and clear weather under the main sail reef the lower sails & set the main sail at 3 wore ship Mount Louie SW b S 5 leagues, fired a gun and made signal to speak a schooner at 9 Mount Louis SW b S 5 leagues St. Anne Point W b S 10 leagues at 1 AM fresh breezes and cloudy with lightening in 1st and 2d reefs topsails at 3 in fore & maintop sail at 6 down topgallant yards at 8 fresh gales set topsails and tacked ship at 10 handed the mizen topsail, hard gales handed fore & main topsail hauled up the fore sail and lay to under the main sail the river Magdalin S b W 8 leagues St. Annes W ½ S 10 leagues.

July 18, 1764 Wednesday SSW, N b E, NNE, NE b N, SW b W

Cape Bozier 6 or 7 leagues

PM fresh gales and clear weather under the main sail reef the courses & set the main sail at 3 wore ship Mount Lieus west & Point Grand Elan SE at 5 set the fore sail at 6 the Extreme point of the land from SE b S 40 W ½ S dist off shore 5 leagues at 8 the River Magdalin SW 6 or 7 leagues and Mount Lieue Point W b S 10 or 11 leagues at 11 wore ship at 12 under fore sail & mizen at 4 AM wore ship at 8 wore ship Grand Etan Vally WS b W 3 or 4 leagues and Cape Rozier SE b S 3 or 4 leagues at 9 bore away, out reefs of the courses and set the close reeft topsails, at 12 Cape Bozier SE b !/2 E 7 leagues hard & weather.

July 19, 1764 Thursday NW, WNW, NNE, W
At single anchor in Gaspie Bay White Rock E b N Fleet Island S b E dist. 4 miles
PM hard gales and squaly weather at 3 Cape Bozier E b S 3 miles at White Rock NW ½ a mile employed turning up the Bay of Gaspie at 11 came too with the best bower in 30 fathom water White Rock 6 NE flat Island S b E dist 4 miles 2 schooners at anchor at 7 AM fresh gales with small rain Boats employed watering the ship, came down and went from the head of the Bay a merchant ship.

July 20, 1764 Friday WSW, NW, W b S
Undersail Cape Bozire NNW 4 leagues
PM moderate and fair weather, the boats employed watering the ship at 9 weighed and came to sail, out reefs the topsails at 10 got up top gallant yards. White Rock NNW one mile at 12 fired 2 guns, at 4 AM strong currents setting to the NE light airs and clear weather at 6 saw a ship & 4 sail in shore standing to the Northward Cape Rozier NNW dist 4 leagues at 11 the island of Bonaventure SW b W 9 leagues Cape Rozier NW b W 9 leagues Cape Ferdon WNW 6 leagues.

July 21, 1764 Saturday SSW
Little Fox River west 3 leagues
PM light airs & clear weather at 4 Cape Feron W b S & Cape Griffin NW 6 or 7 leagues at 6 Island Bonaventure SW b S 10 leagues Cape Boziers W b S 6 leagues at 8 Cape Farione SW b S 7 leagues River Griffon W ½ N 3 leagues northernmost land NW 6 or 7 leagues at 4 AM Great Fox River SW b S 3 leagues
at 6 fired a gun and brought too a Brigg from Plymouth bound to Quebec Great Fox River W b N & Little Fox River West 3 leagues at 12 Grand Etan W Point Magdalen WNW 9 or 10 leagues fair weather.

July 22, 1764 Sunday NW b W, SW, W, W b S, W
Island of Anticoste ESE 11 leagues
PM light airs clear weather at 3 Magdalen Point W b N 4 leagues Grand Valley SW b S 3 leagues at 8 Point Louie WSW ½ W 10 or 11 leagues Grand Valley SSW dist. off shore 3 or 4 leagues at 10 in first & 2d reef fore & main topsail, and close reef mizen topsail fresh breezes with lightening, at 3 AM light breezes, out reefs topsails, at 6 opened a cask of pork No. 2278 210 pieces at 12

moderate & hazey in latitude 49S.

July 23, 1764 Monday W b S, WSW, W, calm
River St. Lawrence Great Island dist 6 leagues
PM fresh breezes and clear weather, at 3, 2 sail in sight at 6 saw the land the Eastward from WNW to ENE at 9 fired a gun and brought too the ship *Ann* from Gaspie to Quebec at 12 Peak Island NW 4 leagues at 4 AM light airs and Cloudy at 6 sounded 16 fathoms muddy ground Great Island N b W & hazy weather at 10 thick fog fired a gun, at 12 Great Island N ½ E distance 5 leagues.

July 24, 1764 Tuesday S, WSW, W, WNW, NE b N
Cape Chatt SSW 6 leagues
PM calm and cloudy weather at 5 fresh breezes and clear, at 6 Seapoint distance WNW 5 leagues at 9 tacked ship at 4 St. Amas River South 6 or 7 leagues at 6 AM tacked ship light breezes and clear, at 10 tacked ship & set steering sails at 12 light airs and foggy.

July 25, 1764 Wednesday SW, S, SW b W, WNW, NW, NE, S
C. Chatt E 7 leagues
PM light breezes and hazy weather, down steering sails at 7 Cape Death W ½ N 6 leagues tacked ship at 8 fresh breezes, Cape Death N b W 5 leagues at 9 squaly in first topsails at 12 thunder & lightening at 3 AM calm with lightening at 5 Cape Cat SW B S 3 or 4 leagues out reefs topsails at 10 tacked ship at 12 fresh breezes & clear weather Cape Cat East dist. 7 leagues.

July 26, 1764 Thursday W, NW, W, SSW, W b S
Cape Maten WSW 5 leagues
PM fresh breezes and cloudy at 4 tacked ship, at 5 Cape Chatt ESE 6 leagues. Most land in sight W b S 7 or 8 leagues at 10 tacked ship Cape Cat East ½ N 6 leagues, at 12 tacked ship & sounded no ground at 60 fathoms at 4 AM the west most land in sight WSW dist. of 8 leagues Point Dawson N at 7 leagues at 7 fresh breezes & cloudy tacked ship & carried away in the mizen vang in the strap of the mizen deck block at 9 Cape Death S b E 9 leagues at 11 tacked ship Cape Matan WSW 4 leagues sounded 18 fathom fine sand.

July 27, 1764 Friday W, W b N, SSW, SW, W b S
Metane River SSW 4 miles
PM moderate & cloudy weather at 2 tacked ship, at 3 tacked ship at 4 River Matano WSW at 4 leagues at 7 calm & foggy fired 2 guns Metana WSW ½ W dist 3 leagues at 12 sounded 80 fathom muddy ground, at 4 AM light breezes & foggy sounded 30 fathom, and Point Kimita WSW 8 or 9 leagues, River Malane SSW 4 miles

at 10 tacked ship.

July 28, 1764 Saturday W, SE, W, W b S

Matan River S b W 3 leagues

PM light breezes and hazy weather, at 3 came too with the Kedge anchor and hawsers in 11 fathom Metan River south dist. 1 ½ miles at 7 weighed and came to sail as if the ship Ann, at 10 sounded 25 fathoms muddy ground, lost a hand line & line overboard at 2 AM tacked ship and sounded 40 fathom, at 3 came too with the stream anchor & hawser in 10 fathom water cleared out a whole cable River Matan S b E 2 miles at 10 fresh breezes and cloudy weighed and got under sail was a sail to the Eastward.

July 29, 1764 Sunday W b N, NW b N, NW b W, NW

Sather Point WSW 2 leagues, N Point of Beek W 5 leagues

PM fresh breezes and hazy weather at 3 tacked ship, and set steering sails at 5 fresh breezes with rain at 6 sounded 45 fathom muddy ground, at 8 sounded 22 fathom the same ground, saw the land bearing from WSW to SE 3 miles off shore, the ship *Ann* in company saw a brigg the Northmost part of Beck 5 leagues.

July 30, 1764 Monday SW, WSW, calm

Island of Beek WSW 2 leagues St. Barnby SE 4 miles

PM fresh breezes and cloudy at 4 Isle Beek WSW 6 or 7 leagues moderate & clear at 6 came too with the stream anchor & hawser in 12 fathom water cleared to a whole cable Isle Beck W b S 5 leagues. Barnby Island S b E 4 or 5 leagues, Beek SW 3 leagues, at 10 came too with stream anchor and hawser in 11 fathom water, Isle Beck W ½ W St. Barniby Iles SE 4 miles at 12 weighed and came to sail.

July 31, 1764 Tuesday W b S, WNW, NW

Island Beck WNW ½ mile

PM light breezes and clear weather at 7 came too with stream anchor & cable in 12 fathom the Island of Beek, West SW dist. 2 miles Cape Original SW b S 3 miles, at 1 AM weighed and came to sail, at 2 sounded from 12 to 13 fathom muddy ground, at 6 came too with the stream anchor and hawser in 12 fathom veered to ½ a cable Isle Beck W b S dist. 1 league at 10 light breezes and cloudy weighed and came to sail Isle Beck WSW.

Aug. 1, 1764 Wednesday W, WSW, N, calm

Isles of Beck East 4 leagues

PM light airs & cloudy sounding from 13 to 20 fathoms muddy ground at 5 came too with the stream anchor and hawser, in 10 fathom water, Isle of Beck E b E 2 leagues. At 11 AM weighed and came to sail, at 3 set steering sails at 4 down steering sails, at

8 came to with the stream anchor and cables in 29 fathoms water came to a whole cable Isle Beek E b W dist 13 leagues at 9 Read the Articles of War & abstract of the new act of Parliament to the ships company at 10 light airs weighed and came to sail the Isle of Beek eastward dist. 3 or 4 leagues.

Aug. 2, 1764 Thursday SW, WSW, W b S, W b N

At anchor Island Beek NE b E dist. 4 leagues

PM light breezes and cloudy with small rain at 5 came too with the stream anchor & hawser in 14 fathoms water, sandy ground veared to a whole cable. Isle Beck SW b W ½ W dist 2 leagues Gerson Island WSW to Senguien Beek NE b E 4 ½ leagues at 9 hard gales & squaly clouds Let go the best bower anchor and veared to a cable down topgallant yards, at 9 AM hard gales with thunder and lightening, at 4 moderate with thick foggs at 8 fresh breezes and foggy.

Aug. 3, 1764 Friday WSW, W, W b S

At anchor Island Beek

PM moderate and hazy weather hove up the best bower and stream anchor and got under sail arrived the ship Ann and a brigg , at 6 found we lost ground came to with the best bower anchor in 4 fathom water sandy ground veared to ½ a cable Sise Point SE b E dist. 4 miles Isle of Beek 13 leagues and Cape Original 11 ½ leagues at 4 AM fresh gales and squaly with rain veared out a whole cable at 6 down topgallant yards.

Aug. 4, 1764 Saturday WNW, WSW, N, SW b W

At anchor Island Beek

PM fresh gales and clear weather, the people Employed drawing yarns and making cloths for the cables, at 4 veered from the ship *Mary* got 1 barrel of beef containing 104 pieces weigh 462 pounds at 12 small rain, at 6 AM fresh gales at 9 sent the boat for wood & water.

Aug. 5, 1764 Sunday

Island of Bask, SSW ½ W 2 leagues

PM moderate & cloudy at 3 weighed and came to sail, turning to the westward at 5 fired a gun shotted at a sloop at a sloop at 6 came too with the stream anchor and hawser in 19 fathom water veared to a whole cable Isle of Beek SW ½ W 2 ½ leagues Isle of Beek E b N 4 ½ leagues off shore dist. 2 leagues. AT 3 AM weighed and came to sail turning to the westward at 6 came too with the stream anchor and hawser in 14 fathom veered to ½ cable Isle of Beck NE b E & Isle of Beek SSW ½ W 2 leagues fresh breezes and cloudy weather.

Aug. 6, 1764 Monday W b S, SW b W, WSW, W
Under sail Condie South ½ a mile
PM fresh gales and cloudy, also squaly let of the best bower and veared to ½ a cable at 7 down topgallant yards, at 9 moderate with rain at 3 AM head up the best bower and stream anchor and came to sail at 6 came too with the stream anchor and hawser in 13 fathom veared a whole cable Island Beek WSW Island Beek NE b S 4 leagues off shore fresh breezes and cloudy.
Aug. 7. 1764 Tuesday WSW, NE, NE b E, ENE
At anchor off Little Cloud Village
PM fresh breezes and cloudy weighed and came to sail at 3 set the steering sail at 6 a baerst of weather at 7 Bask Isle SE ½ E dist 21 miles Guen Isle fromWS b S 1/3 E b S 1 ½ miles Red Island N.W b W 2 leagues at 11 the Celgrines South dist 2 miles at 1 AM fresh gales with thick fog anchored with the best bower in 25 fathoms veared to a whole cable found she did not ride let go the best bower anchor and veered to ½ cable at 4 hove too the small bower anchor and at 6 hove up the best bower and came to sail, at 9 saw the Island of Foundland WSW dist 3 leagues, fired 4 guns a signal for a pilot at 10 came on board a pilot Island of Gander south ½ a mile made sail & stood to the northward.
Aug. 8, 1764 Wednesday NE, SW
Under sail the west part of Gander SW 4 miles
PM Calm & foggy at 9 came too with the best bower anchored in 11 fathom water and veered to ½ a mile Rocky ground little cloud village NW b W dist 1 mile at 5 AM hard gales & squaly with rain found the ship and veered to a whole cable let go the small bower veered to ½ a cable hard rocky ground at 9 past by a sloop from Quebec bound for Boston at 10 began to heave on the best bower. at 11 weighed it and found one of the arms of the anchor gone & 6 fathoms of the cable much rubbed cut it off & began to heave on the small bower.
Aug. 9, 1764 Thursday SW, W
At anchor Cape Paul NW 2 miles
PM hard gales and squaly weather, at 1 hove up the small bower anchor with cable and slack much rubed and buoy & buoy cable gone from the anchor and turn for the Isle of Coudie and lost a hand lead and lone sounding at 4 came too with the small bower anchor in 10 fathom water the Isle of Goodor 1 ½ miles at 9 AM light breezes and clear weighed and came to sail at 12 the west Point of Gander SSW dist 4 miles.
Aug. 10, 1764 Friday calm

At anchor off the Island Orleans St Johns Church N b E 1 ½ miles PM cloudy weather driving up with the tide, at 5 came too with the small bower in 9 fathom water off Little River Little River Church N b E 1 ½ miles at 12 light airs and clear weather weighed and drove up with the tide at 4 AM came too with the small bower in 10 fathom water veered to 2/3 of a cable Cape Pale NW 2 miles at 10 cloudy weighed & drove up with the tide.

Aug. 11, 1764 Saturday calm, SW

At anchor at Quebec

PM calm and cloudy driving up with the tide, at 3 got the boat out & 4 oars ahand rowing towards the Traverse, at 4 got over the Traverse had from half 3 to 5 fathoms in the narrows ½ flood at 6 came too with the small bower anchored in 8 fathoms water off the East end of the Island of Orleans, St. Frances Church W b N dist. 1 mile at 3 AM weighed and came to sail at 5 turning through the narrows between the Island and the main having from 9 to 16 fathoms the tide done came too with the small bower in 14 fathom veered to ½ a cable St. Johns Church N b E dist 1 ½ miles Isle of Madain E b N distance 2 leagues.

Techniques of the survey are suggested by Des Barres as follows: a base line was drawn along a plane in relation to the local shoreline at the extreme ends of the line using a theodolite the surveyor would take angles of sight of objects placed on the opposite which being calculated trigonometrically and protracted in their proper bearings, on paper fixed upon a plain table. Surveyors then repeated the same intersecting the same objets from the same extremities of the base line, by which and other intersections, or series of triangles the surveyor had the distance between an object or banners placed on the shore along the traverse from whence with further intersections performed in the same manner the surveyor determined the true location of features. Repeating the former operations from all the features and islands he had all the angles and distances to agree with previous laid down from earlier observations. From points situated on islands and headlands the surveyor observed other noticeable objects/features as far as they could be distinguished. Next along the shoreline he reexamined the accuracy of every intersected object delineating the true shape of every head land, island, point, bay, rock above water delineating every winding and irregularity. Rocks and breakers were recorded as perfectly as could be. When the map of any part of the coast was completed in this manner, the surveyors immediately provided copies to each survey craft to take in the survey. The sloop was employed in beating off and on, upon the coast, to the distance of ten and twelve miles in the offing (the part of the deep sea seen from the shore) laying down the soundings in their proper bearings and distance, remarking every where the *quality of the bottom.* *The shallop was, in the meantime, kept busy in sounding, and remarking around the headlands, islands, and rocks in the offing; and the boats within the in draught, upwards, to the heads of bays, harbors, etc.*

Aug. 12, 1764 Sunday SW, calm
Moored at Quebec the Citadel NW Point Piers E b N
PM Moderate & clear weather weighed and came to sail turning between the Isle of Orleans & the main Came too with the small bower in 16 fathoms water veered to half a cable Point Livey W b S dist. 2 miles W Point of Orleans NW at 4 AM weighed and came to sail at 7 fired 7 guns to salute the Garisson of Quebec at 8 we anchored with best bower in 16 fathoms water veered away & moored with the small bower to the southward a cable each way the Citadel NSW Point DePieres E b N off Cape Diamond 1 cables length found riding here 3 his Majestys ships the *Mermaid*, the *Garland* & the *Diligence* & several sail of merchant vessels.
Aug. 13, 1764 Monday WSW, calm, SW
Moored at Quebec the Citadel NW
PM fresh breezes & clear weather, sent on shore several boxes and bales directed to the General received on board 217 lb beef for the ships company 1 cask of pease cont: 94 bushels 1 cask of butter 66 lb 1 basket of cheese 29 lb1 butt of Spruce beer Employed variously, received 16 soldiers on board as a party on the survey.
Aug. 14, 1764 Tuesday SW, ENE, SSW
Moored at Quebec the Citadel NW
PM the same weather unloosed the sails to dry and unbent them Employed variously the casks of butter of 66 found it unfit for service. AM sent it onshore to the store the *Mermaid* loosed her fore topsails as did the others.
Aug. 15, 1764 Wednesday SW
Moored at Quebec the Citadel NW
PM fresh gales and squaly with rain Employed cleaning the hold and starting the salt water.
Aug. 16, 1764 Thursday SW, WSW
Moored at Quebec the Citadel NW
PM the same weather as yesterday Employed as before came on

board a Hhd of beer for the ships company.

Aug. 17, 1764 Friday SW, NNE

Moored at Quebec the Citadel NW

PM fresh gales & cloudy, the latter part more moderate & clear weather Employed as before discharged 3 men to His Majestys ship the *Mermaid* per: order of Capt. Dean, at 8 AM the *Mermaid* made a signal to unmoor.

Aug. 18, 1764 Saturday NE

Moored at Quebec the Citadel NW

PM the same weather the people Employed as before Sailed from hence his Majestys ship the *Mermaid*, the *Garland*, & the *Diligence* received on board 255 lb of fresh beef for the ships company, two Hhd of beer 200 lb of bread and 3 firkins of butter containing 198 pounds.

Aug. 19, 1764 Sunday NNE

Moored at Quebec the Citadel NW

PM the same weather People Employed as before.

Aug. 20, 1764 Monday NW, SW

Moored at Quebec the Citadel NW

PM light airs and variable weather Employed as before AM passed round the ship sides with tar absented himself from the ship John Wilkins.

Runaways from the ship early on in the voyage were a serious problem and were treated if apprehended harshly. Being away from ship was a problem when near land and extra precautions were in place to prevent it.

The log documents 25 runaways by name and location for the voyage. Ashore, crew members were under watch of an officer. As the voyage extends over time the number of runaways decreases – this could reflect that the malcontents in the crew all took their chance or that the conditions improved and the crew were less motivated. Record keeping of the ships logs did not change and the regulations did not change suggesting that potential runaways did not exist near the end of the voyage of the Canceaux.

Aug. 21, 1764 Tuesday

Moored at Quebec the Citadel NW

PM the same weather as before, heeled ship to port & payed her with white lead and tallow; AM: Heeled ship to starboard, received on board 65 lb of fresh beef for the ships company.

Aug. 22, 1764 Wednesday NE

Moored at Quebec the Citadel NW
PM the same weather paid the starboard side with white lead and tallow righted ship blacked all mast heads & yards at 6 AM struck yards & topmasts & bent the sheet cable.

Aug. 23, 1764 Thursday WSW
Moored at Quebec the Citadel NW
PM fresh gales with rain, AM moderate & clear got up yards & topmasts and cleared hawse received on board 90 lb of fresh beef for the ships company 1 Hhd of beef, 2 casks of rice cont: 419 lb Employed stowing the hold.

Aug. 24, 1764 Friday WSW
Moored at Quebec the Citadel NW
PM moderate & cloudy at 1, 5 men run away with the boat, John Duggan, Robt. Lock, Wm Johnson, John Cummingham & Saml. Collins at 8 found the boat on the west part of the Island of Orlean Employed as before.

Aug. 25, 1764 Saturday SW
Moored at Quebec the Citadel NW
PM cloudy with thunder & rain AM moderate & clear weather Employed variously received on board 174 lb of fresh beef for the ships company.

Aug. 26, 1764 Sunday variable
Moored at Quebec the Citadel NW The same weather as before Employed variously

Aug. 27, 1764 Monday SW, W
Moored at Quebec the Citadel NW PM moderate & cloudy prest 3 men, AM Employed stowing provisions sent the best bower anchor on shore to be mended.

Aug. 28, 1764 Tuesday W, SW
Moored at Quebec the Citadel NW
PM hard squalles with thunder lightening & rain AM calm & cloudy received on board 28 barrels of beef 19 barrels of pork & 11 firkins of butter Employed shifting 3 tons of Ballast from out the forsl room to the main: hold, recd. on board 225 lb fresh beef for the ships company.

Aug. 29, 1764 Wednesday SW, NNE, SE
Moored at Quebec the Citadel NW PM moderate & cloudy weather Employed fleetting ? the fore shoulder set up the bobstays stayed the foremast & set the shrouds up recd on board 2 Hhds of beer Anchored here a ship from London and a snow from Southampton.

Aug. 30, 1764 Thursday SE, SW

Moored at Quebec the Citadel NW
PM fresh breezes and hazey with rain, Employed variously came in here a sloop and schooner from New England.

Aug. 31, 1764 Friday SE, SW
Moored at Quebec the Citadel NW
PM the same weather Employed scraping the topmasts & topgallant masts AM scraped down the lower masts and payed them with oyle & turpentine.

Varnishing masts with oil of tar and turpentine was a frequent activity of preservation of the masts aboard ship. This kept them from drying out and thus becoming brittle and easily broken.

Sept. 1, 1764 Saturday Var.
Moored at Quebec the Citadel NW
PM mod. with rain came in & anchored here a snow from Cork & a snow from St. Christopher the former with provisions & the latter with rum and sugar received on board 168 lb of fresh beef for the ships company Read the Articles of War and abstract of the new act of Parliament to the ships company.

Sept. 2, 1764 Sunday
Moored at Quebec the Citadel NW
PM moderate & hazy AM fresh gales & cloudy came in & anchored here a brig from London with passengers & goods.

Sept. 3, 1764 Monday
PM mod & fair weather, AM bent the 3 topsails Employed variously.

Sept. 4, 1764 Tuesday
PM fresh breezes and rain received on board 233 lb of fresh beef for the ships company, came in and anchored here a brigantine & schooner from N. York Employed variously, run from the ship John Wattes & John Gask seamen.

Sept 5, 1764 Wednesday
PM fresh breezes & cloudy, AM mod. & cloudy weather Employed variously.

Sept. 6, 1764 Thursday
PM same weather Empd bending the topsails, topg sails jibb and stay sail.

Sept. 7, 1764 Friday
PM fresh breezes and cloudy with rain, completed provisions since the 12 August till the day Vez: fresh beef 3669 lb bread 7761 lb beef 2120 pieces pork 1976 pieces, pease 56 bushells rice 509

pounds beer 5 tons & butter 1599 lb.
Sept. 8, 1764 Saturday
PM moderate & fair weather Employed variously.
Sept. 9, 1764 Sunday
PM the same weather Employed variously
Sept. 10, 1764 Monday
PM Same weather with rain. Recd. on board the best bower anchor & Capt. Hollands goods at 6 loosed the yard arms off topsail a signal for sailing.
Sept. 11, 1764 Tuesday
PM the same weather, AM fresh gales with rain at 5 got down topgallants yards.
Sept. 12. 1764 Wednesday
PM hard gales and squaly with rain at times.
Sept. 13, 1764 Thursday
PM The same weather.
Sept 14, 1764 Friday
PM the same weather AM more mod. & cloudy.
Sept 15, 1764 Saturday
PM moderate & clear weather AM at 6 veered away and unmoored ship hove up to cable on the best bower, at 10 weighed & came to sail at 11 came too with the small bower in 16 fathom veered to 2/3 of a cable Pt. Live ENE 2 miles.
Sept. 16, 1764 Sunday
PM moderate & cloudy weather AM fresh gales & squaly veered to a whole cable hoisted on board 4 bullocks for the use of the ships company at Noon weighed and came to sail.
Sept. 17, 1764 Monday
PM fresh breezes and squaly at 3 spoke 2 briggs one from Louisbourg another from London at 6 came too with the small bower in 5 fathom to 1/3 of a cable Isle Madam ENE 4 or 5 m. St. Johnes Church NW 2 leagues down top gallant yards at 11 veered to ½ a cable AM sent the boat on shore for fresh stocks at 11 weighed and came to & fired a gun for the boat to come off.
Sept. 18, 1764 Tuesday W, calm, SW
PM the same weather at 1 abreast of the Island Madam at 3 came too with the best bower in 3 fathom veered 1 2/3 of a cable at 6 weighed & came to sail opened a cask of beef contg. 56 pieces & a cask of pork contg. 101 pcs. at 8 came too with the best bower in 9 fathom veered to ½ a cable Cape Formont NW 2 miles Isle of Orleans SW b W 2 leagues at 6 AM weighed and came to sail.
Sept. 19, 1764 Wednesday

Moored at Quebec the Citadel NW
First and latter part fresh breezes M. part hard gales & squaly at 2 PM came too with the best bower in 9 fathoms veered to ½ a cable the westernmost part of the Island of Cowdre SW the easternmost part East at 11 veered to a whole cable and let go the small bower under foot, at ½ past 5 AM hove up the small bower and shortend into ½ a cable on the best bower sent the boat on shore for wood.

Sept. 20, 1764 Thursday NW, NE, E, NNW
Moored at Quebec the Citadel NW
PM fresh breezes & cloudy at 2 weighed and came to sail fired a gun for the boat falling down with the tides at ½ past 6 came too with the best bower in 5 fathoms veered to ½ a cable Cape Death E ½ S 2 or 3 miles Great Ramocraska NE b E 3 leagues at 7 AM weighed and came to sail got up topgallant yards.

Sept. 21, 1764 Friday NE
PM light airs & clear weather at 4 came too with the best bower in 9 fathom veered to 2/3 of a cable Great Kamouravea SW b W 4 or 5 miles Pilsguins ENE 1 league at 1 AM Wilm Linch & Danl McKermitt Seamen cut the Pinnace from the stern & made off with her, at 5 made a signal with 10 guns for a boat from the shore ½ past made a raft and sent it on shore in pursuit of the boat at Noon saw a sail in the NE quarter.

Sept. 22, 1764 Saturday NE
PM fresh breezes & cloudy at 2 weighed and came to sail at 5 fired a gun brought too a ship from London bound to Quebec at 7 came too with the best bower in 5 fathom veered to ½ a cable Cape Diable SSE 2 miles Cape Guss W b N 4 leagues at 6 AM weighed and came to sail.

Sept. 23, 1764 Sunday NE
PM mod. with thick fogs at 1 came too with the best bower in 8 fathom veered away and moored ship a cable each way the small bower to the Etward the west most parts of the Island of Coudee in sight SW & dist off shore ½ mile.

Sept. 24 1764 Monday NE
PM the same weather at 2 fired a gun to bring to a snow spoke her from Glasgow bound to Quebec sent the boat on shore for such ? fresh stock.

Sept. 25, 1764 Tuesday ENE
PM fresh breezes & clear weather sent boat on shore for fresh water fired 3 guns shotted to bring too a ship from Piscatua bound to Quebec she spoke an armed schooner bound up the River.

Sept 26, 1764 Wednesday NW, ESE

PM fresh breezes spoted a ship from Cork bound to Quebec Employed watering the ship.

Sept. 27, 1764 Thursday NE, N, varb.

PM light airs and clear weather at ½ past 5 cleared hawser & unmoored ship spoke a brigg from labradore bound to Quebec.

Sept. 28, 1764 Friday NW, NNW

PM fresh gales & squaly at ½ past 1 hove 2/3 of a cable on the best bower at 6 hove up the best bower and let it go again, at 6 AM weighed and came to sail close reef the topsails & down top gallant yards at 10 out 3d & 2d reefs & up topgallant years at 11 out first reef of the topsails.

Sept. 29, 1764 Saturday NNW

PM first part moderate & cloudy at 4 the West End of the Pilgrims W 4 miles at ½ past 6 came too with the small bower in 13 fathom veered to ½ a cable West end of Hare Island NNE 4 miles at 8 in first & 2d reef of the topsail & down T: gallant at 5 AM; weighed & came to sail at 6 out 2 d & first reef of the topsails & up T:G:nts at 9 came too with the small bower veered to 2/3 of a cable spoke the *Shaleur* armed sloop, Brandy Pot Island NNE 2 miles.

Sept. 30, 1764 Sunday NNW, SW

PM fresh breezes & cloudy the Mid: & latter part light breezes & clear at 3 weighed & came to sail , in 1st & 2d reef of the fore sails at 7 the Westward terminus part of Green Island SSE 6 miles at 9 Red Island N 2 leagues at 10 in 2d reef of the T:sails at Mid Island of Beek E: 5 miles at 3 AM out 2d & 1st reefs main topsails at 6 out 1 : reef topsails & set steering sails.

Oct. 1 1764 Monday SW, W b S

PM fresh breezes & clear weathr the mid moderate cloudy at 4 Matan River.

Oct. 2, 1764 Tuesday Varb.

PM light airs & clear weather at 6 Cape Rozier SW b S 10 leagues Grand Valley Point westward 8 leagues read the articles of War & abstract of the new act of Parliament to the ships company.

Oct. 3, 1764 Wednesday SW, NNW

PM light breezes & clear Weath: at 5 first reef T: sails Cape Gaspie S b W 4 leagues.

Oct. 4, 1764 Thursday NNW, NW

PM fresh breezes & clear weath at 4 Bonaventure NW 4 leagues at 8 N 7 or 8 leagues sounded 29 fathom hard ground at 4 AM out the 1st reef T: sails & set steering sails.

Oct. 5, 1764 Friday NE, E

PM the same weather at ½ past 6 came too with the small bower in

7 fathoms veered to ½ a cable westward point of St. Johns NE b E 2 leagues AM mod & clear at 10 weighed and came to sail, Sandy Point SE b E 2 leagues Cape Agolon NE b E 3 leagues.

Oct. 6, 1764 Saturday SE

PM fresh breezes & hazey with rain at 6 came too with the small bower in 6 fathom and veered to ½ a cable Cape Agolon S 3 leagues AM moderate and clear weather at 7 sent on shore one of the Surveyors with a party of men, at 1 weighed & came to sail.

Oct. 7, 1764 Sunday ESE, N, NW

PM fresh gales & hazy with rain at 4 came too with the small bower in 6 fathoms and veered to ¼ a cable, Cape Agolon N b W 2 leagues at 8 veered to a whole cable and got down T:gallant at 8 AM weighed & came to sail, at 8 got up Topgallant fresh breezes & clear weather out 1st reef T:sails Red Head NNW 8 leagues.

Oct. 8, 1764 Monday W, SW

PM fresh breezes & clear weath at 4 Cape Tomantine SSW 3 leagues at 5 Isle St. Peters ESE fired a gun for a pilot at 8 W 3 miles fired a gun for a pilot at 2 AM cloudy with rain came too Point La Joye with the small bower in 16 fathom veered to ½ a cable. The Fort NNW.

Oct. 9, 1764 Tuesday NNW

PM fresh breezes & cloudy at 5 weighed to shift our birth at 6 came too with the small bower in 14 fathom veered to a whole cable & moored with the B. Bower anchor AM Employed as occasion.

Oct. 10, 1764 Wednesday NW

PM fresh breezes & cloudy at 3 anchored here his Majestys sloop *Gaspie* AM mod: with haze anchored here His Majestys ship *Mermaid* delivered on board 2 casks of beer.

Oct. 11, 1764 Thursday WSW

PM mod: & clear weath loosed sails to dry at 2 weighed the stream anchor & veered away and moored with a cable each way Best Bower to the west, The Fort SW b S 1 mile at 5 unbent the courses & stay sails AM Employed as occasion sailed from hence the *Gaspie* sloop.

Oct. 12, 1764 Friday

PM mod. & clear weather AM: fresh gales & cloudy the boats employed sounding the harbour.

Oct. 13, 1764 Saturday NW, NE

These 24 hours fresh gales & clear weather Employed wooding & watering the ship AM dispatched a schooner belonging to the Fort with provisions for 2 surveying partys.

Oct. 14, 1764 Sunday
PM fresh gales & clear weather Employed as before opened a cask of pork its contents 104 pieces short 3 pieces.
Oct. 15, 1764 Monday
The same weather Employed as before.
Oct. 16, 1764 Tuesday W
The 24 hours fresh gales & cloudy weather came in & anchored here his Majestys Armed sloop *Gaspie*.
Oct. 17, 1764 Wednesday WNW, NW
First part Mod: fresh gales & cloudy the latter Mod: & clear received on board 2 casks of beer the boat employed sounding.
Oct. 18, 1764 Thursday WNW
These 24 hours Mod: & clear weather AM Empl sounding harbor.
Oct. 19, 1764 Friday W, SW, S
PM Moderate & clear weather AM fresh gales and cloudy unreeved part of our running riging returned on board the surveyors with their parties also Mr. Brown and the Pilot with the acct. of the loss of the schooner which was dispatched on the 13 instant with provisions for the Surveyors.
Oct. 20, 1764 Saturday S, E, NW
First part fresh gales & clear weath. the latter strong gales & cloudy with rain.
Oct. 21, 1764 Sunday NW
Fresh gales and hazey weather with rain the later fresh gales & clear PM recd. on board 2 casks of beer sailed from hence his majesty's ship *Gaspie*.
Oct. 22, 1764 Monday W, NW
These 24 hours fresh gales & clear weather Employed the ship AM sent the Pinnace with provisions for a party of surveyors.
Oct. 23, 1764 Tuesday SSE
First part fresh gales & cloudy the latter fresh gales & clear PM: got down topgallant masts & riging.
Oct. 24, 1764 Wednesday S
These 24 hours fresh gales & hazey weather with rain AM open'd of beef containing 56 pieces.
Oct. 25, 1764 Thursday SSW, N
PM The same weather AM: strong gales & clear opened a cask of pork containing 52 pieces.
Oct. 26, 1764 Friday N, NNE
These 24 hours fresh gales & clear weather PM Employed watering at 6 the pinnace returned on board at 10 AM: punished Wm Johnston & John Suffock for drunkeness Mutiny and neglect

of duty.

Oct. 27, 1764 Saturday E, S, W

PM: fresh breezes & hazey with rain, got out the powder at 4 AM: unmoored ship & hove into ½ a cable on the same bower at Noon weighed & sailed into Miln Bay.

Oct, 28 1764 Sunday WSW, W, NW

First and latter part fresh gales & hazey with rains the middle part fresh gales & clear, PM unbent three topsails & got down yards & topmasts at 4 cleared the booms & got them on shore AM unbent the sheet & small bower cables and got them on shore at Noon recd. on board a cask of beer.

Oct, 29, 1764 Monday WSW, W, NW

These 24 hours fresh gales & cloudy weathr. with snow PM got out the guns AM sent the sheet & small bower anchors on shore.

Oct. 30, 1764 Tuesday WNW

First part the same weather, the latter part fresh gales & clear Weathr PM: Employ'd clearing the hold, AM punished Cane Williams for drunkeness and neglect of duty loosed sails to dry opened a cask of beef containing 56 pieces.

Oct. 31, 1764 Wednesday WNW

These 24 hours fresh breezes & clear weather PM unbent the topsails AM Employ'd clearing the hold & getting out the Iron ballast at Noon rec'd on board a cask of beer.

*Nov. 1, 1764 to Nov. 6, 1764

Nov. 7, 1764 Wednesday NW, W

Mod.& hazy weather with rain PM got out the mizen mast AM employed raising jeers to get out the fore mast anchored here the *EB Bank* from a cruise.

Nov. 8, 1764 Thursday NW, calm

The same weather got out the fore mast AM: employed shipping the fore mast.

Nov. 9, 1764 Friday E, NE, N

First part moderate & cloudy weather the latter hard gales with ran Empd clearing hold.

Nov. 10, 1764 Saturday N

These 24 hours strong gales with snow AM striped the main mast & got it out.

Nov. 11, 1764 Sunday SW, S

First & latter parts fresh breezes & hazey weather with rain the middle hard gales & foggy Employ'd cleaning the hold.

Nov. 12, 1764 Monday SW, NW
These 24 hours fresh gales & squaly weather Employ'd as before.
Nov. 13, 1764 Tuesday NW
First part Mod. & cloudy weather the latter part fresh gales & clear Emp'd variously.
Nov. 14, 1764 Wednesday NW
These 24 hours fresh gales with snow Employed clearing the hold AM sent a cask of beer on board the *Elibank* & one to Capt. Holland.
Nov. 15, 1764 Thursday NNW
Fresh gales and snow with sleet Employed variously.
Nov. 16, 1764 Friday NW
Fresh gales with frost & snow Employ'd cleaning the hold sailed from hence the *Elibank*.

*Nov. 17 1764 to Nov. 23, 1764

Nov. 24, 1764 Saturday NNW, N
First part fresh gales with snow the latter part mod: & clear wea: PM: Supplied a Surveying party of 14 men with the following provisions Beef, 56 pieces pork, 112 flower 186 lb, suit 26 lb, butter 84 lb, pease 28 gallons, Mellasses 34 gallons AM Employ'd putting on shore the dry provisions.
Nov. 25, 1764 Sunday NNW, N
These 24 hours mod: & fair weather Employed getting out the water casks & iron ballast.
Nov. 26, 1764 Monday N b E
The same weather Employed variously AM: punished Josh Mansfield for neglect of Duty.
Nov. 27, 1764 Tuesday N b W
Fresh gales & clear weather Employed winding the ships cable.
Nov. 28, 1764 Wednesday N b W
Fresh gales & cloudy weather Employed getting up the lower masts to a proper place.
Nov. 29, 1764 Thursday WNW
Fresh breezes & cloudy weather Employed getting the water casks up from the beach and cutting wood for the ships use.
Nov. 30, 1764 Friday NW
The first part fresh gales & cloudy weath. the latter part mod. & clear PM anchored here a schooner from Fort Cumberland.
Dec. 1, 1764 Saturday N
Fresh breezes & cloudy weather Employed variously AM Read the

Articles of War & abstract of the new act of Parliament to the ships company.

Dec. 2, 1764 Sunday NW

The same weather the ships company Employed wooding & the carpenter making Booley hatches for all the hatchways with canvas covers.

* Dec. 3 1764 to Feb. 14, 1765

Feb. 15, 1765 Friday SW, S, NNE

First & middle part fresh gales & cloudy weather with rain the latter fresh breezes with hard frost PM cut up an old main course for tents and coverings for the surveyors to gather with a quantity of Bunts for station marks the ships company Employed with the surveyors & cutting wood.

*Feb. 16, 1765 to Mar. 2, 1765

Mar. 3, 1765 Sunday NE, E

Fresh breezes and cloudy weather PM got on board the short cable AM Went out different party on the survey, supplied the surveyors with a quantity of new canvas & twine for different purposes opened a cask of pork cont:g 104 pieces.

*Mar. 4, 1765 to Mar. 17, 1765

Mar. 18, 1765 Monday WSW, S

Moored in Port Joye

The first part fresh gales with snow, the middle and latter parts mod. & cloudy weathr. PM returned the *Diligent* parties of surveyors, the people employed occasionaly.

*Mar. 19, 1765 to Mar. 31, 1765

April 1, 1765 Monday S, calm

Moored in Port Joye

The first part cloudy weather with snow the middle & latter parts clear the people Employed getting the pinnace clear for the carpenters to repair.

April 2, 1765 Tuesday SE

Moored in Port Joye

First part fresh gales and clear weathr the middle and latter parts Mod. & fair with frost. The carpenters employed as before.

April 3, 1765 Wednesday E

Moored in Port Joye

Mod. and fair weather carpenter Employed as above.

April 4, 1765 Thursday SE

The first part Moderate and fair weather, the middle and latter parts fresh gales, clear, The carpenters Emp. repairing the cutter, people Empd. overhauling the riging.

April 5, 1765 Friday SSE

Moored in Port Joye

The first part fresh gales and clear weather, the middle and latter Modt & ? clear.

April 6, 1765 Saturday varb.

The same weather the carpenter Employed painting and paying the cutters bottom others Employed about the riging.

April 7, 1765 Sunday calm, SSE

Moored in Port Joye

The same weather. PM launched the cutter on purpose to send her to Fort Cumberland. The people employed as before.

April 8, 1765 Monday SSE, SE

Moored in Port Joye

Mod. and cloudy weather the people employed getting the riging, filling the water & getting it onboard.

April 9, 1765 Tuesday SSE

Moored in Port Joye

The same weather the people Employed getting water on board at 1 PM the ice in the river broke up and came away in a body about 2 miles long & 1 mile broad which carried the ship out the cove and with standing the ice being caught all under her & in between her and the shore. It carried her out the harbour as far as Governors Island 6 miles distance at which time she was got clear of the harbor ice at the same time the tide turned and with the assistance of the boat which was taking a longitude all the winter, and jury masts with the studding sails sett on them, got into the same place where she was carried from at ten O'clock the same night without receiving any Damage only the loss of the stream anchor and cable, PM the people employed cutting spars and placing them rounding the ship in order to prevent the ice hurting her as it came and went with the tide.

April 10, 1765 Wednesday NW, NE, N

Moored in Port Joye

Fresh gales and cloudy weathr. the cove filled all round the ship with large pieces of ice which pulled off the sheathing in several places. People employed as before.

In 1761 the British began to use thin sheets of copper nailed to the underwater portion of the bottom to protect the wooden hulls from fouling. When fouling by marine growth was extensive the ship had to be careened and the hull scraped. With coppering, bottoms were clear of barnacles and weeds and the speed of the vessel increased.

April 11, 1765 Thursday NE, NE b N
Moored in Port Joye.
The first part fresh gales and clear weather, the middle and latter more mod. large quantities of ice driving up and down with the tide Employed as occasion.
April 12, 1765 Friday WNW, NW b W
Moored in Port Joye
Fresh airs with snow and hard frost Employed picking oakum. Recd on Bd 1 cask of beer.
April 13, 1765 Saturday N, NW
Moored in Port Joye
The same weather the People employed as before.
April 14, 1765 Sunday NE, NW, W
Moored in Port Joye
Small breezes and clear weathr at 6 PM sent one of the ships boats with an officer to Fort Cumberland with public letters. Employed about the Rigging.
April 15, 1765 Monday varb.
Moored in Port Joye
First & middle part light breezes and clear weathr. latter hazey with snow. The carpenters employed repairing the pinnace, people employed overhauling the rigging.

*April 16, 1765 to April 28, 1765

April 29, 1765 Monday NE
Moored in Port Joye
The same weathr. with snow punished Samuel Collins with 1 dozen of lashes for disobedience & neglect of duty.
April 30, 1765 Tuesday NE
Moored in Port Joye

Fresh gales & clear weathr. the carpenter Empd. repairing the pinnace recd. on board 12 casks of beer.

May 1, 1765 Wednesday NE, E

Moored in Port Joye

Strong gales and clear weathr. People Empd about the rigging, The cutter returned from Fort Cumberland.

May. 2, 1765 Thursday NW, NNW

Moored in Port Joye

Fair & hazey weather. The carpenters Empd. about the boats.

May 3, 1765 Friday NW b N, NW

Moored in Port Joye

The same weather the carpenter Employed as before.

May 4, 1765 Saturday NE

Moored in Port Joye

Same weather Employed as before.

May, 5 1765 Sunday ESE

Moored in Port Joye

Mod. & clear weather the Rivers clear of ice.

May 6, 1765 Monday SSW, SSE, SE

Moored in Port Joye

The same weathr. the carpenters and people employed the ship a float at 11 AM sounded with five fathom water & moored her with a cable each way, the small bower to the eastward & the best bower to the westward the point that forms the river S b E & NW b W.

May 7, 1765 Tuesday NE, NW, NNW

Moored in Port Joye

The same weathr. the people employed aboard the rigging & the carpenters Empd. repairing the boats, at 11 AM the cutter and four men went with the Surveying parties, the river entirely clear of ice.

May 8, 1765 Wednesday ENE, NNE, NE

Moored in Port Joye

The first and middle parts mod. & hazey the latter clear weather People Empd. above, the carpenters employed making topmasts.

*May 9, 1765 to May 14, 1765

May 15, 1765 Wednesday NW, NNW

Moored in Port Joye

Mod. & clear weath the people & carpenters employed as before at 6 PM anchored here His Majestys ships the *Mermaid* &

Albrough from Halifax.
May 16, 1765 Thursday NNW
Moored in Port Joye
The same weath the people & carpenters employed as before.
May 17, 1765 Friday NW, WNW, N
Moored in Port Joye
Fresh gales and cloudy weath the people & carpenters employed as before Recd. from the *Mermaid* and *Albrough* three boats for the use of the Surveyor General.
May 18, 1765 Saturday NW, NE, NNE
Moored in Port Joye
The same weather Recd from the *Albrough* the following provisions: beef 260 pieces, pork 520 pieces, 16 bushells ?
May 19, 1765 Sunday NNW, NW, NNE
Moored in Port Joye
The same weather arrived the schooner *Eliban* David Watts Master Burthen 6 tonns & go to Halifax to bring provisions for the ship.
May 20, 1765 Monday NNW, NW, NNW
Moored in Port Joye
The same weathr people employed getting in the lower masts, at 6 AM clear and four men went on the Survey.
May 21, 1765 Tuesday W, WNW
Moored in Port Joye
The same weathr people Employed as before gott in all the masts.
May 22, 1765 Wednesday WNW
Moored in Port Joye
Light breezes and cloudy the people employed rigging the lower masts AM cleared hawse.
May 23, 1765 Thursday WNW
Moored in Port Joye
The first part the same weather the middle & latter parts Mod. & cloudy weather Employed in overhauling the remnant riging, came on board the Masters of the *Mermaid & Albough* fr Survey the donated provisions & slops that had been *Mermaid* by Batts.
May 24, 1765 Friday varb, W, SW
Moored in Port Joye
The first part Mod. the middle & latter part hard gales and hazey weathr. with rain. AM sailed from hence Mr. Hog with seamen in the schooner & boat on a Survey to the Magdalen Islands also one of the small boats with cutter & four seamen on a Survey to the westward.
May 25, 1765 Saturday SSW

Moored in Port Joye
The same weathr, the people employed clearing the hold & preparing to take the ground, AM cleared hawser.

May 26, 1765 Sunday W
Moored in Port Joye
The first part fresh gales and cloudy weathr the middle and latter Mod. & clear Employed as occasion.

May 27, 1765 Monday varb.
Moored in Port Joye
The same weather people employed about the rigging.

May 28, 1765 Tuesday W, NW, W
Moored in Port Joye
The first part Mod. & fair weather, middle strong gales with rain the latter Mod. & cloudy Employed overhauling the rigging. The carpenters mending taring the tops & yards.

May 29, 1765 Wednesday N, NE, SSE
Moored in Port Joye
Mod & cloudy weathr the people employed getting the tops overhead mast and the fore rigging.

May 30, 1765 Thursday SE
Moored in Port Joye
The first fine and cloudy weather, the latter cloudy with rain, PM sailed from hence his Majestys ship *Mermaid* and *Albough* as did the *Eliban* for the Island of Verte.

May 31, 1765 Friday N, NE, W
Moored in Port Joye
The first and middle parts fresh & breezy and cloudy weathr with rain recd on board bread and water, sett up the main rigging.

June 1, 1765 Saturday S, SE
Moored in Port Joye
The first and middle parts fresh gales and cloudy weathr with rain the latter part more mod. People employed wooding and watering.

June 2, 1765 Sunday SE
Moored in Port Joye
Mod. & clear weathr people employed as occasion. PM anchord here Schooner from Bay of Verte.

June 3, 1765 Monday SW, W
Moored in Port Joye
Fresh gales and cloudy weathr Employed variously carpenters about the topmasts.

June 4, 1765 Tuesday NNE, NE, N b E

Moored in Port Joye
Strong gales and cloudy weath with rain Employed about the rigging, AM recd on board a cask beer.

June 5, 1765 Wednesday NW, NE, N
Moored in Port Joye
The first part light airs and cloudy weath the middle and latter parts fresh breezes and clear weath People Employed on occasion.

June 6, 1765 Thursday S, SW
Moored in Port Joye
First and middle parts fresh breezes and clear weath the latter part rain. People Employed as occasion AM opened a cask of beef contents 73 lb 112 pieces.

June 7, 1765 Friday NNW, NW
Moored in Port Joye
The first and middle parts light airs and cloudy weathr with rain recd on board 1 cask of beer and some water. People employed getting the topmasts off from the shore, carpenters employed repairing the pinnace.

June 8, 1765 Saturday NW b W, NNW
Moored in Port Joye
Light airs and cloudy weath Employed wooding and watering carpenters employed as above, arrived one of the small boats from a survey.

June 9, 1765 Sunday SW, NE
Moored in Port Joye
The first and middle parts strong gales and cloudy weathr with rain, thunder & lightening the latter part Mod & cloudy, employed as occasion.

June 10, 1765 Monday N, E, NE
Moored in Port Joye
Light airs with lightening people employed casehardening the shrouds & rattling up and down The cutter & an officer surveying & sounding the harbor.

June 11, 1765 Tuesday NNE, NE
Moored in Port Joye
Light airs and clear weath PM anchored here His Majesty's Armed Schooner *Magdalen* People employed about the rigging.

June 12, 1765 Wednesday SE, SSE
Moored in Port Joye
The first & middle parts light airs & clear weathr the latter part fresh breezes people employed cathanpening the shrouds AM read the articles of war & abstract of Parliament to the ships comp.

June 13, 1765 Thursday S, S b E
Moored in Port Joye
The first part mod & clear weath the latter part strong gales and cloudy Employed as occasion.
June 14, 1765 Friday W, N b W, WNW
Moored in Port Joye
Strong gales and cloudy weath recd on board 3 casks of water people employed about the rigging punished John Cunningham with 12 lashes for mutinous words and disrespect to his officers.
June 15, 1765 Saturday W, W b N
Moored in Port Joye
The same weath people employed variously AM sailed from hence his majesty's armed schooner *Magdalen*, punished John Suffolk with 24 lashes for mutinous words and disrespect to his officers.
June 16, 1765 Sunday W, W b N
Moored in Port Joye
The same weath people employed on occasion anchored here a schooner from the Bay of Verte.
June 17, 1765 Monday W, W b N
Moored in Port Joye
Mod. & cloudy weath Captain Mowat and six seamen employed sounding the West River.
June 18, 1765 Tuesday N, N b W, W b S
Moored in Port Joye
The first & middle parts fresh breezes and clear weath latter cloudy with cloudy with rain.
June 19, 1765 Wednesday W, W b N, WNW
Moored in Port Joye
The same weath people employed wooding.
June 20, 1765 Thursday N, N b W, NNW
Moored in Port Joye
The same weath PM anchored here the schooner with provisions of all species from Halifax, issued ten yards of bunting for the use of the Surveyors. People employed wooding.
June 21, 1765 Friday W, WNW
Moored in Port Joye
Mod. & cloudy weath recd from the schooner *Elibank* the following species of provisions, beef 40 barrels, pork 20 barrels, butter 25 firkins, bread 19 barrels, pease 6 turies and 7 barrels, Rum 3 penshears ? barrel.
June 22, 1765 Saturday N, WNW, NW

Moored in Port Joye
The first and middle parts mod & cloudy weath the latter strong gales with rain people employed variously.
June 23, 1765 Sunday
NW, SW
Moored in Port Joye
Mod. & cloudy weath with rain people employed variously.
June 24, 1765 Monday W, NW, WNW
Moored in Port Joye
First and middle parts the same weath the latter fresh breezes and clear AM Captain Mowatt and Captain Holland with a party surveyors, in the cutter went on the survey up the NE River, sailed from hence one of the small boats Open'd a barr: of pork opened a cask of pease 44 gallons and a firkin of buttr 90 lb.
June 25, 1765 Tuesday S
Moored in Port Joye
Light airs & calm, returned the pinnace from the head of the N Ethiver. People Empd as occasion opened a cask of beef containing 56 pieces.
June 26, 1765 Wednesday calm, NE
Moored in Port Joye
The first & middle parts calm the latter part fresh breezes with rain employed wooding and watering, and tarring the casks for ground tier of water casks opened 1 cask of beer.
June 27, 1765 Thursday W, SW
Moored in Port Joye
Light airs and mod weath Employed tarring the casks & stowing away provisions recd on board 1 cask of beer.
June 28, 1765 Friday calm, SSW
Moored in Port Joye
The same weath employed getting on board the best bower cable Took up the main anchor & moored with the best bower to the westward a cable each way.
June 29, 1765 Saturday NE
Moored in Port Joye
The first and middle part mod weath the latter fresh gales with thunder & lightening and heavy rain, opened a cask of beef containing 56 pieces at 4 PM employed stowing casks and stores sailed from hence the *Elibank* schooner Quebec.
June 30, 1765 Sunday W
Moored in Port Joye
Mod and clear weather

July 1, 1765 Monday NE, W
Moored in Port Joye
The first and middle parts fresh breezes and clear weath the latter mod. & cloudy employed getting on board the iron ballast and getting water on board, AM read the articles of war and abstract of Parliament to the ships company, opened a cask of pease.

July 2 1765 Tuesday NNE, E
Moored in Port Joye
Fresh breezes with rain people employed on sundries

July 3, 1765 Wednesday E, N, NE
Moored in Port Joye
The first and middle part light breezes the latter part fresh breezes with rain employed getting on board the iron ballast & stowing it away & filling water.

July 4, 1765 Thursday NE, N
Moored in Port Joye
Fresh & cloudy weath with rain, returned on board the cutter with Captain Mowat from soundings, opened a ferkin of the butter. People empd on sundries.

July 5, 1765 Friday W, SW
Moored in Port Joye
Mod breezes and clear weath. Employed getting on board iron ballast & getting the fore and main yards, topsail yards and mizen topmast & getting boom.

July 6 1765 Saturday S, SW
Moored in Port Joye
The first and middle parts light airs and clear weath the latter part fresh breezes Employed rigging the lower yards & filling water for the ground tier.

*July 7 1765 to July 16, 1765

July 17, 1765 Wednesday W b N, W, calm
Moored in Port Joye
First & middle parts fresh breezes and cloudy weath latter light airs with calm People Employed about the rigging & repairing the awning. The carpenter Empd sawing plank in order to repair the forecastle recd onboard 1 cask of beer.

July 18, 1765 Thursday W, NW
Moored in Port Joye
Fresh breezes & clear weath carpenter and people Employed as before opened a cask of beef contents 56 pieces.

July 19, 1765 Friday NW b W, WNW
Moored in Port Joye
The same weath carpenter and people employed as before returned one of the small boats from the eastward, came on board a cooper to repair the casks.

July 20, 1765 Saturday varb, calm
Moored in Port Joye
First part the same weath the middle & latter calm & clear, carpenter & people employed as before & the cooper repairing the water casks. Opened a firken of butter.

July 21 1765 Sunday NNE
Moored in Port Joye
First part light breezes and clear weath middle & latter fresh breezes and cloudy opened a cask of pork contents 112 pieces, short 1 piece.

July 22, 1765 Monday NW
Moored in Port Joye
Fresh breezes and clear weath the carpenter & people employed as before and the cooper repairing the water casks.

July 23, 1765 Tuesday NE, SSW
Moored in Port Joye
The first part the same weath the middle & latter light airs & cloudy empd as before.

July 24, 1765 Wednesday varb.
Moored in Port Joye
Light breezes and cloudy weath sent an officer and 4 seamen in one of the small boats to sound to the east point of the island, carpenter employed as occasion Ships company about the rigging.

July 25, 1765 Thursday W b S, SW
Moored in Port Joye
The same weath opened a cask of beef containing 56 pieces recd on board 2 casks of beer, AM anchored here his Majesty's sloop *Senegall*, & armed schooner *Magdalen* Employed ratting the ground tier & clearing away the hold the carpenter empd as occasion & cooper repairing the water casks.

July 26 1765 Friday W, WNW
Moored in Port Joye
The same weath raffed off 12 casks of water & stowed them away people employed making points and gaskets carpenter & cooper employed as before.

July 27 1765 Saturday W, SW

Moored in Port Joye
Fresh breezes and cloudy weath PM got on board our swivels carpenter & cooper empd.

July 28, 1765 Sunday WSW, S
Moored in Port Joye
Light airs and cloudy weath intermixed with calm, rafted off our guns and hoisted them in, anchored here two transports with troops to relieve the garrison, AM rafted off 30 casks of water employed clearing the hold.

July 29, 1765 Monday SE, E
Moored in Port Joye
The same weath AM sailed hence His Majesty's armed schooner *Magdalen* Ships company employed about the rigging and stowing the hold carpenter & cooper & employed.

July 30, 1765 Tuesday NW, N
Moored in Port Joye
The same weath employed stowing the hold and tarring the ships sides, carpenter & cooper employed AM recd on board 4 casks of beer.

July 31, 1765 Wednesday NW, WNW
Moored in Port Joye
In first part the same weath the middle and latter parts fresh breezes & clear weath recd on board 1 cask of beer employed stowing the hold 7 tarring the rigging carpenter & cooper employed.

Aug. 1, 1765 Thursday NE
Moored in Port Joye
The same weath carpenter & cooper empd ships company empd about the rigging AM read the articles of war & abstract of Parliament to the ships company.

Aug. 2, 1765 Friday NE
Moored in Port Joye
The first part fresh breezes and cloudy weath middle & latter light breezes and clear carpenter cooper & ships company empd as before returned to the Fort 8 casks of pork containing 1792 pounds.

Aug. 3, 1765 Saturday S, SSW
Moored in Port Joye
Light breezes and clouding with rain PM recd on board 1 cask of beer, opened cask of beef contents 56 pieces short 1 piece Ships company employed tarring the rigging carpenter & cooper employed.

Aug. 4, 1765 Sunday S
Moored in Port Joye
First part fresh breezes & cloudy weath middle & latter more mod with haze.
Aug. 5, 1765 Monday SSW
Moored in Port Joye
These 24 hours Mod & clear weath people employed tarring the rigging sent on shore 8 casks of stores which was due the garrison contents 92 pcs.
Aug. 6, 1765 Tuesday SW, W
Same weath sent on shore 750 W of flour which was due the garrison, people & boats employed assisting to embark the troops aboard the transports at 4 pm sailed from hence His Majesty's sloop *Senegal*, sent an officer & seamen in a boat to sound the harbour of Quebec & along the coast to Port La Joye.
Aug. 7, 1765 Wednesday W, WSW
Moored in Port Joye
The first and middle part cloudy weathr. with rain, the latter clear, the people employed making points and gaskets opended a ferkin of butter.
Aug. 8, 1765 Thursday N, NNE
Moored in Port Joye
Fine clear weath People employed putting on platts on the best bower cable.
Aug. 9, 1765 Friday S, SW
Moored in Port Joye
The first and latter parts Mod & clear weath people employed as occasion brought on board 431 fresh beef for the use of the ships company.
Aug. 10 1765 Saturday S, NE
Moored in Port Joye
The first & middle parts fine clear weath the latter fresh breezes and cloudy people employed making points and gaskets.
Aug. 11, 1765 Sunday SW
Moored in Port Joye
These 24 hours fine clear weath.
Aug. 12. 1765 Monday NE, S
Fresh breezes and cloudy weath with rain, at 8 pm got down topgallant yards & punished Wm. Bray & John Suffolk with 24 lashes each for Mut. words.
Aug. 13 1765 Tuesday W, WSW
Moored in Port Joye

The same weath at 7AM got up the topgallant yards people empd variously the carpenter employed calking the ship.

Aug. 14, 1765 Wednesday WNW

Moored in Port Joye

The same weath AM got down topgallant yards carpenters employed as before ships company making points and gasketts.

Aug. 15, 1765 Thursday W, NW, N

Moored in Port Joye

First part fresh gales and clear weath middle and latter more mod & cloudy with rain AM scaled the great guns and swivels recd on board one cask beer Carpenters & ships company employed as before.

Scaling the great guns was done so that any flaky oxide film formed on the metal after heating to high temperatures was removed and the cannon clear of scale. Such scale if not removed could cause premature firing of the powder charge endangering the crew and ship.

Aug. 16, 1765 Friday NW, WNW

Moored in Port Joye

Fresh gales and squally weath with rain AM cut up the poop awning and sailcloth, carpenters empd fixing it & ships company as occasion.

Aug. 17 1765 Saturday NNW, N b W, NW

Moored in Port Joye

The same weath AM recd on board 3 casks of beer carpenter employed as before & ships company about the rigging.

Aug. 18, 1765 Sunday NW

Moored in Port Joye

Light breezes and clear weather.

Aug. 19, 1765 Monday W, SW, SSW

Moored in Port Joye

First part light breezes & clear weath middle & latter fresh breezes & cloudy with rain PM came on board 2 caulkers in order to caulk the ship AM employed caulking the middle deck & ships company empd. variously.

Aug. 20, 1765 Tuesday S, NW, WNW

Moored in Port Joye

First half same weath. middle breezes & cloudy with lightening and thunder employed as before the ships company empd variously

Aug. 21, 1765 Wednesday calm, varb.

Moored in Port Joye
First part clear weath the middle fresh breezes with lightening, the latter part clear weath caulkers employed as before and ships company Empd variously.

Aug. 22, 1765 Thursday var:
Moored in Port Joye
Light breezes & clear weath AM brought off the spare anchor from the shore caulkers employed as before and ships company variously.

Aug. 23 1765 Friday W
Moored in Port Joye
The same weath AM opened a cask of pork containing 112 pieces short 2 a ferkin of butter caulkers employed as before and ships company taking down the lower masts and paying them.

Aug. 24, 1765 Saturday SW
Moored in Port Joye
These 24 hours clear weath carpenters and caulker employed as before the ships company employed variously.

Aug. 25, 1765 Sunday W, S
Moored in Port Joye
These 24 hours clear weath caulkers Employed as before.

Aug. 26, 1765 Monday
Moored in Port Joye
The same weath the Surveyor General purchased a sloop for the use of the survey The carpenters employed repairing her put up a fore topsail & main staysail to make her sails.

Aug. 27, 1765 Tuesday S, NE
Moored in Port Joye
The first and middle parts light airs and clear weath the latter fresh breezes and cloudy carpenters employed on the sloop.

Aug. 28, 1765 Wednesday W
Moored in Port Joye
Clear weath people Employed on sundries & carpenters as before opened casks of beef contents 56 pieces short 1 piece.

Aug. 29, 1765 Thursday NW
Moored in Port Joye
Same weath carpenters employed on the sloop, ship's company Employed about the rigging.

Aug. 30, 1765 Friday NE, W
The first and middle parts cloudy weath with rain the latter clear people Empd. as before.

Aug. 31, 1765 Saturday W

Moored in Port Joye
Clear weath people Employed as before. Sent Mr. Brown with 4 seamen later charge of the sloop *Venus*, opened a cask of provisions & ferkin of butter.

Sept. 1, 1765 Sunday NW, W
Moored in Port Joye
These 24 hours fine clear weath sailed from hence Wm. Brown on the Sloop *Venus* with Wm Wright and Lieut. Pringle for the Coast of Cape Breton, with provisions for 11 men for 10 weeks Opened a cask of butter.

Sept. 2, 1765 Monday W
Moored in Port Joye
The same weath the ships company Employed about the rigging.

Sept. 3, 1765 Tuesday NE
Moored in Port Joye
Cloudy weath with rain people Employed as occasion.

Sept. 4, 1765 Wednesday N, calm
Moored in Port Joye
The first and middle parts cloudy weath the latter part calm & clear Ships compy employed about the rigging opened barrel of beef contents 56 pieces.

Sept. 5, 1765 Thursday NW, WNW
Moored in Port Joye
Fresh breezes and clear weath Employed scraping the ships sides, masts. and setting the rigging fore and aft.

Sept. 6, 1765 Friday varb
Moored in Port Joye
These 24 hours fresh breezes and cloudy weath people Employed on sundries.

Sept. 7, 1765 Saturday W, WSW, SW
Mod & clear weath recd on board from the *Elibants* Schooner 100 barrels of flour containing 22511 pounds.

Sept. 8, 1765 Sunday SW
Moored in Port Joye
The same weath opened a cask of pork containing 112 pieces short 1 piece.

Sept. 9, 1765 Monday WSW
Moored in Port Joye
These 24 hours fresh breezes and cloudy weath. people Employed as occasion.

Sept. 10, 1765 Tuesday SW
Moored in Port Joye

The same weath the boats Employed sounding recd. on board 2 Hhds of beer.

Sept. 11, 1765 Wednesday NW

Moored in Port Joye

The same weath people Employed as occasion.

Sept. 12, 1765 Thursday WNW

Moored in Port Joye

Mod. & clear weath recd on board 428 lb of fresh beef the boats employed sounding.

Sept. 13, 1765 Friday N, varb.

Moored in Port Joye

The same weath sailed from hence the *Elibank* Schooner sent on shore to the garrison 1521 lb of bread.

Sept. 14, 1765 Saturday NE

Moored in Port Joye

Same weath at 5 AM heeled ship to port & scrubbed the bottom payed with razen tallow & brimstone, at 11 heeled at starboard & scrubbed and payed the same way.

Sept. 15, 1765 Sunday NE

Moored in Port Joye

These 24 hours Mod. and fair weath.

Sept. 16, 1765 Monday NE

Moored in Port Joye

The same weath. at 7 AM the Captain went out to sound, employed watering ship & stowing the hold.

Sept. 17, 1765 Tuesday WSW

Moored in Port Joye

Same weath Employed as before.

Sept. 18, 1765 Wednesday SW

Moored in Port Joye

Fresh gales and squally weath. with rain at 9 AM cleared a hawse

Sept. 19, 1765 Thursday WSW, NW

Moored in Port Joye

The same weath people Employed as occasion.

Sept. 20, 1765 Friday NW

Moored in Port Joye

Mod & clear weath the boats Employed sounding at 10 AM unmoored ship & hove short on the small bower.

Sept. 21, 1765 Saturday SW

At signal anchor

Fresh gales and squally weath at 3 PM weighed & came to sail at ½ past came too with the best bower in 10 fathom water &

veered to 1/3 of a cable at 7 sounded that the drove let go the small bower and let hove up the best bower & veered to ½ of a cable Port Amber SW b W ½ a mile opened a ferkin of butter.

Sept. 22, 1765 Sunday W

Moored again Port Joye

Fresh gales and cloudy weath at 4 PM moored ship with the stream anchor and hawser to the southward a cable each way to the island N b W the Governors Island ESE Point from S b E Opened a barrel of beef contents 56 pieces short 1 piece.

Sept. 23, 1765 Monday WNW

Moored in Port Joye

Mod & clear weath The boats Employed sounding the harbour.

Sept. 24, 1765 Tuesday W, WSW

Moored in Port Joye

The same weath at ½ past 9 AM arrived here His Majesty's ship the *Mermaid* Sloop *Senegal* & armed schooner *Magdalen* from a cruize the people employed sounding.

Sept. 25, 1765 Wednesday NW b W

Moored in Port Joye

The first and middle parts Mod & clear the latter fresh breezes and squally, carpenters Employed repairing the pinnace recd on board two tons of water.

Sept. 26, 1765 Thursday N

Moored in Port Joye

The first and middle parts Mod & clear weath the latter fresh gales and squally at 1/2 past 5 AM got down topgallant yards people employed variously carpenters employed on the pinnace opened a cask of pork contents 112 pieces short 1 piece.

Sept. 27, 1765 Friday WNW

Moored in Port Joye

Mod and clear weath people Employed as occasion carpenters employed on the pinnace.

Sept. 28, 1765 Saturday S

Moored in Port Joye

The first and middle parts cloudy the latter Mod and clear Ships company watering & wooding the ship.

Sept. 29, 1765 Sunday W

Moored in Port Joye

The 24 hours fine clear weather.

Sept. 30, 1765 Monday WSW

Moored in Port Joye

These 24 hours Mod & clear weath people employed watering &

wooding the ship carpenters Employed aboard the pinnace opened a barrel of beef contents 56 pieces short one piece.

Oct. 1, 1765 Tuesday SW
Moored in Port Joye
The first part and middle parts clear weath the latter cloudy Employed as before AM Read the articles of War & abstract of the new Act of Parliament to the ships company.

Oct. 2, 1765 Wednesday W
Moored in Port Joye
Fine clear weath at 5 AM Sailed from hence His Majesty's Armed schooner *Magdalen* ships company Empd. as before recd on board five tons of ballast.

Oct. 3, 1765 Thursday W
Moored in Port Joye
The same weath recd from on board the *Mermaid* 3 barrels of pease, ship company Employed wooding Arrived here from the Magdalen Island the ship with Wm Holland and Wm Hogg.

Oct. 4, 1765 Friday N
Moored in Port Joye
The same weather people Employed getting wood on board

Oct. 5, 1765 Saturday WSW, W
Moored in Port Joye
The first and middle parts clear weath the latter fresh breezes at 5 AM sailed from hence His Majesty's ship *Mermaid* & sloop *Senegal* to the eastward people Employed variously.

Oct. 6, 1765 Sunday W
Moored in Port Joye
These 24 hours fresh breezes and clear weather.

Oct. 7, 1765 Monday SW
Moored in Port Joye
First and middle parts little wind the latter fresh breezes and clear weather people Employed getting wood and water on board.

Oct. 8, 1765 Tuesday W, SW
Moored in Port Joye
The first and middle parts fresh breezes & cloudy weath with small rain, the latter more clear, the ships company Employed getting on board the Surveyor members instruments and baggage, opened a barrel of pork cont. 112 pieces short 1.

Oct. 9, 1765 Wednesday S
Moored in Port Joye
The first and middle parts clear weath the latter fresh gales Employed getting the surveyors baggage on board.

Oct. 10, 1765 Thursday SW
Moored in Port Joye
Hard gales with rain, people Employed as before.
Oct. 11, 1765 Friday WSW
Moored in Port Joye
The first and middle parts hard gales the latter more Mod ships company employed as before and getting ready for sea.
Oct. 12, 1765 Saturday WSW
Moored in Port Joye
The first and middle parts fresh gales the latter more mod at 6 PM set the best bower anchor, people Employed getting the Surveyors things on board.
Oct. 13, 1765 Sunday SW
At single anchor in Port Joye
Mod. and cloudy weath PM came on board the Surveyor General and his party with all his baggage at 6 AM unmoored ship at Noon variable weath gott up top gallant yards, opened a cask of calavances.
Masters Log
At single anchor Port Joye SW, N
Mod and cloudy weath PM came on board the Surveyor General and his party with all his baggage at 6 AM unmoored ship, at Noon sight airs sand with variable weath: got up top gallants yards, opened a cask of calavances.

Captain Samuel Holland of the Royal Engineers sent a proposal to the Lords of Commissioners of Trade and Plantation, proposing that a scientific survey be done to encourage land settlement and the fishery in British North America, particularly in the areas recently ceded by France. Such a map would provide accurate maps of the area and would also gather and present detailed descriptions of the land. The proposal as considered in December 1763 by the Lords of the Commissioners of Trade and Plantations, where they referred it to the Privy Council for its consideration on February 4, 1764. By the 10th of that month, King George had approved the proposal.

Oct. 14, 1765 Monday ENE, NNE
At single anchor in Port Joye
PM mod and cloudy weath AM fresh gales and squally weath at 4 PM left the best bower in 12 fathom water & veered to ½ a cable & moored with the stream anchor and cable, Fort Amherst SW at

Noon got down top gallant yards, opened a barrel of beef contents 56 pieces.
Masters Log
At signal anchor Port Joye
PM mod. and cloudy weath AM fresh gales and squally weath at 4 PM lett go the best bower in 12 fathoms water veered to ½ a cable & moored with the stream anchor and cable, Fort Amherst SW at Noon got down top gallant yards, opened a barrel of beef contents 56 pieces.

Oct 15, 1765 Tuesday NNE, N, NW, NNW
Ponnets River No 3 mile
PM fresh gales and clear weath got on board 3 casks of water, at 6 AM began to unmoor ship took up the least bower & hove on to ½ a cable on the stream cable, at 8 weighed and came to sail got up topgallant yards Ponnett River being North Dectarice 3 miles.
Ponnett River N 3 mile.
Masters Log
PM fresh gales and clear weath got on board 5 casks of water, at 6 AM began to unmoor ship sloop of the best bower & hove into ½ a cable on the stream cable, at 8 unmoored and came to sail got up top gallant yards, Ponnett River bearing north distance 3 miles.

Oct. 16, 1765 Wednesday N, NNW
Bear Cape WSW 2 leagues
PM fresh gales and cloudy weath at 4 tacked & took in first three topsails ? sail & came too with the least bower anchor in 16 fathoms water and sandy bottom veered away to a whole cable Bear Cape bearing S b E Wood Island W b N & the East point of the Isle Peetoo SW b W at 10 got on topgallant yards, AM more mod at 9 weighed and came to sail. Got up topgallant yds at 12 Bear Cape bearing WSW dist 2 leagues.
Bear Cape WSW 2 leagues
Masters Log
PM fresh gales and cloudy weath at 4 tacked & took in first reef of topsails shortened sail & came too with the best bower anchor in 16 fathom water hard sandy bottom veered away to a whole cable Bear Cape bearing E b E Wood Island W b N & the East point of Point Peetoo N b W at 10 got down top gallant yards, AM more mod at 9 weighed and came to sail & got up top gallant yards at 12 Bear Cape bearing WSW dist 2 leagues.

Oct. 17, 1765 Thursday N, N b W

Bear Cape WSW

Fair and cloudy weath at 2 PM tacked ship, at 4 tacked at 5 tacked at ½ past tacked and took in the first reef the topsails, Boughton Island N b E at 4 miles head NNW 3 miles Bear Cape SW b S 3 leagues small rain fired a gun a signal for the *Jupiter* in Three Rivers at AM fresh breezes and variable at 11 tacked ship at 6 saw Cape James bearing 9 SSE dist 3 leagues wore ship at 10 Cape St Souis WSW 2 leagues, at 12 the Gut of Canso bearing SE b S 2 leagues.

Masters Log

Mod and cloudy weath at 2 PM tacked ship, at 4 tacked, at 5 tacked at ½ past 6 tacked and took in the first reef the topsails, Boughton Island N b E dist 4 miles head NNW 3 miles Bear Cape SW b S 3 leagues mod & small rain fired a gun a signal for the *Jupiter* in Three Rivers at 1 AM fresh breezes and variable at 1 tacked ship at 6 saw Cape ST. Souies bear 9 SSE dist 3 leagues wore ship at 10 Cape St. Souis WSW 2 ½ leagues at 12 the Gut of Canos bearing SE b S 2 leagues.

Oct. 18, 1765 Friday W, E b E, NE b E

Cape St Souris

Fresh gales and squally weath at got into the Gut & saw a schooner anchored belonging to Quebec bound to Magdalen Islands at 4 came too with the best bower anchor in 10 fathoms water in ship harbour 2 cable lengths from the shore. AM mod & clear weath people cutting wood.

Masters Log

PM fresh gales and squally weath at got into the Gut & saw a schooner at anchor belonging to Quebec bound to Magaden Ilands at 4 came too with the best bower anchor in 10 fathoms water in Ship Harbour 2 cable length from the shore AM mod. & clear weath people Empd cutting wood.

Oct. 19, 1765 Saturday Var:

The same weath winds Variable people employed wooding at 6 AM saw and spoke a schooner from Canso bound to the Three Rivers in the land of St. Johns.

Masters Log

The same weath winds variable people employed wooding at 6 AM saw and spoke a schooner from Canso bound to the three Rivers in the Island of St. Johns.

Oct. 20, 1765 Sunday SSW

Variable and cloudy weath with some rain.

Oct. 21, 1765 Monday SW, SSW

PM the same weath at 8 came in and anchored here his Majesty's armed schooner the *Magdalen* from Halifax AM hard gales and squally weath at 7 she sailed from hence. at 11 lowered down the main top yard and struck top gallant masts.

Oct. 22, 1765 Tuesday WSW

More mod. at 7 PM swayed up the lower yard & got up topgallant yards AM calm & clear weather.

Oct. 23, 1765 Wednesday Var:, WNW

Mod. and cloudy weath at 8 PM came in and anchored here a schooner from the Three Rivers, at 8 AM light airs and variable weather took up the stream anchor & hove short on the best bower anchor at 10 weighed and came to sail at 12 hazey weath with rain the next point of the Gut bearing WNW 1 ½ miles.

Oct. 24, 1765 Thursday NE, NNE, N

PM fresh breezes and hazey weath with rain at 5 the outward most Island of Canso S b W at 7 close reeft the topsails & down topgallant yards at 8 Canso bearing SW b W dist 3 leagues at 1 AM hard gales with a great wave from the eastward at 2 the boat we had at stern filled with a sea & went down & handed the mizen topsails at 3 set the mizen topsail at 10 out 3d & 2d reef topsails at 12 mod & cloudy out the 1st reef topsails.

Oct. 25, 1765 Friday NW, WNW

PM fresh gales and cloudy weath at 7 clear out 1st & 2d reef topsails at 11 tacked ship at 12 sounded no ground at 80 fathom at 2 AM light airs clear at 4 got up topgallant yards at 9 set topmast studding sails & took observation 43, 27 No.

Oct. 26, 1765 Saturday S, NW, N

H.M. Armed Ship *Canceaux* moored in Louisbourg harbor for winter.

PM fresh breezes and fair weath at 4 saw the sand of Cape Breton bearing NW b W to NE b N dist 7 leagues at 8 anchored in Louisbourg Harbour with the beat bower in 7 fathom water light airs & fair weath and riding here His Majesty's Armed Schooner *St. Lawrence* & several merchant vessels. AM opened a firkin of butter, moored ship the east point of the Island battery E ½ S the light house E b W: the Citadel SSW.

Oct. 27, 1765 Sunday NW, NNE

First & middle parts mod & cloudy weath the latter part fresh breezes and clear Opened a barrel of pork contents 112 pieces short 1 piece.

Oct. 28, 1765 Monday NNW

Mod and fair weath Employed landing the Surveyor Generals

baggage.

Oct. 29, 1765 Tuesday NNW

Fresh gales and cloudy weath with rain Employed as before punished Saml Williams with 24 lashes for mutinous words & ? opened a cask of beef contain. 95 pieces.

Oct. 30 1765 Wednesday NNW

Mod and fair weath employed stowing the provisions & ships stores, sailed from hence a brigantine for Spain - Unbent fore and main sail.

Oct. 31, 1765 Thursday NE

Fresh breezes and cloudy weath Employed as before, AM came in & anchored here a sloop from Quebec opened a cask of beef contents 56 pieces a barrel of pork contents of 119 pieces and a ferkin of butter recd on board 3 Hhds of beer.

Nov. 1, 1765 Friday NE, SE

Mod & foggy weath Employed as before, Read the articles of war & abstract of the new act of Parliament to the ships company, opened a ferkin of butter.

Nov. 2, 1765 Saturday SE, S, SW

Mod and foggy weath with rain, AM a gundalowe came a longside and took out long guns & sent them on shore, opened a cask of beef contents 56 pieces.

Nov. 3, 1765 Sunday W, SSE, NW

AM gales and foggy weath with rain at 3 AM drove & let go the small bower anchor and veered away to ½ a cable lowered the fore and main yards down & struck Tgallant masts.

Nov. 4 1765 Monday NW, SSE

PM hard gales and clear weath middle calm the latter hard gales & foggy weath.came in & anchored here three schooners.

Nov. 5, 1765 Tuesday SSE, SW, NNE

PM fresh gales and clear weath. AM mod & cloudy at 7 swayed up the lower yards and topgallant masts.

Nov. 6, 1765 Wednesday NNE, E, SSE

Fresh gales and thick foggs with rain weighed our stream anchor found one of the arms gone, sent all our provisions on shore.

Nov. 7, 1765 Thursday SSE, NNW, NW

PM the same weath AM mod & cloudy loosed sails to dry, The *Jupiter* came along side & took on board our spared sails & some others boatswains stores to be put in store in Louisbourg.

Nov. 8, 1765 Friday Varb.

Fresh gales and cloudy weath with haze and rain sailed from hence His Majesty's Armed schooner *St. Lawrence*.

Nov. 9, 1765 Saturday SSE, calm, NNW
Mod & cloudy weath at 8 AM unmoored ship at 9 hove short on the best bower at 11 weighed & came to sail at Noon Anchored with the best bower anchor in 4 fathom water at the head of the NE harbor.
Nov. 10, 1765 Sunday NW, W, SW
PM fresh gales and clear weath & dried sails & unbent all our sails and made them ? shorten top to masts and got the boom on.

*Nov. 11, 1765 to Nov. 19, 1765

Nov. 20, 1765 Wednesday NNW
Fresh gales and squally weath with snow and frost came in and anchored here His Majesty's armed schooner *St. Lawrence*.

*Nov. 21, 1765 to Dec. 1, 1765

Dec. 2, 1765 Monday varb.
Mod & cloudy weath sailed from hence a schooner for Halifax opened a cask of beef contents 56 pieces & a ferkin of butter.
Dec. 3, 1765 Tuesday ESE
Mod and cloudy weath with snow & hard frost AM fresh gales with snow.
Dec. 4, 1765 Wednesday E, SE, SW
Fresh gales and cloudy with frost.
Dec. 5, 1765 Thursday WNW, NW
Fresh gales and cloudy weath with hard frost punished John Clark with 13 lashes for Drunkenness and mutinous words.
Dec. 6, 1765 Friday NW, NNE
Fresh gales & squally weather with at times, PM moored the pinnace a stern of the ship & unbent her sails for the winter.

*Dec. 7, 1765 to Dec. 13, 1765

Dec. 14, 1765 Saturday SE, NE, N
PM hard gales with thick snow AM clear weath with hard frost clear being a very high tide and great sea did much damage to the fishing craft.
Dec. 15, 1765 Sunday N, NNW
PM hard gale and squally weath AM clear weath with hard frost.
Dec. 16, 1765 Monday NW, N
Fresh gales and clear weath with hard frost.

Dec. 17, 1765 Tuesday NNW
Fresh gales and clear weath, fell through the ice and was drowned Frederick H. Bemand in the Royal Americans & deputy Surveyor to Captain Holland Surveyor General.

*Dec. 18, 1765 to Dec. 22, 1765

Dec. 23, 1765 Monday W b N
The first and middle parts mod and cloudy weath The latter part fresh gales and cloudy at Noon sailed from hence the schooner *Nancy* bound to Madaina, Peter Ramsey Master, opended a cask of beef contents 56 pieces & a ferkin of butter.
Dec. 24, 1765 Tuesday SW
PM hard gales with sleet AM more moderate.
Dec. 25, 1765 Wednesday WSW
PM fresh gales and cloudy weath with show AM mod and cloudy opened a cask of pork containing 112 pieces.
Dec. 26, 1765 Thursday WNW
Fresh gales and clear weath with hard frost came in and anchored here the sloop *York* from N. York, John Wattern, Master with provisions, opened a barrel of beef containing 56 pieces.

*Dec. 27, 1765 to Jan. 2, 1765

Jan. 3, 1766 Friday variable, SSE, S
Moderate and cloudy weath at 4 PM came on to blow very hard with rain and sleet at 10 the ship lost two parts of the stream cable which were her quarter parts and salvaged to her anchored here the ship surrounded broken ice at 10 very hard gales with snow and sleet, at 4 AM more Mod & clear the *Jupiter* take one boat got foul of the ship & carried away her masts.
Jan. 4, 1766 Saturday NW
Mod gales with clear weath and hard frost people Employed getting casks out beer could not get the ship inshore.
Jan. 5, 1766 Sunday NNW
Fresh gales and clear weath with hard frost.
Jan. 6, 1766 Monday variable
Mod and cloudy weather.
Jan 7, 1766 Tuesday WSW, SW
Small breezes and cloudy weath People employed breaking the ice and getting the ship nearer the shore.
Jan. 8, 1766 Wednesday SW, SSE

In mod and cloudy weath, AM fresh gales with some snow and sleet.

Jan 9, 1766 Thursday SSE, WNW

Fresh gales and cloudy weath opened a ferkin of butter.

Jan. 10, 1766 Friday NW

Mod and clear weather with hard frost.

Jan. 11, 1766 Saturday WNW

The same weath sailed from hence the sloop *York* bound for New Orleans.

*Jan 12, 1766 to Jan 21, 1766

Jan 22, 1766 Wednesday WNW, NW

Mod & clear weath the NE harbour froze over at far as Point Tulliken the *St Lawrence* schooner shifted her birth nearer to Point Tuttiken.

Jan. 23, 1766 Thursday WNW

The same weath people Employed variously.

Jan 24, 1766 Friday NW b W

Fresh gales and clear weath discharged Thomas Walfield Seaman Unservable opened a cask of beef contents 56 pieces short 1 piece.

*Jan. 25, 1766 to Feb. 1, 1766

Feb. 2, 1766 Sunday WNW

PM fresh gales and rain AM mod and hard frost the Master and men sailed in the pinnace for Beacones having with them provisions for one month.

*Feb. 3, 1766 to Feb. 7 1766

Feb. 8, 1766 Saturday NE

Fresh gales & cloudy weath with snow PM Sailed from hence the schooner *Charly*, Oates Master for Boston.

*Feb. 9, 1766 to Feb. 21, 1766

Feb. 22, 1766 Saturday NW

The same weath Sent a petty officer and 6 men to Mendcus to to bring down the pinnace.

Feb. 23, 1766 Sunday NNW, NW

Mod and fine weath AM the pinnace returned from Mendcus

Feb. 24, 1766 to Monday SE, S
PM Mod and clear weath AM fresh breezes & cloudy with rain.
Feb. 25, 1766 Tuesday S
Fresh gales and rain the harbour full of drift ice & Noruater to lee seen ice and AM Mod & fine fair weath.
Feb. 26, 1766 Wednesday variable
Mod. and fine weath the harbour side full of ice, a little frost, Captain Holland and his party went out on a survey.
Feb. 27, 1766 Thursday variable
Mod and clear weath at 4 PM Captain Mowat returned with an agreement that he had made seizure of the sloop *George* belonging to Quebec with wine and brandy from St. Peters.
Feb. 28, 1766 Friday SSW, SW
Mod and cloudy weath most of the ice drove out the harbor and with the NE harbour.
Mar. 1, 1766 Saturday SW, variable
Mod and foggy weath all the harbour full of ice AM read the articles of war and abstract of the new act of Parliament to the ships company.
Mar. 2, 1766 Sunday SW, WSW
The same weather.
Mar. 3, 1766 Monday W, NNW
PM Mod and hazey weath AM fresh gales and hard frost with some snow all the ice gone out of the harbour.
Mar. 4, 1766 Tuesday NNW, N
Hard gales & snow with hard frost all the drift ice gone from the stream AM saw a schooner to the east standing to the westward.
Mar. 5, 1766 Wednesday N, NNW
Mod and fair weath with hard frost a great quantity of ice around the ship.
Mar. 6, 1766 Thursday NW, SW
The same weath at 10 AM came in & anchored here His Majestys Armed schooner the *Magdalen* from Halifax.
Mar. 7, 1766 Friday SW, WNW, NW
PM Mod breezes and thick hazey weath with snow AM fresh gales and clear weath with hard frost received from the *Magdalen* Armed schooner the following provisions, bread 2240 pounds, flour 480 lb, and beef 160 pieces, 320 pieces, pease 10 bushells, butter 215 lb, suet 41 ½ cheese 128 pounds.
Mar. 8, 1766 Saturday NW, NNW
Fresh gales and hard frost.
Mar. 9, 1766 Sunday NNW

The same weath at noon came in and anchored here the schooner *Unity*, John Whittly, Master from Boston eight days passage saw a schooner in the east standing in shore.

Mar. 10, 1766 Sunday NW b W

Fresh gales and clear weather.

Mar. 11, 1766 Monday NW, SW

PM the same weath AM fine mod weath with some snow.

Mar. 12, 1766 Tuesday SW

Mod and fair weath Sailed from hence His Majesty's schooner *Magdalen* from the NE harbour.

Mar. 13, 1766 Thursday N, W, WSW

Fresh breezes and dark cloudy weath AM came in and anchored here the schooner *Unity* Oakes master from Boston 18 days passage.

Mar. 14, 1766 Friday SW, S

Fresh gales with snow and sleet AM the harbour full of drift ice. Received on board 1398 pounds of fresh beef for the ships company.

Mar. 15, 1766 Saturday S, NW

Fresh gales with snow and hard frost. The harbour full of ice.

Mar. 16 1766 Sunday NW, N, NNE

Hard gales with frost and snow. The harbour clear of ice.

Mar. 17, 1766 Monday NNE, SW

PM hard gales with frost and snow AM mod and fair weath at 2 PM the ice carried away the *Magdalen* schooner & hauled clear of her cables & got under sail and came here opposite to the town not having anchor or cable to come too with or boat and people employed assisting to get her off.

Mar. 18, 1766 Tuesday SW, SSW, S

PM mod and fair weath AM fresh gales with hazey weath at Noon the *Magdalen* got off after handing her ballast, stores and provisions, people Employed as before.

Mar. 19, 1766 Wednesday S, SW, WNW

Fresh breezes and cloudy weath with snow and sleet People and boat employed Assisting the *Magdalen*.

Mar. 20 1766 Thursday NW, NNW, N

PM fresh gales and clear weath AM moderate the people employed under running the spare cable that we kept in January last.

Mar. 21, 1766 Friday N

Mod and fine fair weath Employed as before got the spare cable on board.

Mar. 22, 1766 Saturday NNE

Mod and clear weath Employed cleaning all the ice and snow off the ships decks, the *St. Lawrence* schooner sailed up to town.

Mar. 23, 1766 Sunday NNE
Moderate and clear weather.

Mar. 24, 1766 Monday SW
Mod and foggy weath Employed getting on board the topmasts at Noon swayed the mizen topmast up and fided it.

Mar. 25, 1766 Tuesday SSW, WSW
Fresh breezes and hazey weath at 4 PM the ice began to come into the harbour got up the fore and main caps and swayed up the topmasts through them and rigged them.

Darcy Lever writing in "The Young Sea Officers Sheet Anchor" (1819) describes swaying under "To Get The Mast Up": The Mast is swayed up by the top-rope, being guyed off the rim of the top by the men there: and when the pole head is sufficiently entered through the cap, the end is cast off (the mast hanging by the stops), and hitched to the eye-bolt in the starboard side of the cap. The Stops are then cut: and the mast hangs by the top-rope, ready for rigging. The rigging is hoisted up by the girt-lines, like the topmast rigging. The masts were hoisted up, a small distance at a time.

Mar. 26, 1766 Wednesday NNE, WNW
Fresh gales and cloudy weath Employed about the rigging AM snow with hard frost.

Mar. 27, 1766 Thursday WNW, SW
PM fresh gales with snow AM mod and fine weath employed clearing between decks and cathanhenning the shrouds.

Mar. 28, 1766 Friday SW, SE, NW
Mod and hazey weath Employed about the rigging.

Mar. 29. 1766 Saturday NW, W
Fresh breezes and cloudy weath Employed getting the hawers in and topsail yards and topgallant mast up.

Mar. 30, 1766 Sunday SW, W
PM fresh breezes and cloudy weath AM mod and thick with snow.

Mar. 31, 1766 Monday NW
PM mod and fair weath Employed about the rigging AM sailed from hence His Majesty's schooner the *Magdalen*.

April 1, 1766 Tuesday NE
PM mod and fair weath AM fresh gales and cloudy weath sailed from hence His Majesty's schooner *St. Lawrence* for Halifax & schooner *Unity* Oakes Master for Boston Employed as before.

April 2, 1766 Wednesday NE
PM the same weath with hard frost AM sailed from hence the schooner *Unity* John Whittly Master for Boston Employed reeving the runing rigging.

April 3. 1766 Thursday NE
Fresh gales and clear weath with hard frost Employed getting the spare topmast and sail on board, read the articles of war and abstract of the new act of Parliament to the ships company got on board the foresail, mizen and jibb and three topsails and bent them.

April 4, 1766 Friday NE, variable
PM the same weath AM moderate Employed above the rigging and filling water. The harbour frozen over at Noon the ice broke up.

April 5, 1766 Saturday variable
Mod and cloudy weath with hard frost. PM Employed as before. AM Employed filling the water fided the topmast and sett the shrouds up.

April 6 1766 Sunday variable
The first part light airs and cloudy weath the latter mod and foggy weath the harbour frozen over hove off from the shore to our anchor in heaving the cable got foul of a wreck and hoisted and lost 35 fathom of our small bower weighed the anchor with the buoy rope.

April 7, 1766 Monday
PM light airs and clear weath AM hard frost at 7 AM weighed & came to sail at 8 came too with the best bower in 5 fathom water opposite the town The citadel flagstaff bearing SW b S the steeple of the hospital SE b S at Noon the ships draught of water, forward 10ft:6in aft 9ft:11in difference 17 inches.

April 8, 1766 Tuesday
Mod breezes and clear weath Employed getting ballast on board, shifted 12 piggs of iron ballast from the main hold to the town, at 27 minutes past 8 PM saw a comet or blazing star bearing by the compass NW b W being about 30 degrees high, at 33 minutes past 10 the comet disappeared at 7 AM got up top top gallant yards the carpenters employed on the *Jupiter* got on board 1 Hhd of beer.

April 9, 1766 Wednesday
Mod and cloudy weath Employed as before at 6 PM got down top gallant yards at 6 AM got them up The harbour full of drift ice, carpenters empd. as before.

April 10, 1766 Thursday
Fresh gales and hazey weath with rain at 4 PM got down topgallant yards and lash yards and topmasts.
April 11, 1766 Friday
PM fresh gales and hazey weath with rain AM moderate people employed making of points and gasketts Recd on board one Hhd of beer.
April 12, 1766 Saturday
Mod and foggy weath people employed as before.
April 13, 1766 Sunday
Moderate and foggy weather.
April 14, 1766 Monday
PM light airs and foggy weather AM fresh breezes and clear weath at 6 swayed up yards and topmast, & got up topgallant yards handed sails to dry at 10 The ice began drive out of the harbour at Noon the ship cleared of ice.
April 15, 1766 Tuesday
PM fresh breezes and clear weath AM mod with fresh drift ice around the ship at 4 PM sent and brought our guns on board Employed hoisting them in AM bent the mainsail, main top sail, mizen middle and mizen and fore stay & sprit sails.
April 16, 1766 Wednesday
PM mod and foggy weath AM fresh gales and squally with rain The harbour full of drift ice Recd on board 8 Hhds of beer and stored it in the hold.
April 17, 1766 Thursday
Fresh breezes and cloudy weath Employed getting wood and water on board got all our spare sails and provisions on board from the shore the harbour clear of Ice.
April 18, 1766 Friday
The same weath Employed variously at 8 AM fired a gun and hoisted the foretop sail a signal for sailing
April 19, 1766 Saturday
Mod and cloudy weath employed variously ships draught of water forward 10 feet 3 inches aft 11 feet 4 inches difference 1 foot 1 inch.
April 20, 1766 Sunday
The same weather at 5 AM unmoored ship at Noon weighed and came to sail.
April 21, 1766 Monday SW, ENE, SW
Light airs and variable anchored with the best bower bower 8in the north east harbour in 6 fathom soft ground veered out

½ a cable Point Tulletsen bearing ½ E. The flag staff at the Citadel in Louisbourg SW Grand Battery W b N at 11 weighed and came to sail.

April 22, 1766 Tuesday N b E, NNW, NW, N

PM fresh gales and clear weath at 2 took in first reef topsail at 6 got down topgallant yards at 7 land in sight of the land at 2 AM the same weath tacked ship at 6 saw the land bearing from NW to N b N at 7 tacked ship at 8 out reef topsails at 12 mod and hazey weath tacked ship Canso WNW dist 7 or 8 leagues observation 45 degree 9 m.

April 23, 1766 Wednesday SW, calm, NE, NW

Light breezes and cloudy weath Canso bearing W b N about 4 or 5 leagues at 7 took in one reef topsails at 5 AM light breezes with snow at 7 took reefs topsail, at 2 past 10 got up topgallant yards fresh breezes & clear & obser. 44.35 No.

April 24, 1766 Thursday W, NW, W

Light breezes and cloudy weath at 4 PM fresh gales took in all the reefs in the topsails and topgallant yards Saw 2 sails standing to the eastward at 6 tacked the westernmost land in sight at W 72 N the easternmost land ENE off shore 1 mile at AM out first reef topsails saw 2 sail in the AM fresh gales and clear weath spoke a schooner from Halifax banks point obser: 14 ?

April 25, 1766 Friday W, NW

PM fresh gales and pleasant at 2 saw land bearing from WNW to NE dist. 3 leagues at 5 tacked ship the land to the west and W b S and to the eastward E b N dist between 4 miles and 3 miles at 9 squally handed the fore and mizen topsails, at 10 AM mod and cloudy weath at 3 sett the fore and mizen topsail at 6 light airs with a swell from the westward out reefs top sails, got up the topmast rigging fore and aft at 8 fresh gales and clear weath set first and 2d reef topsails, at ½ past tacked to the northward, at 11 spoke a schooner from Falmouth bound to the Isle of Sable, latitude of observation 44.25 No.

April 26, 1766 Saturday W b S, NW, W

PM fresh gales and clear weath at 2 saw the land bearing from W b N to NE strong gales at 3 tacked ship, off shore 3 or 4 leagues at 3 AM small breezes & clear weath got up the top gallant yards at 11 tacked ship at 6 fresh gales and clear weath at 44. 05 North.

April 27, 1766 Sunday N, NE, ESE

PM mod breezes and clear weath at 2 fresh breezes at 3 saw the land bearing from NW to SE b E at 8 mod the extreme of the land from W b W to ESE at 11 Cape Samborough lighthouse bearing west at 12 brought too with the topsails masts at 5 AM saw a sail and stood for Halifax Harbour at 1/2 past 8 saluted the Admiral with 13 guns and came too with our best bower anchor in 9 fathom water in Halifax harbour where we found His Majesty's ship *Mermaid* with the White flag at the mizon topmast in the Right honorable Lord Colvil Rear Admiral of the White with His Majesty's following ships the *Mermaid, Alboregn, Squire Mc Donegall*, with the *St. Lawrence*, and *Gaspie* sloop Armed vessels.

April 28, 1766 Monday E, ESE, E b N

Fresh gales and hazey cloudy weath AM hard gales with rain & foggy AM came on board the Master intended to transport the ship to the wharf Employed transporting the ship to the careening warf.

Ships after long voyages needed work on their bottoms and were hove down or careened. In this major activity guns and stores were landed, ballast removed and yards were lowered and topmasts and topgallant masts were struck. Openings were closed and caulked and battens nailed on deck for footing on the steep angles of the deck. Anchored at bow and stern for stability, the shrouds on the lower masts were strengthened with spars on the opposite side as the hull work. The masts were reinforced with tackle and additional spars lashed to the lower mastheads and through the gunports reduced the strain on the hull and facilitated tipping the hull over to expose the bottom enabling scraping, caulking, painting and carpentry work as needed. When bracing was complete heavy tackle was secured to the fore and main mastheads and massive blocks on shore. The line was wound on capstans and the ship pulled over on her side where crews on stages or rafts did the work. Hull sheathing was used on the Canceaux.

April 29, 1766 Tuesday E b N, SE, SW

PM mod and thick fogg at 11 gott alongside the warf and moored with the 2d bower found a cut upon the bower and one upon the quarter with a last to the warf AM clear and loosed sails to dry Employed unbending the sails and getting the stores on shore.

April 30, 1766 Wednesday WSW

Fresh breezes and clear weath Employed unrigging the ship came on board caulkers to caulk the ship.

May 1, 1766 Thursday variable

Mod and clear weath employed as before and clearing the hold, carpenters and caulkers employed on the ship Read the articles of war and abstract of the New act of Parliament to the ships company.

May 2, 1766 Friday NNE

Mod breezes and clear weath Employed getting the ballast out carpenters and caulkers employed as before.

May 3, 1766 Saturday NNE

Same weath Employed as before.

May 4, 1766 Sunday NE

Mod breezes and clear weath Employed as before.

May 5, 1766 Monday

The same weath at Noon cleared the hold of all the ballast carpenters and caulkers Employed as before.

May 6, 1766 Tuesday

Fresh gales with rain People Employed over hauling the rigging caulkers employed between decks AM came in and anchored here a brigantine from Lisbon 41 days passage.

May 7, 1766 Wednesday SE

Fresh gales and hazey weath with rain people Employed as before.

May 8 , 1766 Thursday

The same weath Employed as before.

PM fresh gales and cloudy weath people, carpenters and caulkers

May 9, 1766 Friday

PM fresh gales and cloudy weathr. People, carpenters, and caulkers Employed as before AM mod and fair weath at 10 hove down the ship got out the larboard side at Noon, sighted the Admiral made a signal for all to come on board.

May 10, 1766 Saturday

Mod and fair weath people Employed shifting the guns to heave the other side out at 8 AM heave over the starboard side at 12 hauled out.

May 11, 1766 Sunday

The same weath people employed about the rigging & getting on shore all the rigging.

May 12, 1766 Monday

The same weath people employed about the rigging and getting the ballast in carpenters and caulkers Employed as before.

May 13, 1766 Tuesday

The same weath People employed painting the ship and hoisting in the ground tier the carpenters and caulkers employed as before hauled off from the warf the guns of sloop.

May 14, 1766 Wednesday

PM mod and fair weath AM fresh breezes people Employed getting on board ballast and rigging the ship carpenters and caulkers Employed as before.

May 15, 1766 Thursday
Mod and fair weath people & & Employed as before AM came on board painters in order to paint the ship, Three men John Clarke, John Williams, & Jack May deserted themselves from duty.

May 16 1766 Friday
Fresh gales and cloudy weath people, carpenters && Employed as before PM sailed from here His Majesty's schooner *St. Lawrence* recd. on board 20 barrels of beef and 23 barrels of pork.

May 17, 1766 Saturday
The same weath with rain people employed variously painters employed painting the cables veered on the following provisions flours 1 barrels, vinegar, Hhd containing 62 gall. suet 4 barrels with 2 new cables.

May 18, 1766 Sunday
PM mod with rain AM fresh gales and cloudy weath came in and anchored spoke a brigantine from Dublin, Recd on board a new stream cable and 1 new ground hawser.

May 19, 1766 Monday variable
The same weath people Employed getting the boatswain's and carpenters stores on board and scraping the sides.

May 20, 1766 Tuesday
Fresh gales and clear weath Employed variously The painters painting the ship, a long boat came along side with provisions.

The British navy paint scheme was usually a light yellow or varnished brown having a black band above the copper sheathing. Navy ships were often painted red or brown inboard on bulwarks and overheads to make the blood splatters less noticeable. Spars were varnished brown, masts painted black with the standing rigging, block and deadeyes tarred black

May 21, 1766 Wednesday
Fresh gales and squally weath with rain AM employed hoisting in the provisions and stowing them away AM Employed bending the sails & getting on board the boatswains & carpenters stores, get provisions recd on board up all as follows: bread 176 lb beef 656 pieces, pork 1627 pieces, butter 201 lb, rum 324 gallons, ease bushells oatmeal 41 bushells, cheese 7182 lbs, rice 551 lb, vinegar 160 gallons.

May 22, 1766 Thursday NNE
Same weath recd on board, boards and other stores for the Surveyor General Empd scraping the lower masts, at 10 His Majesty's ship the *Mermaid* made a signal for a Court Marshall, scraped the sides and payed them and varnished masts with ye oil of Tar.

May 23, 1766 Friday NE
The same weath Employed getting on board Boatswains stores, punished Daniel Stern & Tom Bagly with 50 lashes for desertion by the sentence of a Courts Marshall.

May 24, 1766 Saturday NE
The same weath Employed scraping the sides at Noon rain Received on board 122 lb of fresh beef for the ships company.

May 25, 1766 Sunday variable
Mod breezes and variable weath.

May 26, 1766 Monday NNE
PM mod and cloudy weath AM fresh breezes and squally at 10 hauled off from the warf and bay with the stream cable part to the splice to the best bower, offing came in and anchored here his Majesty's armed schooner *St. Lawrence*

May 27, 1766 Tuesday NE, SE, S
Fresh gales and squally weath Employed putting the decks to right and placing the rigging AM recd on board a new whale boat with masts, sails, and rope for the use of the survey.

May 28, 1766 Wednesday S, SE
Mod and fair weath AM weighed and came to sail at Noon anchored with the best bower anchor in 12 fathoms water veered to 1/3 of a cable and moored her with the stream anchor and cable. The Citadel WSW Georges Island SE b E distance off there 1 cable length.

May 29, 1766 Thursday S
Mod and hazey weath Employed setting up the topmast rigging and making points and gaskets sailed from hence His Majesty's armed schooner the *St. Lawrence* with 15 guns as did the Admiral and all the fleet.

May 30, 1766 Friday S, SE
Mod & fair weath people employed variously at 9 AM the *Mermaid* made a signal for a court marshall.

May 31, 1766 Saturday SE, ESE
Moderate and hazey weath with rain People Employed variously.

June 1, 1766 Sunday SSE
Fresh breezes and hazey weath with rain, came in here a brig from

Cork AM read the articles of war and abstract of the new act of Parliament to the ships company.

June 2, 1766 Monday SSE

PM the same weath AM mod and foggy at 10 the Admiral made a signal to sail handed sails to dry.

June 3, 1766 Tuesday SW

Mod and cloudy weath Employed variously the Admiral made a signal for all to sail.

June 4, 1766 Wednesday WSW

Mod and clear weath came in and anchored here His Majesty's ship the (no name in log) Employed variously His Majesty's ship the *Rumnay* and the Fleet were all directed to observe it bring the Kings Birth Day and fired 21 guns.

June 5, 1766 Thursday SW

Fresh gales and cloudy weath at 8 AM the Admiral made a signal for a court marshal on Lawrence May Seaman belonging to the *Canceaux*, at ½ past 10 the signal was made on board the Admiral for the punishment which was 50 lashes a longside the end. and 50 lashes alongside the *Canceaux*.

June 6, 1766 Friday WSW

Fresh gales and squally weath with rain took in first reef topsails at 3 PM weighed and came to sail Employed serving out at 8 thick fogg Cape Sambrough bearing W b E 3 leagues at 4 AM out the topsails and set topgallant and sail, at 12 brought too and sounded no ground at 70 fathom.

June 7, 1766 Saturday WSW, S, SW

Fresh breezes and foggy weath at 6 PM sounded 80 fathom soft mud at 6 light breezes with rain at 6 sounded 70 fathom soft mud mixed with sand at 8 sounded 70 fathom with soft mud. In first reef topsails at 10 sounded 70 fathom soft mud at 12 calm with rain sounded 70 fathom soft mud at 4 AM light breezes with thick fogg at 10 out the reef topsails and sett the mizen driver at 12 sounded 96 fathom soft mud.

June 8, 1766 Sunday SW, W, SW

PM mod and foggy weath at 6 the breeze sprung up at north in fresh and set 2d reef top sails at 8 light breezes and clear weath at 2 AM sounded 38 fathom gravel mixed with sand and at 3 saw the land and bearing from NW b W to NNE off shore 3 leagues at 8 saw Port Nos bearing W hauled up at 12 fresh breeze and thick fogg.

June 9, 1766 Monday SW

PM fresh breezes and thick fogg tacked ship at 4 sailed at 6 tacked at 8 tacked & took in 1st reef topsails at 10 in 2d reef fore topsail at 12 fresh gales tacked at 3 AM cloudy saw a sail bearing NNE which proved to be His Majesty's armed schooner *Magdalen* at 3 saw the land which proved to be Louisbourg at 10 anchored in Louisbourg harbour with the best bower the *Magdalen* in company found lying here His Majesty's armed schooner the *St. Lawrence*.

June 10, 1766 Tuesday SW

Fresh breezes and clear weath weighed and came to sail shifted our birth and anchored here with the best bower in 5 fathom water sandy bottom veered to ½ a cable moored with the stream anchor and cable the flagstaff W b S The steeple of the hospital S b E dist of ¼ of a mile.

*June 11, 1766 to June 16, 1766

June 17, 1766 Tuesday SW, N

The same weath at 6 PM came on board the Surveyor General AM moderate clear weath sailed from hence His Majesty's schooners the *Magdalen* and *St. Lawrence* the former to the westward and the latter to the eastward.

June 18, 1766 Wednesday WSW

Mod and fine clear weath at 5 AM unmoored ship and hove short on the best bower at 7 weighed and came to sail at Noon Port Nova Rock NNW ¼ of mile.

June 19, 1766 Thursday NE, N

Mod and hazey weath at 2 PM Flint Island bearing ESE dist 4 miles at 6 the west ? head of Spanish River W 2 leagues at 9 calm anchored with the stream anchor and cable in 10 fathom water veered to 2/3 of a cable the more point south 3 miles, Bradore point NNW 5 or 6 miles, at 5 AM weighed and came to sail at 7 anchored with the best bower in Spanish River in 9 fathom water of mud, veered away and moored ship a cable way NE & SW the best bower of the NE, the house on the point bearing NE b N the outward point of the Island N b E ¼ of a mile the W point W b S one mile. Employed unbending the sails.

June 20, 1766 Friday WSW

Fresh breezes and clear weath Employed sounding the cables. Captain Holland & his party went out on a Survey delivered to him 60 yards of old canvas 97 yards of bunting, one deep sea lead and line to each hand, carpenters Employed fitting out a boat for the Survey, came in here the *Jupiter* boat.

June 21, 1766 Saturday W b S
Same weath finished rounding the cables heaving rounded 7 fathoms each cable 10 AM went away on a Survey Mr. Sproul and his party having 1 midshipman, 2 seamen with him, 10 in number with 3 months provisions, 65 yards old canvas tents, deep water lead and line one each & 1 hand lead each 2 hand lines 1 lanthorn, spare cable, 89 yards of bunting for colours 3 reels twine, 3 sail needles, 2 pad locks , 1 graple rope 35 fathom sailed the *Jupiter* boat.

June 22, 1766 Sunday SW
The same weath Captain Holland and his Party returned from Surveying.

June 23, 1766 Monday WSW
The same weath at 10 AM Captain Holland and his party went out on a Survey as did Captain Mowat with the pinnace. Having 7 days provisions with them punished James Williams with 24 lashes for disobeyance of orders.

June 24, 1766 Tuesday WSW
The same weath Employed cutting wood and getting it on board sent the boat up the river for spruce.

June 25, 1766 Wednesday variable
The same weath Employed scraping and cleaning between decks punished Wm. Presser with 24 lashes for theft.

June 26, 1766 Thursday variable
Mod breezes Employed cutting wood and getting it on board.

June 27, 1766 Friday variable
Light airs and cloudy weath with thunder and rain at 5 PM Captain Holland and his party returned from Surveying as did Captain Mowat.

June 28, 1766 Saturday NNW
Mod and fair weath at 4 PM came on board a shallop from Niginish with the news of His Majesty's armed schooner *St. Lawrence* and five men with news the *St. Lawrence* schooner was blownup the day before by lightening by which these men were wounded. The ship sets in 6 fathom water Captain Dundas lost his four low guns three men got safe on shore but lost everything they had, at 6 the shallop sailed with the following provisions for Captain Dundas. bread 27 lb beef 56 pounds pork 112, butter 70 lbs and rum 36 gallon.

June 29, 1766 Sunday W
Fresh breezes and squally weath Employed variously. The Surveyor General went away on a survey toward Fredore.

June 30, 1766 Monday S
Mod and clear weath Employed variously.
July 1, 1766 Tuesday
The same weathr read the articles of war and abstract of the new abstract of Parliament to the ships company.
July 2, 1766 Wednesay SW
The same weath at 6 PM began to bend our sails at 4 AM unmoored ship at four & weighed and came to sail.
July 3, 1766 Thursday WSW
Fresh gales and cloudy weath at 4 PM Cape Fumey bearing N b W 6 leagues at 6 Signal Island SW 7 leagues, fired 3 guns for a pilot at ½ past 7 the Island at 3 cable length wore ship and stood off took in first & 2d reef topsails at 4 wore ship at 6 spoke the boat with the Master of the *St. Lawrence* and three people on board to assist us at 8 the Island WSW 4 or 5 leagues at 10 fired 2 shots and brought too a fishing schooner from the Straights of Bellisle. At Noon the Island ENE ½ a mile.
July 4, 1766 Friday W
Nigonish Harb.
Same weath at 4 AM anchored with the best bower in 13 fathom water hard mudy ground at 8 AM moored ship over the wreck Employed sweeping the wreck with her cables.
July 5, 1766 Saturday Var.
Mod and cloudy weath Employed on the warp broke a nine inch cable trying to weigh her.
July 6, 1766 Sunday SW
Mod and clear weath Employed as before but all to no purposes as her quarter deck was 18 feet under water and could not weigh best bower anchor.
July 7, 1766 Monday SSW
Fresh gales and squally with rain could do nothing on the wreck on account of the weath punished Wm. Base with 24 lashes for mutinous words.
July 8, 1766 Tuesday WNW
Fresh gales and variable at 10 AM Captain Dundas and some of his people went away in a shallop to Louisbourg leaving him Master and 6 men with us.
July 9, 1766 Wednesday NW
Hard gales and squally weath with a very great sea from the NE at 8 PM came in here Mr. Gututes boat with Mr. Wright Deputy Surveyor and his party at 9 AM unmoored ship at Noon got under

sail found our cables much rubbed in several parts.

July 10, 1766 Thursday NW, SW

PM fresh gales and squally weath at 2 Cape Tumey bearing WNW 2 leagues Apple ? Cape WSW 3 miles at 5 we anchored in Spanish River with our best bower in 8 ½ fathom water soft ground Moored ship a cable each way the best bower to the NE and the small to the SW. The house on the point NNE dist ½ mile. The W point WSW 1 mile AM mod and cloudy unbent the sails.

July 11, 1766 Friday variable

The same weath Employed variously.

July 12, 1766 Saturday WSW

The same weath Employed making points and gasketts.

July 13, 1766 Sunday SW

The same weath at 4 PM The master and seamen with three weeks provisions sent in the pinnace in the sound and take the navigable remarks of Captain Hollands Survey.

*July 14, 1766 to July 29, 1766

July 30, 1766 Wednesday SW

The same weath. at Noon the Master and his party in the pinnace came on board from sounding and making remarks.

July 31, 1766 Thursday WSW

The same weath 1 AM came the *Jupiter* with Mr. Wright and his party from Surveying the west and north part of Cape Breton Empd sounding the Harbour.

Aug. 1, 1766 Friday WNW

Fresh breezes and cloudy weath Employed as before and getting wood on board AM Read the Articles of War and new Abstract of Parliament to the Ships Company.

Aug. 2, 1766 Saturday SW

Fresh breezes and cloudy weath Employed bending the sails and setting the lower and topmast rigging fore and aft.

Aug. 3, 1766 Sunday varib

PM mod and cloudy weath AM calm at 8 began to unmoor ship at 10 took up the small bower anchor up and hauled short on the best bower came in and anchored here 2 fishing schooners.

Aug. 4, 1766 Monday WNW, calm

PM light airs and cloudy weath at 2 weighed and came to sail at 4 Apple Cape NW b N dist 2 miles at 8 the fleet point WNW 3 miles at 1 AM thick fogg and anchored with the stream anchor in 20 fathom water hard bottom at 6 mod and clear weath weighed and came to sail at Noon the coal mines WNN 3 miles 13 sail of schooners in sight the shoreline WNW by ESE from ? land to Spanish River.

Aug. 5, 1766 Tuesday NNW, N

Fresh breezes and clear weath at 3 PM going thorough between Scatarea ? and Menadee ? at 6 anchored in Louisbourg harbour with the best bower in 4 ½ fathom water the flagstaff SW b W the Hospital S b E off shore one cable length Punished James Williams with 24 lashes for disobedience of orders. The Surveyor General and his party went on shore with their baggage.

Aug. 6, 1776 Wednesday SW

Fresh breezes and cloudy weath with rain Employed variously came in here the *Jupiter* boat with Mr. Wright and his party arrived Mr. Pringle & his party.

Aug. 7, 1766 Thursday SW, NNW

Mod and clear weath the carpenters employed repairing the *Jupiter* and boats.

Aug. 8, 1766 Friday NE

Fresh breezes and cloudy weath carpenters Employed as before.

Aug. 9, 1766 Saturday SSW

Fresh breezes and hazey weath carpenters Employed as before.

Aug. 10, 1766 Sunday SW

Fresh gale and foggy weath carpenters Employed as before.

Aug. 11. 1766 Monday WSW

The same weather carpenters Employed as before.

Aug. 12 1766 Tuesday W

The same weath carpenters Employed as before fired 21 guns it being the Prince of Wales's Birth day.

Aug. 13, 1766 Wednesday SW

Mod and hazey weath delivered to Mr. Wright and party 13 in number Mr. Watts and seamen entered 12 weeks provisions of all species being bound to the Island of Antesesta in the Gulf of St. Lawrence to winter. Delivered unto Mr. Pringle & party Mr. Chase & Scurrien encluded being 13 in number 10 or 11 on the provisions of all species they being bound to the Bay of Chaleur to winter. Sailed from hence the schooner that was hired to carry him and the provisions away.

Aug. 14, 1766 Thursday variable

Mod and clear weath at 5 AM saw a ship in the offing maned the pinnace and sent her on board at Noon the boat returned and found her to be His Majesty's ship *Lauenston* with Admiral Dursell, Vice Admiral of the blue bound to Halifax to relieve

Admiral Colvill Came in here several people and schooner.
Aug. 15, 1766 Friday NW
Fresh gales and clear weath.
Aug. 16, 1766 Saturday NW
Hard gales and cloudy weath with rain AM saw a ship in the offing standing to the Eastward with her main topmast down.
Aug. 17, 1766 Sunday WSW
Fresh gales and hazey weath with rain Employed variously.
Aug. 18, 1766 Monday variable
PM the same gales AM mod and cloudy.
Aug. 19, 1766 Tuesday WSW
Fresh gales and hazey weath AM sailed from hence the *Jupiter* with Mr. Wrights party for Anticosta.
Aug. 20, 1766 Wednesday variable
Mod and clear weath Employed variously. The carpenters at work on a shallop which was hired in the service.
Aug. 21, 1766 Thursday NNE
Same weath Carpenters employed as before.
Aug. 22, 1766 Friday SW
Fresh breezes and clear weath the Surveyor General with his party and seamen with 2 boats went from hence to Survey the Island of Hatarce and Mases River.
Aug. 23, 1766 Saturday WSW
Mod and hazey weath Employed fixing a shallop to go sounding came in sail of fishing schooners, punished John Toliss with 4 lashes for unhelpfulmess and disrespect to his officers.

*Aug. 24, 1766 to Sept. 2, 1766

Sept. 3, 1766 Wednesday SSE, SE, E
PM fresh gales and squally weath with rain, AM hard gales at 10 shroud yards and topmasts, at 11 found the ship hove with a cable and a half on the best bower, let go the sheet anchor and veered out to 1/3 of a cable and brought her to anchor in 13 feet water and found to 5 feet, a great sea setting into the harbour all the small vessels drove and one on shore.

*Sept. 4, 1766 to Sept. 13, 1766

Sept. 14, 1766 Sunday S, N, NE
PM light airs and clear weath AM fresh breezes with thunder and lightening. Capt. Harvard returned from soundings the Lake

Bradore in one of the whale boats.

*Sept. 15, 1766 to Sept. 24, 1766

Sept. 25, 1766 Thursday N
PM cloudy weath AM clear sent Mr. Brown with a party in a whale boat to sound for the survey people Employed variously.

Sept. 26, 1766 Friday SW
Fine clear weath people Employed as occasion.

Sept. 27, 1766 Saturday SW
The same weath at 11 AM Captain Mowat went away in the pinnace sounding came in and anchored here a brig from Boston.

Sept. 28, 1766 Sunday SW
PM dark cloudy weath AM clear.

Sept. 29, 1766 Monday S, SW
PM cloudy weath AM fresh breezes with rain arrived here a schooner from Halifax People Employed variously.

Sept. 30, 1766 Tuesday W
PM clear weath people Employed as occasion anchored here 3 schooners from Spanish River.

Oct. 1, 1766 Wednesday SW
PM cloudy wear AM clear Captain Mowat returned from sounding.

Oct. 2 1766 Thursday W
PM Clear weath Employed clean the ship fore and aft deserted with ye pinnace Menaduk Wm. Isaac, Boatswain mate and John Careley seaman who rowed the pinnace and the following things, 2 hand leads and one deck lead hand line and lead, 1 knights compass and the boats sails.

Oct. 3, 1766 Friday W
PM fine clear weath AM cloudy with rain Read the articles of war and the abstract of act of Parliament to the ships company carpenters Employed repairing the rudder people Employed variously came in and anchored the schooner *Dolphin* from Quebec.

Oct. 4, 1766 Saturday WNW
Carpenters Employed as occasion arrived here 2 schooners from the Banks.

Oct. 5, 1766 Sunday NE, N, NW
Fresh gales and cloudy Weath AM clear at 4 PM Mr. Brown went away in the whale boat to finish the soundings to the westward.

Oct. 6, 1766 Monday E

PM light airs and clear weath AM hard gales & cloudy with rain Employed variously.

Oct. 7, 1766 Tuesday W, SW

The same weath People Employed unreeving the running rigging.

Oct. 8, 1766 Wednesday

PM hard gales and cloudy weath AM mod with rain Emp. as occasion.

Oct. 9, 1766 Thursday W, NW

Fine clear weath people Employed cleaning the ships fore and aft Carpenters employed repairing the boats.

*Oct. 10, 1766 to Oct. 30, 1766

Oct. 31, 1766 Friday WSW

Fresh gales arrived here His Majesty's schooner *St. John* from Halifax.

Nov. 1, 1766 Saturday WSW, NW

Fresh gales and clear weath sailed His Majesty's schooner *St. John* at the same time arrived here one of the Surveyors boats from sounding. Read the articles of war and new abstract of Parliament to the ships company.

Nov. 2, 1766 Sunday W, WNW

The same weath people Employed variously, boats Employed sounding the harbour & taking the naval remarks.

Nov. 3, 1766 Monday NW

Fresh breezes AM strong gales clear weath carpenters Employed repairing boats.

Nov. 4, 1766 Tuesday NW

The same weather carpenters Employed as before.

Nov. 5, 1766 Wednesday SW, NNW

PM mod and hazey weath AM strong breezes and rain. The ships company employed as before fired 21 guns being Gun Powder Treason Day.

Nov. 6, 1766 Thursday SW, WNW

PM fresh gales with rain AM mod 2 boats empd sounding this harbour.

*Nov. 7, 1766 to Nov. 16, 1766

Nov. 17, 1766 Monday N, NE

The same weath carpenters and people employed about the boats Recd on board Hhds beer, arrived here His Majesty's schooner

St. John from a cruize.

Nov. 18, 1766 Tuesday NE

Fresh gales with snow and hale. Sailed from hence a schooner to St. Johns with plan of Cape Breton.

Nov. 19, 1766 Wednesday NNE

The same weath carpenters and people Employed repairing the boats & sails.

Nov. 20, 1766 Thursday NNW

Mod and cloudy weather employed as before.

Nov. 21, 1766 Friday W, SW

Fresh gales and cloudy weath with snow and hail, arrived here a brig from Newfoundland bound to Boston at the same time the schooner with the plans put back here.

Nov. 22, 1766 Saturday NNW, N

The same weath the plans were removed from the schooner into the brig bound for Boston and sailed immediately.

Nov. 23, 1766 Sunday W

Mod and hazey weath with snow at times sailed from hence a schooner.

Nov. 24, 1766 Monday SW, S b W

Mod weath at 6 AM unmoored ship at 9 got under sail and went into St. Lawrence cove in the NE Harbour & moored ship head and stern under 4 cables the best bower to the westward and the small bower to the northward.

Nov. 25, 1766 Tuesday WSW

Fresh gales and squally weath with rain & snow got out two of the *St. Lawrence* cables for stern mooring unbent the topsails sett jibb and driver, people employed unrigging the ship.

*Nov. 26, 1766 to Jan. 19, 1767

Jan. 20, 1767 Tuesday NW

Louisbourg Harbour: NE

Mod and fine fair weath came in here and anchored here the schooner *Kitty* Hatch Master from Boston with dead meat on 29 days passage.

*Jan. 21, 1767 to Jan. 29, 1767

Jan. 30, 1767 Friday NW b N

Louisbourg Harbour NE

Do. Weathr came n here from Halifax the schooner *Warem* Hogon Master 4 days passage

*Jan. 31, 1767 to Feb. 2, 1767

Feb. 3, 1767 Tuesday NNW
Louisbourg Harbour: NE
The same weath came in from Halifax the schooner *Lucy*, Perkins master with provisions for the ship & fresh beef && for a markett.

*Feb. 4, 1767 to Mar. 1, 1767

Mar. 2, 1767 Monday variable, N
Mod and fair weath at 4 AM sailed from hence the schooner *Lucy* for Halifax.
Mar. 3, 1767 Tuesday NNW, calm, WSW
PM Mod and clear weath sailed from hence the schooner *Kitty* for Boston. AM fresh breezes and cloudy weath. Returned the schooner *Kitty*.

*Mar. 4, 1767 to Mar. 7, 1767

Mar. 8, 1767 Sunday NW, NNE
PM fresh breezes with hard frost at 6 AM sailed from hence the schooner *Kitty* in PM bound for Boston.

*Mar. 9, 1767 to Mar. 30, 1767

Mar. 31, 1767 Tuesday ESE, SW
PM clear weath with hard frost Empd rigging the ship the NE harbour full of drift ice Empd repairing the roundings of the of the cables many cut among ice.
April 1, 1767 Wednesday SW, calm, S
PM Light breezes & Fine clear weathr, Middle calm with hard frost. AM fine clear weathr with fresh breezes. NE Harbour still froze over. Employed rigging the ship got the fore and main top gallant masts up. Read the articles of war and the New Abstract of Parliament to the ships to the ships company.
April 2, 1767 Thursday SE, calm, varib
PM fresh breezes and clear weathr. Middle calm with hard frost AM Mod and clear weathr employed about rigging and cleaning the hold of empty water casks. At 10 do. Got up top gallant yards.

Recd 104 fm of 2 inch rope for main and fore topsail hallerds the old much wore and decayed converted the old hallerds rounding the cables amongst.

April 3, 1767 Friday Var., SSE

Mod & cloudy weath. Winds variable the Middle and latter part hard gales and & rain. The harbour full of drift. Employed variously

April 4, 1767 Saturday SSE, WSW

PM Hard gales and clear weathr. With hard frost part of the drift ice drove out of the harbour. AM mod & cloudy weath & rain people Empd variously.

April 5, 1767 Sunday WNW

Fresh gales & clear weath with hard frost. People employed variously.

April 6, 1767 Monday WNW, calm. WSW

Do. Gales & squally with frost People Empd about the rigging. Do recd new fore top sail buntline 1 ½ inch 44 fm Do. Recd new top tackle falls 3 inch 74 fm Do. Recd fore bowline 2 ½ inch 36 fm Do. Cable falls 9 inch 36 fm. Do Recd main bowline 2 ½ inch 34 fm do. Main clew garnets 2 ½ inch 56 fm all being much ware converted them for rounding for ye cables and mooring of boats. Recd on board 3 hoghead of beer containing 189 gallons.

April 7, 1767 Tuesday WNW

Mod & fair weath Empd as before about the rigging.

April 8, 1767 Wednesday WNW, NNW

Fresh breezes & clear weath with frost Empd variously. Sailed hance a small schooner for Halifax Hogon Master do. Arived a sloop from England bound a fishing.

April 9, 1767 Thursday Var., SSE

PM fresh gales & clear weath AM mod with dark cloudy weath & rain winds variable people empd variously do. bent the three topsails & sett up the topmast rigging fore and aft.

April 10 1767 Friday SSE, WSW

PM fresh gales & rain the ice all broke round the ship. AM fresh breezes & clear weath Empd clearing the ice from about the ship & stowing the hold 39 hoghead and gunge casks full of water.

April 11, 1767 Saturday WNW, ENE, NW

PM clear weathr AM dark cloudy weath with rain Empd as before winds var.

April 12, 1767 Sunday NW, SW

PM dark cloudy weath AM mod & clear people Empd variously Most of the ice is drove out of the harbour found the ship ditto lost the hawse in the ice.

April 13, 1767 Monday SW, calm, var.

PM fresh gales & cloudy weathr. Middle part calm AM fresh gales with rain and variable. Empd getting stone ballast on board drift Ice about the ship.

April 14, 1767 Tuesday SE, S, WSW

Strong gales with heavy rains & winds from the SSE to the WSW at 6 PM got down Top gallant yards AM hard gales & squally with snow & hail people Empd variously.

April 15, 1767 Wednesday WSW, Var., SW

PM fresh gales clear weath Middle mod AM fresh gales & hazey weathr at 5 do. hove out of the Cove to set our anchor at Noon weighed & came to sail found the best bower buoy and rope carried away with the ice.

April 16, 1767 Thursday WNW, WSW, SW

PM fresh gales & hazey weathr. Empd turning the ship up to the town at ½ past 3 do. came too with the B Bower before the town of Louisbourg in 5 fathoms water shingle bottom. AM mod & hazey weathr at 8 do. got up topgallant yards moored N & south with the stream hawser fast to the shore. The flag staff on the city house SW b S the spire of the hospital S b E dist. Off shore one cables length. People employed variously.

April 17, 1767 Friday SW, NNW

PM strong gales at 3 got down top gallant yards with heavy rain. AM do. Gales and clear weath with hard frost at 2 lowered the lower yards down & let go the small bower anchor under foot. People Empd variously .

April 18, 1767 Saturday WNW, WSW, SW

PM hard gales & clear weathr hard frost. AM mod & thick hazey weath with some rain came in here the sloop *Kitty* from New York for Quebec at 6 do. swayed up the lower yards & top gall. masts do. & hoisted in all the guns recd 11 hogsheads of beer contg 693 galls.

April 19, 1767 Sunday SW

PM fresh gales & thick hazey weath with several hard claps of thunder & lightening AM mod & foggy with heavy rain.

April 20, 1767 Monday SW, calm, N

PM mod & thick fogg with rain the Middle calm with rain. AM strong gales with sleet & snow & hard frost at 5 do. lowered down the lower yards down & struck gallt. masts do. Came in here 3 fishing schooners from the eastward Empd variously.

April 21, 1767 Tuesday NNE, calm, Var.

PM strong gales & clear weath with frost AM mod & clear weath winds variable 6 do. swayed up the lower yards & top gallt masts and yards at 9 begun to unmoor fired gun at 11 weighed and came to sail at noon Employed turning ship out.

April 22, 1767 Wednesday Var.

Light airs and clear weathr. Winds variable at 3 PM came too in the NE Harbour with the B Bower in 6 fm water veered to 1/3 of a cable Rusoles store house on Point bearing S ½ E at 6 AM bent the main sail People employed variously.

April 23, 1767 Thursday SSE, SW

Light airs and variable with thick fogg People Empd variously.

April 24, 1767 Friday Var., SW

PM thick fogg AM Mod and clear weathr sail maker Empd mending the fore stay sail that was eat by ratts.

April 25, 1767 Saturday WSW

PM mod breezes & clear weathr. The middle calm & cloudy AM light airs & variable.

April 26, 1767 Sunday Var., NE

Dark cloudy weathr

Small breezes sprang up to eastward weighed and came to sail got clear out of the harbour light house bearing Cabarouse Point bearing NE b N dist. 4 leagues

Lost sight of the land

Fresh gales and squally with rain took in the 1 & 2 reefs topsails

Out 2nd reefs topsails

Saw the land bearing from the NW to the NNE

Do gales and hazey weath lat Obs 44.44N

Course S 59N dist 26 leagues Cabarous Point NE b e dist 30 leagues.

PM fresh gales & clear weath Middle & latter light airs & clear. 3 PM weighed & came to sail at 11 AM Cabarouse Point SE b N distance 4 leagues. At 9 AM saw the land bearing from NW to NNE.

April 27, 1767 Monday Var.

Fresh gales and clear weathr.

Do weathr.

Do. Saw Sambro Head bearing W b S dist 4 leagues

More mod in the 2 reefs top sails and hauled the wind.

Light airs and clear weathr.

Saw the light house bearing W b S.

Calm and clear weathr Sombro Light house bearing W b N dist. 5 or 6 leagues.

PM weath at 6 PM all sand Head bearing W b S dist 4 leagues at 4 AM saw the light house bearing W b S.

April 28, 1767 Tuesday Var.

Light airs and cloudy weathr
Do. Airs and variable
Got into Halifax Harbour do. Fired 11 guns a salute
Do anchor off the Kings wharf or dock yard with the best bower in 11 fm water found here his Majesty's ship *Mermaid* and *St. John's* schooner at the careening warf.
Employed unbending bending sails etc.
PM cloudy weath at 6 PM got into Halifax harbour fired 11 guns a salute anchored off the docks with the Bt. Bower in 11 fam water found here his Majesty's ship *Mermaid* & the *St. John* schooner at the careening yard.

*April 29, 1767 to May 10, 1767

May 11, 1767 Monday SSE

Mod & fine clear weathr Employd as before, at 6 AM came on Board carpenters & caulkers.

May 12, 1767 Tuesday S b E

Do. Weather Employd as before, do aire our spare sails, found several cut with the ratts.

May 13, 1767 Wednesday variable

Fresh breezes with hazey weathr, Winds variable employd hoisting Out the iron ballast.

May 14, 1767 Thursday SSE

Mod & cloudy weathr Employd as before carpenters & caulkers as before.

May 15, 1767 Friday S

Do. Weathr got out all the ballast, Employd variously carpenters Found the foremast gone in the partners, at work as before.

May 16, 1767 Saturday WNW, W

Mod fine clear weathr Employd getting the careening geer on Board & fixing it. Carpenters & caulkers as before. Read the articles of war & etc to the ships company.

May 17, 1767 Sunday variable

Do. Weathr at 2 PM hove down the ship keel out, at 4 do. Righted ship, employd shifting the geer.

May 18, 1767 Monday WSW

Dark cloudy weathr with some rain, employd as before, punished Jas. Creek with 24 lashes for drunkeness & neglect of duty.

May 19, 1767 Tuesday SW
Fresh breezes & clear weathr at 3 PM hove down the ship keel out At ½ past 5 righted ship, AM employd returning the careening geer.
May 20, 1767 Wednesday variable
Mod and fine clear weathr, at 6 PM got out the foremast it being found unfit for service, carpenters and caulkers employed.
May 21, 1767 Thursday WSW, N
PM mod with rain, middle and latter parts hard gales & clear weathr. Employd getting in the ballast.
May 22, 1767 Friday SW
Mod and fine clear weath Employed getting in the ballast, carpenters and caulkers employed as before.
May 23, 1767 Saturday WSW
Mod breezes and clear weath Employed as before at 9 AM haul off from the wharfe His Majesty's ship *Mermaid.*
May 24, 1767 Sunday WSW, W
Do. Weathr got in all our ballast. Carpenters Employed as before.
May 25, 1767 Monday variable
Fresh gales & cloudy with some rain People employed over hauling the rigging, carpenters & caulkers as before.
May 26, 1767 Tuesday E
Fresh gales & squally with rain, at 10 AM got in the foremast Carpenters & caulkers as before. Mod weath with heavy rain Employed as before fitting new topmast rigging, carpenters at 8 AM got in the topmast.
May 27, 1767 Wednesday ENE
Do. Weathr with heavy rain, Employd over hauling the rigging & fitting new topmast shrouds. Carpenters as before.
Employed as before got on board beef for the ships company.
May 28, 1767 Thursday WSW
Do. Weathr employed as before, recd two hogsheads of beer containing 126 gallons.
May 29, 1767 Friday variable
Do. Weathr, employd as before sailed hence His Majesty's ship *Mermaid.*
May 30, 1767 Saturday NNW
Mod & fine fair weathr employd as before, recd on board 177 pounds of fresh beef for the ships company.

*May 31, 1767 to June 18, 1767

June 19, 1767 Friday SW, S
PM mod & cloudy weathr AM fresh gales & rain, came in & anchored here His Majesty's ship *Mermaid & Garland*, employed as before.

*June 20, 1767 to June 25, 1767

June 26, 1767 Friday calm
Light airs & calm with thick fogg employd variously, recd On board one new pinnace & whale boats.
June 27, 1767 Saturday SSW, NNW
PM calm with thick fogg AM fresh gales & clear weathr at 10 do. Cast off from the wharfe & got under sail, at ½ past came to with The best bower in 8 ½ fm soft mud the church steeple W b S Georges Island SSE one & half cables length from the shore do received on board the following provisions viz.

Bread	4060 pounds	oatmeal	55 gallons
Beer	754 gallons	rice	1556 pounds
Beef	1051 pounds	butter	956 pounds
Pork	2560 pounds	cheese	1912 pounds
Pease	75 ½ gallons	vinegar	120 gallons

June 28, 1767 Sunday NW, calm, variable
PM fresh gales & clear weather, AM calm employd variously & getting gunners stores on board, scaled the guns
June 29, 1767 Monday SW b S, SW
Fresh breezes & cloudy weathr
Weigh'd & came to sail as did His majesty's ship *Garland*
Employed turning out lost sight of the
Sambro light house bearing W dist 5 leagues
Cloudy weathr.
Set the fore top mast steering sail.
Fresh gales & hazey set the fore steering sail.
June 30, 1767 Tuesday SW, SSE, SW b W,
Fresh gales & hazey weathr carried away the fore top mast
Steering sail boom
Canso bore N b E dist 3 leagues
Little winds & do weathr
Island St. Esprit N b E dist 2 leagues close reef the topsails
Brough too with our head to the South-ward with the main
Topsail to the mast fresh gales & thick fogg.
Mod & hazey weathr out all reefs the topsails & made a sail at ½ past 5 saw the land which proved to the Caberuse Point which is 3

leagues from Louisbourg.
Anchored in Louisbourg Harbour with the best bower in 5 fam water the flagg staff on the citydale SW b S 2 cables length from the shore.
Thick fogg with rain.

July 1, 1767 Wednesday SW
Fresh gales & thick fogg with rain PM employd as occasion, AM Employd rounding the cables.

July 2, 1767 Thursday WSW
Do. Gales & do. Weathr Employd variously loos'd sails to dry.

July 3, 1767 Friday SW
Do. Weathr employd getting on board the Surveyor Generals things.

July 4, 1767 Saturday variable
Do. Weathr with rain Employd as before, Mr. Brown with 4 men In the cutter went a sounding.

July 5, 1767 Sunday SW
Fresh gales & hazey weathr with rain employd as before.

July 6, 1767 Monday WSW
Fresh breezes & foggy employed variously.

July 7, 1767 Tuesday variable
Thick drizling weathr employd variously

July 8, 1767 Wednesday SW
Do weathr employd as occasion received on board three Hhds of beer, containing 189 gallons

July 9, 1767 Thursday WSW
Thick drizling weathr, employd variously loos'e sails to dry.

July 10, 1767 Friday SW b W
Light airs with thick fogg & rain.

July 11, 1767 Saturday WSW
Fresh breezes & ditto weathr returned the cutter from sounding.

July 12, 1767 Sunday SW
Ditto weathr came on board the Surveyor General & all his baggage.

July 13, 1767 Monday SW
Mod. & thick fogg, employd variously.

July 14, 1767 Tuesday WSW
Fresh breezes with fogg & rain.

July 15, 1767 Wednesday WSW, NW
PM do weathr AM mod & clear employd variously loosed sails To dry. Read the Articles of War & to the ships company.

July 16, 1767 Thursday S

Mod & clear weathr loosd sails to dry. Came in here a brigantine from the Isle Rey with salt.

July 17, 1767 Friday SSW

Mod & thick fogg, received 2 casks of beer on board contg: 126 gallons.

July 18, 1767 Saturday SW

Do. Weathr.

July 19, 1767 Sunday WSW

Fresh breezes & thick fogg in terms intermixed with rain exercized great guns & small arms & fired at a mark.

July 20, 1767 Monday WSW, NNE

PM do weathr AM mod & cloudy weathr employd variously loos'd sails to dry.

July 21, 1767 Tuesday variable

PM light airs & variable with rain AM fresh breezes & heavy rain.

July 22, 1767 Wednesday SE, S, SSW

Thick fogg with rain received on board 8 Hhds of beer contg: 504 galls.

July 23, 1767 Thursday SW

Fresh gales & very thick fogg.

July 24, 1767 Friday do.

Do. Weathr employd as occasion.

July 25, 1767 Saturday do.

Do. Weathr loos'd sails to dry, unmoor's ship.

July 26, 1767 Sunday SSW

Light airs & very thick fogg.

July 27, 1767 Monday SSW, SW

Light airs & cloudy weathr

Weighed & came to sail.

Port Nova Gore E ½ N 1 ½ leagues lost sight of the land with a thick fogg.

Do. Weathr.

Fresh breezes & cloudy saw a sloop No. of us.

Clear saw the land bearing from WSW to NNW.

Fresh breezes & clear weathr. Lat: Observed 46.39 N.

July 28, 1767 Tuesday W, WSW, variable, W b S, WSW, variable

Fresh breezes & hazey weathr.

Cape North bearing NNW ½ W Island St. Paul NE b N dist off shore 2 ½ leagues.

In the 1st reefs topsails Tried the current found it to run to the SE Qrtr 2 ½ knotts, the 2d day of the Moon.

Fresh breezes & cloudy weathr do Cape bore SW 2 leagues.

Hard squally, handed the topsails.
Fresh gales & squally with lightening.
Took the 2d reef topsails, set the topsails.
Do gales & cloudy weathr.
Out 2d reef the topsails.
Saw the land Magalan do. Point bearing W do. Saw the Bird Islands bear NE at ½ past 11 saw the Island Bryon bearg NW at Noon do Islands W one league.

July 29, 1767 Wednesday variable

Mod & cloudy with rain.
Island Bryon bearing SSW dist 2 ½ leagues.
Do. Weathr.
Do weathr in the 2d reefs topsails.
Clear with flashes of lighning from the No.
Fresh breezes & clear weather.
At ½ past 8 came on a heavy squall with thunder & rain do.
Hand'd the topsails& down topgallt yards.
Hard gales & squally haul'd the mains & fore sail up under the mizen & forestaysail.
Strong gales & clear weathr Latde Obsd 48.32

July 30, 1767 Thursday WSW, NNW, NW, N b W NNW, SSW

Strong gales & clear weathr at 2 set the main & fore courses.
Fresh gales & clear weathr.
Wore ship
Do weathr wore ship saw a sloop to the Eastward.
Sat the main topsail.
Sat the fore & mizn: tops out all reefs the topsails.
Light airs & variable got up topgallt yards Lat obsd 47:46
Tack'd ship

July 31, 1767 Friday variable, SW, SE, SW, S

Light airs & clear weathr.
Saw the high land over Island Bonaventure bearing NNW 15 leagues dist.
Small breezes & dark cloudy weathr.
Light breezes & cloudy, shortened sail took in 1st reefs the topsails.
Out reefs topsails & made sail
Fresh gales & hazey with rain the Island Bonaventure W b N dist 2 leagues.
At Noon anchored in Gaspee Basin in 10 fam water soft bottom, Cr. Deans house SE b S found the *Jupiter* boat here with Mr. Wright & party from Anticosta.

Aug. 1, 1767 Saturday variable, S, SSW

Fresh gales and hazey weathr with heavy rains Employd variously and moored ship.

Aug. 2, 1767 Sunday NW, S

Cloudy weath with rain at times Employed variously

Aug. 3, 1767 Monday SSW

Mod & cloudy with rain at times Employd as occasion.

Aug. 4, 1767 Tuesday variable

Fresh breezes with heavy rains received on board 5 Hhds of beer containg: 315 galls:

Aug. 5, 1767 Wednesday do.

Mod & clear weathr at 8 AM weigh'd & came to sail at 9 Join'd us Mr. Pringle & his party from Chaleur Bay who finished the Survey of do.

Aug. 6, 1767 Thursday do.

Mod & cloudy weathr, winds variable at 3 PM anchored in 10 fm water.

Aug. 7, 1767 Friday SE

Fresh gales & foggy with rain.

Aug. 8, 1767 Saturday do.

Fresh gales & thick fogg with rain, at Noon weigh'd & came to Sail, left Mr. Sproul with a party to Survey Gaspee & the south side of the river St. Lawrence,

Aug. 9, 1767 Sunday SE

Do. Gales & foggy Employed turning out of Gaspee Bay.
At Noon Cape Ferillon NW one mile.

Aug. 10, 1767 Monday SE, ESE

Fresh breezes & thick fogg with rain.
Cape Rozier W dist 4 miles.
Do. Weathr.
Mod with rain & thick fogg.
Was lost on the Survey of Chaleur Bay the following provisions viz;

viz;	bread 352	pounds
	Beef 29	"
	Pork 29	"
	Butter 24	"
	Pease 12	gall.
	Rice 8	"
	Rum 12	"

Saw Magdalane River SSW one mile.

Aug. 11, 1767 Tuesday E, ENE, calm SW b W

Fresh gales & thick fogg with rain.
Do. Weathr

Do. Weathr haul'd down the steering sails
Do. Weathr.
Sounded no ground at 150 fam.
Do. Weathr sounded no ground.
Calm & variable.
Light airs & foggy.
Aug. 12, 1767 Wednesday SW, W, variable
Light airs & foggy winds variable.
Sounded 18 fam hard bottom 1/2 past saw the land.
Tack'd at 4 anchor'd in 15 fam water with the best bower Matane River SW b W 3 miles.
Calm & foggy weathr the tide began to run to the westward: weighd & came to sail.
Came to with the best bower in 10 fam water near the same place we weigh'd from bearings as before.
Small breezes & clear weather.
Fresh breezes & clear weathr.
Aug. 13, 1767 Thursday WNW, varible, NW, W
Mod & dark cloudy weathr.
Weigh'd & came to sail.
Squally employd turning to wind.
Anchor'd with the best bower in 17 fam water hard bottom to the eastward of where we weigh'd from last about 2 miles Matan River SW b S 5 miles off shore one mile.
Fresh breezes & clear weather.
Do. Weather.
Aug. 14, 1767 Friday W, WSW, W b S, W b N, W b S, SW, W
Mod & clear weathr.
Weigh's & came to sail do. Capt. Holland & his party settoff For Quebec in a whale boat in order to survey part of the way.
Mod & fine clear weathr River Matan SSE 3 ½ leagues.
Aug. 15, 1767 Saturday calm, SE, SSW, calm, E
Mod & clear weathr.
Do. A small breeze sprung up at SE.
Dark cloudy weathr.
Light airs & hazey weathr.
Mod & hazey with rain.
Saw the Island Bis bearing W dist 4 leagues Barnaby Island SW b S 2 leagues.
Fogy with rain Bic Point W b N ½ leagues.
Aug. 16, 1767 Sunday E b N, variable, calm, WSW, W b S
Fresh breezes & thick hazey weathr with rain.

Mod & dark cloudy weathr with rain came to with the best bower in 12 fam water Basque Island SW b S dist. One mile Green Island WSW.
Do. Weathr.
Light airs & variable.
Dizling rain.
Do. Weathr.
Weigh'd & came to sail.
Came to with the best bower in 4 ½ fam water clay bottom, Basque Island WNW 1 ½ miles.
Aug. 17, 1767 Monday WSW, variable, NE, ESE
Mod & clear weathr.
Weigh'd & came to sail.
Came to with the small bower in 10 fam water soft bottom Apple Island SSW one mile
Servd rum to the ships company the beer being out.
Light airs & clear weigh'd & came to sail set steering sails.
Fresh breezes with rain W end of Green Islands.
Fresh breezes and clear weath with breezes with rain at 6 PM signaled and came to sail
Apple Island SSW one mile, at 8 AM weighed and came to sail.
Aug. 18, 1767 Tuesday ENE, NNE, calm, NW, N
Fresh gales with heavy rains & thick weather.
Do. Weathr Hare Island N. 3 miles
Carried away the foretop mast steering sail & was lost.
Do. Weathr.
Came to with the small bower in 8 ½ fam soft bottom.
The Hamarases Islands ENE
Cape Diable SE 2 miles
Light airs & variable weigh'd & came to sail.
Fresh gales & squally the Island Coudre the Bay NNW 1 ½ leagues going up the south channel.
Aug. 19, 1767 Wednesday NNW, SW, WNW, W, SW, WSW
Fresh gales & squally,
Do. Weathr.
More mod E end of Goose Island NW in 5.6.7 fam soft bottom.
Came to with the small bower in 5 fam water soft bottom, the W end of Goose Island NW Church Steeple on the S shore S b E.
Fresh gales with rain.
Do. Weathr weigh'd & came to sail Employd turning thru the Channel.
Moderate & cloudy weathr.

Fresh gales with rain and squally, at 9 AM anchored with the small bower in 5 Fam. water soft mud the west end of Goose Island NW
Church steeple on the S shore S b E, at 9 AM weighed and came to sail. Employed turning ship the channel lost oar to fix boat flying the line finished a tore sail and mizen
sail for the jibs for schooner.

Aug. 20, 1767 Thursday WSW, NNE, NW

Mod. & cloudy weathr. Employd turning through the channel at ½ past. Anchored with the best bower in 8 fam soft bottom.
Weigh'd & came to sail.
Light breezes & clear weathr west end Island Orleans NW ½ mile at 1 came to with the best bower in 10 fam water veer'd away & moor'd ship a cable each way Cape Diamond SW b W Church Steeple in the Upper Town west found riding here 3 transports with troops and several merchant vessels. Saluted the garrison with 13 guns.
Moderate and cloudy weath at 2 anchored with the best bower in 8 fam water soft bottom at 5 weighed and came to sail at Mr. Wright the N end of Orleans NW half a mile at 3 came to with the B. Bower in 10 fathoms water veered away and anchored ship found lying here 3 transports with troops and several more merchant vessels saluted the garrison with 13 guns.

Aug. 21, 1767 Friday variable

Moderate and cloudy weath with thunder lightening and rain AM Read the articles of war & to the ships Company.

Aug. 22, 1767 Saturday NW, NNE, WSW

Fresh breezes and cloudy Employed drying the sheets. AM unbend the main & fore courses topgallant sails & spritsail topgallant & mizen topmast staysails Recd. on board one Hhds beer containing 64 gallons for the ships company.

*Aug. 23, 1767 to Sept. 1, 1767

Sept. 2, 1767 Wednesday SW

Mod & fair weathr, sail'd hence three transports with troops on board for England Employd as occasion
Ditto weath sailed hence three transports with troops for England

Sept. 3, 1767 Thursday WSW, variable

Fresh breezes and cloudy with flying showers of rain.
Read the articles of War & the new abstract of Parliament to the ships company.

Sept. 4, 1767 Friday W
Ditto weath Employed as occasion, anchored here a brigantine from England.
Do. Weathr people employed as occasion, came in here a brigg From Plymouth.

*Sept. 5, 1767 to Sept. 7, 1767

Sept. 8, 1767 Tuesday WSW
Moderate and cloudy weath People employed as occasion, Recd on board one Hhd of beer containg: 63 gall. AM in veering the boat astern she sunk & lost 4 oars and a boathook.
Sept. 9, 1767 Wednesday variable
Moderate and fine weath Employed as occasion.
Sept. 10, 1767 Thursday ESE
Moderate & flying cloudy weathr. at ½ past one fired 13 guns to salute the governor, at 5 do fired 13 guns to salute do.

*Sept. 11, 1767 to Oct. 9, 1767

Oct. 10, 1767 Saturday SW
Fresh breezes & cloudy weathr. Recd on board 89 lbs of fresh Beef for the ships company. Deserted from the ship John Robinson & John Gentec.
Oct. 11, 1767 Sunday WNW
Fresh breezes & hard frost. Recd on board 4 Hhds beer cong: 252 gall.
Oct. 12, 1767 Monday ENE
Fresh gales with hail snow & sleet recd 205 lbs fresh beef for the Ships company.
Oct. 13, 1767 Tuesday NNW
More mod winds variable, ground all covered with snow with hard frosts.
Oct. 14, 1767 Wednesday NNE, WSW
Mod & clear weathr with frost recd on board fresh beef for the ships company 103 lbs fresh beef Recd in all for the ships company 3322 pounds do received the followings provisions/viz:

Bread	11543 pounds
Beer	53 tons & 85 gall.
Beef	943 pieces
Pork	416 pieces
Oatmeal	16 bush. & 1 gall.

Butter 300 pounds

Oct. 15, 1767 Thursday WSW

Mod breezes with hard frost PM, unmoored ship at 11 AM fired A gun & loos'd the topsails a signal for sailing at Noon weigh'd & came to sail.

Oct. 16, 1767 Friday WSW, NNW, WSW

Mod with very cold weathr at 4 PM St. John's Church NW ½ mile at ½ past 6 came over the Traverse at ½ past 7. Came to with the small bower in 9 fam water, soft bottom Cape Torment NW b N 1 mile at 10 AM weigh'd & came to sail, Read the articles of war &c to the ships company. At Noon Cape Torment WSW dist 2 leagues.

Oct. 17, 1767 Saturday variable

Light airs & clear weathr winds variable at 10 PM came too with the best bower anchor in Coudre road in 5 fam at low water, the westermost ledge at low water WSW. Capn Bushee house S b W the eastermost point St. Paul Bay NW b W. NW Bluff on the Island SW 1/ S: soft bottom.

Oct. 18, 1767 Sunday do.

Small breezes & clear weathr winds variable, boasts employd getting off wood from Coudre.

Oct. 19, 1767 Monday do.

Do. Weathr at 8 PM anchor'd here, one brigg, one schooner, & one sloop from Quebec for London, sighted our anchor found it foul, moor'd with the stream anchor & cable. At 10 AM anchor's here the ship *Laton* from Quebec for London.

Oct 20, 1767 Tuesday E

Moored in Halifax Harbour with the stream anchor.

PM light airs and cloudy weath AM fresh breezes with fogg and rain people employed on occasion.

Oct. 21, 1767 Wednesday calm

Calm & thick Hazey weath with rain, Recd on board 400 weight of beef for the ships company. Employed variously

Oct. 22, 1767 Thursday calm with fogg, NW

PM ditto weath Free 8 fathom under the hull and brought too a brig which proved to be the *Charming Peggy* Alexander Calicerice Master, belonging to London last from Guernsey loaded with ? of Gineracy ? sent an officer on board and sized her AM weath cloudy and hazey

Masters Log

PM fired 8 three pounders with shott at & brought to a brigg which proved to be the *Charming Peggy*, Alexander Caldler Master belonging to London from Guernsey last loaded with claret - ginavea & soap, sent an officer & three men & siezed her.

Oct. 23, 1767 Friday variable

Light and fogg. Winds variable.

Oct. 24, 1767 Saturday variable, calm, WSW

Light airs and clear weath winds variable, at ½ past 1 AM weighed and came to sail, in company the prize & a sloop from New York at 8 came too with the best bower anchor in 10 fam water veered away ½ cable, at 6 AM weigh'd & came to sail at ½ past 8 came too with the small bower in 1 ½ fam high water, soft bottom, Cape Torment NW b W, Burnt Cape NE b N Rat Island the east end S: West end Burnt ledge E ½ No. dist off shore ¾ mile.

Oct. 25, 1767 Sunday WSW, calm, variable

PM fresh breezes and cloudy weath. At 3 PM weighed and came to sail in company. Employed turning the ship, at 10 anchored with the small bower in 11 fathom water soft ground ? clear to NNE ? half a mile at 5 AM weighed and came to sail ? at 10 anchored again in 13 fathom soft bottom. St. John's Church NNE off shore ½ mile, at 5 AM, weigh'd & came to sail in company as before, at 10 came too with the small bower in 9 fam soft bottom, Mod weather winds variable.

Oct. 26, 1767 Monday variable

Moored at careening wharf Halifax, NS

Moderate and fine clear weath. At ½ past 5 PM weighed and came to sail in company as before. At 9 anchored at Quebec, as did the prize, Cape Diamond SW B W ½ W the church steeple in the upper town W ½ N: found several merchant vessels here.

Oct. 27, 1767 Tuesday do.

Moderate and clear weath winds variable. People employed as occasion.

Oct. 28, 1767 Wednesday WNW

Ditto weath Employed variously.

Oct. 29, 1767 Thursday NW, NE

Do. Weathr AM hard gales with some show, got down topgallant yards, & lower'd the lower yards down.

PM moderate weath and gales.

Oct. 30, 1767 Friday variable, NE

PM strong gales and cloudy weath AM more moderate & clear, swayed up the lower yards.

Oct. 31, 1767 Saturday variable

Moderate and fine fair weath. Winds variable 2 AM Departed this

life William Johnston, Seaman.
Nov. 1, 1767 Sunday WSW
Ditto weath.
Nov. 2, 1767 Monday WNW
Ditto weath with gales and squally employed as occasion
Fresh gales & squally weath.
Nov. 3, 1767 Tuesday NNE
Hard gales and squally
Do. gales & do. weath Employd as occasion
Nov. 4, 1767 Wednesday NE
Moderate breezes with snow AM Fresh breezes and snow with hard frost AM People employed variously Moderate and clear weath Ditto weath Employed as occasion along side of the wharf. Fresh breezes and snow with hard frost AM people employed variously Fresh gales and hard frost people employed on occasion
Fresh gales with Moderate weath and
Moderate and cloudy weath with fresh employed as occasion
PM with and cloudy AM fresh gales with snow and sleet
Fresh airs with snow
Moderate and cloudy
Ditto weath Employed on occasion
Hard gales & squally with snow, struck the topmasts
Nov. 5, 1767 Thursday SSW
PM hard gales and snow with hard frost, AM more modt
Fired 15 guns in commemoration of Gun Powder Treason.
Nov. 6 1767 Friday SW
Modt. & cloudy with hard frost, got up yards & topmasts
Nov. 7 1767 Saturday WSW
Fresh breezes with snow, the brigg *Peggie* Prize haul'd along The wharfe & she & her cargo was sold at publick vendue.

*Nov. 8, 1767 to Nov. 20, 1767

Nov. 21, 1767 Saturday variable, WSW to WNW
PM, modt & variable, do unmoor'd ship, & hove short on the Best bower, AM fresh gales & cloudy, at 8 do weighed & came To sail, at noon St. John's church W b N dist 2 miles.
Nov. 22, 1767 Sunday variable, ENE
PM fresh breezes & variable, at ½ past 2 past the traverse, at 1 AM, anchor'd in Coudre Road, near Bushee's house bearing So; The ledges outter point W b S in 5 ½ fam at low water, found At anchor here one brigg, one sloop & one schooner.

Nov. 23, 1767 Monday ENE, variable
Modt. Breezes & variable at 10 AM anchor'd the brigg for London, do sailed hence the brigg & schooner received on board 140 pounds of fresh beef for the ships company do. Got up Top gallant yards.

Nov. 24, 1767 Tuesday NE
Fresh gales & cloudy weath with hard frost people & boats Employ'd cutting wood & bringing it on board, the brigg & Schooner return'd.

Nov. 25, 1767 Wednesday NNE, SW
PM moderate & cloudy weath People employ'd as before.
AM fresh gales & hazey, at 9 weigh'd & came to sail as did Two briggs one schooner & one sloop Goose Cape NNW.

Nov. 26, 1767 Thursday SW, WSW, NW, NNW, N
Fresh gales & thick cloudy weather.
Thick snow hand'd top-gallt sails & got down the yards do Close reef'd the fore & mizen topsails & the 1st reef the maintops at 5 the West point of Green Island SSW 2 miles at 6 the NE part of do Island S b W 2 ½ miles.
In company as before.
Do. Weathr.
Saw the land of the south shore.
Fresh gales & clear weath 3 sail in sight.
Out all reefs & got up topgallt yards.
At noon light breezes with a swell from the eastd
Cape Chatt E b S Cape de Mont Pelles No:

Nov. 27, 1767 Friday N, N b E, SE b E, var.
Light airs & cloudy weath.
Cape Chatt SSE 3 leagues, the Etmost land in sight on the south Shore bearing the Etmost land on the North whore bearing N b W.
Light airs
Light airs & variable 6 sail in sight
Mount Louis River SSE 7 miles.
Do. Airs Mount Louis River SSW 4 leagues.

Nov. 28, 1767 Saturday NE, W, SW, WSW, NW
Fresh breezes & hazey weath.
Fresh gales with snow. Mount Louis River SW.
Took in all the reefs the topsails & handed them, last of all the vessels
Thick snow.
Do. Weathr wore ship & lay too under the foresail & mizen.
Strong gales & squally thick of snow.

Saw the land on the south shore very strong gales.

Nov. 29, 1767 Sunday NW

Strong gales & squally under a foresail.
Do. Gales was Cape Rozier bearing SSE dist 3 leagues
Haul'd in under the Cape & came too with the small
Bower anchor in 7 fam water hard bottom veer'd a
Whole cable, Cape Forelong bearing S ½ W Cape Rezier
NNW a point of trees WNW.
Very hard squalls found the ship drove, the sea very
High that it made a passage over us, was oblig'd to
Cut away the anchor; having about 6 fath of cable,
Within board, do. Hoisted the forestay sail to try to
Wear, but it blow'd to pieces loos'd the foresail
But still found she would not wear, cut the mizen
Jeers & peek halliards to get the darrick down
& the mizen blow'd to pieces at 12 got her before
the wind under the foresail a very hard frost the
ship a body of ice, she could not lay too, the sea
being very high.
Lat: Obs: 47.21 No.

Nov. 30, 1767 Monday NW, SW

Strong gales & cloudy
Saw the land bearing SE dist 4 leagues which proved
To be Dead mans Island near the Magdalen Island
Haul'd under the SE part of Magdalen Island do. Wore
& lay too under the mizen staysail
Reeft the foresail & set it with a skirt of the mizen staysail.
Do gales, saw Cape Louisbourg SSW, do saw Justicore
Island bearg ENE saw a sloop a stern.
Enter'd the Gut of Canso.

Dec. 1, 1767 Tuesday NW

Anchored the ship in the Gut of Canso
Fresh gales and cloudy weath at 1 AM came too with the best
bower ½ of a cable in 2 fathom of water Employed cleaning the
decks.
Strong gales came too with the best bower anchor
In ship Harbour in 5 fam water in the Gut of Canso saw 3 sloops
As anchor under the west shore.
Do. Gales Employed cleaning the decks

Dec. 2, 1767 Wednesday NW, variable

PM hard gales AM more moderate Employed loading wooding.
PM hard gales with frost, AM more mod. Employ'd getting wood

on board, pass'd by & went thro' the Gutt a large ship.

Dec. 3, 1767 Thursday W

Moderate breezes PM

Mod breezes & variable with rain Employ'd variously

Dec. 4, 1767 Friday variable

Lying in Gut of Canseu

Moderate breezes and cloudy with hard frost AM Ship in board of the *Fair Freedom* a whaler bound to Gaspey with all species for provisions on board Ensign Sproul and party 1 Gastuy in the party of Mr. Waite Midshipman. AM weighed and came to sail.

Masters Log

Mod breezes & cloudy with hard frost, PM sailed from hence the sloop *Fair Freedom* a whaler bound to Gaspee Mr. Watts Midshipman on board with provisions for Mr. Sproul & his party who winter'd there, AM weigh'd & came to sail at noon the West part of Madam bearg SSE the west point of the Gutt So dist 2 ½ miles.

Dec. 5, 1767 Saturday NW

Fresh gales with snow, at 5 PM anchored with the best bower in 1 fathom water set 1 mod ? the E shore of the Gut of Canso Bear Island bearing SW 2 cables length. At 8 AM weighed and came to sail, at Noon anchored in Cape Canso Cove, Gut of Canso. Fresh gales with snow, at 5 PM came too with the best Bower in 7 fam water soft bottom under the S shore of the Gutt, the small Island bearg SSW dist 2 cables length at 8 AM weigh'd & came to sail.

Dec. 6, 1767 Sunday NW

Moored Gut of Canso

Mod with gales and cloudy weath with hard frost. Employed mooring the ship current strong at times from Gut of Canso with the ice.

These 24 hours modt weathr & cloudy with hard frost Employed variously.

Dec. 7, 1767 Monday NW

Fresh gales bad weath at 1 AM Wm Hogg Master went in shallop to Louisbourg with a surveying party. People employed variously.

These 24 hours for the most part baffling weathr at 3 PM Mr. Hogg Master went in a shallop to Louisbourg & took 4 hands with him, in order to bring from thence a Surveying party in the *Venus* schooner, people employ'd variously

Dec. 8, 1767 Tuesday variable

First part moderate breezes and cloudy weather with hard frost, latter fresh breezes with hail and hazey weath AM unbent the sails, AM came back the ship *Fair Freedom* and second half provisions not able to get to Gaspee Employed getting on board the provisions.
These 24 hours for the most part fine weath with hard frost loos'd sails to dry people employ'd variously.
Dec. 9, 1767 Wednesday NW
Fresh breezes and cloudy weath with rain AM Employed variously
The first & middle parts of these 24 hours gentle breezes & cloudy with hard frost latter part fresh breezes with thick hazey weath, PM unbent the sails, AM came back the sloop *Fair Freedom* with Mr. Watts Midshipm. Not being able to get to Gaspee with the provisions.
Dec. 10, 1767 Thursday variable
Clear and fine weath Employed unreeving the running rigging and clearing the hold.

*Dec. 11, 1767 to Jan. 6, 1768

Jan. 7, 1768 Thursday SE, calm
PM fresh gales with snow AM strong gales, all the ice drove out of the Bay People employed cleaning ice of the ship.
The first part of these 24 hours fresh gales with snow, middle part calm with snow, latter part strong gales with snow all the ice drove out of the bay. Employd occasionally.
Jan. 8, 1768 Friday NW, NW b W
Fresh gales with hard frost These 24 hours.
The first part of these 24 hours strong gales with frost & snow, middle & latter parts fresh gales with frost. Employd occasionally.
Jan. 9, 1768 Saturday NW
These 24 hours for the most part strong gales and squally with hard frost Employd occasionally.
Jan. 10, 1768 Sunday NW, calm
The first & middle parts of these 24 hours fresh gales with hard frost, latter part fine calm clear weathr with frost Employd occasionally.
Jan. 11, 1768 Monday SW, calm, variable
These 24 hours little winds & variable intermixt with calm, PM drove in here a great deal of loose ice, employd occasionally.

Jan. 12, 1768 Tuesday calm

These 24 hours for the most part fine calm weathr. AM most part of the loose ice drove out again. Employd occasionally.

Jan. 13, 1768 Wednesday calm, variable, SE

These 24, hours dark cloudy weath PM drove in here a great deal of Ice. AM came back Wm Hogg with the Surveyor Party from Louisbourg, most of the ice drove out again, employed making a ? Came on board smith. Breaking ice, lost over board by accident a double headed maul, which left from the gunnel of the ship. These 24 hours for the most part, little winds & variable, intermixed with calms & dark cloudy weathr with frost. Employed occasionally.

Jan. 14, 1768 Thursday SE, variable, calm

Fresh gales and cloudy weath. AM Read the articles of war to the Ships company.

These 24 hours for the most part little wind & variable. Intermixt with calms & dark cloudy weathr with some snow. PM, drove in here a great deal of ice, AM, came back the shallop that went for the *Venus* & surveying party, most of the ice drove out again. Employd occasionally.

*Jan. 15, 1768 to Feb. 15, 1768

Feb. 16, 1768 Tuesday

Fresh gales and clear weath with hard frost People employed variously carpenters Empd about the boats.

Feb. 17, 1768 Wednesday

Ditto weath great quantities of ice drove through the Gut of Canso.

Feb. 18, 1768 Thursday

PM fresh gales with frost Middle calm latter light airs and variable. great quantities of drift ice about the ship, AM employed rigging

Feb. 19, 1768 Friday NW, calm, variable

PM fresh gales with frost, middle calm. AM light airs & variable with great quantities of drift ice, at 10 do began to rigg the ship do got up the topgallt mast & mizon topp mast.

Feb. 20, 1768 Saturday variable, WNW

PM light airs & variable. AM small breezes & cloudy with some rain do. Got the topsail yard across in the tops with the ties, lifts, halliards & braces reeved.

Feb. 21, 1768 Sunday variable, SW, variable

PM light airs & variable with hazey cloudy weath & rain. Middle fresh gales & squally with rain, AM mod & cloudy with rain at times, winds variable, employd cleaning between decks & washing fore & aft.

Feb. 22, 1768 Monday variable, WNW, SSE

Light airs & cloudy winds variable Employd about the rigging came in here the schooner Venus.

Feb. 23, 1768 Tuesday variable

Fresh breezes & cloudy winds variable employd as before.

Feb. 24, 1768 Wednesday S

Fresh gales with show & strong frost, great quantities of drift ice.

Feb. 25, 1768 Thursday E, NW

Fresh gales & extreem hard frost the Bay all frozen over to which walk'd ashore on the ice, hoisted out the masts of the schooner, employd variously.

Feb. 26, 1768 Friday variable

Mod breezes & clear weathr with hard frost, made ice clear over to the passage, employd getting wood on board cooper employd trimming the casks for water carpenter employd about the *Venus* schooner.

Feb. 27, 1768 Saturday do.

Mod breezes & clear weathr with very hard frost Employd as before.

Feb. 28, 1768 Sunday do.

Mod & fine clear weather winds variable, got up yards and topmasts & set up the topmast rigging fore and aft.

Feb. 29, 1768 Monday SW, SSW, SW

PM do weathr do bent the topsail. AM light airs & very heavy rains, people employd making points & gaskets.

Mar. 1, 1768 Tuesday SW, calm, SSE

Moderate and fine weathr AM fresh breezes People employed getting wood onboard.? the lee and get the provisions, on board. PM light airs & rain, middle part calm AM mod breezes & fine soft weathr, do loos'd sails to dry, employd getting wood on board & broke the ice & got the boat ashore.

Mar. 2, 1768 Wednesday SSE

Fresh breezes and cloudy weath with rain at times Employed as occasion AM read the articles of war to the ships company.

Mar. 3, 1768 Thursday SSW, NW

Moderate and cloudy weath with thick fog first and middle parts latter part. Most of the ice drove out of the cove People employed about the rigging.

Mar. 4, 1768 Friday NW

First and middle parts fresh gales latter ditto with snow a great deal of drift about the ship Employed as before.

Mar. 5, 1768 Saturday

PM fresh gales and clear weath with hard frost Employed getting ready hoving the ship with the PM got her length.

Mar. 6, 1768 Sunday WSW

At single anchor at Canso Cove.

Ditto gales and clear weath Employed bending the rest of our sails.

Mar. 7, 1768 Monday SW

PM fresh gales and clear weath with extreme hard frost,

AM fresh gales and clear with hard frost. Ice made all over the bay, at Noon part of the ice drove out of the shore to the ship. The anchor and cable were lost overboard. The winds drove the ice out could not save them.

Mar. 8, 1768 Tuesday

Fresh gales with extreme hard frost, at the bay froze over employed variously. All bent the main sail.

Mar. 9, 1768 Wednesday

Ditto weath first and middle parts little more mild Employed variously.

Mar. 10, 1768 Thursday variable

Fresh breezes and cloudy weath with hard frost. Employed getting the shingle ballast on board.

Mar. 11, 1768 Friday SE

Fresh gales and thick hazey weath and rain. Employed variously. Ice as before.

Mar. 12, 1768 Saturday

Moderate and foggy weath with rain gales.

Mar. 13, 1768 Sunday

PM moderate and fogg. Middle calm with rain. AM moderate breezes with snow at Noon all the ice drove out of the Cove.

Mar. 14, 1768 Monday E

Fresh gales and cloudy with snow Employed reeving of running rigging &c.

Mar. 15, 1768 Tuesday WNW

First and latter part fresh gales and cloudy, middle clear weath hard frost Employed about the rigging and making ready for sea.

Mar. 16, 1768 Wednesday SW

Mod breezes with very hard frost, the bay all over Ice. AM Up sails.

Mar. 17, 1768 Thursday WNW

Bay full of Drift ice in sight, Employed in tying the lead hand line of 1300 ft.

Mar. 18, 1768 Friday

Canso Island

PM fresh gales and very cold weath. middle calm with hard frost, latter moderate cloudy with at 10 AM ? and came to sail found buoy & rope ? AM east of Canso Gut a lead line also 2 leagues sounding &.

Mar. 19, 1768 Saturday

First and middle parts fresh winds and cloudy weath AM

Mar. 20, 1768 Sunday

Latter strong gales and squally, weighed and came to sail.

Mar. 21, 1768 Monday

Strong gales and squally with rain AM snow, latter part fresh gales with hard frost at 1 PM ? saluted load all the 13 guns, anchored at 5 PM, yards and topmasts, got down topgallant yards ? here the running with a Broad and pendant and the surveyors.

Mar. 22, 1768 Tuesday

Fresh gales and cloudy weath with hard frost. AM dryed sheets and unbent.

Mar. 23, 1768 Wednesday NW

Fresh gales and clear weath Reced on board fresh beef for the ships company. Employed variously.

Mar. 24, 1768 Thursday NW

Alongside of the careening wharf

First and latter parts fresh hazey weath cloudy, Middle gales at 6 AM ? and the ? the ? side of the careening wharf.

Mar. 25, 1768 Friday

Fresh gales and cloudy weath Employed variously.

Mar. 26, 1768 Saturday NNW

Fresh gales with hard frost. Employed getting the ground jeer AM came on board caulkers to consult with ship also carpenters repaired the galley.

Mar. 27, 1768 Sunday

Fresh gales and cold weath. Came in here His Majesty's ship *St. Lawrence*

Mar. 28, 1768 Monday

Moderate breezes & cloudy weathr. Came in here a schooner.

Mar. 29, 1768 Tuesday

Moderate breezy and variable Caulkers as before AM employed about the rigging and getting on shore boatswains stores, Sailed hence his Majesty's armed schooner the *Halifax*.

Mar. 30, 1768 Wednesday
Ditto weath caulkers and people as before.
Mar. 31, 1768 Thursday
Moderate and cloudy weath caulkers as before. AM got up yards and topmasts. Employed variously
Recd on board fresh beef for the ships company.
April 1, 1768 Friday
Fresh and variable airs with moderate weath, latter hard gales with rain and sleet. People employed making points and gaskets.

A gasket is a cord or canvas strap used to secure a furled sail to a yard, boom or gaff. A reef is a means to reduce the size of a sail by tucking in a part and tying it to or rolling it around a yard. It is secured to a point of which there are several across the sail in a reinforced reef band by a cord that is tied to secure the sail with a square knot.

April 2, 1768 Saturday
Very strong gales, with sleet and rain at 5 PM sheet yard and topmast and topgallant masts, mizen top mast and the lower yards upon deck, the small craft about the town , recd great damage also main yard damaged, people employed about the ship.
April 3, 1768 Sunday
hard gales and squally with hard frost employed variously recd on board beef.
April 4, 1768 Monday
PM hard gales middle and latter more moderate AM people employed about the rigging.
April 5, 1768 Tuesday
Fresh gales and cloudy with hard frost Employed about the rigging , AM read the articles of war to the ships company, Employed reeving new running rigging the old retained.
April 6, 1768 Wednesday NW
Moderate gales with hard frost Employed as before.
April 7, 1768 Thursday NNW
Ditto weath Employed stowing our ground floor with water AM recd on board beef, at 9 AM fell from yard between the ship and the wharf and was drowned Lawrence May Seaman AM setup yards and topmast and set the rigging up fore and aft.
April 8, 1768 Friday WSW
Moored at careening wharf
Fresh gales with hard frost. Employed as before about rigging.

April 9, 1768 Saturday
PM moderate with hard frost Empd as occasion.
April 10, 1768 Sunday NW
Fresh gales and cloudy weath
April 11, 1768 Monday variable
Moderate with rain at times very cold Employed variously
April 12, 1768 Tuesday WSW
Fresh gales and clear weath Employed variously caulkers and carpenters on boats also a small bower anchor old lost and cables.
April 13, 1768 Wednesday NNW
Do breeze with hard frost employed as before.
April 14, 1768 Thursday
Fresh breezes with hard winds & variable. Employed about the rigging, recd on board beef.
April 15, 1768 Friday SSW
Strong gales and clear weath employed as before.
April 16, 1768 Saturday
Ditto weath Employed as before.
April 17, 1768 Sunday
Ditto weath with fresh breezes
April 18, 1768 Monday
Fresh breezes and clear weathr AM recd on board all our provisions
April 19, 1768 Tuesday
Fresh breezes and clear weath AM recd on board all our provisions also ? under William Holland commanding ?
April 20, 1768 Wednesday
Moderate and cold weath at 11
April 21, 1768 Thursday
At single anchor ?
Mod. airs and variable Latter came too with
the best bower in 12 fm water and veered to 1 of a cable.
April 22, 1768 Friday
Light airs and hazey weath Employed about the rigging and clearing the hold. Punished (name not indicated) seaman with 12 lashes for disobedience & neglect of duty.
April 23, 1768 Saturday
The first part mod. & thick foggy, people employed making points and gaskets
April 24, 1768 Sunday
Fresh breezes with a thick fogg. Winds variable. AM salted the guns. Employed up making ready for sail.

April 25, 1768 Monday
Meddore Head NNE 3 miles
Moderate and foggy weath at 3 PM weighed and came to sail, employed turning out of the harbour, at 10 anchored in 16 fathom water used the Bt. Bower ? at ½ past 6 weighed and came to sail, at 7 AM Sambro Head ? NNE

April 26, 1768 Tuesday
Moored in Canso Harbor at single anchor
Moderate gales and cloudy weath at 7 AM Whitehead N b W 2 leagues, set studding sails, at 9 down Employed turning into Canso Harbour at Noon anchored in Canso Harbour with the B. Bower found 18 sail of whalers here.

April 27, 1768 Wednesday
Fresh gales and squally weath at 8 got down Topgallant yards and lowered the lower sails, veered to half a cable and let go the small bower under foot, at 10 AM hauled up the small Bower & the ship struck and held fast a little, at 11 hove her off. Sailed hence with the whale boat to the Gut of Canso, up lower yards.

April 28, 1768 Thursday
At single anchor outside of ? Moderate and cloudy weath at ½ past 4 AM weighed and came to sail, at 9 AM anchored in Yarmouth Harbour, fired 7 guns a signal, for a pilot, at ¼ past 7 unmoored.

April 29, 1768 Friday
Sounded in 9 fathom water soft ground anchored with the B. Bower & veered to 2/3 of a cable.

April 30, 1768 Saturday
Moored with the stream anchor Yarmouth Harbour
Fresh breezes and clear weath at 4 PM weighed and came to sail went farther up the Canso harbour 6 fathom water veered away to half a cable and anchored with the stream anchor and came in here his Majesty's Armed Schooner *St. Lawrence*

May 1, 1768 Sunday
Fresh breezes and clear

May 2, 1768 Monday
Moored with the stream anchor in Yarmouth Harbour
PM moderate and clear weath, AM fresh gales and thick weath, at 6 AM sailed hence his Majesty's Armed Schooner *St. Lawrence*.

May 3, 1768 Tuesday
PM moderate and thick weather, AM Fresh gales and cloudy weath, at 6 AM anchored here the *St. Lawrence*, at 8 AM sailed hence the *St. Lawrence* at Noon Read the articles of war & to the ships company.

May 4, 1768 Wednesday
Moderate breezes and cloudy weath AM employed on the sundries, AM Dryed sails at Noon anchored here his Majesty's armed Schooner the *St. John*
May 5, 1768 Thursday
Moderate and clear weath latter, first hazey with sleet and rain. Employed variously, AM came on board Adm ? and took charge of the ship
May 6, 1768 Friday
? here latter with ? Employed ? sailed hence the ?
May 7, 1768 Saturday
Ditto weath and squally, AM hove the shallop to sound from the Gut to Louisbourg Employed sounding with the ship boat and cutter.
May 8, 1768 Sunday
Fresh gales and moderate weath middle and latter part breezes and cloudy AM anchored off Nunachet Harbour in 10 fathom water.
May 9, 1768 Monday
Ditto weath and clear weath Employed variously.
May 10, 1768 Tuesday
Ditto weath and breezy
May 11, 1768 Wednesday
Moderate and cloudy weath. Employed turning up and down the bay.
May 12, 1768 Thursday
Ditto weath at 6 PM
Bay AM cleared at 11
in order to bend her.
May 13, 1768 Friday
Moderate and fair weath let out sails to dry at Noon weighed and came to sail
May 14, 1768 Saturday
Ditto weath Employed as before.
May 15, 1768 Sunday
Fresh breezes and cloudy with heavy rain Employed as before of Nuseachal.
May 16, 1768 Monday
Fresh breezes and clear weath AM Emp spoke brigg employed sounding
May 17, 1768 Tuesday SW
At single anchor in the harbor of Yarmouth
Fresh breezes and clear weath ship and boats employed

sounding the harbour

May 18, 1768 Wednesday

Ditto weath employed drying sails

May 19, 1768 Thursday NW

Fresh breezes and cloudy weath rain Employed sounding AM cloudy employed in shallop in sounding

May 20, 1768 Friday S, SE

Do. Weathr return'd one of the shallops from sounding, moor'd ship with the stream anchor.

May 21, 1768 Saturday SW

Mod & cloudy Employd variously.

May 22, 1768 Sunday N, NNE

First part do. Weathr middle & latter mod: & clear.

May 23, 1768 Monday NE, SE

Fresh breezes & cloudy with some rain Return'd the other shallop from sounding.

May 24, 1768 Tuesday N, W, WNW

First part fresh gales & clear, middle & latter more mod. & clear AM sent a shallop to the west to sound, employd variously.

May 25, 1768 Wednesday S, SE, ESE

Do. Weathr AM sent shallop to the west to sound & sett the Rock in the Bay of Narechot.

May 26, 1768 Thursday E b S, E, E b N

First part fresh gales & clear weathr middle & latter fresh breezes with rain.

May 27, 1768 Friday variable

These 24 hours light breezes with rain & fogg at 3 PM unmoor'd ship & hove in to ½ a cable on the stream anchor at 6 return's the shallop from sounding.

May 28, 1768 Saturday S b W

Do. Weathr.

May 29, 1768 Sunday S, SE

First part do. Weathr middle & latter fine clear weathr at noon weigh'd & came to sail.

May 30, 1768 Monday S, calm

First part do. Weathr middle & latter calm & cloudy with rain at ½ past 3 PM came too in the Gutt of Canso with the best bower in 10 fam water. Veer'd to 1/3 of a cable Bear Island SE ½ S dist. Off shore 2 cables length .

May 31, 1768 Tuesday variable, NW

First part light airs with thunder, lightning & rain, middle calm & clear latter light breezes with rain Employd wooding.

June 1, 1768 Wednesday WNW, W, S

First & middle parts light airs & cloudy, latter small breezes & do. Weathr at 9 AM weigh'd & came to sail at Noon running thro the Gut.

June 2, 1768 Thursday SE, S, SSW, SSE, SE, ESE

Fresh breezes & cloudy set steering sails.

Do. Weathr.

Down steering sails in a squall at ½ past up topmast steering sails.

Lost the fore topmast steering sail occasion'd by the boom breaking in 1st reef both topsails Bear Cape N b E end of Sutton Island SW b S do. Breezes with rain.

Fresh breezes with rain.

Do. Weathr.

Lost a logg & two lines.

Do. Weathr Cape Ebmoort SE b E 4 or 5 miles.

June 3, 1768 Friday E, NE, NNE

Fresh breezes with rain.

Do. Weathr.

½ past came to with the small bower in 7 fam water sandy bottom & veer'd to ½ a cable Northmost point in sight NNE ½ E & West point S b E 3 or 4 miles dist off shore ½ a mile.

Do. Breezes with thunder lighting and rain.

Weigh'd & came to sail, do bore away to the S.

Mod with haze Nermost point in sight NNE ½ E & W point SE.

June 4, 1768 Saturday NE, ENE, E

Fresh breezes with rain

Came too with the small bower in 4 ½ fam water sandy bottom W. point NW ½ N point of Shoal off do. Point NW b W.

Do. Weathr. Weigh'd & came to sail to shift our berth.

June 5, 1768 Sunday E b S, SSE, S b W

Fresh breezes with rain.

Came too with the small bower in 7 fam water sandy bottom & veer'd to ½ a cable W. point.

Weigh'd & came to sail.

Cape No SE b S 6 or 7 leagues more mod & clear with a swell from the ESE.

June 6, 1768 Monday

Light breezes and clear, middle squally with thunder and Lightening.

Saw the Island of Bonaventure NNE ½ E about 4 leagues.

June 7, 1768 Tuesday SSE, ESE, E, NNW

Moderate breezes with rain and hazey at 9 AM anchored

in Gaspey Bay with the best bower in 10 fathom water the Old Wife SE b E St. Johns head N b W shore half a miles at 10 AM weighed and turned up the Bay, found here Mr. Sproul.

Throughout these 24 hours mod breezes with rain & haze at 9 PM Came too in Gaspee Bay with the best Bower in 10 fam water & veer'd & veer'd to ½ a cables Old Wife SE b E & S St. Johns head N b W ½ W dist off shore 2 miles at 10 AM weigh'd & turn'd up the bay found here Mr. Sproule & party.

June 8, 1768 Wednesday NNW

Ditto weath at 2 PM anchored in 11 fms water with the best bower in the Bay. Punished Andrew Ghescahes with 12 lashes four mutinous expressions.

Do. Weathr at 2 PM came too in 11 fam water with the best bower & Veer'd to ½ a cable.Punish'd Jno Churchill with 12 lashes for mutinous words.

June 9, 1768 Thursday NE

First and middle calm, middle fresh breezes and clear weath at 4 AM weighed turning up the bay, at 1 PM anchored in 13 fam water, at 6 AM weighed and came to sail at 10 anchored in Gaspey Basin with the B.B. in 10 fam water, with our hawse cable in order to weigh the *Jupiter* schooner, which sunk last fall People employed weighing the *Jupiter*.

June 10, 1768 Friday

Fine weath PM weighed the *Jupiter* and towed near shore with cable gone also part of her rigging and mast.

June 11. 1768 Saturday SE

In Gaspey Basin at anchor

Fresh breezes and cloudy AM carpenter employed setting up masts in the *Jupiter* schooner that were carried with the ice where sunk. People employed setting up rigging for the *Jupiter* Employed from the same on repairing the *Jupiters* 1st hole.

June 12, 1768 Sunday variable

Ditto weath carpenters employed upon the *Jupiter*. People as before repairing the ship.

June 13, 1768 Monday

Ditto weath carpenters employed as before, AM dryed sails unbent sails.

June 14, 1768 Tuesday

Ditto weath Employed as before and rigging the *Jupiter*.

June 15, 1768 Wednesday S

Ditto weath employed as before and painting the *Jupiter* schooner

June 16, 1768 Thursday NE
Ditto weath with rain at times employed as before.
June 17, 1768 Friday SE
Fresh gales with rain. Carpenters employed upon the schooner & whale boats.
June 18, 1768 Saturday ESE
Ditto weath AM carpenters employed as before at 10 AM the *Jupiter* & whole boat sailed with Ensign George Sproul and Wm Duncan Hodge further recd *St. Lawrence* party delivered them sundry stores and amunition for signals &.
June 19, 1768 Sunday ESE
Moderate and cloudy weath ships boats employed sounding the Bay of Gaspey.
June 20, 1768 Monday ENE
Fresh breezes and thick cloudy weath Employed as before carpenters employed repairing surveying boats.
June 21, 1768 Tuesday NW
Ditto weath the boats and carpenters as before, AM Al Megg Turner from Hian ? of the brig being condemned shot.
June 22, 1768 Wednesday ESE
Fresh gales and hazey weath Employed as before
June 23, 1768 Thursday WSW
Ditto weath Employed as before AM Mr. Watts sailed from the Bay of Chateau in the schooner hired for that purpose to sound and make the Naval Remarks
June 24, 1768 Friday variable
PM moderate and clear weath AM fresh gales with rain employed as before people Employed on sundries.
June 25, 1768 Saturday NNW
Fresh gales and squally weath at 5 AM Two men went in the cutter to the outer harbour La Tuch at 7 AM surveyors up in a squal and James Smith & Alex Nesbit were drowned, the boat found by fishermen returned afterward whereas the lost sails, the grapeling rope 4 fath line boathook. At 10 AM came on board fishermen to give the report of the manner the boat was found and brought her on board.
June 26, 1768 Sunday NNW, NW
Fresh gales and cloudy Employed variously
June 27, 1768 Monday variable
Moderate and clear weath carpenters employed on one of the whale boats.
June 28, 1768 Tuesday ditto

Fresh breezes with rain carpenters employed as before employed worming the rigging and scraping the ship side & lost overbd three scrapers

June 29, 1768 Wednesday NW

Fresh breezes and cloudy weath carpenter employed repairing the sheathing of the *Canceaux* bow and under the wales, employed turning the rigging & yards &&.

*June 30, 1768 to July 12, 1768

July 13. 1768 Wednesday variable, NW

Moored in Gaspey Harbour

Fresh gales and Mod weath at 11 read the articles of war to the ships company with the abstract of act of Parliament punished Patrick Walls for disobedience of orders with 12 lashes, Employed masting of the main mast tops and 6

July 14, 1768 Thursday variable

Moderate and cloudy weath scrape ship the mast and graple and pay her sides with tarr,

July 15, 1768 Friday

Fresh gales with rain Employed variously.

July 16, 1768 Saturday variable

Moderate and cloudy weath hard sleet La tuch scraped and foretops with tallow

July 17, 1768 Sunday

Moderate and fair weath Employed making ready for sea AM bent the sails.

July 18, 1768 Monday

Moderate and cloudy with rain, Employed getting of water on board.

July 19, 1768 Tuesday

PM Moderate and cloudy AM fresh gales with rain, Employed as occasion getting on board prov. getting ship ready for sea.

July 20, 1768 Wednesday variable

Mod. and cloudy weath AM Employed warping the ship out of the Basin at ½ past 11 the ship ran aground, carried out her B. Bower anchor in order to heave her off at high water.

July 21, 1768 Thursday

Moderate and cloudy weath at 2 AM hove of the ship and lay at the anchor at 12 weighed and came to sail, at 8 anchored in 12 fams water with the Bs. Bower. Custom House N b E off shore 2 cables caught a breeze recd N b W and far of call and between in setting up the rigging the lower and topmast.

July 22, 1768 Friday variable

PM moderate and cloudy weath AM fresh gales and cloudy weath rain employed about the rigging

*July 23, 1768 to July 28, 1768

July 29, 1768 Friday

Moderate and cloudy weath at 4 AM weighed and came to sail, as did the snow from buoy rope and wood buoy.

July 30, 1768 Saturday SSE, WSW, NE

PM weath with breezes and hazey, middle and latter light airs and variable. AM Cape Vreices SSW 2 leagues at 4 PM Cape Rozcer WSW and a very great current setting to the westward.

July 31, 1768 Sunday SE, calm, NW

West point of the Island of Anticoste

First part light airs and variable, middle and latter parts Breezes and clear weath. 9 PM calm anchored with the stream anchor to stop current gravel bottom in 25 fathoms, at 4 weighed and came to sail, at 7 calm anchored again to stop in 21 fath ground, Fox River WSW half a mile, at 10 found the current back and drawd us to the west and at 12 AM found the current set to the westward at 9 AM weighed and came to sail, left the snow at anchor.

Aug. 1, 1768 Monday NW, SE

Grand coley

Fresh breezes and cloudy weath these 24 hours, at 9 AM set studing sails.

Aug. 2, 1768 Tuesday calm, NW

Mod. weath at 1 AM down studing sails, sounded no ground at 100 fam, at 5 PM employed mending sails, at 1 AM down ditto, at 10 thick fogg

Aug. 3, 1768 Wednesday WNW

PM moderate breezes with a thick fogg, middle and latter clear weath AM ? row to the H? at 8 AM Grand Coley SSE b W 5 miles AM ? occasioned by a strong current setting to the G:C.

Aug. 4, 1768 Thursday WSW, N b W, S b E

West Point of northernmost Cape 5 or 6 leagues

First part fresh gales and latter fair at 7 at 6 AM at 11 AM set studding sails.

Aug. 5, 1768 Friday S, SE

Cape Day NW b W 7 or 7 leagues

Fresh breezes and clear weath. at 1 PM saw land bearing NW 8 leagues at 1 AM set studding sails.

Aug. 6, 1768 Saturday SE, variable, S

Moderate airs and cloudy weath at 6 PM down studding sails ? Cape D ? NW 6 or 7 leagues, at 4 AM heavy rain & squally took in 2 reefs topsails. Employed rigging the sprit sail and sprit yard.

Aug. 7, 1768 Sunday variable

Cape Soll ? S b W 6 or 7 leagues

First part fresh breezes and cloudy, middle and latter light airs and calm at times 1 AM saw smoke upon the shore which we took for ill at 11 and went to surveying made the signal and fired 6 three pounders Employed standing of and on, at 5 light airs then found them to be *Jupiter*, made sail out all reefs at 8 AM sounded at 1 with 10 fathoms line.

Aug. 8, 1768 Monday

Light airs and cloudy weath first part middle fresh gales and gales squally latter fresh gales and clear weath at 6 rigged the sprit sail topsail yard and bent a topgallant yard for the spritsail & topsail, at 8 veered studding sails, at this night sounded no ground AM spoke a sloop from Quebec to Boston at 11 AM anchored with the stream anchor in 10 fathom water soft bottom

Aug. 9, 1768 Tueday

Moored Canso SSW

Fresh gales and squally weath with a great sea. At 2 PM light airs came to under the garrison & ? reef the topsails and set them, at 9 handed the topsails and gallants and got up the topgallant yard spritsail & topsail yard, at ½ past 10 AM wore ship at ½ past 1 AM handed the topsails in pressing up to the maintop at 4 bent another topsail and set the topsails. Sailmakers Employed repairing the maintop sail.

Aug. 10, 1768 Wednesday NE

Fresh breezes and cloudy weath. at 10 AM saw the Island of Buinuber bearing SW. Sailmaker employed as before.

Aug. 11, 1768 Thursday variable, E

Isle of Back 3 miles

Moderate and clear weath saw the Island Bich N about 3 leagues, at 1 PM fired 2 guns shotted and brought too a schooner from Cadez for Quebec with a mast had been out 12 weeks and out of provisions. Supplyd them with pork and bread, checks they were to return at Quebec. At 11 down studding sails at 4 AM anchored with the stream anchor in 22 fam soft mudy clay. At 7 weighed and came to sail, set studing sails.

Aug. 12 1768 Friday variable

Westward of Grand Isle SSE ½ mile

Light airs first and middle part, latter fresh gales and cloudy weath at 3 PM anchored with the stream anchor in 12 fam water west end Bic half a mile at 7 weighed and came to to sail set studing sails, at 9 hauled down at 4 saw the Isle of Basque SSW 3 miles, at 8 Green Island the east end SSW The Tide being strong the ship did not go any ahead supplies going 10 knots

Aug. 13, 1768 Saturday NE

PM fresh gales with moderate weath and heavy rains middle and latter fresh breezes at 1 PM saw Brandy Potts hove to & shortened sail ? with the breeze in ¼ fathom that cover, at low water & less 3 ? Brandy Pott Island NE this AM most just of Hearn Island SW ½ 1 degree of 2 miles, Sailmaker employed repairing of main topsail and ?

Aug. 14, 1768 Sunday

Moderate and fresh gales ? boats employed sounding from Harbour and over to the shore, at 3 AM load schooner from the Strait of Belleisle with ballast at 6 anchored with the Bt. Br. in 8 fm low water of spring tide found it rise and fall 13 feet here sandy in ? fm, E end of the Pilgrim, SW White Island NNE W end of Harbour Island NW b W. Employed repairing the main topsail

Aug. 15, 1768 Monday

Moderate breezes and clear weath. At 4 AM sail maker repair the main topsail ?

Aug. 16, 1768 Tuesday

Moderate and clear weath AM fired 3 guns shotted and brought too a ship from the coast Labradore his Majesty's Armed ship schooner the *St. John* bound for the Bun

Aug. 17, 1768 Wednesday

Fresh breezes and cloudy weath at 3 PM weighed and came to sail. At 7 past set stream anchor in 16 fam to the Pilgrim SE Gut of C one of SW soft ground & the current does not run so strong Cable on flood at any part of the channel, Boats employed sounding.

Aug. 18, 1768 Thursday

PM fresh breezes AM light airs and variable, at 2 PM weighed and came to sail from Bay Ni ? W b S , at 9 anchored with the Bt. Br in 24 fm water soft bottom. Employed of the Isle of Coudre S dist 6 mile. At 3 AM anchored and came to at ½ past 9 came too with the Bt: Bower in 7 fam soft mud Cape

Goose E b N Point of Coudre

Aug. 19 1768 Friday E, calm

Moderate and cloudy weath the first part showers of rain AM fired 2 shotted and brought too a schooner from Boston for Quebec Employed variously.

Aug. 20, 1768 Saturday

PM light airs and calm. At 4 weighed and came to sail came too with the bower in 11 fam water with rocky bottom, Grand Colee

Aug. 21, 1768 Sunday

Fresh breezes and cloudy weath flashes of lightening and some rain, at 4 fired a gun a signal for surveying boat at 7 to weigh and come to sail at 7 ship moored with the best bower in 9 fam water soft bottom Cape Toinion SW b W got Cape Coulee end of Rett Island at 6 AM weighed and came to sail at Noon came too with the best bower in 6 fm of water people employed Island of Orleans W b S.

Aug. 22, 1768 Monday

Light airs with suny hot weath AM ditto weath with thunder lightening and hard rain at 11 a very hard squall at 7 PM weighed and came to to sail and turning to Orleans at 11 came too with the best bower in 7 fam water hard ground At ? Church on Orleans NW ? Point N b W AM weighed and came to sail weath and dark cloudy, at 11 AM a very hard squall attended with very loud thunder and heavy rain, which split the jib and caused part of the sheet of ditto to split. Anchored in 9 fam water hard bottom St. Francis at End of Isle Hasan, SE b S Sailmaker employed repairing the gib and the sails after the squal.

Aug. 23, 1768 Tuesday

Fresh breezes and cloudy weath with showers of rain, at 4 AM weighed and came to sail.

Aug. 24, 1768 Wednesday

Fresh gales and squaly weath, at 3 AM gave a signal for a surveying boat at 4 anchored at Quebec in 11 fam water muddy ground

Aug. 25, 1768 Thursday variable

PM Moderate and cloudy weath with some rain latter part employed as before

Aug. 26, 1768 Friday

Moderate and fair weath, Dryd sails and unbent the courses and top sail, sail maker as before.

Aug. 27, 1768 Saturday

Fresh gales with rain, Employed moving a cable ? way NE ? and anchored the Colysale, SW Church steeple upper town W b S, Saint of the Town NW b W ? of shore at half a cable length, sail maker finished People employed making survey tent and repair main top gallant ?

*Aug. 28, 1768 to Sept. 14, 1768

Sept. 15, 1768 Thursday
Fresh breezes and cloudy weath AM arrived here Mr. Watts Mid. from taking naval remarks of the Bay of Chaleur &c.

Sept. 16, 1768 Friday squally
Moderate and cloudy weath Employed fitting out the whale boats.

Sept. 17, 1768 Saturday SSW, NNW
PM Ditto weath with rain AM fresh weath Dryd sails

Sept. 18, 1768 Sunday NW
Moderate and fine weath Recd on board provisions of different species.

Sept. 19, 1768 Monday NW
Employed overhauling the rigging & AM ditto weath dryd sails.

Sept. 20, 1768 Tuesday
Ditto weath AM recd on board fresh beef, carpenters employed refitting the boats of the survey.

Sept. 21, 1768 Wednesday
Moderate and cloudy weath Employed in the hold AM arrived Ensign Georges ? with party from Surveying the S part of the River St. Lawrence also Mr. ? with a party from surveying about the mouth of the River Siguney People employed as before.

Sept. 22, 1768 Thursday NE, SE
Moderate weath AM recd on board provisions of several species with fresh beef for the ships company AM in the hold Fired 10 guns being his Majesty's Coronation.

Sept. 23, 1768 Friday SW, SSW
Fresh breezes and cloudy weath. AM completed Mr. Hogg, Master with a months provisions of all species for 60 men to make three the Naval Remarks about the Isle of Coudre Employed about the rigging.

Fresh breezes & cloudy weathr. PM completed Mr. Hogg Master with one months provisions of all species for himself & five men to go take the Naval remarks about the Isle of Coudre & in a shallop, AM employd about the rigging.

Sept. 24, 1768 Saturday SW, SSW

Fresh Breezes and cloudy weath flying showers of rain, PM people usefully employed AM sailed hence Mr. Hogg Master for Isle of Coudre, to take the Naval remarks &c. the Carpenters employed refitting the whale boats.

Naval Remarks were the recording of descriptions of the lands of the survey including vegetation, structures, roads, fence lines, landings that would be compiled and noted of the preliminary drafts of a map and later shown on the finalized map being prepared by Mr. DesBarre.

Sept. 25, 1768 Sunday SE, SW

First part fresh breezes and cloudy latter part gales and squally, PM recd on board sundry provisions at Noon sent two whale boats down the North Channel between the island Orleans and the main, to sound & take keep the Naval Remarks under the direction of two surveyors/petty officers.

Sept. 26, 1768 Monday variable

Moderate and fine weath.

Sept. 27, 1768 Tuesday

Ditto weath.

Sept. 28, 1768 Wednesday SSE

Moderate gales and cloudy weath AM recd on board provisions of different species AM employed on occasion.

Sept. 29, 1768 Thursday NNE

Moderate and cloudy weath PM employed pressing of yarns and making of spun yarn AM breezes here provisions the Naval Remarks of the seven islands and survey the north shore of St. Lawrence in the *Jupiter* schooner and gave an account of the anchorage and their taking the distance from the shores.

Arrived here Mr. Brown Mids from taking the Naval Remarks of the seven Islands & part of the North Shore of the River St. Lawrence in the *Jupiter* schooner & gave an account of loosing an anchor & cable off Managogan Shoal.

Sept. 30, 1768 Friday variable

Fresh breezes and cloudy with some rain AM dryd sails at 4 PM Employed about repairing and making of supplies Carpenters upon the whale boats & recd on board fresh beef hauled the *Jupiter* ashore to be repaired.

Fresh breezes & cloudy weathr with some rain, AM carpenters employd refitting the *Jupiter* schooner, people employd about do.

Oct. 1, 1768 Saturday
Fresh breezes and clear weath carpenters employed on the *Jupiter*.
Oct. 2, 1768 Sunday
First part cloudy with heavy showers of rain AM Moderate and fair weath. AM dryd sails, carpenters as before.
Oct. 3, 1768 Monday SE, SE b E, S b E
Moderate and fine weath latter rain, carpenters and people employed on the *Jupiter* schooner, PM anchored here two boats and men taking the Naval Remarks of the N. and between Orleans and the main.
Mod & fine weathr the first part, fresh gales with rain the middle & latter parts, PM people usefully employd, AM carpenters & people employd about the *Jupiter* schooner, arriv'd here the two whale boats from taking the Naval remarks of the North Channel.
Oct. 4, 1768 Tuesday
Moderate and fine weath AM completion the *Jupiter* with provisions also the latter for to take the Naval Remarks of the South Channel between Orleans & the main.
Oct. 5, 1768 Wednesday
These 24 hours fresh gales and cloudy weath with flying showers of rain people usefully employed.
Oct. 6, 1768 Thursday
Moderate and cloudy weath AM dryd sails AM recd on board provisions of all species Carpenters on the whale boats.
Oct. 7, 1768 Friday
Moderate and cloudy weath with some rain. AM carpenters repairing the whale boats the people employed variously
Oct. 8, 1768 Saturday
Moderate and fair dryd sails, recd on board provisions of all species, AM employed getting on board provisions of all species in a schooner for two surveying parties who are to sound in the River St. John off Anticosti.
Oct. 9 1768 Sunday
Moderate and cloudy weath Employed as before.
Oct. 10, 1768 Monday
Moderate and cloudy weath AM employed putting on board provision for the Surveyors and repairing of sails
Oct. 11, 1768 Tuesday calm, W, WSW
Moored at Quebec
Fresh breeze and cloudy weath AM employed storing everything for the Surveying party that was going away
Oct. 12, 1768 Wednesday NW, W

Ditto weath PM employed on sounding, AM sailed hence for the River St. John, two surveying boats

Oct. 13, 1768 Thursday SSW

Moderate and cloudy weath with rain Recd on board fresh beef AM returned the pinnace making some Naval Remarks of the snow or between Orleans and the main fort

*Oct. 14, 1768 to Oct. 26, 1768

Oct. 27, 1768 Thursday

Moderate and cloudy with small snow, AM anchored here at 1 sloop taking the Remarks of the Isle of Gendre, at 2 AM worked the ship in to Coudesac.

Oct. 28, 1768 Friday

Fresh gales with hard frost, Employed getting the yards & topmasts on then upon the wharf, hauled up the pinnace, and a whale boat which was store in to the boat house.

Oct. 29, 1768 Saturday variable

Moderate and cloudy weath unhung the rudder and covered it on shore, Employed rounding of cables and hawses being warn parts bad parts & with descard running and standing rigging being rubbed & cut with the ice in the winter.

Oct. 30, 1768 Sunday NW

Fresh gales with snow and sleet, middle and latter fresh gales and clear weath Employed as before at 3 AM broke from our B Bower Bouy being moored to it The ship ground on the shore to pass, among the rocks above Caudesac.

Oct. 31, 1768 Monday NW

Fresh gales & cloudy weath AM got the cutter on to the Kings yard. Employed as before.

Nov. 1, 1768 Tuesday variable

The moderate and cloudy weath AM Ditto with some snow, AM cut the clenehis ? bower cable the anchor, lying ? 1 low water of clenehis them ?

Nov. 2, 1768 Wednesday

Ditto weath Employed getting out the iron ballast AM Employed at low water doing the hawser cable & as far as the anchor with descard running rigging to ? from ? gott with these with winter.

Nov. 3, 1768 Thursday NE

Laid up for the winter in Harbour of Quebec

Fresh gales with rain and sleet with snow. Employed repairing the cable and hawses as needed.

*Nov. 4, 1768 to Nov. 19, 1768

Nov. 20, 1768 Sunday
Fresh breezes and cloudy weath Sailed hence the snow *Dolphen* for the Straits.
Nov. 21, 1768 Monday
Ditto weath with hard frost, sailed hence a sloop and schooner for Boston. Recd on board Monday provisions.

*Nov. 22, 1768 to Feb. 2, 1769

Feb. 3, 1769 Friday SW
Ditto weath AM Captain Holland and party went up the river Montmarary a surveying party arrived here
Feb. 4, 1769 Saturday
Moderate and clear weath. Employed overhauling the rigging &c
Feb. 5 , 1769 Sunday SW
Ditto weath This day pass and repassed men & horses over the river.

*Feb. 6, 1769 to Feb. 9, 1769

Feb. 10, 1769 Friday NW
These 24 hours very severe frost no possibility of marking, AM Captain Holland returned.

*Feb. 11, 1769 to Feb. 20, 1769

Feb. 21, 1769 Tuesday NW
Ditto weath AM Departed this life of the sea Tom Colevard Reno, Seaman.
Feb. 22, 1769 Wednesday
Fresh gales with a great of snow, AM Mr. Sprale went down the River with man to Survey and chart of the S. shore with a months provisions of all species &.

*Feb. 23, 1769 to Feb. 27, 1769

Feb. 28, 1769 Tuesday NW
Mod. weath People employed drawing of yarns and making of Spunyarn. AM recd fresh beef for the ships company.

Through over bd broke to pieces with the frost two crocks.

*Mar. 1, 1769 to Mar. 18, 1769

Mar. 19, 1769 Sunday NW
Moderate weath with the great ? of snow at 2 AM Lieutenant Sproul returned with his party from surveying the shore of the River St. Lawrence.

Mar. 20, 1769 Monday WNW
These 24 hours light and clear with very strong frost. Observed the latitude: at 16 degrees 47 minutes and 15 seconds North. People employed logging in the snow for plank to repair the ship.

Mar. 21, 1769 Tuesday NW
First part thick weath with snow, middle and latter do with a trace, Employed as before.

Mar. 22. 1769 Wednesday NW
Fresh breezes and cloudy weath these 24 hours People variously employed.

Mar. 23, 1769 Thursday
Moderate and cloudy weath. Employed about the rigging.

Mar. 24, 1769 Friday NW
Moderate and clear. Do. Employed

Mar. 25, 1769 Saturday NW
Fresh breezes and clear weath these 24 hours, people employed about the rigging &. recd on board fresh beef & beer for the ships company. AM hired carpenters employed scraping of plank &c.

Mar. 26, 1769 Sunday NW
Fresh gales and cloudy with snow AM Employed sawing of plank and board for the repair of the craft and ship. People employed about the rigging.

Mar. 27, 1769 Monday NE
These 24 hours fresh breezes and cloudy weath Carpenters employed as before.

Mar. 28, 1769 Tuesday SE
Fresh gales with thick weath. and snow, people employed logging for planks in the snow to repair the ship and surveying craft.

Mar. 29, 1769 Wednesday NW
Fresh breezes and clear weath Carpenters employed sawing of plank & board repair ship and craft.

Mar. 30, 1769 Thursday NW
Ditto weath. Carpenters employed as before people employed

clearing the ice from ? in order to get her repaired, recd on board the 20 Nov. 68 ? 31 March 69 and 10 68, beer 30 tons, pork 875 pieces, pease 13 bushels, rice 2137 pounds, fresh beef 7143 pounds, vinegar 80 gallons, batter 13 HG, ferkin butter & cheese & butter ?.firkins.

Mar. 31, 1769 Friday N

These 24 hours, light airs and clear weath people employed overhauling the rigging and slack, carpenters employed on the *Jupiter* schooner.

April 1, 1769 Saturday variable

Moderate and fair weath. AM people employed digging the ballast out of the *Jupiter.*

April 2, 1769 Sunday variable

Moderate and fair weath. The shiftings of ice round the ship abaft 9 feet 1 inch same forward.

April 3, 1769 Monday variable

AM moderate and fine weath. AM fresh gales and cloudy weath with rain, Employed as necessary.

April 4, 1769 Tuesday ESE

Fresh gales and cloudy with rain at times, at 10 AM came on board several carpenters to work on the ship.

April 5, 1769 Wednesday SE

PM more moderate, AM fresh gales weath rain, carpenter as before People employed making okam.

"Okam" old rope fiber after being pulled apart was reused as a filler in the caulking of seams.

April 6, 1769 Thursday S

Fresh gales with heavy rain intermixed with sleet & hail.

April 7, 1769 Friday NNE

Ditto gales with a great deal of snow People as before.

April 8, 1769 Saturday NE

Fresh gales with snow and sleet AM do. gales and cloudy weath AM a very fresh sea none as high this winter, carpenter at work on the ship.

April 9, 1769 Sunday

Moderate and cloudy weath.

April 10, 1769 Monday

Moderate and clear weath. People employed repairing of our sails, Carpenters at work on the craft and ship, People employed about the rigging.

April 11. 1769 Tuesday variable

Ditto weath Carpenters as before, people employed variously, recd on board sundry provisions.

April 12, 1769 Wednesday SE

Fresh gales with sleet and snow, employed as before.

April 13, 1769 Thursday

PM ditto weath AM Moderate and cloudy, carpenters as before, People about the rigging.

April 14, 1769 Friday variable

Moderate and fair weath., carpenters and people as before. AM dryd and weather allow its mend the following sails much cut and gett well rolls, flying jib, M. top w layd mizen & staysail, main course & foretopsail, a mizen topsail not repairable & dryd, stowing the bad sails uppermost in order to get them repaired.

April 15, 1769 Saturday E

Fresh breezes and cloudy with rain and very cold weath. Carpenters employed on the survey schooner.

April 16, 1769 Sunday

Fresh gales with snow sleet and rain. AM more moderate.

April 17, 1769 Monday

Fresh gales with hard frost intermixed with snow, AM carpenters employed on the ship boat, and people about the rigging, came on board a sail maker to replace the sails.

April 18, 1769 Tuesday NE

Ditto weath with very hard frost. Carpenter, people & sail maker employed as before.

April 19, 1769 Wednesday

Moderate and clear weath Employed as before.

April 20, 1769 Thursday

PM moderate and clear weath. AM fresh breezes and clear weath. Employed getting the main top mast on Bd, do. shipped the foremast and rigging the fore yard as new. Carpenters & empd.

April 21, 1769 Friday

Fresh breezes with hard frost. AM New sized and sewed the lynes (lines) of the fore shrouds. employed about the fore rigging and turning of do. Carpenters, sail maker as before.

April 22, 1769 Saturday SW

Moderate and clear weath with hard frost. People employed about the main rigging and taring of it: carpenters and sail maker as before.

April 23, 1769 Sunday variable

PM Moderate and cloudy weath inclinable to rain. AM do.
April 24, 1768 Monday
PM moderate breezes with heavy rain. AM fresh gales with rain, carpenters & sail makers as before, people employed making points & gaskets, ratting the shrouds and mast.
April 25, 1769 Tuesday
PM moderate and fine weath. AM the guchermo ? to have amotion, ? at 11 AM began to moderate from calm the river broke, carpenters & sail maker as before. People employed about the rigging.
April 26, 1769 Wednesday
Moderate and cloudy weath with rain, 1 time. Caulker, carpenter, & sail maker employed recd on board for ships company employ variously.
April 27, 1769 Thursday variable, SE, ESE
At Quebec in dock
Clear and fine weath AM got up the tops and caps and topmasts up through stays of a masthead Caulkers, carpenters, and sail makers and every guard AM moved the ice gone without the vessel.
April 28, 1769 Friday NE, ENE
Fresh breezes and clear weath, caulkers, carpenters, & sail maker as before, people employed about the rigging.
April 29, 1769 Saturday ENE
Moderate breezes and clear weath with frost ? as before, employed about the rigging reeving of running rigging.
April 30, 1769 Sunday NE
Moored at the Kings Wharf in Quebec
Moderate and cloudy weath, all the drift ice gone, AM transported the ship along side of the Kings Wharf. Employed about the rigging AM as before.
May 1, 1769 Monday variable, NNE
At Quebec
PM moderate breezes and fine clear weath AM fresh gales caulkers and carpenters at work in the ship, sail makers repairing the sails and the people employed variously. Read the articles of War and the Abstract of the late act of parliament to the Ships company.
May 2, 1769 Tuesday NE, ENE
PM hard gales and clear weather AM more moderate, caulkers carpenters and sail makers employed as before people employed digging under the ship for the carpenters to put on some of the false keel it being gone carried out the stream anchor and hawsers

to low water mark for a stern fast for the ship.

In this procedure, when in port the ship would be worked into a convenient low water area and anchored or secured. When the tide went out at low water, the ship would come to rest on its bottom exposed for hull work. For work on the false keel (a major timber fastened outward of the ships keel) the ships carpenter crew would tunnel under the ship along the keel and when found to remove the damaged false keel or replace missing portions. With return of the tide the vessel would again float free and then be moved into open water.

May 3, 1769 Wednesday NE
Fresh gales and cloudy weath. carpenters and caulkers employed on the ship Sailmakers as before, people employed digging under the ship for carpenters to work.
May 4, 1769 Thursday NNE
Moderate breezes and clear weather Sailmakers employed as before people fixing and reeving the running rigging.
May 5, 1769 Friday NE
Moderate and clear no ice to be seen in the river caulkers and carpenters employed on the boats sail makers as before people employed variously.
May 6, 1769 Saturday NNE
Ditto weath. Caulkers, carpenters &c employed as before.
May 7, 1769 Sunday variable
Quebec, Kings Wharf
Do. weath at 8 AM transported the ship alongside the Kings Wharf Do. came down a brig from Montreal.
May 8, 1769 Monday do.
Do. weather Caulkers, carpenters and sail makers employed as before, people employed rigging the ship got the lower and topsail yards across &c.
May 9, 1769 Tuesday do.
Do. weather, carpenters caulkers & sail makers employed as before people employed rigging the ship.
May 10, 1769 Wednesday do.
PM light airs and variable. AM hard gales and cloudy with some hail and rain carpenters and sail makers as before people employed variously, this morning had a remarkable high tide.
May 11. 1769 Thursday NE

Fresh gales and cloudy weather, carpenters employed repairing the boats the people employed variously.

May 12, 1769 Friday ESE

Do. weather carpenters employed as before people employed about the rigging Reeved new top tackle fall the old being much are and unfit for service.

May 13, 1769 Saturday ENE, SSW

PM fresh gales and cloudy with rain, middle calm and variable. AM fresh breezes and clear weather carpenters employed as before people variously.

May 14, 1769 Sunday NW

Fresh breezes with hard frost snow and hail and extreme cold.

May 15, 1769 Monday NW

At the Kings Wharf, Quebec

Fresh gales with hard frosts Carpenters employed on the boats, sail makers employed making and repairing boats sails for the surveyors people employed variously.

May 16, 1769 Tuesday variable

Moderate breezes and cloudy weath carpenters sail makers and people employed as before.

May 17, 1769 Wednesday Ditto, NE

Moderate breezes and cloudy with some rain carpenters & sail makers employed as before the people employed variously.

May 18, 1769 Thursday NE, ENE

Fresh breezes with rain at times carpenters employed as before people employed variously received some provisions and beer on board.

May 19, 1769 Friday ENE

Light airs intermixed with calm carpenters employed as before swayed the yards & topmasts up employed fitting the rigging.

May 20, 1769 Saturday variable

Do. weather at 7 PM struck yards & topmasts carpenters employed as before people employed variously.

May 21, 1769 Sunday ENE

Ditto weath carpenters employed as before.

May 22, 1769 Monday Ditto

Ditto weath carpenters employed on the boats do. gravd one side and payed with pitch and tar.

May 23, 1769 Tuesday variable

Do. weather carpenter & caulkers employed on the ship people employed variously.

May 24, 1769 Wednesday Ditto

Fresh breezes with heavy rains.
May 25, 1769 Thursday NE, var.
Do. weather AM arrived here two ships from London in ballast,
May 26, 1769 Friday var.
PM fresh gales and thick hazy weather with heavy rains arrived here a brig from London and a sloop from New York AM moderate & cloudy came up here a brig and 2 ships from London, a sloop from New York and a brig from Guernsey Carpenter employed on the ships bottom & survey boats people emp. variously.
May 27, 1769 Saturday E
Fresh breezes and cloudy weath carpenters and caulkers empd as before people employed variously AM a sloop ran aboard of the *Jupiter* boat and carried away his bowsprit and foremast with the jibb sheet and halyards, and broke her cable and lost then its spar, came up a brig, sloop & schooner, employed creeping for the anchor.
May 28, 1769 Sunday SW
Fresh gales and clear at 7 PM put a new foremast & bowsprit in the *Jupiter* boat with another anchor and a new jibb, at 11 AM sailed hence the *Jupiter* and two whale boats with AM Mr. Sproule Depy Surveyor to the coast of Labradore on the No. side the River St. Lawrence on a survey sent *Polly* surveyor C. Siamin with the party, delivered them provisions for 3 months also ½ a barrel of powder so this ordnance stores to assist another party of wanted who wintered down the river.
May 29, 1769 Monday NE
At the Kings Wharf Quebec
Moderate and fair weath carpenters finished the bottom and payed it employed getting all the stores onboard came in here two brigs from New York and a sloop & a schooner from Boston.
May 30, 1769 Tuesday do.
PM moderate and cloudy AM fresh gales with rain carpenters employed on the ships and boats people employed hoisting in and stowing away the ground tier of water hoisted in our guns.
May 31, 1769 Wednesday do.
PM fresh gales with rain, came in here a ship and a snow from London and a sloop and schooner from Boston carpenters employed as before people employed variously AM employed creeping for the schooners anchor but to no purpose.
June 1. 1769 Thursday do., variable

PM fresh gales with rains AM more moderate people employed variously bent all our sails except the mainsail.

June 2, 1769 Friday SW

Moderate and fair weather carpenter employed on the ships boats people employed variously Read the article of war and abstract of the act of Parliament to the ships company. Ships draught of water forward 12 feet 2 inches abaft 13 feet 1 inches.

June 3, 1769 Saturday SW

Off in the stream

PM weather at 1 AM hauled off the ships from the wharf to her anchors carried out the stream anchor and cable to steady her, scaled the guns got the yards and topmasts up and the top gallant yards a cross; employed sweeping for the *Jupiters* anchor as of occasion its found and carried off.

June 4, 1769 Sunday variable, ENE

PM moderate & hazey AM fresh gales and clear. Came in a ship from London and a schooner from Bristol fired a salute of 21 guns it being the Kings birthday.

June 5, 1769 Monday NE

Off St. Patricks Harbour

Fresh gales with rain people employed variously. AM unmoored ship at 8 weighed and came to sail, at Noon anchored off St. Patricks hole in 7 fathoms water soft bottom the east point of Orleans NE b E west point W b W moored ship with the stream anchor and cable ships boats employd sounding the south channel of Orleans.

June 6, 1769 Tuesday variable

Moderate and cloudy weath two of the ships boats employed as before.

June 7, 1769 Wednesday E

PM moderate and cloudy weather with some rain, AM pleasant weather. Boats employed as before.

June 8 1769 Thursday variable

Off St. Patricks Hole

Moderate and fine pleasant weather ruffed & scraped the sides and payd them with tar went past us a snow, sloop and schooner down the river, a boat employed sounding received a letter from Mr. Blaskowitz Deputy Surveyor of the loss of a a whale boat and all her provisions, arms &.

June 9, 1769 Friday var. ESE

Moderate and cloudy passed by a schooner from New York and 2 sloops going down the River.

June 10, 1769 Saturday ESE, SW
Light airs and variable with rain AM strong gales and squally people employed in the boats sounding.
June 11, 1769 Sunday WSW, WNW
Fresh gales and squally with heavy rains cleared hawse.
June 12, 1769 Monday SW
PM moderate & cloudy with rain AM fresh gales and flying clouds boats empd as before
June 13 1769 Tuesday
PM fresh gales and squally AM striped the lower masts payd them with turpentine and oil and the top masts and top gallant masts with tallow.
June 14 1769 Wednesday
Moderate and cloudy weath employed sounding, 4 men left onboard besides the Captain & pilot, the master and all the gentlemen gone a sounding.
June 15, 1769 Thursday
Moderate and fine weath. boats employed as before.
June 16, 1769 Friday
Moderate and cloudy with inclinable to rain fitted out two whale boats and went away Captain Holland Party up the Lakes of St. Charles and two seamen gave them ammunition etc for signals.
June 17, 1769 Saturday
Moderate and cloudy with rain at times past by a schooner from Boston boats employed as before.
June 18, 1769 Sunday E, ENE
PM light airs and heavy cloudy weath with rain at times AM hard gales with heavy rains past by a sloop from Boston.
June 19, 1769 Monday SW, NE
PM fresh gales with rain AM more moderate and cloudy boats employed as before past by down the river two lumber loaded vessels for London.
June 20, 1769 Tuesday var.
Moderate inclinable to rain the weath very warm boats employed as before.
June 21, 1769 Wednesday
Moderate and fine pleasant weath boats employed as before.
June 22, 1769 Thursday var., NW
PM moderate breezes and cloudy fresh gales and squally at 8 came in and anchored the boat that had been sounding with the Master and one of his ships.
June 23, 1769 Friday NW

Fresh breezes with rain the boats went away sounding under the South Shore having 11 days provisions with them.

June 24, 1769 Saturday NW, WSW.
Moderate and cloudy weath cleared anchor passed by a ship from Plymouth and a brigg from New York with flour.

June 25, 1769 Sunday var.
Ditto weath.

June 26, 1769 Monday ESE
Fresh breezes and cloudy with rain boats employed as before.

June 27, 1769 Tuesday
PM hard gales with many rains AM moderate and cloudy with boats employed as before.

June 28, 1769 Wednesday
Moderate and clear weath boats employed as before cleared hawse .

June 29, 1769 Thursday SE, E, SW
Ditto weath PM came on board Mr. Watts with the cutter who had two days before lost grapling and rope a sounding lead and line and two oars.

June 30, 1769 Friday var.
Moderate and cloudy weath passed the cutters logs with another grapling and rope and sounding lead sent her to sounding again converted the *Jupiters* old mainsail and jibb into a surveying tents.

July 1, 1769 Saturday E
Ditto weath read the articles of war and the new abstract of parliament to the ships company, Punished Bolat Watts with 30 lashes for drunkness neglect of duty and mutinous expressions.

July 2, 1769 Sunday SE
Moderate and clear weath boats employed as before.

July 3, 1769 Monday Var., ENE
Fresh gales with hazey rain passed by a sloop and schooner from Boston with rum and provisions.

July 4, 1769 Tuesday E, var.
PM moderate AM more moderate boats employed as before.

July 5, 1769 Wednesday var.
Light airs and clear weath boats employed as before fired 2 guns at a sloop and schooner bound for Boston both loaded with provisions.

July 6, 1769 Thursday
Light breezes and clear with boats employed as before.

July 7, 1769 Friday

Fresh and cloudy weath with rain boats as before cleared hawse.

July 8, 1769 Saturday var.

Off St. Patricks Hole

Moderate and fair weath AM came on board the Master and the pinnace from sounding.

July 9, 1769 Sunday do., ENE

PM moderate and fine weath AM fresh gales with Rain.

July 10, 1769 Monday var.

Moderate breezes and cloudy weath boats employed sounding the master went away in the pinnace a sounding.

July 11, 1769 Tuesday N, ENE

PM Moderate and cloudy AM fresh gales and cloudy with thunder lightening and heavy rains Boats employed as before.

July 12, 1769 Wednesday E

Moderate and cloudy weath some rain Boats as before at 4 AM came on board Mr. Watts in the cutter for provisions PM went away again.

July 13, 1769 Thursday SW, calm

Moderate and fair weath boats employed as before cutt up 50 fathom of 3 inch rope for making logs of iron ballast and parts for buoys, to intersect from the shore.

July 14, 1769 Friday calm

Calm weath boats as before Reeved a new cat fall the old so warn out sling 5 loggs of a line ballast to buoy gaskets on the traverse near Cape Torment.

July 15, 1769 Saturday Var.

Light airs and variable employed as before.

July 16, 1769 Sunday N

Fair weath employed sounding off St. Micheals Church.

July 17, 1769 Monday WSW

Off the E point of the Isle of Orleans

Fair weath at 10 AM unmoored at ½ past weighed and sounded with the ship down the north side of the river. At 5 PM anchored off the E Point of Orleans the boats employed sounding the traverse.

July 18, 1769 Tuesday var.

Fresh breezes and cloudy weath these 24 hours the Ship and boat employed sounding.

July 19, 1769 Wednesday W, NW

Sounding on the St. Lawrence

Fresh gales and squally at 11 AM weighed and went a sounding the St. Lawrence the boats employed sounding lost 2 oars out of the boat in a squall the two running so strong could not take them up.

July 20, 1769 Thursday NW, calm, NE

Off the eastern point of Orleans anchored

Fair weath 6 PM anchored off the E point of Orleans Isle north of shore 2 cables length, boats employ'd as before.

July 21, 1769 Friday variable

Sounding on the St. Lawrence

Fresh gales and cloudy with rain thunder and lightening AM weighed and sounded on the traverse as did the boats.

July 22, 1769 Saturday NE

Ditto weath at 6 AM came too in 7 Fathm water St. Frances Church to 7 or 8 miles dist. off shore ¼ mile at 7 AM weighed and put fore awing up, the river at noon and anchored off St Patricks Church in 11 fathom water a cables length shore the boats employed as before.

July 23, 1769 Sunday W

Fair weath, the ship and boats employed a sounding at 2 PM weighed and went a sounding at 8 came too off the E point of Orleans Island in 2 fathm water sent the boats to take up the bouys and found both of them first occasionally by the strength of the tides breaking the buoy ropes.

July 24, 1769 Monday E

Fresh breezes and cloudy at 7 AM weighed and sounded down the river the boats sounded in the traverse passed by a brigg from Halifax.

July 25, 1769 Tuesday SW, SE

Ditto weath at 11 PM came too in St. Patricks Hole in 9 fath. water and moored a stream cable to the westward the boats employed sounding.

July 26, 1769 Wednesday E

Light airs and clear unmoored and sounded the river at 6 PM came too off the E point of Orleans in 6 fath water the boats sounding on the traverse.

July 27, 1769 Thursday do.

PM light airs and cloudy AM fresh gales and squally the boats employed as before.

July 28. 1769 Friday NE, E

Fresh gales and squally at 10 AM weighed and came to sail employed as before.

July 29, 1769 Saturday N, E

Fresh gales and squally weath these 24 hours at 2 PM came

too in 7 fath. water on the south channel the boats employed sounding.

July 30, 1769 Sunday E, NE

PM fresh gales and cloudy weath AM light airs with rain received on board 2 Hhds of beer for the ships company & passed by a ship from Falmouth.

July 31, 1769 Monday E, NE

Fresh breezes and cloudy weath with much rain these 24 hours, spoke a schooner on the west for Quebec

Aug. 1, 1769 Tuesday N

Fair these 24 hours spoke a sloop from Boston bound to Quebec.

Aug,. 2, 1769 Wednesday E

Ditto weath past by a brig down the river to take in fish at Mount Louis.

Aug. 3, 1769 Thursday SW

Fresh breezes and squally weath these 24 hours with showers at times the boats employed sounding on the traverse.

Aug. 4, 1769 Friday var.

Sounding of the Isle of Orleans

PM fresh breezes with squally weath AM light airs with much rain at 2 AM weigh and sounded in the river as did the boats at 9 came too above the traverse passed by a sloop bound from Quebec to Boston.

Aug. 5, 1769 Saturday do.

Light airs and part cloudy weath these 24 hours at 9 AM weighed and came too and sounded on the traverse as did the boats at ½ past 12 came too at the E end of muddy ground.

Aug. 6, 1769 Sunday E

Fresh gales and squally weath these 24 hours at 4 PM weighed and sounded to St. Patrick Hole and anchored in 8 fath water the boats employed sounding. Read the articles of war and the new abstract of Parliament to the ships company.

Aug. 7, 1769 Monday do.

Ditto the boats employed as before received on board 2 Hhg of beer for the ships company.

Aug. 8, 1769 Tuesday do.

Ditto weath employed as before at 9 AM passed by His Majesty's ship *Glasgow* for Quebec.

Aug. 9, 1769 Wednesday var.

Light airs and cloudy weath. At 4 PM passed by a brigg

from London and a schooner from Labrador for Quebec employed as before.

Aug. 10, 1769 Thursday var.
Moderate weath the ship and boats employed sounding the river.

Aug. 11, 1769 Friday do.
Moderate at 2 PM sailed down the river a brigg from Quebec bound to Philadelphia at 10 spoke a ship from London bound to Quebec and a sloop and a brigg people employed as before.

Aug. 12, 1769 Saturday calm
Ditto weath the boats and people employed as before at 4 PM fired a gun at and brought too a ship from Port Beuno to Quebec with wine.

Aug. 13, 1769 Sunday E, do., SW
Light airs and hazey weath AM fresh breezes and squally at 3 PM weighed and sounded in the south channel at 8 PM came too off the west end the Isle Madame in 9 fath water at 5 AM weighed and came to sail and sound down to Gross Isle at 10 came too in 5 fath abaft of the E shore of the Island.

Aug. 14, 1769 Monday SE, W, E
Fresh gales and cloudy weath with rain at times, at 4 PM weighed and went a sounding south Channel at 7 Do. came too off Goose Island in 8 fath clay bottom and anchored in ½ a cable at 6 AM weighed and came to sound at do. the cutter over run by this ship getting over her stern and lost 3 pigs of iron ballast out of her with 4 oars and one leather bucket at noon came too at the W end of Craine Island in 8 fath.

Aug. 15, 1769 Tuesday ENE
Anchored at St. Patricks Hole
Hard gales and squally weather with rain at 8 PM weighed and came to sail up the river at midnight came too in Patricks Hole in 9 fath veered to 2 cables on the small bower at 5 AM moored with the stream anchor and cable the boat employed as before.

Aug. 16, 1769 Wednesday E, ESW
Fresh gales and thick hazey weath. These 24 hours receivd on board 2 Hhds of beer for the ships company employed as before.

Aug. 17, 1769 Thursday var.
Anchored above the traverse.
Moderate and cloudy weath at 2 past one AM unmoored ship at 2 do. weighed and came to sail at 5 do. fired a gun at and brought too a brigg from Falmouth bound to Quebec with wine

at 7 came too above the traverse in 7 fath. water and veered to ½ a cable on the small bower employed as before.

Aug. 18, 1769 Friday
Off Cape Torment
Light airs and clear weath these 24 hours at 9 weighed and went a sounding on the traverse at 7 PM weighed and came too below Cape Torment in 9 fathm clay bottom boat employed as before.

Aug. 19, 1769 Saturday SW
Anchored Cape Sable 153.30 W W point of Couire
Ditto weath weighed and came to sail and sound the south Channel before Cape Corment at 8 PM anchored abrest of Cape Slarfience in 16 fathm water at 6 AM weighed and came to sail and sounded towards Coudre at 10 do. came too in Coudre Road in 20 fathm water Cape Linbile NE 53.30 West

Aug. 20, 1769 Sunday S
Moored at Coudre
Ditto breezes and cloudy weath at 9 PM moored ship a whole cable and the small bower and a third on the best bower to the Eastward when moored Cape Diablo N 55 W from the traverse SW Benches house S b W employed as before.

Aug. 21, 1769 Monday do.
Ditto weath heavy rains recd on board provisions of Mr. Sproule and party the boats employed sounding at 9 AM arrived here the sloop *Rose* for Boston.

Aug. 22, 1769 Tuesday SW, SE
Weath hazey at 7 PM down top gallant yard employed as before received on board Hhd of beer.

Aug. 23, 1769 Wednesday NW, SW
Ditto employed sounding round the Island of Corcers lost one oar out of the boat.

Aug. 24, 1769 Thursday var.
Fresh airs and people employed as before.

Aug. 25, 1769 Friday
PM light airs and cloudy weath AM fresh gales and cloudy with rain at 10 AM replace 2 new hawsers the old being warn out, employed as before.

Aug. 26, 1769 Saturday
These 24 hours light airs and at times calm, the boats employed sounding traverse.

Aug. 27, 1769 Sunday
The boats employed sounding the south traverse.

Aug. 28, 1769 Monday var.
Moored in Coudre Head
Ditto weath employed sounding to the Northwest of Causea at midnight saw a comet in the 16th sight and is the Pluaves.
Aug. 29, 1769 Tuesday do.
Mod. with rain and clear weath these 24 hours the boat employed surveying recd on board beer for the ships company.
Aug. 30, 1769 Wednesday do.
PM first part do weath the latter fresh breezes and squally at 4 PM fired a gun at and brought too a schooner from Boston bound to Quebec.
Aug. 31, 1769 Thursday do.
Light airs and clear weath the boats employed as before at ½ past 3 AM fired a gun at and brought too a brigg from New York bound to Quebec.
Sept. 1, 1769 Friday calm
Ditto at 1 PM fired a gun at and brought too a schooner from the Labradore coast bound to Quebec
Sept. 2, 1769 Saturday NE, SW
Fresh breezes and thick weath with rain at times at 8 AM passed by down the river the *Lagten* a merchant ship for London.
Sept. 3, 1769 Sunday NE
Light airs and thick fogg with much rain at times employed as before.
Sept. 4, 1769 Monday SW
PM moderate AM fresh gales and cloudy at 8 AM went down the river the *Carletons* from Quebec bound to Louisbourg employed as before.
Sept. 5, 1769 Tuesday do.
Down the boats employed as before.
Sept. 6, 1769 Wednesday var.
People employed as before.
Sept. 7, 1769 Thursday SW
Fresh gales and cloudy weath with some rain these 24 hours a 6 AM spoke his Majesty's ship *Glasgow* from Quebec bound down the river employed as before.
Sept. 8, 1769 Friday var.
PM clear at 5 PM fired a gun and brought too a schooner from Boston bound to Quebec weath latter at 11 AM fired a gun and brought too a schooner from New York bound to Quebec. The boats employed sounding at noon arrived here the *Jupiter* schooner with James Hingan and gave an account of the half barrel of

powder and sent in the boats.
Sept. 9, 1769 Saturday NNE
Fresh gales and thick weath with much rain and squally at times at 6 AM fired 3 guns and brought too 2 sloops from New York and one schooner from Plata del Polde bound to Quebec, the boats employed sounding.
Sept. 10, 1769 Sunday SW
Fresh gales and cloudy weath employed as before.
Sept. 11, 1769 Monday var.
Light airs and clear weath intermixed with calm, passed by a schooner from Quebec do. employed.
Sept. 12, 1769 Tuesday do.
Ditto weathr employed as before.
Sept. 13, 1769 Wednesday do.
Passed by here a brigg from Quebec bound to London employed as before.
Sept. 14, 1769 Thursday var.
Moored in Coutre Road anchored on the shore side.
Sent the boats employed sounding, the carpenter employed as before, passed the *Jupiter* schooner boat.
Sept. 15, 1769 Friday do.
First part ditto weath, the latter fresh gales and cloudy at 2 PM unmoored at 3 weighed and came to sail and a schooner the north channel at 10 do. came too in 9 fath. above Cape ?
½ past one weighed and came to sail at 7 AM
Sept. 16, 1769 Saturday SW
Fresh breezes and clear weath at 2 PM weighed and came to sail and sound on the river at 3 came too abreast of St. Johns Channel with the small bower 13 fath at 4 AM weighed and came to sail and sounded the river from the boats.
Sept. 17, 1769 Sunday S, SW
Employed making soundings at 3 PM came too on the north side of the river in 9 fathom water recd on board beef for the ships company.
Sept. 18, 1769 Monday SW
Boats employed as before.
Sept. 19, 1769 Tuesday var.
PM fresh gales at 11 PM fresh gales and cloudy with rain the boats employed sounding.
Sept. 20, 1769 Wednesday SW
Cape Waillard NNE 1 ½ miles
PM fresh gales and cloudy with rain at times hard 9 AM weighed

and came too sail at 10 sounding over the traverse : SE Burnt Cape NNE ½ E in 52 fathoms water at Noon Cape Williams NNE dist 4 miles.

Sept. 21, 1769 Thursday SSW, SE

Anchored off Coudre

PM fresh gales and cloudy weath at 4 PM anchored at Coudre with the best bower in 7 fath Latter employed sounding and watering AM more moderate fired at 2 ships and brought too a brigg and a sloop bound to Boston.

Sept. 22, 1769 Friday SW, var., W

Moderate breezes at 11 AM weighed and came to sail employed sounding between shore and the island

Sept. 23, 1769 Saturday W, WNW

Westernmost part of Hare Island Ledge NNW 1 ½ miles

PM moderate and fair weath at 8 AM anchored with the best bower in 7 fath sandy bottom it went of the great Coroination Islands bearing St. Pat. E at a distance of do. SE b W at 6 do. weighed and came too making soundings between the side and at noon the Westernmost point of Cau Island lying NNW ½ mile.

Sept. 24, 1769 Sunday WNW, W, SSW

Fresh breezes and cloudy employed sounding between Dan Island ledge and the Pilgrim at PM anchored off the Brandy port in 5 fath of water sand and muddy bottom and the point of Brandy Pot bearing SW b W at 10 AM weighed and came to employed sounding between Mare and Green Islands.

Sept. 25, 1769 Monday SW, var.

PM employed as before between Green and Red Island found the current allways sett and spoke at schooner and a brigg from New York with provisions for Quebec.

Sept. 26, 1769 Tuesday do.

Anchored Apple Island bearing SW ½ L at out 1 ½ mile.

PM people employed as before the boats employed surveying in and about the Islands at 4 anchored with the best bower in 7 fath hard bottom Apple Island SW 2 leagues

Sept. 27 1769 Wednesday do.

PM moderate weath and cloudy boats employed a sounding in and about Apple Island.

Sept. 28, 1769 Thursday SW, S

Anchored Baigne Island

Fresh breezes and cloudy with rain at times at 2 weighed and came to sail employed as before at 10 AM anchored in 12 fathom sand and muddy bottom Basque Island at 1 PM the boats employed a sounding about the Island.

Sept. 29, 1769 Friday var.

Anchored West end of Big Island NE b N

Fresh gales and cloudy at 2 PM weighed and came too sail, employed as before at 7 anchored off Big Island in 9 fath sand mixed with stones the Wtward Island NW b N 3 leagues 2 shott at and brought too a snow from Falmouth to Quebec with wine.

Sept. 30 1769 Saturday SW, W

PM employed as before at noon weighed and came to sail at 9 AM moored in 10 fath soft bottom, end of island bearing SW b S.

Oct. 1, 1769 Sunday WSW

Moderate airs boats Employed as before.

Oct. 2, 1769 Monday WNW, N

PM moderate and clear AM fresh gales with rain & haze, fired a shott & brought too a schooner from Boston to Quebec with provisions.

Oct. 3, 1769 Tuesday ENE

Fresh gales & hazey with a great sea.

Oct. 4, 1769 Wednesday NE, do. SW

Red Island NNW

PM moderate & clear at 2 PM weighed and came to sail Employed sounding between west of Barnaby Island at 9 do. bore up at 11 AM anchored in 24 fath Apple Island bearing S at end of Guin Island bearing SW b S Red Island NNW at 7 do. weighed & came to sail at Noon Red Island NNW.

Oct. 5, 1769 Thursday SW, NW, NNW

Anchored NE ½ N Red Island ENE

Fresh gales & cloudy with rain sleet at 7 anch. in 14 fm sand with small shells Red Island W b N ½ N Red Island ENE at 8 AM fired a gun at & brought too a brigg from New York for Quebec provisions.

Oct. 6, 1769 Friday SSW

Anchored off the Brandy Potts.

PM gales with sleet & snow at 7 PM weighed & came to sail at 10 came too with the best bower 8 fath water soft bottom the outer Brandy Potts SW ½ W White Island NNE fired 2 gun & brought too a snow from Ayal with wine for Quebec.

Oct. 7, 1769 Saturday

Fresh gales with snow & hard frost Employed variously.

Oct. 8, 1769 Sunday WNW

Fresh gales & do. weath.

Oct. 9, 1769 Monday W, SW

Mod. weighed & came to sail Empd sounding fired 3 shott a brigg from New York bound to Quebec.

Oct. 10, 1769 Tuesday SW

Anchored between Pilgrims

Fresh gales & cloudy with rain at 4 AM anchored in10 fm soft bottom the east Pilgrim SE b E the great Camararka SW ½ W.

Oct. 11, 1769 Wednesday SW, S, WNW

Breezes & cloudy Boats Emp. as before fired a gun at and brought too a sloop from Boston to Quebec with rum & provisions &.

Oct. 12, 1769 Thursday WSW, NNW

Fair and cloudy boats Empd as before.

Oct. 13, 1769 Friday SSW

PM Fresh & mod. parts mod & var. latter hard gales with frost sleet & snow at 4 AM veered to a whole length the best bower at 6 let go the small cable and veered away to 2/3 of a cable & 2 on the B. Bower with very hard squall got down the top gallant mast & lowered down the lower yard.

Oct. 14, 1769 Saturday NNW

Anchored between the Pilgrim & Camararka

Strong gales & squally with hard frost at 2 PM struck the top masts the cutter oversett & sank in 20 fathoms 2 masts & 2 sails rudder & tiller 2 tin gallon kegs grapling & do. rope.

Oct. 15, 1769 Sunday var.

Sounding W Goose Cape

Gales & do. weath AM more mod. at 5 do. hove in up on both cables at 8 took up the small br. to ½ a cable on the best bower found the best bower cable much rubbed in several places at 10 got up yards & top masts at Noon weighed & came to sail do. sent the pinnace in each of the cutter. Ship Employed sounding

Oct. 16, 1769 Monday SW, W

Anchored in Cnidre Road

Fresh breezes & cloudy at 4 PM came too with the Best Bower in 19 fm veered to a whole cable of Goose Cape NW b W Cape Coudra WNW at 7 AM the pinnace returned with the cutter much damaged among the rocks on the S. shore do. weighed & came to sail Employed sounding at noon anchored with the best bower in Caudre Road Banhis House S b W the sawmill on the N 7 fath N ½ E.

Oct. 17, 1769 Tuesday NNE

Fresh gales & squally with hard frost Empd wooding & watering.

Oct. 18, 1769 Wednesday SSW
Mod. with snow Empd as before fired 2 guns at & brough too a brigg & sloop the latter from Boston the former from New York with rum & provisions &.
Oct. 19, 1769 Thursday WNW
Fresh gales with thick snow past by two ships from London.
Oct. 20, 1769 Friday SW
First & mid parts Mod. & snow latter fresh gales & fair weath. with hard frost PM unmoored & hove in to ½ a cable on the best bower at 7 do in 1 & 2 Reefs of the top sails at 2 weighed & came to sail Employed sounding with the ship between Coudra & Goose Cape.
Oct. 21, 1769 Saturday W, var.
Mod. & cloudy at ½ past 7 came too with the best bower in 18 fm veered to ½ a cable hard bottom Goose Cap NE the Body of Coudre Island N b S ½ S the S part of Coudra Island SW b S ½ S the river Quelle SE b E ¾ E at 10 do. Blows hard at 12 hard gales & squally with snow & hard frost AM strong gales with snow & sleet at 4 do. found the ship. Down the small bower veered away to a whole cable & one cable & ¾ on the best bower found ship in 30 fm hard bottom at 7 do. the best bower cable parted Do. began to heave in on small bower at ½ past 9 the anchor began to come home at 11 got the small bower The wind made a very great sea Set the fore sail fore & mizon stay sail & mizon at noon near Coudre NW Cape S Rock SE b E St. Anne Church ESE.
Oct. 22, 1769 Sunday SSW, W, NNW
Anchored between Coude & Goose Is.
Strong gales with sleet & snow at 2 do the So. Rock bearing with one cables length ½ past came too with the small bower in 9 fm under Goose Island soft bottom. Et end of Goose Island, ES Rock ENE Bellinger Church E b S ½ miles.
Oct. 23, 1769 Monday NW SSW
Gales and squally with sleet & snow attended with hard frost.
Oct. 24, 1769 Tuesday var.
Fresh gales & cloudy AM more moderate.
Oct. 25, 1769 Wednesday var.
Anchored off Goose Island
Fresh breezes & var at 8 AM sent away the *Jupiter* schooners boat in quest of the best bower anchor & cable ships boat Employed sounding.
Oct. 26, 1769 Thursday NW
Mod. & fair weath Empd as before.

Oct. 27, 1769 Friday var.
Light airs with dark cloudy weath & some snow Employed as before.

Oct. 28, 1769 Saturday do.
Small breezes & cloudy at 8 AM weighed & came to sail Empd sounding between Crane & Goose Islands & the S shore having from 3 to 10 fm soft bottom.

Oct. 29, 1769 Sunday NNE, ENE
Moored at Patriks Hole
Fresh gales with thick snow ½ past 2 brought up for the Island of Orleans at 3 do. under the yard of the top sail at 5 came too with the small bower in 8 fm soft bottom moored the ship with the anchor & cable a cable each way Empd starting the ground two of water and bring the water casks on shore at Patricks Hole the Wtmost point SW b S.

Oct. 30, 1769 Monday SW
Gales with very hard frost. Empd unrigging the ship at 8 AM returned the *Jupiter* boat and heard an account they could not find three anchors & had most 2 parts of Studding sail halyards 15 fm of boats grapling rope.

Oct. 31, 1769 Tuesday NNW
Fresh gales with hard frost all the sails frozen that we cannot undo them.

Nov. 1, 1769 Wednesday WSW
Fair moderate Employed unbending the yards past by one brigg & 2 sloops from Boston and New York.

Nov. 2, 1769 Thursday var.
Fresh breezes & cloudy with some snow got down the top masts past by a ship for Boston.

Nov. 3, 1769 Friday
First and mid parts do. Breezes latter light airs & var. AM hauled the ship into St Patricks Hole this place is a sandy level bottom & a good safe place for a vessel to lay up in, coming in is a ledge of rocks runs clear across the harbors mouth and seen at low water at times has you will carry in 12 or 14 feet over the rocks it, flows E by W full & change the shore the current runs up with ½ past 7 it fall 4 or 5 feet up & down by the shore be with slack water in the middle of the channel a very fine fresh water run these might be a very fine dry harbour as the water leaves our ship.

Nov. 4, 1769 Saturday NW
Breezes with hard frost & snow Employed taking out part of our iron ballast & storing do.

Nov. 5, 1769 Sunday do.
Frost with sleet & snow Empd as before.
Nov. 6, 1769 Monday WNW, SW
People Empd. mooring the ship for the winter one bower cable out a head fast to one do. out a cable to an anchor two six inch hawsers out upon each side two 4 ½ inch do. upon each bow.
Nov. 7, 1769 Tuesday E
Anchored in St. Patricks Hole
Fresh gales & cloudy Empd variously.
Nov. 8, 1769 Wednesday do.
Gales & clear weath with hard frost.
Nov. 9, 1769 Thursday
Ditto breezes & cloudy Employed variously received the following provisions from the 1 Nov. to the 9th do. for the surveying parties of the ships company (viz) bread 13019 bus tons Rum 90 gallons fresh beef 3016 lbs 1477 pieces of beef 2215 pieces of pork 52 bushels butter 1294 for butter & cheese rice 2852 lbs vinegar 120 gallons.

*Nov. 10, 1769 to April 9, 1770

April 10, 1770 Tuesday var.
Anchored St. Patricks Hole
Mod. & clear with hard frost carpenters Empd as before caulkers Empd caulking the decks the company Empd variously.
April 11, 1770 Wednesday WNW
Fresh breezes and cloudy caulkers as before Ships company Empd cutting the ice around the ship.
April 12, 1770 Thursday W, NW
Moderate and clear with frost caulkers as before people Empd rigging the top masts.
April 13, 1770 Friday var.
Ditto weather caulkers as before AM got up the top gallant masts & rigg'd them.
April 14, 1770 Saturday do.
Ditto weather Empd variously.
April 15, 1770 Sunday do.
Fine pleasant weather caulkers as before people empd variously.
April 16, 1770 Monday do.
Ditto weath caulkers as before people empd cutting the ice without the ship.
April 17, 1770 Tuesday ENE, ESE

Ditto weath. caulkers Empd caulking the ship. Ships company empd as before.

April 18, 1770 Wednesday ESE, var.

Mod. weath Employd as before Ice & snow going fast from the ship.

*April 19, 1770 to April 24, 1770

April 25, 1770 Wednesday W

Fresh airs & cloudy weath Empd variously Punished George Davis with 12 lashes for neglect of duty & going on shore without leave.

April 26, 1770 Thursday var.

PM mod. weath hard frost empd cutting away the ice.

April 27, 1770 Friday do.

Fresh breezes & cloudy with rain at 7 AM hauled the ships stem about ½ a cable length out the draught of water 9 foot 10 in. Aft 8 ft 10 in. forward.

April 28, 1770 Saturday ESE

Ditto weath Empd heaving off the ship Broke the capstan Carpenter empd mending do. Graple do. hoisting the iron ballast on board.

The Canceasux was equipped with a capstan and a windlass which were used for heavy pulling of ground tackle and elements of the rigging (see ship plan). The log entries reflects that the ship had difficulty with the capstan and windlass frequently.

April 29, 1770 Sunday WSW

Fresh breezes with rain Carpenter Empd making Bilge ways to free air the ship. People Empd making room for iron ballast on board. AM came in here a small sloop that had wintered on the south side of the river this morning was the highest tide we have had these springs it being the third day the changes being most part of the ice as drove out of the cove.

April 30, 1770 Monday do.

Fresh breezes with thick haze intermixed with drizling rain Carpenters Empd fixing in the bilge ways The ship people Empd variously.

May 1, 1770 Tuesday var.

Fresh gales with frost this forenoon at high water the ice before & above Quebec broke up & came down in great quantities

Carpenters Employd repairing the capstan ships company empd getting the iron ballast in Read the articles of war & abstract of Parliament to the ships company.

May 2, 1770 Wednesday var.

Anchored in St. Patricks Hole

Mod. & fair Caulkers & carpenters Empd about the boats People employd getting in the shingle ballast.

May 3, 1770 Thursday WSW

Mod. weath caulkers Empd as before sail maker Employd mending the jibb & main top mast stay sail. People empd as before.

May 4, 1770 Friday var.

Mod. weath caulkers & carpenters as before sail maker as before People Empd as before a great deal of drift ice in the river.

May 5, 1770 Saturday do.

Ditto weath caulkers & carpenters empd as before sailmaker as before People empd getting the top sail yards great quantities of drift Ice in the river.

May 6, 1770 Sunday do., NE

Mod. weath AM fresh gales with dark cloudy weath & rain not so much drift ice as yesterday.

May 7, 1770 Monday NE

Fresh gales with rain little drift ice in the river Sail maker empd as before cut up the fore courses for hammocks for the ships company being most of them rotten & decayed.

May 8, 1770 Tuesday ENE

Fresh gales & fair caulkers & sail makers Empd as before ships company Empd variously little drift ice in the river.

May 9, 1770 Wednesday ENE

Ditto weath caulkers employed breaming & paying one side of the ships bottom with patch of tar sail maker Empd making sails, tents and marks for the use of the Surveyors on board. All the drift ice gone.

May 10, 1770 Thursday NE

Ditto weather caulkers Empd breaming & paying the other of the ship as before.

Breaming consisting of removal and burning of the stuff which is collected on the ship's bottom during a long voyage according to Darcy Leaver in his Lever's Young Sea Officer's Sheet Anchor.

May 11, 1770 Friday do.

Off on stream

Weath do. Bent the top sails at 8 PM hauled the ship out in the stream do. came too with the Bt. Br. in 9 fath at low water.

May 12, 1770 Saturday var.

Ditto & fair Empd bendng the remainder of the sails caulkers empd about the boats sail makers empd as before.

May 13, 1770 Sunday ENE

PM light airs & var. AM fresh gales & clear.

May 14, 1770 Monday var.

Mod. weath AM lightening var. caulkers & sail makers Empd as before.

May 15, 1770 Tuesday do.

Mod. & fair Empd staying the lower sails & setting up the rigging fore & aft. Reeved several lanyards to the fore & main shrouds the old decayed & unfit for service.

May 16, 1770 Wednesday do, NE

Fresh airs & var. Empd scraping the sides & paying them with oyl of turpentine.

May 17, 1770 Thursday var., ENE

PM cloudy weath with some thunder & lightening Empd getting on board wood &.

May 18, 1770 Friday ENE

Fresh breezes with dark cloudy weath Thunder lightening & rain at times.

May 19, 1770 Saturday var.

Ditto weather AM mod. & fair Empd. scraping the lower masts & pay'd them with oyl of turpentine.

May 20, 1770 Sunday do.

Turning up to Quebec & clear ½ past 10 AM unmoored ship at at 11 weighed & came to sail Employd turning up the ship at Noon W Point of Orleans NW ½ N part Livy Church S b E ½ E.

May 21, 1770 Monday do.

Moored off Quebec

Light airs & variable Empd as before ½ past 4 PM came too with the best bower in 18 fm at 2/3 of a cable Citadel bearing SW Point Levy Church E ½ S at 3 AM weighed & came to sail with the tide at 10 moored ship a cable each way best bower NE b N small do. S Citadel SW b W one cable length from the N. corner of the King's wharf.

May 22, 1770 Tuesday do.

Ditto weather Empd squaring the ratlings fore & aft.

May 23, 1770 Wednesday do.

Gusty weath with thunder & rain Empd variously.

May 24, 1770 Thursday var. E
Moored at Quebec
Ditto cloudy with some rain AM fresh gales & AM at 10 do. down top gallant yards Employed variously Ditto sailed by us a ship from London to Montreal.
May 25, 1770 Friday ENE
Fresh gales & squally with some rain Employed variously.
May 26, 1770 Saturday E
Ditto weath PM came in here the ship *Quebec* Bourhe Master from London Empd taking on board some of Capt. Holland baggage.
May 27, 1770 Sunday var.
Fresh gales & var. with some thunder & rain AM more moderate Employd variously.
May 28, 1770 Monday ESE
Fresh gales & cloudy Employd taking on board baggage belonging to the surveyors.
May 29, 1770 Tuesday ENE
Fresh gales & cloudy with rain at times at 9 AM found the ship Draught has brought both cables ahead do. began haul up the small bower at 10 got up do. bower & began to heave up best bower ½ past 11 had hove a part when a larger brigg came on board of us and carried away all the starboard quarter gallery, Quarter deck rails rigging sails laniards of the mizen & shrouds main braces mizen vang & halliards.
May 30, 1770 Wednesday E
Hard gales & squally at ½ past 1 got clear of the brigg who lost one anchor & cable sprit sail yard jibb boom head & part of head. Being a weather lids hove up the best bower at 5 do. came too with the best bower ? round a cable each way the citadel W b S, N corner of the Kings Wharf NW b W 1 ½ cables ? from the Kings Wharf.
May 31, 1770 Thursday var.
Mod & clear weath loosd sails to dry Employd taking on board baggage at Noon furled sails carpenters employd repairing galley & quarter deck rails do found the main top gallant yard Rotten & decayed do. found the main mast much decayed at the after part above cap.
June 1, 1770 Friday do., ENE
Moderate breezes & variable AM fresh gales with rain at times Carpenters Empd as before ships company variously.
June 2, 1770 Saturday NE
Fresh breezes & cloudy carpenters empd as before & making

a top gallant yard People Employed taking on board provisions. Read the articles of War & new abstract of Parliament to the ships company.

June 3, 1770 Sunday var.

Fresh gales & cloudy came in here a snow from London for Montreal Smith Master & a schooner from the West Indies. Scaled the guns fore and aft.

June 4, 1770 Monday do.

Ditto weath cloudy Carpenters Empd as before People got the new main top gallant yard on board do. got up the top gallant yard. Fired 21 guns it being the kings Birthday.

June 5, 1770 Tuesday do.

Ditto weather AM came in here a brigg & a sloop from New York carpenters Empd as before.

June 6, 1770 Wednesday NNE

Gales & rain with thunder & lightening got down top gallant yards.

June 7, 1770 Thursday SSW

Fresh gales & cloudy winds var. Empd taking on board baggage came in here 2 schooners with rum from Boston.

June 8, 1770 Friday NW

Weath moderate Carpenters empd as before.

June 9, 1770 Saturday var.

Mod. & clear Empd as before.

June 10, 1770 Sunday ENE

Mod. & cloudy with rain at times.

June 11, 1770 Monday ENE, E

Ditto weath came in here a sloop & schooner from Boston Empd variously.

June 12, 1770 Tuesday var.

Moderate AM loosed sails to dry got up top gallant yards Empd variously.

June 13, 1770 Wednesday ESE

Moored at Quebec

Fresh breezes & clear AM clear weath recd on board the following species of provisions Viz 12657 pounds fresh beef 11020 pieces salt do, 420 pieces pork 630 pieces salt do, pease 10 ½ bushels raisen 12 gals., 1093 pounds beer 35 tons 2 gall, vinegar 100 gall. Empd hoisting in do. provisions.

June 14, 1770 Thursday ENE

Fresh gales & cloudy ½ past came in here His Majestys ship *Rose* and *St. John* armed schooner from Boston

June 15, 1770 Friday var.

Fresh gales AM moderate at 8 do. got up top gallt yards at 9 do. began to unmoor at 10 got up the small bower anchor & hove up the B. B. & came to sail came on board the Surveyor General & all his deputies with their baggage.

June 16, 1770 Saturday do.
Anchored at St. Patricks Hole
Light airs & variable ½ past 2 mod. came too with the best bower in 111 ½ fm at ½ past 4 weighed and came to sail with the *Rose* and *St. John* at Quebec with several merchant vessels at 10 do. came too with the best bower in 10 ½ fm soft bottom. Saw on the south shore bearings S. St. Lawrence Church E.

June 17, 1770 Sunday do.
Mod airs & cloudy AM heavy rains & dark cloudy weath fired 3 shott at & brought too one brigg & 2 sloops from New York for Quebec with provisions.

June 18, 1770 Monday do.
Fresh airs & clear weath

June 19, 1770 Tuesday do.
Cloudy with hard squalls thunder lightening & rain.

June 20, 1770 Wednesday do.
Fresh airs & var. Empd getting on board spruce beer & water at 8 AM unmoored ship & hove short on the best bower.

June 21, 1770 Thursday do.
Cape Goose NNE 2 leagues
Fair & cloudy with rain at times ½ past 3 weighed & came to sail at 4 St. John Church NNW 4 ½ mile. ½ past 9 came too with the best bower in 9 fath soft bottom off the Marshe Island ¼ mile from the shore at 9 AM weighed and came to sail at 10 do. going over the S traverse found it very irregular at Noon Cape Goose NNE 2 leagues.

June 22, 1770 Friday do.
Anchored under Star Island
Strong gales & squally at 9 do. came too with the Best Bower in 18 fm soft bottom under Hare Island & Pilgrim SSW Brandy Pott ENE dist off shore 3 ½ mi. past by a brigg & sloop for Quebec with provisions from Boston & New York AM more mod & fair.

June 23, 1770 Saturday NE, W, SW
Anchored at Bic Island
Moderate & clear at 3 sett weighed & came to sail ½ past 5 Red Island NNW 2 ½ m. at 8 came too in 23 fm soft bottom Bic Island E b N ½ N at end of Barque Island SW b S at 6 AM weighed &

came to sail at 10 do. Anchored in 7 fm soft bottom opposite the Wood & watering place fired 2 shott & brought too a brigg from Glasgow to Quebec with merchandize.

June 24, 1770 Sunday var.
Fresh gales & squally with heavy rain Mid part very hard squalls with rain AM more mod with thick fogg got on board a boat load of water fired 2 shott & brought too a sloop from the Grenadines bound to Quebec.

June 25, 1770 Monday do.
Light airs & thick fogg at 3 PM weighed & came to sail at 4 cleard up Barnaby SW further point ESE dist. off shore 3 PM ENE at 8 PM Mount Camille SE b S at 6 AM Cape Chat E ½ S 7 or 8 leagues do. set steering sails at 10 landed one of the Surveyors about 2 ½ leagues to the W'ward of Cape Chat to make some observations

June 26, 1770 Tuesday WSW
Cape Rozier SE ½, 1 ½ leagues.
Mid part fresh breezes & clear latter light airs & cloudy at 2 PM came on board the boat with the surveyors set sail & stood for the N shore at 9 ? Cape Peter Bou W b S ¾ S, Cape Chat SSE do. Bou away at 3 AM set sails at 4 Magdalen River S b E ½ E 2 ½ leagues at 8 do. fired 2 shott & brought too a snow from Boston bound to Quebec.

June 27, 1770 Wednesday var., calm, NNE
Bonaventure NE b N, 6 leagues
Fresh breezes & hazey with fogg at times found the current set to the Noward 2 ½ or 3 m. an hour at 8 PM in do down the top sails at 6 AM saw the land which proved to be Cape Rozier bearing SW b W 3 m. Cape Ferrillion SSW found a current set to the Northward all night at 8 Old Wife off Cape Ferrillion NNW 3 m. at 9 going through between shore & the island Percy set the driver & steering sails.

June 28. 1770 Thursday NE, calm, S b W
Etmost land in sight NW & sough most S b W
First part fresh gales & clear mid light breezes & cloudy latter do. breezes & hazey at 2 PM Island of Mescou WSW do. island NW fired 2 shott & brought too schooners proved to be 2 fishing vessels at 8 down steering sails sounded 25 fm sandy bottom.

June 29, 1770 Friday S, S b E
First & mid part fresh gales with rain latter fresh breezes & cloudy at 6 PM in 1st & 2d reefs fore & mizon sails & 2d reef main top sail down top gallant yards sounded 25 fath sandy bottom at 8

sounded 30 fath heavy swell from the Etward at 2 AM handed the fore top sail & out reefs there the main topsail at 8 handed the top sails under the fore sail & mizon do. sounded 35 fath at 10 set the top sails 7 let all reefs & top gallant yards.

June 30, 1770 Saturday NW b W, NW, N b W

The No. point of St. Johns Island NW b W 2 ½ lea. First part fresh breezes & clear Mid & latter fresh gales & clear at 2 PM saw the No. pt of St. John Island bearing 5 leagues at 6 King ship fired 2 shott & brought too a brigg bound to Boston at 8 No. point of do. Island WNW 3 at 9 ? ship at 10 in AM & & 2 reefs of the top sails and down top gallant yards ½ past 12 ship at 6 out reefs of the top sails at 11 bore away for the east point of St. Johns North point NW b W 2 ½ leagues at 9 got up top gallant yards & made sail.

July 1, 1770 Sunday NW, calm, ENE

Et. Point of St. Johns Island E 2 leagues

First and latter parts light breezes & clear mid do. breezes & cloudy at 8 PM shortened sail at 4 AM saw 3 schooners to the Eastward of us at 8 do. fired a shott & brought too a schooner from Boston bound to Quebec.

July 2, 1770 Monday var. S

Anchored at 7 Latter turning to windward at 8 PM came too with the stream anchor & cable in 23 fath. soft bottom East point St. Johns Island S b W at 4 AM weighed & came to sail at 8 East point of do. Island W b S.

July 3, 1770 Tuesday SSE, SE

Breezes & fair at 11 turning head going into the three rivers SW b W Broughten Island WSW at 6 PM got into the three rivers and anchored in 5 fath water soft bottom Goose Neck point ESE 2 cables length fishing stage SE b S. AM hard gales & squally got down top gallant yards Read the articles of war and abstract of Parliment to the ships compy.

July 4, 1770 Wednesday SE, var.

Hard gales & squally weath with rain AM more mod. do. got up top gallant yards.

July 5, 1770 Thursday var.

Bear Cape WSW 2 miles

Moderate breezes & clear at 5 PM weighed and came to sail at 6 Panmure Head WSW ¼ mile at 8 Bear Cape WSW 2 miles do. anchored in 10 fath water bearing as before.

July 6, 1770 Friday do.

Anchored Bear Cape

PM fair at 3 AM weighed and came to sail Employd turning

windward and at 11 do. came too with the stream anchor and hawser in 21 fm soft bottom Wood Island WSW eastward of Pictou Island S b W Bear Cape NE.

July 7, 1770 Saturday SW, W, var.

Anchored at Port Harbour

Mod. & var. at 4 PM weighed and came to sail at east Wood Islands ENE 3 miles½ past 10 came too with best bower in 15 fath soft bottom Point Parim ? NNW 2 leagues at 6 AM weighed and came to sail at 9 PM E b S ½ past 10 Governors Island E ½ past 11 came too with the best bower in 11 fath soft bottom ? harbour Fort ? SW b S.

July 8, 1770 Sunday var.

Mod. & cloudy moored ship with the stream anchor & hawser.

July 9, 1770 Monday SW, NW

Breezes & squally with rain Employd fitting out the *Jupiter* schooner boat and two row boats for the surveying parties going out to survey the other parts of Nova Scotia.

July 10, 1770 Tuesday WNW, NW

Gales & squally with heavy rains at AM very hard squally Broke adrift one of the surveying whale boats and fitted having in her 2 sprit sails 2 mast five oars 1 grapling & rope 2 iron bound 10 gallon Keggs.& hook & one buoy line.

July 11, 1770 Wednesday var.

Squalls AM moderate & cloudy swayed up the lower yards & loosed sails to dry Empd variously do. with cutter and search of the whale boat at Noon furled sails. Supplied the *Jupiter* schooner boat with rope of all sizes, some canvas, twine and other gunning, carpenters stores for use of the survey.

July 12, 1770 Thursday do.

Hard breezes & var. PM returned the cutter with an account they had seen some pieces of the whale boat but no part of his caulking to be found.

July 13, 1770 Friday var.

Moor'd in Port Harbour

Light airs & var. with dark cloudy weath Employed getting the surveying party ready for service being prepared to sett out the ships cutter to go in place of the whale boat that was lost.

July 14, 1770 Saturday do.

Mod & dark cloudy weath AM very hard gusts of wind all round the compass attended with heavy claps of thunder, lightening hail & rain came in and anchored here His Majesty's ship *Rose.*

July 15, 1770 Sunday do.

PM do weath AM moderate & clear loos'd sails to dry at Noon furled sails came in & anchored here His Majesty's schooner *St. John.*

July 16, 1770 Monday do.

Moderate & sultry hott weath Empd getting water on board the surveyors on shore making observations.

July 17, 1770 Tuesday do.

Fresh airs & cloudy weath Empd as before AM sailed hence His Majeaty's Ship *Rose* & *St. John* bound for Halifax.

July 18, 1770 Wednesday do., S, WSW

Wood Island NW 4 miles

Mod. Weath at 5 PM weighed & came to sail at 8 do. anchored in 9 fath water soft bottom East point of the land off Port Joy NNW Capt. Hollands house NW. At 6 weighed & came to sail saw a sloop in NW quarter fired 2 gun & brought too a sloop & schooner from New York bound to Quebec.

July 19, 1770 Thursday SW, WSW

Gut of Canso SE b E 2 ½ leagues

Mod. breezes & cloudy with rain At 3 PM Bear Cape N b W at 8 Cape Jervis SSW dist, 2 miles N entrance Gut SE ½ S at 11 PM anchored with the Bt Br in 21 fath soft mud Cape Lewis NW ½ N Gutt SE ½ S at 8 AM weighed & came to sail Gutt mouth SE b S 2 ½ leagues.

July 20, 1770 Friday var., SW, WNW

Anchored in Ship harbour

Light aire & var. at 4 do. Gutt entrance SE dist 3 miles ½ past 6 do. anchored with the Bt Br in 13 fm under the west shore at 8 weighed and came to sail at 10 anchored in 10 fath under Cape Mon then at 2 AM weighed and came to sail AM anchored in Staisles Paris Cove in 10 fath. at 9 weighed and came to sail at Noon anchored in 11 fath. in Ship Harbour fresh gales & squally with thunder lightening & rain.

July 21, 1770 Saturday SSE, W, NW

Anchored in the entrance of Douglas Bay

First part hard squalls with thunder lightening & rain AM hard gales with thick thick haze at 10 set 1st and 2d reefs of the top sails do weighed and came to sail found the Bt Br buoy of *Rose* was away by the Rooks and lost do lost out of the pinnace 2 at Noon came too with the best bower in 11 fath hard bottom in the entrance of Douglass Bay Southmost point of the Gutt of Canso south most Pt NW b W ½ miles from the sound fired a gun & brought too a brigg from the West Indies bound to Quebec with molasses.

July 22, 1770 Sunday NW b N

Going through the harbour

Fresh gales & squally at 9 AM weighed & came to sail.

July 23, 1770 Monday NW, W, SW b W

Cape Samborough S 72:00 W dist 30 leagues

First part fresh breezes & clear mid Mod with thick fogg latter do. & cloudy at 1 PM Old Harry Ledge 4 mile saw His Majesty's schooner *St. John* at 4 White Point N b E 3 leagues do. tacked (Tkd) at 6 Tkd point NW 4 mi at 9 Tkd Torban Point N b W 2 or 3 miles at 2 AM Tkd and up top gallant yard at 6 sounded with black soft mud at 8 Tkd at Noon sounded 80 faths.

July 24, 1770 Tuesday SW, W, WNW

First and mid parts light airs with fogg at times latter fresh gales & squally at 2 PM fired gun signal sounded 56 fath gray sand mixed with small stones at 5 fired a gun signal in a fogg at 7 sounded and 85 fm gray specks at 3 AM saw the land bearing from WNW to the NE b E saw the *St John* schooner at 7 PM fly all and clear the top sails up & hand them at 9 set the top sails.

July 25, 1770 Wednesday NW

Cape Samborough 10 or 11 leagues ? N 8.0 w do land 5 or 6 leagues Latter parts frsh breezes & clear mid light airs & clear at 4 PM Tkd at 5 joined company the schooner *St. John* at Braun Harbour NNE 2 ½ leagues at 9 AM fired a gun & brought too a schooner from Boston bound to Quebec.

July 26, 1770 Thursday SW b W, W b N, W b S

At Halifax

Fresh breezes & clear at 3 AM saw the light of Sambrough bearing W b N at 6 Sambrough head W 3 miles ½ past 10 saluted the commander with 15 guns at 11 anchord in the Halifax Harbour found lying here His Majesty's Ship *Ramesay* Commander Hood with the *Mermaid* & *Rose*.

July 27, 1770 Friday SW, W

Fresh gales & squally weath PM hauled along side the careening wharf AM carpenters Empd about side.

July 28, 1770 Saturday var.

Moderate & fair clear weath PM came in here His Majesty's Schooner *St. John* do struck the main mast People Employed variously.

July 29, 1770 Sunday do.

Fresh gales & cloudy.

July 30, 1770 Monday do.

Fresh and fine weath. A survey taken of the boats and stores.

July 31, 1770 Tuesday NW

Fresh breezes & foggy Empd returning decay'd stores.

Aug. 1, 1770 Wednesday NNW

Light breezes and clear AM came in His Majesty's sloop *Bonett* & ships company Empd variously.

Aug. 2, 1770 Thursday var.

Moderate and cloudy with rain AM came in His Majesty's schooner *St. Lawrence* Employd getting on board boatswains stores.

Aug. 3, 1770 Friday do.

Cloudy weath came in here two of His Majesty's ships *Deal Castle* & *Glasgow*. Empd variously.

Aug. 4, 1770 Saturday SW

Mod. & clear weath AM hauled off from the wharf Empd variously.

Aug. 5, 1770 Sunday var.

Fresh breezes & cloudy with rain Read the articles of war to the ships company.

Aug. 6, 1770 Monday SW, SSW

Fresh breezes & hazey Employd getting on board carpenters & boatswains stores.

Aug. 7, 1770 Tuesday NW

Divels Island east of Cape Sambro SW

Mod weather with heavy rain ½ past 9 AM cleared up do. sailed hence His Majesty's ship *Mermaid* and at 10 weighed & came to sail.

Aug. 8, 1770 Wednesday W, var.

Sambro light house E b N 3 leagues.

First part fresh breezes & hazey mid & latter small breezes & clear at 1 PM in 1st reef of the top, came up with us the *Young Canadian* at 4 past by one of His Majesty's sloops of war going into harbour came on board a pilot for this & New England coast at 8 light House bearing W b N 4 or 5 leagues at mid light house NNW at 4 AM worked ship & out reefs of the top sails Several sloops in sight.

Aug. 9. 1770 Thursday SW b W, calm, SW

Fresh breezes & clear at 1 PM the High Land of Ashepitegan WNW½ N at 8 lost sight of land at 4 saw the high land of St. Nau Bussing NNE 9 or 10 leagues Saw a sloop standing to the westward fired 2 shott & brought too a sloop from Halifax to New York.

Aug. 10, 1770 Friday SW b W, calm
Anchored in Liverpool Harb.
First and middle parts fresh breezy & clear latter light airs intermixed with calm at 2 PM saw entrance of Liverpool Harbour at 4 fired 6 guns a signal for Mr. Des Barres surveying schooner come into Liverpool Harbour at 8 anchored with the best bower in 14 fm water sandy bottom head of this harbour S b W ½ W Coffins Island E ½ S at 5 AM weighed & came to sail Empd hauling the ship up the harbor at 11 anchored with the best bower in 11 fath at low water Point West shore S 30 Epoint on the eastern shore Eastern 30 South found Mr. Des Bares with two Survey schooners one large cutter with his parties.
Aug. 11, 1770 Saturday SW
Fresh gales & clear Employd getting on board wood & water.
Aug. 12, 1770 Sunday W, calm, SW
In Liverpool Harbour
First part fresh gales & cloudy Mid calm latter fresh gales & clear Empd as before.
Aug. 13, 1770 Monday var.
Cape Negro W dist. 9 miles
First part light airs & var. with heavy rains Mid calm latter fresh breezes & cloudy weighed and came to sail fired 2 shott & brought too a brigg from Newfoundland. bound to New York with ballast & fish departed from the latitude of 44,04 N at 8 PM Island NNW dist. 2 miles at Noon Observd & found the latitude to be 43.37 Cape bearing S ½ 6.00 W dist. 9 miles which makes the Latitude of Cape Negro to be 44.31 N
Aug. 14, 1770 Tuesday NW b W, WNW
First part fresh gales & clear mid and latter fresh breezes & clear at 2 PM Cape Negro N b W ½ W abreast 6 miles in1st reef of the top sails at 5 Tkd Cape Negro N ½ E 3 or 4 mile at 7 westernmost in sight S 55 Wt at 8 Cape Negro NNW 5 or 6 leagues Suns Magnitick Amplitude N 82 E at 8 AM top sail vessel standing to the Eastward at 9 Tkd sounded 58 fath gray sand mixed small black stones.
Aug. 15, 1770 Wednesday SW b W, ESE, ENE
First and middle parts light airs & cloudy latter fresh gales with haze & rain at 10 PM sounded with gray sand mixt with small black stones at 12 sounded 30 fath at 1 sounded 36 fath soft bottom at 6 AM saw a ship in the NW quarter do. hauld up & gave chase at 8 fired 4 guns brought too a sloop from Falmouth bound for Halifax.

Aug. 16, 1770 Thursday ENE, NW b W, N
First part do. weath mid and latter light & clear at 1 PM in 1st reef of the topsails sounded 96 fath muddy bottom at 6 AM out reefs at 8 Tkd ship.

Aug. 17, 1770 Friday SW b W, SSW, SSE
Bone Island S b E ½ E, Nuble Island SW b W 4 or 5 miles.
First and latter parts fresh breezes & clear Mid fresh gales& hazey at 9 PM in 1st and 2d reefs top sails fired 2 guns & brought too a schooner from the West Indies bound to Boston in 3d reefs of the top sails at 5 AM out reefs of the top sails saw the land bearing SW b W dist. off shore 3 or 4 leagues at 9 Tkd ship.

Aug. 18, 1770 Saturday S b E, SE b E
Anchored in Piscataqua River
Light airs & var. at 2 PM Tkd ship at 4 Tkd carried through this channel from 16 to 6.5 ½ and rocky bottom at 7 got into Piscataway Harbour & came too with the best bower in 10 fm water hard bottom flag staff on the fort SSE church steeple on the island side SSW church on the Kittery side NW b N.

Aug. 19 1770 Sunday WNW
First part foggy past by one ship & brigg for London sailed from hence three schooners

Aug. 20, 1770 Monday var.
Mod. & clear AM thick hazey weather with rain at times Loosed sails to dry.

Aug. 21. 1770 Tuesday do.
Fresh gales with rain at times employd landing the Surveyor Generals baggage.

Aug. 22, 1770 Wednesday ESE
Mod. & fair weather Empd as before came in here a brigg & sloop from the West Indies began loading rum for the ships company.

Aug. 23, 1770 Thursday NNW
Fresh breezes & clear Empd as before sailed from hence a ship & brigg for England.

Aug. 24, 1770 Friday do.
Moderate & cloudy with some rain Employd fitting out a surveying party to go eastward sailed hence His Majesty's armed schooner *Halifax* for Boston.

Aug. 25, 1770 Saturday SW
Moored in Piscataqua
Fresh breezes & clear Empd as before came in & anchored here 2 brigs.

Aug. 26, 1770 Sunday SW
Fresh gales & cloudy Punished James Swanson seaman with 12 lashes for drunkeness and mutinous expressions.
Aug. 27, 1770 Monday do.
Moderate & fair weather Employd setting out a party with boats stores provisions & empd watering the ship & drying sails.
Aug. 28, 1770 Tuesday do.
Ditto weather Punished Alexander Andinon with 12 lashes drunkenness & misbehavior
Aug. 29, 1770 Wednesday W
Fresh breezes & clear AM sailed hence Mr. Sproule with his party for Canso Bay in order to begin his survey having provisions stores & for 9 months employd completing work of Captain Holland with provisions stores & for the same time.
Aug. 30, 1770 Thursday var.
Light airs & var. Employd as before.
Aug. 31, 1770 Friday SW b S
Fresh breezes & clear Employd variously.
Sept. 1, 1770 Saturday SE b S
Ditto weath came in here a brigg and a sloop from the West Indies
Sept. 2, 1770 Sunday SSE
Ditto weath Employd getting on board wood & water Read the articles of War to the ships company.
Sept. 3, 1770 Monday var., calm, SSE
Fresh airs & var at 5 AM unmoored ship at 7 weighed & came to sail Star Island bearing SSE this island is one of the Isle of Shoals Observd the Latitude to be 43.3 N which the Entrance Piscataqua is far down the Best Daughts 20 miles to the Northward of whence it is.
Sept. 4, 1770 Tuesday S b E
Mod. breezes & hazey with fogg at times 2 PM Star Island SW b W 1 ½ leagues Bone Island 2 v½ E 2 leagues at 3 Star Island W ½ S 5 leagues at 6 Cape Ann SW ½ S.
Sept. 5, 1770 Wednesday SW, W b N
Cape Sable NE ½ E dist. 3 leagues.
Mod. breezes & hazey with thick fogg at 9 AM saw the land bearing from the N to the dist about 7 leagues.
Sept. 6, 1770 Thursday NNE, NNW
Sambro Head NE b N 3 miles.
First part fresh gales & clear mid mod & clear latter fresh gales & squally at 2 PM Cape Negro dist. 2 ½ leagues ½ past 6 lay too at

7 made sail at 8 lost sight of land, 5 AM saw the land of Cape Sambro N b W at 6 Sambro light house NE 7 leagues at 10 Sambro light house N b W 1 ½. In 1st reef of the top sails Sambro head NE b N 3 mi. at Noon turning into Halifax harbour.

Sept. 7, 1770 Friday NNW, NNE
Turning into Halifax
Fresh gales and squally Employd turning into Halifax Harbour.

Sept. 8, 1770 Saturday var.
Alongside the Kings Wharf
Fresh gales & clear Employd at before at 8 came too with the best bower in 10 fath. in Major Beach AM more mod at 6 weighed & came to sail Employd as before at 10 got in the dock yard along side the wharf His Majesty's ship *Romney* & *Dial Castle* here.

Sept. 9, 1770 Sunday do.
Light aire & var. Empd landing some of the ships stores such as anchors & cables.

Sept. 10, 1770 Monday do.
Fresh breezes & fair weath Empd taking on board Kings stores & surveyors baggage.

Sept. 11, 1770 Tuesday do.
Fair weath Empd taking on board provisions & water & at Noon hauled from the wharf in here His majesty's ship *Boston.*

Sept. 12, 1770 Wednesday N, NW, S
Anchored in harbour Georges Island
Ditto weath Empd as before received on board 18 invalids from the hospital belonging to different ships and 19 invalids belonging to different regiments at 6 weighed & came to sail as did His Majesty's ship *Deal Castle* came too in 13 fath without Georges Island as did the *Deal Castle.*

Sept. 13, 1770 Thursday S, NW
Cape Sambro light house SW distance 6 miles.
Light airs & var. at 5 AM weighed & came to sail as did the *Deal Castle* at Noon lost sight of the *Deal.*

Sept. 14, 1770 Friday E
First parts Mod & cloudy with some lightening latter fresh gales at 4 PM Sambro light house WNW at shortened the fore & mizon top sails.

Sept. 15, 1770 Saturday E b N, E b S
First and mid parts fresh gales & squally with rain at times latter more mod & cloudy at 2 PM hauled in fore sail & lay too under the main mast at 11 hauled up the main sail & lay to under the

mizon at 6 set the main sail & set it at 9 balanced the mizon at 8 AM set the fore sail at 10 set the Main top.

Sept. 16, 1770 Sunday E

Cape Samborough N b E 38 2/3 leagues.

First and mid parts more mod & hazey with fogg at times latter light airs & clear a great swale from west was heard at 9 AM move ship & set the fore & mizon top sails do. out all reefs of the top sails and main sail at Noon up top gallant yards.

Sept. 17, 1770 Monday SE, E, calm

Fresh breezes & cloudy with rain at times at 6 PM in 1st and 2d reefs of the top sails & down top gallant move ships head all round compass at 8 AM fath gray fine sand.

Sept. 18, 1770 Tuesday N b E, W, WSW

Fresh weath at 2 PM out reefs of the top sails and up top gallant yards at 5 AM set steering sails at 11 saw ships in the southern quarter and standing to the eastward & the other together northward

Sept. 19, 1770 Wednesday SW, W b N, N b W

First part do. weath mid & latter fresh gales & squally at 6 PM down steering sails at Midday clear ruff up sails & handed mizon do. at 6 AM spoke two sloops from New Foundland bound to Boston.

Sept. 20, 1770 Thursday NW b N, var.

Fresh gales & clear with lightning at times at 6 PM shortened sail at 5 AM made sail a swell passed.

Sept. 21, 1770 Friday W b N, W

First and latter parts do. weath mod & fair at 6 PM shortened sail at 6 AM saw 2 sail to the westward spotted a schooner from Marblehead bound to the Grand Bank.

Sept 22, 1770 Saturday SW, S, calm

Gales & cloudy at 6 PM shortened sail & in 1st reef both top sails at 6 AM out reefs of the sails at 8 sounded 42 fath gray sand take the ?

Sept. 23 1770 Sunday calm, SSW

Cloudy with fogg at times at 3 PM hove too with the top sails to the west Ships head to the west and ½ past 3 sail at 7 in 1st reefs of the top sails at 9 am set steering sails saw a ship in the SE quarter.

Sept. 24, 1770 Monday WSW, W b N, WSW

First and mid parts Do weath latter fresh breezes & thick fogg at 1 PM fired 2 guns shotted & brought too a ship from Bordeau bound to St. Peter Island at 11 sounded 31 fath course gray sand mixed with small stones at 3 AM sounded 28 fath gray sand at 6 set main sails.

Sept. 25, 1770 Tuesday W b S, WNW

First do. weath mid fresh gales & squally latter do. gales & strong squalls at 6 PM carried away the main top sail steering sail bent reefs the fore & mizon top sails & handed them & on reef all top sails as 8 AM in 3rd main T.S: & handed and ? the close reef F. F. sail fore sail & fore stay sail.

Sept. 26, 1770 Wednesday NW, NNW

At 1 PM split the fore stay sail, sail maker Empd mending it at 8 AM reefs the fore sail at 10 set fore top sail under the fore sail sprit sail & fore stay sail.

Sept. 27, 1770 Thursday NE, N

Cape Sambrough N 89.25 W 32.15

Is part fresh gales & squally with rain mid Mod latter fresh breezes & clear at 11 PM reefd main sail & set it ½ past 5 handed the fore sail & lay too under the main sail at 10 set the fore sail at 6 AM set the top sails at 8 out reef s of the fore & Main sail at 9 out 3 do. & 2 d reef of the sails.

Sept. 28, 1770 Friday NE b E, calm, S b E

Fresh breezes & cloudy at 6 PM in 1st reefs of the top sails at 6 AM out reefs & up top gallant yards bent the fore stay sail.

Sept 29, 1770 Saturday SSW, S b E

Cape Samborough 37 leagues

First and latter parts fresh breezes & cloudy Mid strong gales with rain at 6 PM in 1 and 2 reefs. Top sails at 11 handed the mizon top sail at 12 handed the main sail & main top sail split the stay sail sailmaker employed mending it at 8 AM got down top gallant yard at 9 set the fore top sail at noon let the fore & main top sails.

Sept. 30, 1770 Sunday NW, N b E

Fresh breezes & squally with rain at times a great sea from the southward at 1 PM out reefs top sails at 6 close reefs the fore top sail and in 1st & 2d reefs main top sail 8 AM out all reefs.

Oct. 1, 1770 Monday N b E, N

Fresh gales & cloudy at 6 PM close reeft the top sails 8 out reefs of the top sails at 2 split the main top mast stay sail at 7 AM saw a schooner in the SE quarter standing to eastward at Noon out 2d reef of the fore top sail.

Oct. 2, 1770 Tuesday NW b N

First and mid parts do. weath latter more mod a great swell form the northward at 6 PM post a logg with 3 lines in 2d & 3d reefs of the top sails & handed mizon do. at 8 handed the Main sail at 6 made sail out 3d reefs of the top sails & set the mizon top sail & main sail at 7 out 2d reef of the top sails.

Oct. 3, 1770 Wednesday NW b W

1st part fresh gales & cloudy mid & latter light airs & ver. with some rain at 6 PM in 1st & 2d reef of the top sails at 6 AM out reefs at 10 up top gallant yards.

Oct. 4, 1770 Thursday WSW, W

Fresh breezes & cloudy at 8 PM in 1st and 2d reefs of the top sails at 5 AM set steering sails & 1st reef for top sail.

Oct. 5, 1770 Friday WSW

PM saw a ship in the E quarter at 7 PM bow away to speak the ship fired 2 guns at the ship at 1 AM fired a gun & brought too the ship two vessels from N. Carolina bound to Glasgow. AM a great swell from the NNW.

Oct. 6, 1770 Saturday SW b S

Cloudy with a swell from the NW at 2 AM in 1st and 2d reef of the top sails at 6 saw 2 sails in the E quarter & one in the southern quarter fired 4 guns & brought too a ship from Virginia bound to Spain. Out reefs of the top sails & set steering sails.

Oct. 7, 1770 Sunday S, SSW

Mild do. weath mod & later fresh breezes & hazey at 6 PM in 1st & 2d reefs of the top sails PM out 2d reef main top sail.

Oct. 8, 1770 Monday S b W

Fresh breezes & hazey with rain at times at 4 AM out 1st reef of the top sails do let the fore steering sail and down at 8 AM saw a sail in the southern quarter and to the eastward do. saw a sail in the west quarter at 3 PM first sight of land to the southward.

Oct. 9, 1770 Tuesday SW, SSW, S

Fresh breezes & hazey at 4 PM spoke a brigg from the Banks of New Foundland bound Havre de Grace at 6 hove too & sounded and ground at 160 fm of line in 1st reef fore top sail AM sounded 75 fm gray sand at Noon saw a sail to the southward standing to the westward.

Oct. 10, 1770 Wednesday SSW

Fresh breezes & cloudy with haze at 4 PM sounded 60 fm fine gray sand saw 2 sail to the eastward the ship *Renown* & a small schooner in company from Liverpool bound to Guinia in 2d & 3d reef top sail & down top gallant yards at mid sounded 75 fm fine white sand at 4 AM out 3d & 2d reefs from top sails & up top gallant yards sounded 72 fm with white sand.

Oct. 11, 1770 Thursday N b E, WNW

Berry Head ESE
Fresh & hazy with rain ½ past 2 PM close reefs the top sails brought too & sounded 55 fath white sand saw the land bearing NE b N 4 or 5 leagues which proved to be the Island of Scilly at 4 leagues bearing NNW ½ E 3 leagues Down top gallant yards at 6 out 3 reef of the top sails at 1 AM light bearing N b W 5 or 6 leagues at 6 out all reefs & up top gallant yards & SW sails the Dead Man NW 7 leagues the Eastern Point ENE 3 leagues at 10 Mast Point E b N ? NW b N Ram Head NE b E 5 leagues.

Oct. 12, 1770 Friday W b N, W b S

Fresh gales & squally at 4 PM W b N 11 league Berry Head N b E at 6 in 1st reef of the top sails and the main sail at 9 Portland light ENE 5 or 6 leagues at mid do. light NW b N 4 leagues. AM lay too main top sail to the mast at 11 Puirill Point
NNE 4 leagues ½ past wore ship Point S 2 ½ cable length past lower road & found His Majesty's sloop *Speg* ? at an anchor with several merchant vessels.

The Canceaux returned to England with sick soldiers and to undergo repairs in the shipyard at Woolrich, England.

Oct. 13, 1770 Saturday WSW, SW

Giteeker NW & South sea E b N
Fresh gales & squally at 1 PM came too with the best bower on the Mather Bank in 3 ½ fath water soft bottom at 11 do. weighed & came to sail ½ past saluted the Admiral with 13 guns in loading the gun one seaman was shott & fell overboard & was drownd found lying here His Majesty's ship *Achilles* Admiral Grasy with the *Centaur*, *Bellona*, *Stagyil*, ? *St. Antonio*, *Rippon* and *Mercury*, at came too at Spithead in 7 fm water.

Oct. 14, 1770 Sunday SW b W

Gales & cloudy sent on these all the invalid soldiers. Employd variously.

Oct. 15, 1770 Monday SSE, SW

First and latter parts Mod & cloudy mid hard gales & squally at 6 AM struck yards & topmasts and top gallants a signal.

Oct. 16, 1770 Tuesday SSE

Gales & squally with rain AM sailed hence His Majesty's ship (not named) .

Oct. 17, 1770 Wednesday

Moderate & cloudy with rain anchored here an westward bound Dutch East India man.

Oct. 18, 1770 Thursday
Gales with heavy rain at times AM got up yards & top masts Anchored here His Majesty's ship *Bellisle*. Employd variously.
Oct. 19, 1770 Friday
Ditto weath PM down yards & top masts received on board Hhds of beer containing 414 gallons.
Oct. 20, 1770 Saturday
Moderate & clear AM got up yards & top masts received on board 180 pounds of fresh beef for the use of the ships company.
Oct. 21, 1770 Sunday var.
Fresh gales & squally with rain down yards & top masts.
Oct. 22, 1770 Monday SSE, SSW
First part moderate & cloudy with rain and calm & clear latter strong gales & squally & heavy rains.
Oct. 23, 1770 Tuesday SW, var. WNW
First and mid parts do. weath latter more mod & cloudy AM up yards & top masts and loosed sails to dry at Noon furld sails Received on board 111 pounds of fresh beef for the use of the ships company.
Oct. 24, 1770 Wednesday var.
Moderate & cloudy with rain Employd variously fired 15 guns as did all the fleet on the occasion of the Admiral shifting his flag to Vice of the Red.
Oct. 25, 1770 Thursday S, NW
Fresh gales & squally with rain employd variously.
Oct. 26, 1770 Friday var.
Cloudy with rain got up yards and top mast anchord here His Majesty's ship (not listed) from the West Indies.
Oct. 27, 1770 Saturday WSW
Fresh breezes & cloudy with rain Employd variously.
Oct. 28, 1770 Sunday var.
Fresh breezes & cloudy with heavy rains AM Admiral Giary shifted his flag on board *St. Antonio* at 8 unmoored at Noon weighed & came to sail.
Oct. 29, 1770 Monday SW, NW
Dover Castle N b w, town N b W 1 ½ mile
Fresh breezes & cloudy with rain at times at 1 PM standing off & on at 4 bow away through buoys ½ past 5 Dunnore W b S 5 leagues at 6 AM Beachy Head NNE 3 leagues at 10 NNE 1 mile fired 2 guns a signal for a pilot at Noon came on board a pilot.
Oct. 30, 1770 Tuesday NW, WNW

Anchored in the Downs
Gales & clear at 4 PM turning into the Downs found 3 Kings sloops at anchor in the little Downs in 6 fm with soft bottom at 6 AM weighed & came to sail. At 8 north Foreland NNW at 11 came too with the best bower in 8 fm water sandy bottom Foreland SE b S Margaret Church NW dist. off them 2 miles.

Oct. 31, 1770 Wednesday N b W
Gales & cloudy with rain at 6 PM weighed & came to sail at 9 anchored with the best bower of N. Foreland E b S.

Nov. 1, 1770 Thursday N
Gales & squally with rain PM veerd to a whole cable.

Nov. 2, 1770 Friday NNW, var.
First and mid parts do. weath latter more mod at 7 AM weighed & came to came to sail Employd turning to windward got through the Buoy's do. anchored in 5 fm water 16 feet at low water the buoy of the Spaniard SW ½ mile.

Nov. 3, 1770 Saturday do.
In the river.
Mod & fair at 2 PM anchored with the best bower in
11 ½ fm at 7 weighed & came to sail at 11 anchored off beach.

Nov. 4, 1770 Sunday
At 7 AM weighed & came to sail Employed turning to windward at Noon past by Gravesend.

Nov. 5, 1770 Monday
Anchored in Gallions Reach
At 3 PM anchored in long reach at 11 weighed & came to sail turning to windward at 2 anchored in Gallions Reach & steadied her with the stream anchor & hawsers.

Nov. 6, 1770 Tuesday var.
In Gallions Reach Fresh airs & drizling rain.

*Nov. 7, 1770 to Nov. 11, 1770

Nov. 12, 1770 Monday NW
First and latter parts Mod & cloudy mid hard gales with rain the ship brought home the stream anchor Came on board to carry the ship up to Woolwich.

Nov. 13, 1770 Tuesday WSW
Mod with rain.

Nov. 14, 1770 Wednesday SW
The AM came along side a vessel to carry the gunns & gunners stores Employd getting out the guns & stores out.

Nov. 15, 1770 Thursday var.
At Woolwich
Fresh gales & hazy with rain at 8 AM came on board a pilot to carry the ship to Woolwich do. shift the ship with cable & hove up & came to sail ½ past 11 hauled along side the *Ronouse* Frigate found laying here with His Majesty's ship *Trident & Captain.*
Nov. 16, 1770 Friday WSW
Fresh gales & cloudy with rain Empd returning the anchors & cables
Nov. 17, 1770 Saturday SW
Carpenter Empd unrigging the ship.

*Nov. 18, 1770 to Nov. 23, 1770

Nov. 24, 1770 Saturday WNW, var.
Employed unmooring the ship sent those of our people to sick quarters.

*Nov. 25, 1770 to Dec. 11, 1770

Dec. 12, 1770 Wednesday do., var. NW
Fresh airs the first part, the latter part fresh gales squally, the yawl broke adrift from the ship anchored.
Dec. 13, 1770 Thursday NW, calm
First part moderate weath the latter more moderate AM sent the people in search of the yawl.
Dec. 14, 1770 Friday var.
Mod. the first part, the latter fresh gales, our people employed on board the *Intrepid.*

*Dec. 15, 1770 to Dec. 19, 1770

Dec. 20, 1770 Thursday do.
Mat Lund, a midshipman and our men in the *Intrepid*.

*Dec. 21, 1770 to Dec. 30, 1770

Dec. 31, 1770 Monday var., ENE
Moderate cloudy the first part, the middle light airs with rain, the latter fresh gales and cloudy.

Canceaux Records

Expenses paid to:

Joseph Mansfield
James Main
John Churchhill
William Hogg
Joseph Gei ?
Daniel Jackson
J. Huntley
Jno Houre
P.M. Brock
M Johnston
Lawrence May
John Smith
? Becksjove
Jn Raisling
JC Hughs
Edw Read
JM Becks

Tickets & certificates made out on board of H.M.S. *Canseaux*

Name:	Reason:
Daniel Jackson	unsble
John Moore	Death
Wm Johnsten	Death
John Smith	Drownd
Alex Nesbet	Drownd
Lawrence Nay	Drownd
John Rawling	unsble
James Hughen	unable
Edward Reed	Sm: Pox

Jan. 1, 1771 Tuesday W

Moderate and fair weath Employed getting the ship clear for dock - received on board fresh beef for the ships company.

In February, A.S. Canceaux was moved to dock where her lines were taken off and the plans and drawings prepared.

*Jan. 2, 1771 to May 17, 1771

May 18, 1771 Saturday variable

Fresh breezes and clear weather Empd variously AM came on

board the master for William Hogg.

*May 19, 1771 to May 28, 1771

May 29, 1771 Wednesday W b N
Do breezes at 2 PM cast off and came to sail at 3 do, came too with the best bower in 5 fathom water in Gallins Reach the launch carried out the small bower and moored ship the Devils house WSW, Woolwich church steeple SW b W AM came along side the gun hoy with the guns and gunners stores. Do. employed hoisting them in.

May 30, 1771 Thursday WNW
Fresh gales and squally with rain at times Employed variously.

May 31, 1771 Friday variously
Do gales and clear weather Employed as before.

June 1, 1771 Saturday NW
Do gales and black clouds came on board a pilot to carry us down Read the articles of war and abstracts to the ships company.

June 2, 1771 Sunday variously
More mod at 6 AM began to unmoor, at 9 unmoored ship and hove short on the best bower scaled the guns and swivels.

June 3, 1771 Monday variable
Mod. and fair weather wind variable at 2 PM weighed and came to sail, at 3 under sail took in 16 ½ barrels of powder at 9 anchored in 7 fm soft bottom in sea reach at 5 weighed and came to sail, at 9 came too with the best bower in 8 fm water at the Nove soft bottom.

June 4, 1771 Tuesday variable
Slight breezes and variable at 11 AM discharged all the yachts men and received from the *Resolution* 15 seamen at Noon sailed.

June 5, 1771 Wednesday variable
Light airs and variable at 1 PM fired 21 guns as did the *Resolution* it being the Kings Birth Day at 5 came through the Nove at 9 anchored with the Bt Br in 9 fm water N. Forland SE b S at 6 weighed and came to sail at 11 anchored in the Downs with the best bower in 8 fathom water North foreland SW b S over castle NW, North Forland NNE.

June 6, 1771 Thursday variable
Light airs and clear weather at 10 AM weighed and came to sail Employed working to windward at Noon south Forland N b W ½ a mile.

June 7, 1771 Friday variable

Dover Castle NNE
Light airs and fine clear weather at 2 PM anchored in Dover Roade in 9 fathom water with the best bower south Forland ENE Dover Castle N ½ E dist. of shore about ½ a mile weighed and came to sail at 4 anchored with the stream anchor and cable in 16 fm water Dover Castle NE b N Folkstone N b E dist. off shore 4 or 5 miles at 10 weighed and came to sail - turning to windward Dover Castle NNE

June 8, 1771 Saturday
variable
Dunnore SW b W Culver Cliff 5 or 6 miles
First part cloudy weath middle and latter fresh breezes and clear weath at 5 PM came to with the stream anchor in 21 fms at 6 weighed and came to sail, at 7 let steering sails at 8 Dungeness Light N b E 3 miles, at 4 AM Beachy Head NE b E 6 0r 7 leagues - at Noon Dunmore SW b W Culver Cliff W b N 5 or 6 miles.

June 9, 1771 Sunday variable
Moored at Spithead - So. Sea Castle NE b E Gilkirken NNW
Light breezes and fair weath at 1 PM saluted Vice Admiral Pye of the Red aboard his Majesty's ship *Barfleur* with 15 guns do. came to at Spithead with the Bt. Br. in 8 fm water & moored ship with the stream anchor - So. Sea Castle NE b E Gilkecker NNW found here his Majesty's ships as follows *Balfleur*, *Captain*, *Admiral Montague*, *Lennos*, *Terrible*, *Egmont*, *Prudent*, *Worcester*, *Royal Oak* with several frigates & sloops.

June 10, 1771 Monday do.
Light airs and fair, at day light found six men run from the ship who had got onshore in some shore boat, the ships boats hoisted in - AM sent onshore 29 barrels in *Lennox's* longboat to be filled.

June 11, 1771 Tuesday do.
Light breezes at 2 PM the longboat came alongside with the water returned by do. 15 Hhds & 1 butt - at 8 AM Adm. Montague made the signal to unmoor, at 11 made a signal to weigh; ½ past do. weighed as did the *Tamur* and *Swann* Sloops; the *Canceaux* not having received the seamen in lieu of those run could not weigh at the same time.

June 12, 1771 Wednesday do.
Light airs and variable AM received 7 men from the *Terrible* and sent them onshore with an officer to receive their wages for the above ship - at 10 AM hove short lying waiting for the men -

Adm: Montague made the signal for sailing at St. Holems.

June 13, 1771 Thursday do.

At single anchor

Light airs and hazey at 2 AM received onboard 6 puncheons beer, recd. 3 Hhds: - at 3 weighed, at 4 the officer returned with the men, anchored with the Bt. Br. no wind, *Admiral* out of sight - at 6 weighed, at 7 anchored again it being very hazey, at 4 AM weighed hazey weath, at 7 anchored again - broke 12 handspikes and 2 barrs in heaving up the anchor at Spithead.

June 14, 1771 Friday W b S, W, NW b W

Light airs and hazey, foggy weath, at 1 AM weighed and came to sail, at Culver Cliff NW 6 or 7 PM - at ½ past 7 anchored with the stream anchor in 25 fms: Catherine Point NW ½ N 7 leagues - got down F.T.yards - at 12 weighed and came to sail, thick hazey weath - at 4 AM got up T.G. yards N 6 standing to the Southward in hopes of seeing the *Admiral.*

June 15, 1771 Saturday W b N, WNW, NW, N b W

Carkets SW b S dist 3 or 4 miles

First part mod. and hazey weath latter light airs and variable. at 2 PM saw 3 sail from the masthead in the SW Qr: which we supposed to be the *Admiral* - all sails set - at 7 Cape la Roque S b W & Isld of Alderrey SW 4 or 5 leagues - little wind the tide running very strong to the southward at 10 anchored with the stream anchor in 34 fm hard bottom at 12 weighed and came to sail, found one of the arms of the stream anchor gone. At 4 AM Caskets SSW at 8 Caskets S ½ E 3 or 4 mile very light airs & hazey weath no sight of the *Admiral.*

June 16, 1771 Sunday WNW, calm, variable

At anchor under Sark Island NE part of Do. Island NNW, and do. end WNW dist4 or 5 miles. First part light airs inclinable to calm, middle very hazey blowing a very hard gale - latter blowing hard with a very high sea - at 3 PM the tide running very strong to the SW anchored with the spare anchor and stream cable in 35 fms - Caskets bearing ESE 5 or 6 miles. At 10 the tide running very strong, veered out to a cable. At 1 AM the wind flew round to the NW, in heaving up the stream cable parted about 3 from the hawse - set the courses and lose reefd topsails - in tops sails the ship not being able to carry sail to clear Guernsey - bore away under the foresail at 6 AM anchored with the Bt Br in 31 fm under sail Island and veered to two cables, the gale still increasing and the sea running very high the NE and of Sark Island NNW, the Wt end of do. WNW at 4 or 5 miles - the westward end of Jersey S b W ½ W, at 9 struck topgallant masts to reef the foresail.

June 17, 1771 Monday NNW

Moored in St. Hilary Bay Island of Jersey Elizabeth Castle NNE, Norman pt. WNW do. off shore abt. 3 miles. First part blowing a violent storm of wind, with a very following sea, latter more mod. at 2 PM parted the Bt. Br. about 5 fms from the hawse reefed and set the foresail & bore away for Jersey, at 6 hauled round Norman Pt. ½ ? anchored with the small Br. in 20 fm. & veered out to a cable, let go the sheet anchor under foot struck yards & topmasts found in the road his Majs: Frigate *Glory*, at 8 AM fired 2 guns and made a signal for a boat. at 11 got 30 men from the *Glory* to assist us in getting under sail with our yards and topmasts & to get the ship further in shore.

June 18, 1771 Tuesday W

Anchored in St. Hilary Bay Elizabeth Castle ESE Norman Pt. W b S off shore abt 1 ½ mile.

These 24 hours, fresh gales and squally, at 3 PM set up the lower and topmasts rigging fore and aft at 6 hove up the sheet anchor and hove to ½ a cable on the small Br; at 9 weighed and turned the ship into a proper anchoring place at 11 anchored with the small Br. in 8 fm and veered to ½ a cable - Elizabeth Castle SE Norman Pt. W b S distant off shore abt. 1 mile & a half joined the small Br. cable much rubbed and cut with rocks, one place 7 fm from the anchor two strands cut. Cut the cable and new bent it.

June 19, 1771 Wednesday do.

These 24 hours fresh gales and thick hazy weath wind westerly PM sent onboard of the *Glory* by her own boats, six Hhds: of beer - AM people employed making points and gaskets.

June 20, 1771 Thursday variable

Light airs and hazey weath the wind variable Received from the *Glory* a stream cable and anchor and six handspikes.

June 21, 1771 Friday do.

Do. weath people empd making points & gaskets AM loosed sails to dry. At 11 AM weighed and came to sail.

June 22, 1771 Saturday NW

At single anchor Sark Island: SE 5 or 6 miles.

First part light breezes and clear, latter light airs at 6 PM fired a gun shotted to bring too a sloop - empd turning to windward at 4 AM brought Sark Island and the western end of Jersey to the same bearing as when the Bt. Br. cable parted, but could see nothing of the buoy at 9 AM anchored with the stream anchor to stop tide - Sark Island SE distant 5 or 6 mile.

June 23, 1771 Sunday variable, W

At single anchor

Light airs and variable at 4 PM weighed and came to sail, at 10 anchored to stop tide with the stream anchor in 35 fm at 4 AM weighed & came to sail, empd turning to windward at 11 anchored to stop tide.

June 24, 1771 Monday W, NNE

Guernsey SE b E dist abt. 8 leagues.

First part light airs inclinable to calm; latter light breezes & clear; at 6 AM weighed and came to to sail, at 1 AM anchored to stop tide, at 5 weighed & came to sail, in 1st reefs topsails & set topgallant sails, 10 cout 1st reefs topsails

June 25, 1771 Tuesday NE b N, N b E, NW

Lizard N 20:58 E dist 4 leagues.

First part mod and clear, latter fine pleasant weath at 11 PM the Eddystone light NW abt 5 leagues at 5 AM set steering sails & driver at Noon all sails set.

June 26, 1771 Wednesday E b N, E

Light breezes and fair weath at 3 PM bent the spritsail & spritsl topsail at 5 set maintop gallant steering sail at 3 AM set spritsail

June 27, 1771 Thursday E, N b W

First part mod breezes and fair weath middle fresh breezes & cloudy latter light airs and clear at 2 PM unbent the cables and stowed the anchors at 3 AM saw a sail in the SE 2 standing to the eastward at 8 hauled down the steerng sails.

June 28, 1771 Friday N, N b W, calm, SW b W, SW b S

First and middle parts light airs & cloudy inclinable to calm, latter light breezes and cloudy at 6 PM handed topgallant sails & reeft topsails at 7 AM out reefs topgallant & set topgallant sails.

June 29, 1771 Saturday variable

First part fresh breezes with showers or rain; latter light airs & cloudy at 1 PM fired 2 guns shotted and brought too the Brig *Fame*. Isle Derby Mn from Newbury 22 days passage at 3 PM in topgallant sail & spritsails topsail at 4 set topgallant sails, at 6 passed by a sail standing to the eastward, at 9 handed topgallant sails, and in 1st reefs topsails - wore ship at 8 AM set topyard sails - employed twisting foxes to make matts for the yards.

June 30, 1771 Sunday variable

First part light airs and cloudy. latter fresh breezes and fair. At 6 AM saw a ship bearing SE b S standing to the westward - at Noon all sails set one sail in sight. Survey'd & condomn'd 457 gns beer 75 pieces pork, 50 lbs cheese & 43 lbs butter.

July 1, 1771 Monday N b E, N b W, NNW

First part light breezes and cloudy, latter mod and fair at 1 PM in S sails at 8 in southerly sails, 1st reeft & topsails & handled spritsail and spritsail tops at 3 AM set top yards and sails, at 6 out 1st topgallant & set & spritsail & spritsail topsail at 11 handed spritsails and spritsail topsail.

July 2, 1771 Tuesday NNW, WNW

Light breezes and cloudy at 8 PM in 1st reefs. Topsails at 4 AM Tkd, at 10 saw a sail in the NE 2nd standing to the Northward at Noon Tkd.

July 3, 1771 Wednesday variable

First part fresh breezes and fair, Middle hazey with rain, latter fresh gales and cloudy at 2 PM spoke a ship called the *Hannah* from London to Boston Rt. Jarvis Master at midnight handed topgallant sail, at 1 AM squally lose reeft, fore & miz: topsails a great head sea, at 4 saw & *Hannah* bearing NW ½ W ½ pt 8 out 3 and 2 reefs of topsails fore & mizon.At 10 lost a logg & 3 lines occasioned by breaking in hauling them in.

July 4, 1771 Thursday N b E, NNE, E

First part fresh breezes and fair, latter light airs & variable at 7 PM out 1st reef main & mizon topsails AM Employed occasionly

July 5, 1771 Friday SSE, variable, W, WSW

First part light airs and clear, latter light breezes and cloudy at 8 PM took in the small sails and 1st reeft topsails, at 2 AM down drivers at 4 saw the *Hannah* SW at 9 set topgallant sails & driver Tkd occasionally.

July 6, 1771 Saturday variable

First part light airs and fair weath middle hazey, latter mod. & fair weath at 2 AM Tkd ship at 7 the *Hannah* south, at 8 a great swell from the westward.

July 7, 1771 Sunday variable

First part thick hazey weath middle foggy, with light airs & a great swell from the NW Latter light airs and foggy at 1 PM passed a brig steering to the eastward at 2 down topgallant yards & in spritsails & yard at 8 PM at 4 AM the *Hannah* NE b E at 5 up top gallant yards and set the sails at 8 do.

July 8, 1771 Monday WSW, W b N, W, WSW

First part mod breezes & thick hazey weath with rain, latter fresh breezy and clear at 7 PM 1st reeft topsail ½ past 8 Tkd at 12 Tkd at 6 AM set topg. sails at 8 handed do. at Noon lost sight of the *Hannah*.

July 9, 1771 Tuesday WSW, W, variable
Fresh breezes and cloudy at 2 PM passed a snow steering to the eastward at 8 a great swell from the NW at 6 AM Tkd ship set Topgallant sails ½ past 11 Tkd Empd making matts for the yards.

July 10, 1771 Wednesday WSW, W, W b S
Fresh breezes and cloudy at 8 PM handed topgallant sails, at 2 AM 2d reeft main tops AM served brandy to the ships company the beer being expended at Noon passed a brig standing to the eastward.

July 11, 1771 Thursday WSW, NW b W, NNW
First part fresh breezes and cloudy, middle squally with drizling rain latter fresh gales and cloudy at 4 PM a heavy swell from NW at 6 in 2d reefs main & mizontops and close reeft foretops, at 7 down Topgallant yards, at 8 handed topsails at 5 AM wore ship & set topsails.
At 6 out 3d reef fore & 2 reef mizontops at 7 out all reefs

July 12, 1771 Friday NW, SSE, SW b W, WSW
First part light bowwows and fair, middle light airs and cloudy, latter fresh gales and haze, at 3 PM got up T.G. yds & sails, a great swell from the NW at 7 handed topgt sails at 10 AM 2: reeft topsails.

July 13, 1771 Saturday WSW, SW b W, SW b S
Fresh gales and hazey a great swell from the westward at 3 PM in 2 reefs topsails fore, at 7 handed fore & mizon top sails & in 2d reefs maintop sails, passed a brig standing to the southward at 5 AM set fore & misontop sails at 10 handed misontop sail.

July 14, 1771 Sunday variable
Fresh gales and squally with rain, at 7 PM hauled up the mainsail, at 7 wore ship and handed the topsails, at 11set mainsail, at 4 AM set topsails at 6 wore ship at 9 got out 3 reefs maintop sail at 11 in handed mizontop sail at Noon handed fore and maintopsails.

July 15, 1771 Monday W, WNW, NW b W, NW, NNW
First part fresh gales and squally with a great swell from westward latter mod and fair weath ½ past 8 PM wore ship, at 1 AM set maintopsail at 4 set fore & mizon top sail at 5 out 3 reefs fore & maintop sails & 2d mizon top sail at 4 out all reefs up T.G. yards at 9 set T.G sails & driver at 10 got the spritsail yard across and set do. sail.

July 16, 1771 Tuesday NNW, calm
Slight breezes & cloudy weath latter calm at Noon hauled down futtock shrouds and set up maintop mast shrouds exercised

great guns & .

July 17, 1771 Wednesday calm, wterly, variable
Hazey weath latter fresh breezes and cloudy at 5 AM spoke a brig from New Fd Land Variation azimuth 25.46 west.

July 18, 1771 Thursday W b W, W b N, NW b W, NW
First part mod and fair weath middle squally, latter fresh breezes hazey weath at 1 PM a sail in sight standing to the westward, at 5 in 2d reefs fore & maintop sails handed mizon topsail at 8 down T.G. yards at 10 in 3d reefs fore & main top sails at 11 handed the foretop sails thick hazey weath at 4 AM set foretop sails at 6 PM set mizon top sails at 7 out 3d reefs maintops sail & 2d reefs mizon top sail at 9 out 3d & 2d reefs foretop sails & 2d reef maintop sail got in T.G. yards at Noon a brigg in sight standing to the westward.

July 19, 1771 Friday NW, N, calm, WSW
First part fresh breezes, middle hazey, latter light breezes & hazey weath at 5 PM set T.G. sails, at 2 AM set the driver at 9 out reefs top sails.

July 20, 1771 Saturday WSW, SW b W, SW b S, SW b W
First part light breezes and clear, middle thick hazey weath latter fresh breezes and cloudy at 10 PM handed T.G. sails, at 12 set do.

July 21, 1771 Sunday SW b W, variable, SSW, SW b W
First and middle parts fresh breezes & thick hazey weath latter little winds and cloudy at 7 PM in 2d reefs topsails at 8 Tkd at 9 Tkd at 6 AM out reefs topsails and out do. sprits & sprit top sail

July 22, 1771 Monday SW b W, W b S, calm, variable, W
First part light breezes and fair middle light airs & hazey weath breezes and clear at 4 AM set studding sails at 7 passed a schooner standing to the eastward at 8 hauled down steering sails Empd making points.

July 23, 1771 Tuesday WNW, W b N, W, W b S
Fresh breezes and clear weath at 6 PM 2d reefs topsails at 9 AM set topgallant sails at 10 saw a sail to the westward steering to the eastward at ½ past 11 Tkd.

July 24, 1771 Wednesday W b S, SW b W, SW, SW b W
Fresh gales and with a great sea from the westward at 1 PM spoke a brig from Nantucket for London handed T.G. sails & 2d reeft F. & M. top sails at 6 down T.G. yds in spritsail tops yd at 2 AM handed mizon topsail at 9 set do.

July 25, 1771 Thursday variable
First part fresh gales and hazey middle thick misty weath latter

fresh gales and fine clear weath at 10 PM Tkd out 2d reefs Top sails & set jibb and driver at 2 AM set maintop sail & set do. sail down driver at 4 out 2d feets T.S. up foretop gallant yards and set do. sail set do. spritsail out spritsails topsail yards do. set do. sail at 9 set steering sail.

July 26, 1771 Friday ENE, E b S, ESE
First part light breezes and clear weath Middle mod and cloudy latter fresh gales and hazy with heavy rain, at 5 AM carried away the fore top mast. Steering sail boom at 9 set the fore & foretopmast steering sails sails at Noon hauled down T.G. steering sails.

July 27, 1771 Saturday ESE, calm, variable
First fresh gales with drizling rain; middle light airs inclinable to calm with thick misty weath latter light winds and cloudy at 8 PM down steering sails handed T.G. sails & in 2d reefs topsails at 6 AM out reefs & set T.G. sails at 9 saw sail standing to the eastward.

July 28, 1771 Sunday WNW, variable, NW b N, NW, NW b W, N
Fresh gales and squally uncertain weath with rain at times at 1 PM set reefs Fore & maintops sails at 2 in 2d reefs main top sail at 3 in 2d reefs topsails at 6 in spritsail topsail yard & down T.G. yards close reeft topsails at 8 Tkd at 9 handed mizon topsail at 11 handed foretopsail at 12 wore ship at 4 AM set foretop sail at 5 out 3 & 2 reefs topsail & set the jibb and mizontop sail a great sea from the westward at 8 handed mizon topsail at 10 set do. at 11 close reefted sails & handed mizontop sail.

July 29, 1771 Monday N b E, N
First part fresh gales and squaly middle fresh gales and cloudy, latter fresh gales and fair weath at 2 PM split the foretop mast stay sail unbent it a great sea from the Northward at 6 AM out 3 reefs F. & M.topsails at 8 set isotope sail at 9 out 2d reefs mizontop sail set lift jibb and spritsail at 10 saw a ship standing to the eastward sail maker empd repairing the fore top mast stay sail at Noon lost a logg and 2 lines saw a sail to the westward standing to eastward.

July 30, 1771 Tuesday NE, NNE, N, N b W
First part fresh gales and cloudy, middle mod and fair, latter mod. breezes and cloudy weath at 5 PM out 2d reefs F.& main topsails at 4 AM set up T. G. yards and & set sails at 7 set driver & out 2d reefs topsails sail maker empd as before at Noon sounded no ground.

July 31, 1771 Wednesday N b E, NNE, N b W, variable
First and middle parts mod and fair weath latter light airs

inclinable to calm at 2 PM fired 2 gunns shotted, brought to, and spoke a ship from Maryland to Glasgow variation azimuth 23: 46 W at 4 passed a brigg and schooner standing to the eastward. at 5 out 2d reefs mizon topsail at 1 AM sounded 38 fm fine sand at 3 spoke a French brig belonging to Diep, a fisherman sail maker finished the foretop mast stay sail several sail in sight.

Aug. 1, 1771 Thursday SW, SSW, variable NE
First part light breezes and fair weath Middle light winds and hazey with drizling rain latter fresh breezes and cloudy weath PM read the articles of war & ½ past 6 brought to in 2d reefs topsail at 7 made sail at 5 AM set steering sails at 8 AM thick foggy weath fired a gun as a signal at Noon served out lines and hooks to the ships company.

Aug. 2, 1771 Friday NW, ENE, variable, SW b S
First part fresh breezes and hazey weath, middle light winds & clear weath latter fresh breezes and clear weath at 7 PM handed sprit sail & sprit sail topsail at 4 AM down steering sails, at 8 saw a sail standing to the eastward.

Aug. 3, 1771 Saturday variable
First part fresh breezes, middle do. breezes with small rain latter mod & fair with a sea from the westward at 2 PM handed T.G. sails at 8 2d reef top sails & got down T.G. yards at 12 handed misontop sail at 4 AM Tks at 5 set top sail at ½ past 6 out 2d reefs topsails, got up T.G. yards & set sails.

Aug. 4, 1771 Sunday variable
First part fresh breezes with clear weath middle light winds & clear weath latter calm with clear weath at 7 AM variation amp. 17: 00 west at 3 AM saw a ship to the northward steering to the eastward Empd setting up the main rigging.

Aug. 5, 1771 Monday SSE, variable, calm, W
First light airs and clear weath at 5 PM set steering sails at 6 hauled down ½ past 7 2d reeft topsails.

Aug. 6, 1771 Tuesday W, SW b W, WSW
Fresh breezes and hazey weath at 2 PM down driver & handed T.G. sails at 5 set T.G. sails at 9 handed do. at Noon sounded no ground.

Aug. 7, 1771 Wednesday W b W, SW b W, W b W, SW b W
Fresh breezes and thick foggy weath ½ past 8 PM 2d reeft Fore & maintops & Tkd½ past 9 AM Tkd ship at 11 out reefs topsails.

Aug. 8, 1771 Thursday SW b W, variable, ENE, E
Cape Ann N87:5 W dist 144 leagues

Light winds and thick hazey weath with drizling rain at 8 PM Tkd at 5 AM set steering sails.

Aug. 9, 1771 Friday E, variable, N b W NW
Do. N88: 43 W dist 119 leagues
First part fresh breezes and hazey, middle little wind and foggy latter mod breezes and cloudy weath at 4 PM bent the Bt Br cable at 3 AM hauled down steering sails at 9 saw a sail in the NW quarter.

Aug. 10, 1771 Saturday NW, variable, WSW
Light winds and cloudy latter do. with squalls rain at 2AM Tkd at 4 saw a sail in SE quarter at 8 saw a sail in the NW quarter.

Aug. 11, 1771 Sunday variable
Do. N86:20 W dist 89 leagues
Light breezes and fair pleasant weath at 2 PM Tkd at 4 a snow in in the SW quarter all standing to the Westward at 7 set steering sail at Noon all sails set.

Aug. 12, 1771 Monday variable
Do. N. 89:02 W dist 79 leagues
First part fresh breezes & squally with clear weath middle calm latter light winds and clear weath ½ past 1 PM split the jigg unbent and bent another; at 3 fired 2 gunns and brought too a ship brigg & schooner the ship proved to be the *Hannah* at 5 AM variation ? amp: N:00W at 8 3 sail in sight two in the NW & one in the SW quarter Sailmaker Empd repairing the jibb.

Aug. 13, 1771 Tuesday variable WSW W b S
Mod breezes and fair weath at 2 PM Tkd at 4 Tkd Departed this life Peter Sambell carpenter at 6 2d reeft topsails read the burial service and past the body of Peter Sambell overboard into the sea at 7 variation amp: N: 4 W at 12 sounded 66 fms pebble stones at 5 AM variation amp 11: 20 W at 7 several sail do. to and sent a boat on the *Hannah* at 11 hoisted in do. boat and made sail Sailmaker empd as before.

Aug. 14, 1771 Wednesday variable
Cape Sable N 19:54 W dist: 15 leagues
First part mod breezes and pleasant weath middle squally with foggy and rainy weath latter mod do. with thick foggy weath PM finished the jibb & bent it and unbent the other at 5 do. fired 2 guns and brought to a schooner, at 8 brought too at 9 made sail at 12 Tkd ship 2d reeft Top sails at ½ past 3 AM split maintop mast staysail & unbent do. at 7 out 2d reefs Topsail, at 8 fired 2 guns shotted to bring to a schooner at 9 thick foggy weath fired a gun as a signal being our Cape Sable fishing bank at 11 fired a

gun for a signal at 12 fired a gun for do.

Aug. 15, 1771 Thursday W b S, W, WSW, W b S
First and middle parts light airs and thick foggy weath latter fresh breezes and clear at 4 PM fired a as a signal in a fogg at 8 fired a gun as a signal in a fogg at 4 AM Tkd at 6 passed the ship *Hannah* standing to the eastward Got up T.G. yards at 10 fired a gun & brought to a schooner Empd repairing main mast stay sail.

Aug. 16, 1771 Friday
Variable first part fresh breezes and hazey weath middle light breezes and clear latter light airs and cloudy at 2 PM saw the land which proved to be about Cape Sable at 4 Tkd Cape Blanch N b E 3 leagues: Cape Negro NE b N about 5 leagues Cape Sable WNW about 4 or 5 leagues at 7 variations ? amp 11:00 W at 4 AM up T.G. yards calm ships head to southward at 9 hoisted out the boat & scrubb'd ship between wind and water at Noon hoisted in the boat sail maker empd repairing maintop mast staysail.

Aug. 17, 1771 Saturday calm, NW b W, NW, NW b N, NW, NW
Cape Ann N 79:56 W do, 52 leagues First part calm and clear weath Middle and latter fresh breezes & clear at 4 the land about Cape Sable NNW do. 6 or 7 leagues at 4 set T.G. sails at 5 handed do. at 11 in 2d reefs fore & main Top sails: sail maker finished maintop mast staysail bent do.

Aug. 18, 1771 Sunday variable
Fresh breezes and clear weath at 2 PM close reefd topsails at 7 out 2d & 3d reefs do. at ½ past do. Tkd Variation amp: to: 58 W at 9 AM set jibb, at ½ past 10 Tkd a great sea from the westward at noon set driver.

Aug. 19, 1771 Monday variable
First part light breezes and clear weath latter light airs and cloudy at 7 PM variation amp: 10:55 W at 8 Tkd ship AM people empd cleaning between decks.

Aug. 20, 1771 Tuesday SW, variable, calm, NNE, NE
First and latter parts light airs and clear weath middle cloudy & calm at 3 PM fired 2 guns brought too and spoke a brig from Boston for Firryland at 6 2d reef Top sail at 5 AM out do. at 7 set steering sails at Noon in Empd with *Hannah.*

Aug. 21, 1771 Wednesday NE, SE, varaible, SW
First part light breezes and clear weath middle light breezes and foggy weath latter fresh breezes and fair weath at 2 AM hauled down steering sails, variation amps: 11: 07W.

Aug. 22, 1771 Thursday SW, SW b W, SW
First part fresh breezes and clear weath latter mod & hazey at 5

PM 2d reefs Top sail at 7 hauled T.S. sails fired a gun brought too & spoke the *Hannah* at 12 Tkd at 2 AM Tkd,

Aug. 23, 1771 Friday SSW, variable, WSW

Cape Ann NW b N dist 5 leagues.

Mod breezes and clear weath latter light breezes at 1 PM saw the land bearing from WNW to NW b N in about Piscataqua, at 4 saw Cape Ann SW b W dist 7 or 8 leagues at 6 Isle of Shoals WNW dist 7 or 8 miles at 7 Tkd at 3 AM Tkd at 6 Tkd at 8 Cape Ann W b N dist: about 5 leagues at Noon C. Ann NW b N distant about 5 leagues.

Aug. 24, 1771 Saturday W, WSW, WNW, variable, calm, NE

Moored in Boston Harbour about small islands from the shore.

Light breezes and clear weath at ½ past 1 PM spoke His Majesty's ship the *Gibralter*, at 2 brought to and reefed from do. 61 pieces beef at 6 made sail ½ past 7 saw Cape Ann NW ½ N 8 or 9 miles at 9

Tkd at 3 AM set steering sails & ? at 5 bore away for the light house at 6 fired a gun for a pilot at came onbd do. at 8 abreast of the lighthouse down steering sails, at 11 saluted *Adm: Montague* with 13 guns he returned do. with 11, ½ past 11 came too with our Bt Br and moored with the stream anchor & hawser in 7 fm water do. from those abt. 1 mile found riding here the *Captain*, *Adm. Montague* and the *Salisbury*, *Commandore Gambier*.

Aug. 25 1771 Sunday Eterly

Fresh breezes & cloudy midday hazey showers PM received on board ½ a cord of wood - AM signal for all his Lieutenants Recd onboard 140 lbs of fresh beef.

Aug. 26, 1771 Monday do.

Light breezes & pleasant weath AM loosed sails to dry Signaled onboard the Admiral Punishment of some deserters belonging to the *Swan* sloop.

Aug. 27, 1771 Tuesday E, SE

Moored in Boston Harbour

Do. weath PM sent our sick men ashore to the hospital Empd drying our small sails AM our signal for a petty officer arrived here his Majesty's schooner *Halifax*.

Aug. 28, 1771 Wednesday variable

Light breezes cloudy, at 10 PM came in here his Majesty's sloop *Beaver* Empd variously.

Aug. 29, 1771 Thursday do.

Light airs with thunder lightening & rain, latter fair, Empd occasionally.

Aug. 30, 1771 Friday NW
Light winds with calms & clear weath AM unbent our sails - sail'd hence his Majesty's ship *Commodore Gambier* with the rope frigate & the *Senegal* sloop for Halifax received onboard a firkin of butter, a cask of pease & Hhd of bread.

Aug. 31, 1771 Saturday NW, NE
Do. weath PM employed unreeving our running rigging Recd on board a Hhd of beer for the ships use AM Empd about rigging received on board 109 lbs of fresh beef signaled for all lieutenants.

Sept. 1, 1771 Sunday variable
Do. employed about rigging & blacking the yards & mast heads AM sailed hence the ship & schooner Read the articles of war to the ships company.

Sept. 2, 1771 Monday SE
First part light winds & clear latter thick hazey weath PM sent a sick man ashore to the hospital AM received the guard from the *Beaver* Empd about the rigging.

Sept. 3, 1771 Tuesday variable
Fresh gales & hazey with heavy latter light winds & fair AM returned the guard to the *Admiral*. Recd 83 lbs of fresh beef Employed taring the rigging.

Sept. 4, 1771 Wednesday variable
Light winds & fair weath latter parts hazey Employed ratting down the rigging & getting water aboard.

Sept. 5, 1771 Thursday do.
Do. employed watering AM received 8 hands from the *Swan* to assist us with the rigging. received the guard.

Sept. 6, 1771 Friday do.
Fresh breezes & hazey with misting rain PM employed about our rigging returned the hands onboard the *Swan*. AM returned the guard to the *Admiral*.

Sept. 7, 1771 Saturday ENE
Fresh breezes & hazey weather Employed variously AM recd on board 141 lbs of fresh beef received 13 men out of the *Swan* to assist us with our rigging.

Sept. 8, 1771 Sunday NE, E b S
Fresh breezes & cloudy, middle with drizling rain PM returned the above men to the *Swan* AM cleaned ship fore and aft.

Sept. 9, 1771 Monday NE, NW
Fresh breezes & cloudy PM came in his Majesty's sloop *Kingfisher* AM returned a Hhd of beer not fit to drink.

Sept. 10, 1771 Tuesday variable
Light windy & cloudy Employd as necessary AM received the guard from the *Beaver* Empd scraping the topmast & greasing them with tallow.
Sept. 11, 1771 Wednesday NW, N
Fresh gales & cloudy PM signal for all the Lieutenants our signal for a petty officers PM returned the guard to the *Admiral* employed about the rigging & scraping lower masts & paying them.
Sept 12, 1771 Thursday WSW, W, SW
Light winds & fair AM signal for exercising great guns & small arms fired 8 3 lb shot 2 swivel & six pounders and balls at a mark.
Sept. 13, 1771 Friday wterly
First part gales & fair PM received a cask of beer AM recd 2.5 lbs of fresh beef received 2 hands from the *Captain* to assist us in scraping our sides.
Sept. 14, 1771 Saturday W
Slight winds and fair AM recd 105 lbs for fr. beef recd 6 hands from the *Captain* to assist us to scraping ship blacking our yards & scrubbing our bottom Empd paying the sides and whales with tarr.
Sept. 15, 1771 Sunday NW, E
Do. weath recd onbd a cask of pork Empld variously AM received the guard from the *Beaver*.
Sept. 16, 1771 Monday
Light windy & fair AM returned the guard signal for excerising the marines ashore do. for all lieutenants empd tarring the rigging & the wooding of the masts & ca.
Sept. 17, 1771 Tuesday variable
Light winds & hazey with mosting weather & rain PM empd getting water aboard AM stowing it.
Sept. 18, 1771 Wednesday WNW
Light winds & cloudy PM our signal for a petty officer Empd as necessary AM received 60 pounds of fresh beef.
Sept. 19 1771 Thursday W b N
Light winds & fair Empd as necessary, carry'd out a bower to ye westward & got on board the stream anchor & hawser.
Sept. 20, 1771 Friday do.
Do. weath Empd getting up the boatswains stores to be surveyed recd on board cask of beer AM recd onboard the guard.
Sept. 21, 1771 Saturday Wterly
Do. weath Empd stowing away the boatswains stores being surveyd AM returnd the guard to the *Admiral* recd 66 lbs of

fresh beef.

Sept. 22, 1771 Sunday W, NE

Do. weath latter part fresh breezes & cloudy PM signal 1 or all Lieutenants come in here His Majesty's sloop *Martin* & saluted the *Admiral* returned do. AM signal for all lieutenants come in His Majesty's Sloop *Tamer* Empd variously.

Sept. 23 1771 Monday NE

Do weath PM recd on board from the *Martin* 9 cables AM recd some boatswain stores from the *Tamer* came in His Majesty's sloop *Viper*.

Sept . 24, 1771 Tuesday NE, NW

Fresh breezes & cloudy latter clear saluted for the Kings coronation as did the rest of the fleet Empd variously Received 136 lbs of fresh beef.

Sept. 25, 1771 Wednesday variable

Do weath Empd variously AM sailed hence his majesty's sloops *Swan* & *Martin* Received the guard from the *Beaver*.

Sept. 26, 1771 Thursday do.

Light winds & variable PM recd on board a cask of beer AM returned the guard to the *Admiral*.

Sept. 27, 1771 Friday do.

Do weath Empd variously AM recd onboard 8 bags of bread Signal for exercising the marines on shore Came in a Deputy Surveyor with a party.

This is the first mention of marines in the logs of the Canceaux. While not mentioned until now they were part of the ships company and found in a ratio of one marine to every four sailors. With the extensive discipline problems mentioned in the logs, the marines were an armed guard force to control the seamen. As the times began to change they were considered a fighting force aboard ship used many time ashore.

Sept 28, 1771 Saturday SW

Fresh breezes & squally with cloudy weath AM our signal for a petty officer received on board 121 lbs of fresh beef.

Sept. 29, 1771 Sunday WSW, NW

Fresh gales & cloudy PM recd on board a cask of beer AM at 2 AM scraped yards & topmasts.

Sept 30, 1771 Monday NW

Fresh breezes & clear at 6 AM up lower yards & topmasts. Sail'd hence his Majesty's sloop *Viper* Signal for all lieutenants Punished

John Tarral for neglect of duty Mutinous expressions, recd the guard from the *Beaver* came in the surveying sloop *Jupiter*.

Oct. 1, 1771 Tuesday NW

Light winds & clear weath PM employd setting up the bobstays & staging the foremast AM returned ye guard to the *Admiral* sailed hence his Majesty's sloop *Kingfisher* signal for exercising the marines ashore Empd setting up the main rigging recd 126 lbs of fresh beef read the articles of war to the ships company.

Oct. 2, 1771 Wednesday WNW, W b S

Light winds and clear PM empd recd our provisions & stowing them away. AM empd variously.

Oct. 3, 1771 Thursday NW, N

Do weath Empd variously AM came in his Majesty's schooner *Sultana* a Deputy Surveyor & party with boat empd surveying the harbour. AM recd the guard from the *Beaver*.

Oct. 4, 1771 Friday WNW, W, WNW

Moderate & fair weath Empd fitting out the *Jupiter* sloop for sea surveyors Empd as before Recd onbd: 2 months provisions viz. bread 3782 lbs pork 9 barrels contg 998 pieces Beef 1 barrel contg 60 pieces, pease 5 barrels contg 17 bushels and a half, Rice 2 casks contg 99 lbs neat, 3 firkins of butter contg 218 pounds received 95 lbs of fresh beef for the use of the ships company. AM returned the guard to the *Admiral*.

Oct. 5, 1771 Saturday NNW, NW

Mod & cloudy weath AM do weath saild hence the *Jupiter* surveying sloop with provisions for ye surveying parties *Surveyor* Empd as before recd 136 lbs of fresh beef for the ships company.

Oct. 6, 1771 Sunday NW

Do weath AM employed cleaning between decks.

Oct. 7, 1771 Monday variable

Do. weath Empd occasionally recd a cask of beer AM recd guard from ye *Beaver*. Surveyors empd as before.

Oct. 8, 1771 Tuesday NW

Fresh gales & cloudy weath latter strong gales and cloudy PM struck yards & topmasts returned guard to the *Admiral* recd 80 lbs of fresh beef for the ships company.

Oct. 9, 1771 Wednesday

Mod & cloudy PM got up yards & topmasts Empd occasionally Surveyors as before.

Oct. 10, 1771 Thursday W

Do weath Empd clearing and cleaning between decks,

surveyors Employed as before. AM received guard from the *Beaver.*

Oct. 11, 1771 Friday WSW, SE

First and middle parts do. weath latter do. weath with rain Sailed hence his Majesty's schooner *Sultana* AM returned the guards to the *Admiral* Surveyors empd as before Received 154 lbs of fresh beef for the ships company.

Oct. 12, 1771 Saturday NW

First part mod & cloudy latter strong gales & squally Struck yards and topmasts.

Oct. 13, 1771 Sunday do.

First part fresh gales and clear weather, latter moderate and clear.

Oct. 14, 1771 Monday variable

Light airs and cloudy Sailed hence his Majesty's sloop *Beaver* got up yards and topmasts Recd 25 lbs of fresh beef for the ships company Surveyors Empd as before.

Oct. 15, 1771 Tuesday Wterly

Mod and cloudy AM returned the guard to the *Admiral* People employed occasionally Surveyors as before.

Oct. 16, 1771 Wednesday E b N, SE

Fresh breezes and clear weath latter squally with rain Empd variously.

Oct. 17, 1771 Thursday S, SSW

First part fresh gales and hazey latter light winds and clear AM received the guard from the *Tamar* recd 152 lbs fresh beef.

Oct. 18, 1771 Friday N, ENE

Light winds and cloudy AM returned the guard to the *Admiral.*

Oct. 19, 1771 Saturday variable

Do weath Empd variously Longboat Empd watering. AM our signal for an officer.

Oct. 20, 1771 Sunday do.

Do weath AM cleaned ship fore and aft

Oct. 21, 1771 Monday SSE, S

Mod and cloudy PM punished Jn, Baden and Jno Farral, each for drunkenness neglect of duty and mutanious expressions.

Oct. 22, 1771 Tuesday NE

Fresh breezes and clear weath Empld bending sails received 12 men from *Admiral* to assist us in do. AM received the guard from the *Tamer.*

Oct. 23, 1771 Wednesday variable

Light airs and variable with calm PM came in his Majesty's frigate *Tartar* AM returned guard to the *Admiral* came in ye surveying sloop *Jupiter*. Returned the 12 men to the *Admiral* Empd bending sails Signal out for all Lieutanants Recd 80 lbs of fresh beef.

Oct. 24, 1771 Thursday NW

Light airs and variable with calm latter fresh breezes and clear PM recd a cask of beer longboat empd watering AM signal out for exercising marines ashore recd 100 lbs of fresh beef.

Oct. 25, 1771 Friday NW, W

Fresh gales and fair weath Arrived here his Majesty's ship *Gibralter* recd on board the guard.

Oct. 26, 1771 Saturday W, S

Fresh breezes and fair weath at 1 PM fired 19 guns being the Anniversary of his Majesty assession to the throne Recd a cask of beer. AM sailed hence his Majesty's sloop *Tamar* and *St. John* Armed schooner. Recd 129 lbs of fresh beef.

Oct. 27, 1771 Sunday E, WSW

Do. weath PM came in his Majesty's sloop *Beaver* and *Swan* AM cleaned ship fore and aft.

Oct. 28, 1771 Monday WNW

Fresh breezes and cloudy AM our signal for an officer Recd 84 lbs fresh beef, 2 firkins of butter and a cask of beer. Empd unmooring to give birth to the *Tartar* frigate.

Oct. 29, 1771 Tuesday NW

Fresh breeze and cloudy latter part light wind and clear PM empd mooring ship. AM signal out onboard the *Tartar* for a Court Martial Empd taking in wood for the ship use. Recd 172 lbs of fresh beef.

Oct. 30, 1771 Wednesday NNE

Moored in Boston Harbour

Stiff breezes and clear. latter on light wind and foggy PM received 8 casks of pork and 2 firkins of butter recd I firkin of do. AM signal requested onbd the *Tartar* for a court martial General signal for assistance. Recd some boatswain stores from the *Swan* sloop.

Oct. 31, 1771 Thursday SW, W

Fresh gales and cloudy, latter strong gales and hazey with rain, arrived here his Majesty's ships ? and *Mermaid* recd 2 casks of beer, at 11 down yards and topmasts general signal for Petty Officer

Nov. 1, 1771 Friday NW, N

Fresh gales and fair, latter light winds and clear. PM recd cask of beer & 2000 wt of bread for the ships company. AM recd 200 lbs of beef. Signal out for exercising marines ashore. Read the articles of war and abstract to the ships company. At 8 AM got up lower yds and topmasts.

Nov. 2, 1771 Saturday NNE, E

First part light winds and fair, latter fresh breezes and cloudy AM recd 112 lbs fresh beef. Empd making points and gaskets.

Nov. 3, 1771 Sunday SE, NNE. NNW

Heavy gales with thick hazey weath and rain at 9 PM struck yards and topmasts at ½ past 6 AM struck T.G. masts. PM came in his Majesty's ship *Deal Castle* at 7 AM he saluted and stove our pinnace and cutter with their woods and broke 26 pains of glass.

Nov. 4, 1771 Monday W b N

First part strong gales and hazey, with drizling rain, latter more mod and clear AM general signal for a boat with an officer at 8 up lower 2 yards, topmasts and T.G. masts General signal for all Lieutanants carpenters empd mending the boats.

Nov. 5, 1771 Tuesday do,

Light winds and fair Empd clearing the decks and preparing for sea PM recd 230 lbs fr beef. PM signal for all Lieutanants. Recd onbd some carpenters & boatswains stores. Carpenters empd as before.

Nov. 6, 1771 Wednesday NW, W b S

Stiff breezes and fair weath at 1 PM fired 13 gun being the anniversary of Gun Powder Treason. Recd 2 casks of beer. AM unmoored ship, our signal out for an officer. Sailed hence his majesty's sloop *Swan.*

Nov. 7, 1771 Thursday NW, WSW

At single anchor Castle William W b S abt 12 mile

First part fresh breezes, middle and latter light airs and fair. At 2 PM hove up our small bower anchor, and came to below the shipping with our Bt Br at 9 AM weighed and sail'd at Noon came to off Long Island dist. 1 mile. Castle William W b S about 1 ½ mile.

Nov. 8, 1771 Friday variable, NE

Moored do. bearings

Light winds and calms with cloudy weath latter part strong gales and hazey at Noon let our small Br. and veered away to a whole cable on our Bt. Br. and half do. on our small Br Down lower yds.

Nov. 9, 1771 Saturday NE. NNW

Fresh gales and hazey with sleet. At 5 PM struck T.G. masts.

Nov. 10, 1771 Sunday WNW, SW
Half Way Rock NNW abt 2 leagues
First part fresh gales and cloudy, middle and latter light winds & clear weath. At 5 PM up lower yards & T.G. masts. At 4 AM hove up our Bt Br anchor, & hove short on the small, at 6 weighed and sailed, up T.G. yard and out do. sails at 9 abreast of the Lighthouse all sails set, at Noon Half Way Rock NNW abt. 2 leagues. Read the articles of war and punished Henry Johnston with 12 lashes for mutinous expressions.

Nov. 11, 1771 Monday SW b W, W, W b N
Hortehers Island S. Pilgrim Hill SSW dist. about 2 leagues.
First part stiff breezes and cloudy, middle light winds and clear, latter fresh breezes and fair weath at ½ past 3 PM came to with our Bt Br in 7 fms water, in Cape Ann Harbour. Normans Row SW b W eastern most point S ½ W the Church NNE do. of shore ½ a mile ½ past 5 let go our small bower anchor and wore away upon both cables down T.G. yards. At 4 AM hove up our small Bower & short on our Bt Br At 6 weighed and found one of the arms of our Bt Br gone at 8 up T.G. yards at 10 Thatchers Island NNW about 1 ½ mile, at Noon Thatchers Island, S. Pidgeon Hill SSW distance about 2 leagues.

Nov. 12, 1771 Tuesday variable, ENE
Piscataqua Lighthouse N b W ½ W 3 miles.
Modt. and fair, at 2 PM Pidgeon Hills S. Isles of Shoals NNE about 5 miles at 8 Piscataqua Lighthouse N b W, Isle of Shoals E b N 4 leagues at 12 came to in Piscataqua Entrance in 9 fm Isle of Shoals SE b S Lighthouse N ½ W about 2 miles at 11 AM weighed and came to sail at Noon the Lighthouse N b W ½ W about 8 miles.

Nov. 13, 1771 Wednesday variable
Moored off Kittery Point Piscataqua River Lighthouse S b E dist off shore ½ cables length.
Light winds with calm & fair weath at ½ past 3 PM came to off Kittery Point with our Bt Br in 13 fm and moored with our small Bower. Lighthouse S b E Kittery Point WNW dist of shore about ½ a cable length. AM employed variously.

Nov. 14, 1771 Thursday calm
First part cloudy latter thick foggy weath Empd working junk paid the long boats bottom with tar and tallow.

Nov. 15, 1771 Friday variable
Moored off Kittery Point as before.
First part light winds and foggy, latter strong gales and cloudy,

at 9 AM down our T.G. masts. Fired 2 gun shotted &
brough to a sloop & schooner from the Mole of St Nichols.

Nov. 16, 1771 Saturday S b E, calm
Light winds and fair weath at 9 AM up lower yds & T.G. masts.

Nov. 17, 1771 Sunday variable
Fresh breezes and cloudy. Middle and latter stormy gales and clear, at 11 PM down yards & T.G. masts, at 8 AM up do. fired 2 guns shotted & brough to a sloop from St. Statius.

Nov. 18, 1771 Monday W
Moored in Spruce Creek Piscataqua River Kittery Church E
Modt and fair weath AM hove up our Bt Br anchor and on small do. warped into Spruce Creek Empd mooring ship Kittery Church SE.

Nov. 19, 1771 Tuesday S, W b N
Hard gales and hazey, latter more modt with misty weath at ½ past 8 PM down lower yards and topmasts. AM Empd mooring ship.

Nov. 20, 1771 Wednesday WNW
Strong gales and clear Empd as necessary.

Nov. 21, 1771 Thursday NW
Do. weath Empd variously.

Nov. 22, 1771 Friday do,
Do. weath latter more modt AM loosed sails to dry.

Nov. 23, 1771 Saturday calm
Calm with fair weath PM Empd. unbending sails. Read the articles of war & punished Jno Hary & Geo. Inslon for drunkeness & neglect of duty.

*Nov. 24, 1771 to Dec. 12, 1771

Dec. 13, 1771 Friday NE, W
First part strong gales and hazey with snow and hail, latter modt and clear PM punished Jno Baden and Jon Scot with 12 lashes each for drunkeness.

Dec. 14 1771 Saturday WNW
Modt and fair weath Empd variously.

Dec. 15, 1771 Sunday NNE, N
Fresh breezes with strong frost and cloudy weath PM empd variously AM read the articles of war and punished Jno Baden for drunkeness and neglect of duty with 12 lashes.

*Dec. 16, 1771 to Jan 11, 1772

Jan. 12, 1772 Sunday SSW
Fresh breezes and snow Arrived here a large mast ship from London 11 weeks passage Lost a hand lead.

After harvesting, the great mast pines (Pinus Strobus) of the coast of Maine were moved overland or by river to mast landings to be floated to ports such Falmouth. The center of the Falmouth mast trade was Stroudwater at the top of the Fore River estuary. Here the "great sticks" were prepared and loaded aboard mast ships. Masts were a strategic commodity for the British fleets and was under the control and protection of the navy. Masts and spars were the parts of ships that were most frequently damaged or lost in storms at sea. In shipyards masts were needed for vessels under construction, a major supply was essential. New England was the source for pine masts while the Baltic forests provided spruce for spars. These were the prime mast sources for the Royal Navy. Masts normally lasted approximately twelve years before the resin dried up and they lost their strength and resilience (flexibility). Severe weather including frequent hurricanes played havoc on the British fleets during the mid 1700's
Both legs of a mast ship voyage were important as after carrying masts to England, the ship carrying passengers and cargos of manufactured goods would return to New England.

*Jan. 13, 1772 to Mar. 16, 1772

Mar. 17, 1772 Tuesday SSW, W, WNW, NW
PM fresh gales with snow, AM modt and clear weath hard frost Empd fitting out the *Jupiter* Sailmaker empd repairing the *Jupiter* sails.
Mar. 18, 1772 Wednesday NW, SW
PM fresh gales and cloudy AM modt and clear weath empd ballasting the *Polly* and *Jupiter*.
Mar. 19, 1772 Thursday variable
Light winds and fair weath with calm Empd getting the *Jupiter* ready for sea.

*Mar. 20, 1772 to Mar. 26, 1772

Mar. 27, 1772 Friday variable
Light airs and fair AM sailed hence the *Jupiter* surveying schooner Empd clearing our decks &c.

Mar. 28, 1772 Saturday NNE
Light winds and cloudy Carpenters repairing the boats.
Mar. 29, 1772 Sunday NE, ESE
Light airs and variable with cloudy weath latter strong gales and squally with rain & sleet.
Mar. 30, 1772 Monday ENE
Heavy gales and hazey with snow and small rain.
Mar. 31, 1772 Tuesday NE, N
Strong gales with snow latter or light winds & fair carpenters as before.
April 1, 1772 Wednesday variable
Light winds and fair weath AM sent our broken bower anchor and kedge do. on board his Majesties sloop *Swan* bound to Halifax to be returned .
April 2, 1772 Thursday do., ESE
Light winds and fair latter fresh breezes and hazey.
April 3, 1772 Friday NE
Strong gales and hazey middle and latter heavy gales with snow & sleet.
April 4, 1772 Saturday do., NNE
Heavy gales and hazey latter more modt with clear weath.
April 5, 1772 Sunday var.
Light airs with calms and clear weath Empd working up junk.
April 6, 1772 Monday do., SSE
Do. weath AM empd variously carpr. repairing the boats.
April 7, 1772 Tuesday variable
Do. weath Empd as before.
April 8, 1772 Wednesday do., SSE
Do. weath latter cloudy at 8 PM came in the *Polly* schooner at 1 AM came in the *Jupiter* Empd getting out of the latter some carpenters and boatswains stores.
April 9, 1772 Thursday SE, NE
Fresh breezes and cloudy latter heavy gales and hazey with rain.
April 10, 1772 Friday NE, N
Heavy gales and hazey with rain latter modt and clear weath carpr Employed repairing the boats.
April 11, 1772 Saturday var.
Light winds and fair at 4 AM signal onbd the *Swan* for assistance.
April 12, 1772 Sunday do.
Light winds and hazey with calms Latter rain at 2 came down and anchored of Kittery Point the *Swan* sloop.
April 13, 1772 Monday NW

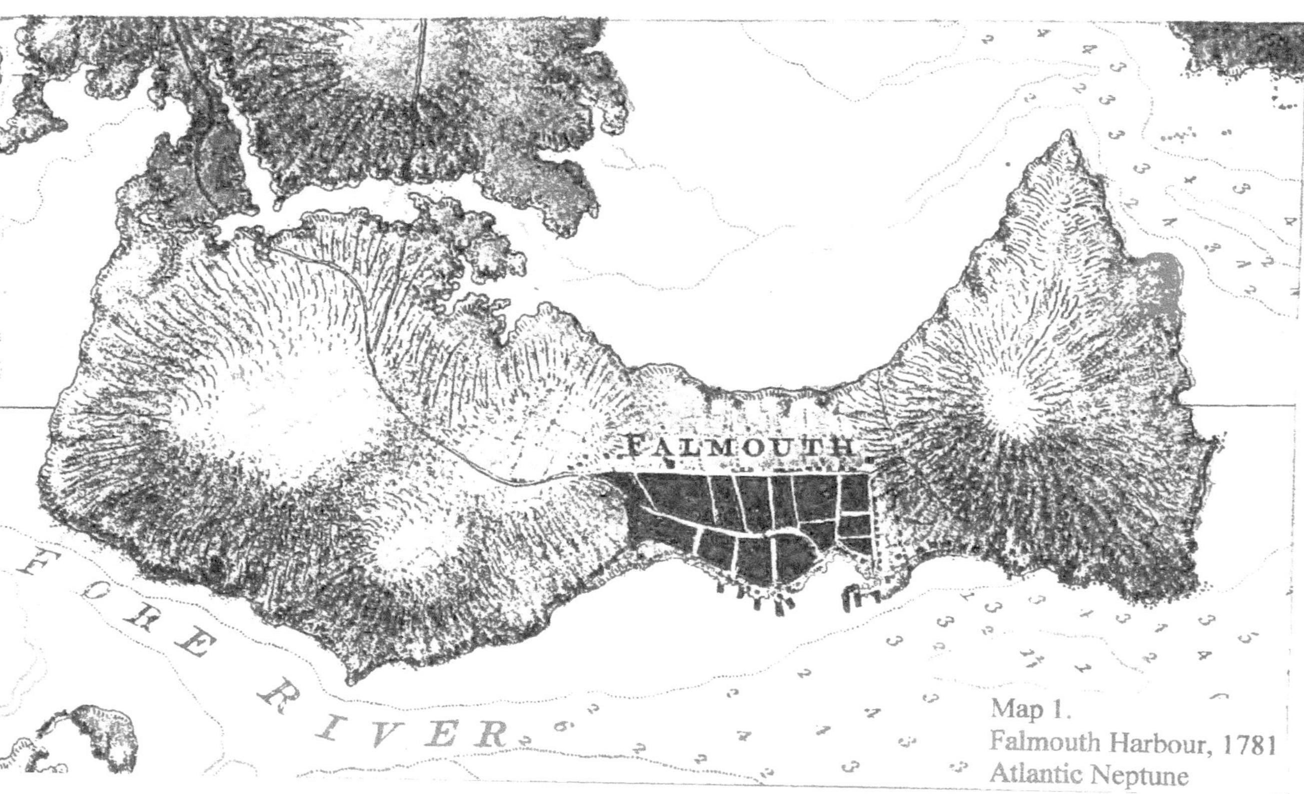

Map 1.
Falmouth Harbour, 1781
Atlantic Neptune

Map 2.
Chart of Portland Sound to Cape Small 1776
Atlantic Neptune

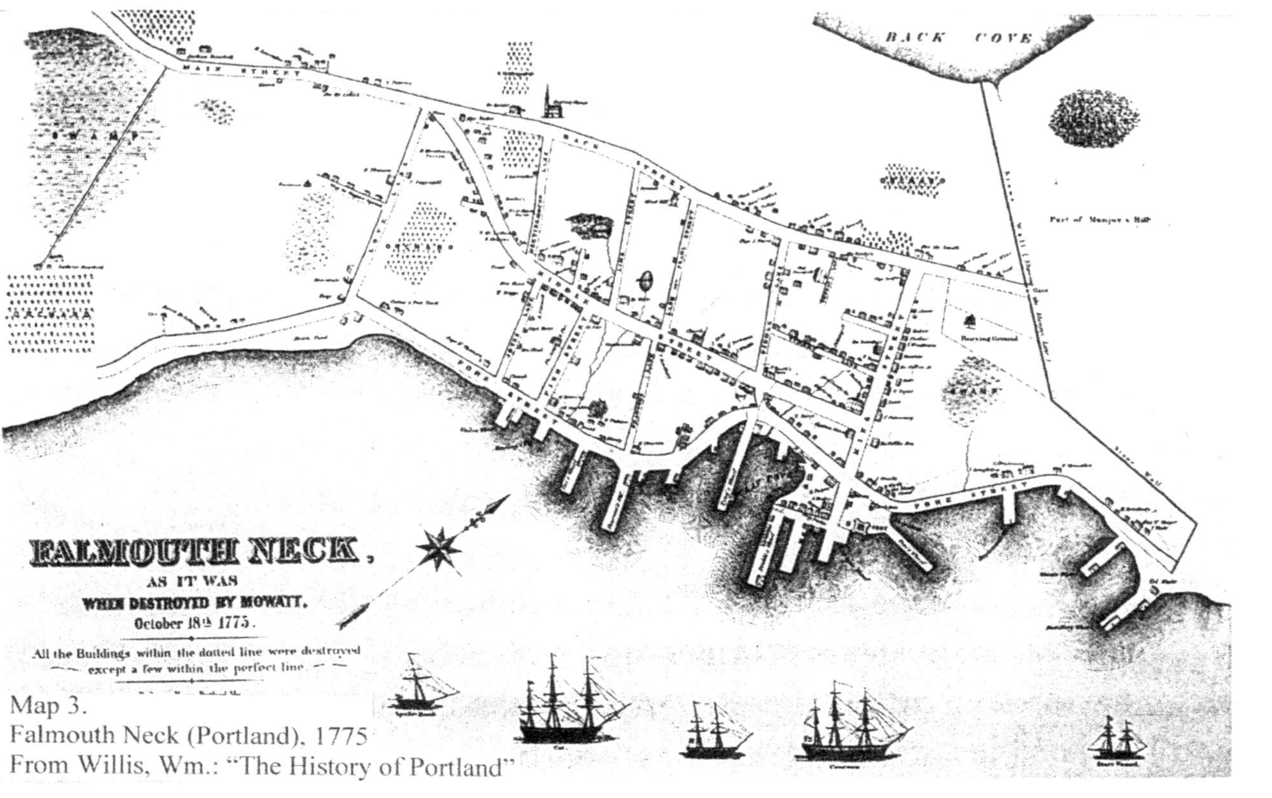

Map 3.
Falmouth Neck (Portland), 1775
From Willis, Wm.: "The History of Portland"

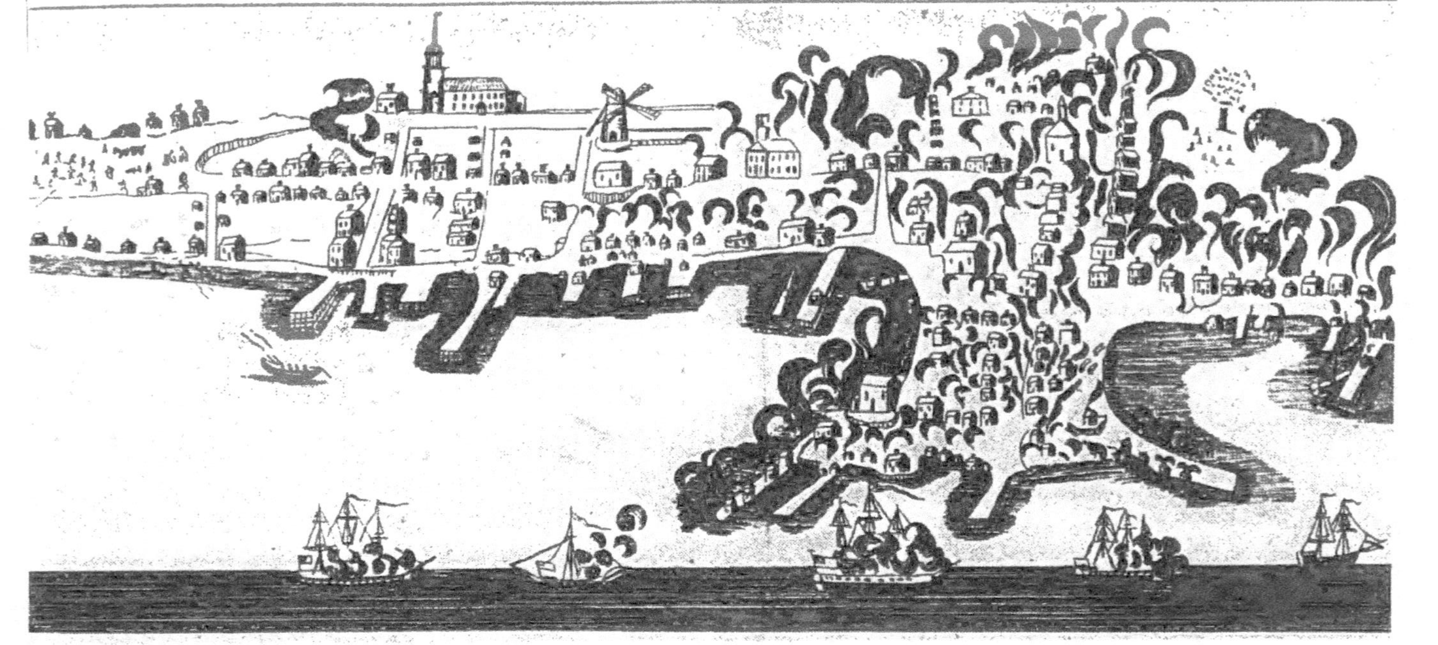

Map 4.
The Town of Falmouth, Burnt by Captain Moet Octbr 18th 1775.

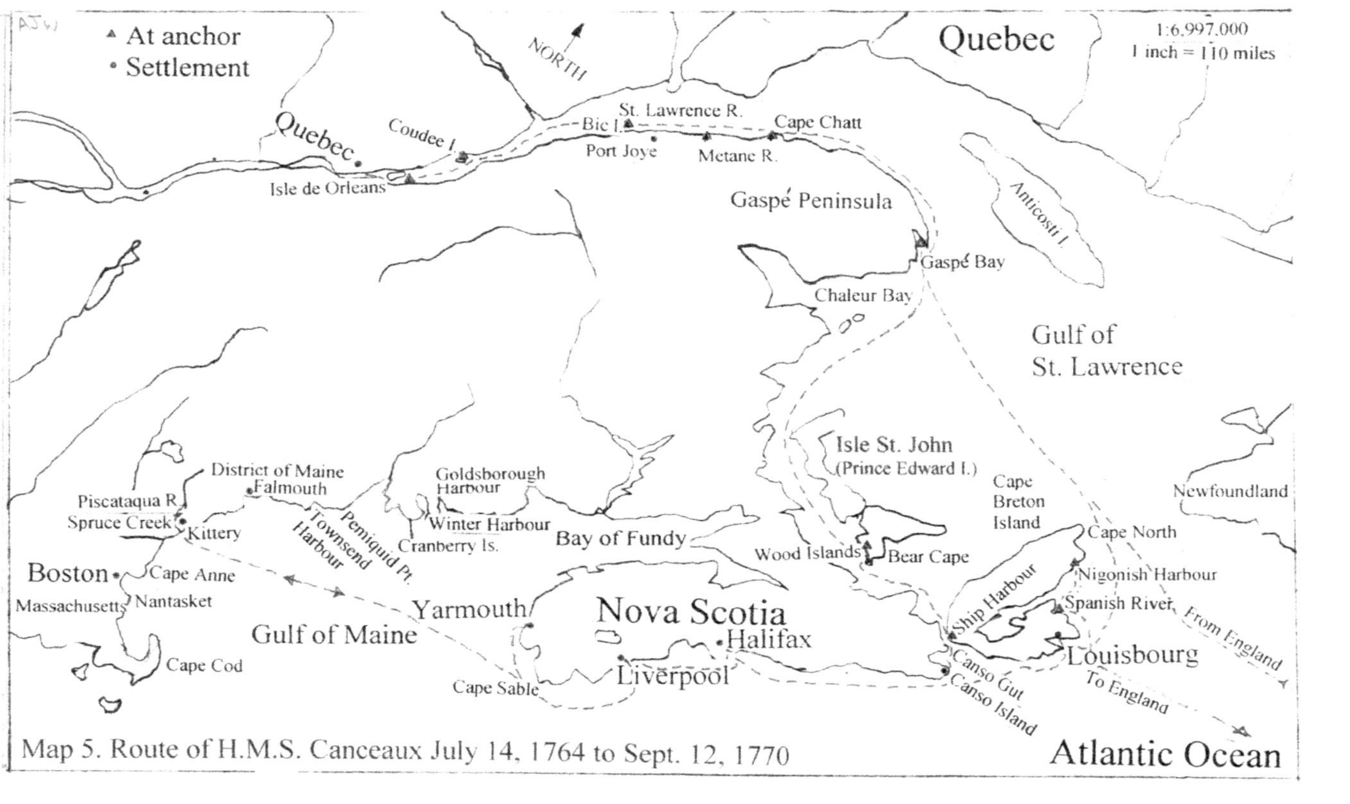

Map 5. Route of H.M.S. Canceaux July 14, 1764 to Sept. 12, 1770

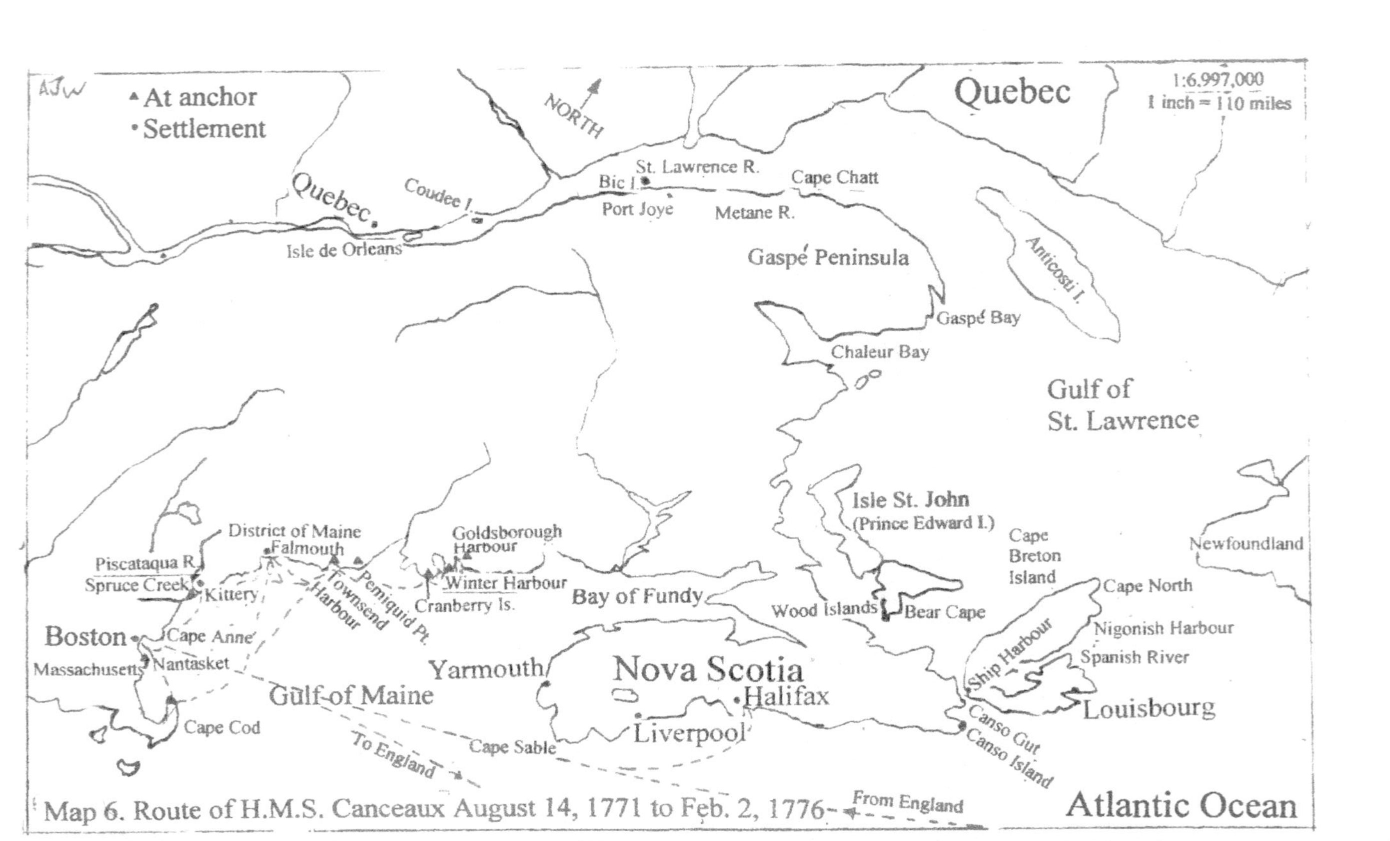

Map 6. Route of H.M.S. Canceaux August 14, 1771 to Feb. 2, 1776

Illustration 1.
Henry Mowat, Samuel Holland, Joseph Frederick Wallet DesBarres

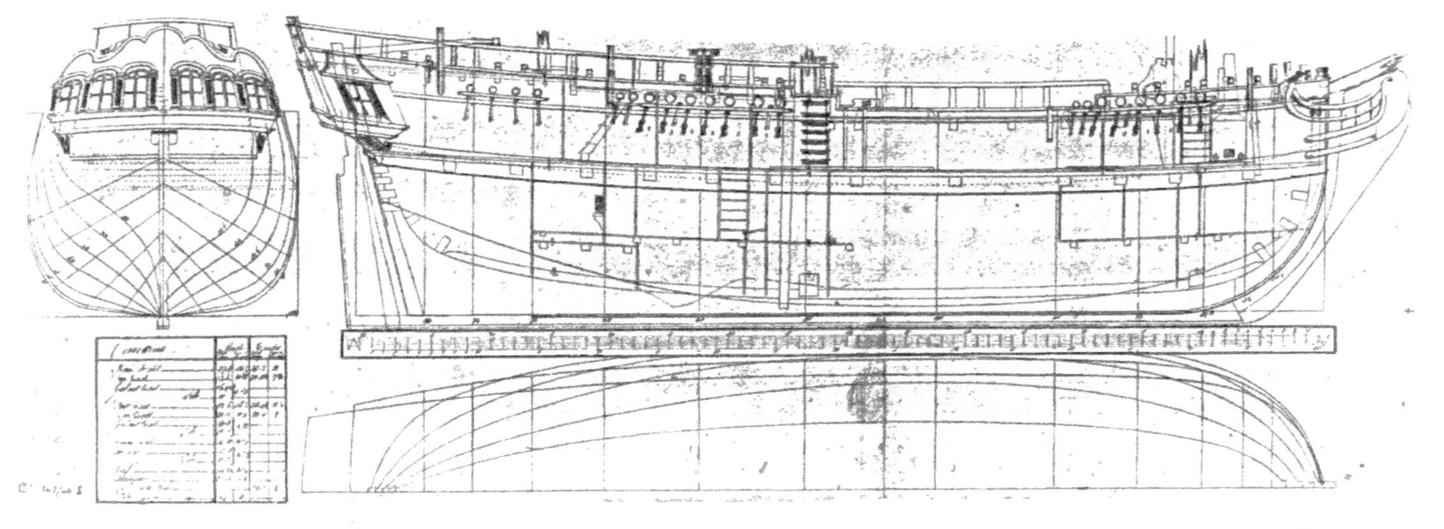

Illustration 2.
Profile of hull and cross sections of H.M.S. Canceaux
Courtesy of the National Maritime Museum, Greenwich, London, England

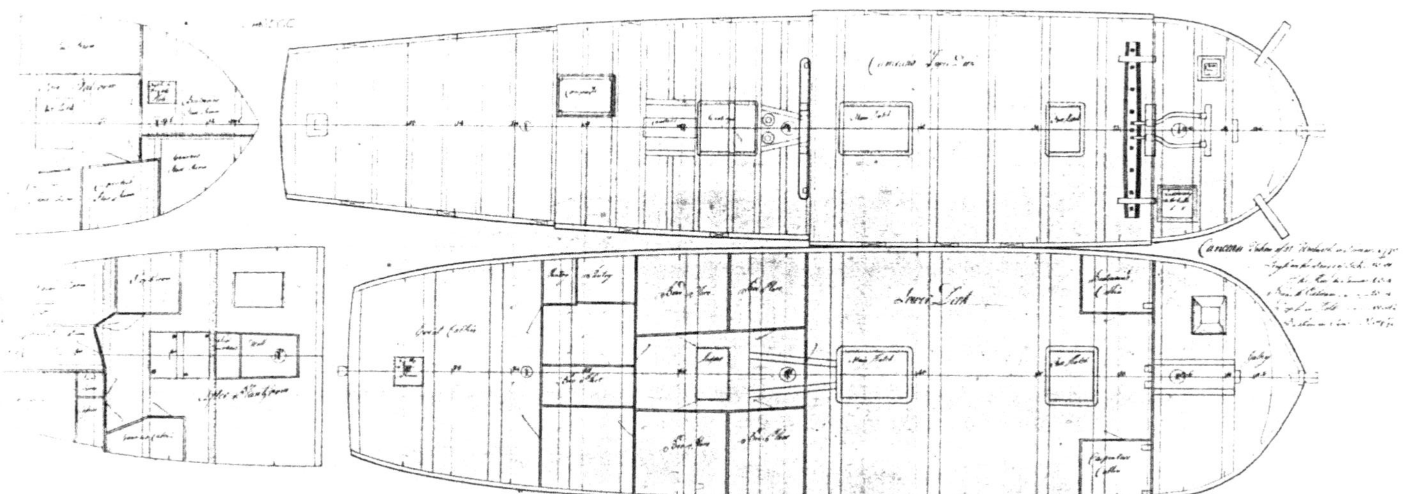

Illustration 3.
Deck plans of H.M.S. Canceaux
Courtesy of the National Maritime Museum, Greenwich, London, England

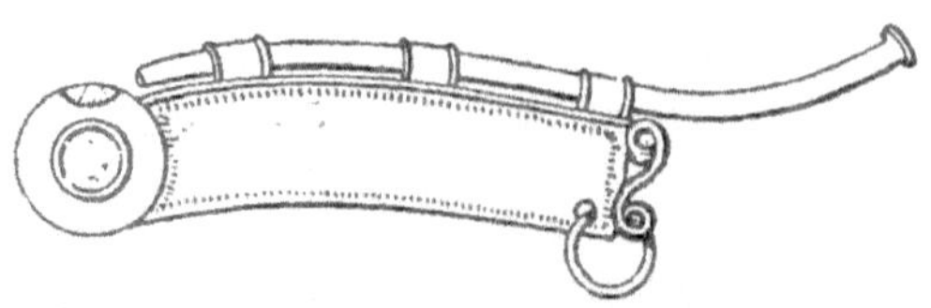

Illustration 4.
Bosun's Pipe late 18th Cent.

Boatswain Pipe

The various calls and orders conveyed by the pipe include:

TO BE PASSED: Piped to command silence before passing an order or information.

ALL HANDS: Piped to call all hand's attention, also for calling the first, mid and morning watches.

BOAT CALL: Piped to call away a boat, also to call a division or divisions to quarters.

CALL MATES: Piped by the boatswain to assemble his mates.

STAND-BY: Piped for set taut, stand-by and lay on.

HOIST AWAY: Piped in hoisting boats. In hoisting generally and in the walk away with cat or fish falls; always preceded by the pipe "stand-by".

HAUL: Piped to keep men pulling together.

BELAY: Piped to cease hauling and make fast; and also to cease an order just piped.

HEAVE AROUND: Piped for mess gear; also to heave around a capstan.

VEER: Piped to ease away, walk back and slack away.

LAY UP: Piped to send men aloft.

LAY OUT: Piped to lay out manning yards or rail; also to trice up and out booms.

PIPING THE SIDE: Accompanies appropriate side honors.

Fresh gales and cloudy latter parts light winds and fair weath at 4 AM sailed hence his Majesty's sloop *Swan*, Carpt. as before.

April 14, 1772 Tuesday SW

Modt and fair weath middle rain carpr. as before.

April 15, 1772 Wednesday do.

Fresh gales and fair weath do. empd.

April 16, 1772 Thursday SW, SSE

Do. weath latter part strong gales and hazey with rain.

April 17, 1772 Friday do. W

Fresh gales and hazey with rain latter modt and cloudy Empd. variously.

April 18, 1772 Saturday NW

Modt and fair sail maker empd making tents for the survey opened a cask of beef 2 pces short.

April 19, 1772 Sunday ESE

Do. weath PM Empld overhauling our shrouds & blacking the yards & topmast heads Sailmakers as before.

April 20, 1772 Monday ENE

Light winds and cloudy latter fresh gales with snow.

April 21, 1772 Tuesday NW

Fresh gales with rain, latter clear Empd overhauling the rigging & tarring it.

April 22, 1772 Wednesday NW, S

Light winds and hazey Empd as before.

April 23, 1772 Thursday SSW, W

Do. weath Empd as before.

April 24, 1772 Friday WNW

First part fresh gales and squally latter modt and fair do. empd.

April 25, 1772 Saturday do., WNW, S.

Fresh breezes and fair weath AM empd getting provisions and sails out of the *Polly* schooner.

April 26, 1772 Sunday do. S

Fresh breezes and cloudy latter light winds and clear weath Empd getting provisions of the *Polly*.

April 27, 1772 Monday var.

Light winds and foggy Empd about ye rigging & sailed hence the *Polly* schooner.

April 28, 1772 Tuesday do.

Do. weath Empd scraping the topmasts &.

April 29, 1772 Wednesday Soerly

Do. weath Empd getting the rigging and rigging overhead.

April 30, 1772 Thursday SSW

Light winds and hazey Employed about ye rigging.
May 1, 1772 Friday SSW, W
Do. weath at 8 PM squally with thunder and lightening Empd ? Came in *Polly* schooner.
May 2, 1772 Saturday NW
Light breezes and fair Empd about the rigging.
May 3, 1772 Sunday N, S
Fresh breezes and fair Empd about the riggng.
May 4, 1772 Monday S
Do. weath latter hazey with small rain Empd variously
May 5 ,1772 Tuesday
Do. weath Employed variously.
May 6, 1772 Wednesday SW
Fresh breezes and cloudy weath empd putting provisions onbd the *Polly* & *Jupiter* for the surveying partys.
May 7, 1772 Thursday SSE
Fresh gales and hazey at 8 AM sail'd the *Polly* & *Jupiter* with surveying parties, but the wind being to ye eastward they could not get out, & was obliged to anchor off New castle.
May 8, 1772 Friday SE
These 24 hours fresh gales and squally with rain at times the people necessarily empd. PM struck the T.G. masts.
May 9, 1772 Saturday Soerly, NW
First and middle parts fresh gales and squally with rain latter modt gales and fair weath at 7 PM struck yards and topmasts at 7 AM sailed the *Polly* & *Jupiter* to the eastward with Mr.Wright and Blaskowit Deputy Surveyor and their parties.
May 10, 1772 Sunday NW
These 24 hours fresh gales and fair weath.
May 11, 1772 Monday WNW
Modt breezes and fair at 8 AM got up T.G. masts and swayd up yards and topmasts.
May 12, 1772 Tuesday Noerly
Light breezes and cloudy People empd reeving the running rigging .
May 13, 1772 Wednesday NW
Do. weath Empd as above.
May 14, 1772 Thursday NNW
Fresh breezes and clear weath recd from onbd the sloop three cord of wood and one cord of bark for the ships use.
May 15, 1772 Friday Wterly
Do. weath the people necessarily Employed.

May 16, 1772 Saturday WSW
Light breezes and cloudy, with showers at times.
May 17, 1772 Sunday Wterly
Modt breezes and fair weath.
May 18, 1772 Monday do., Soerly, NW
First and latter parts modt and fair middle fresh breezes with showers AM the caulkers came onbd and began to caulk the Quarter deck.
May 19, 1772 Tuesday var.
Light breezes and fair weath the wind variable caulkers Empd as above. Sail makers empd making new sails for the new surveying boats.
May 20, 1772 Wednesday NW
These 24 hours light breezes and fair weath. Caulkers empd caulking decks the people necessarily employed.
May 21. 1772 Thursday Wterly
Light breezes and fair weath caulkers Empd caulking the galley & between decks.
May 22, 1772 Friday WSW
Fresh breezes and cloudy people necessarily empd. caulkers about the main deck.
May 23, 1772 Satuday SW
Do. weath caulkers empd about the forecastle sail makers empd making tents.
May 24, 1772 Sunday Soerly
Light breezes and hazey.
May 25, 1772 Monday SE
These 24 hours fresh breezes and hazey with rain.
May 26, 1772 Tuesday Eterly
Fresh breezes and thick hazey weath with rain People empd clearing between decks.
May 27, 1772 Wednesday SE
Do. weath the people necessarily empd.
May 28, 1772 Thursday Soerly
Modt breezes and cloudy with rain AM hawled the pinnace ashore to be repaired.
May 29, 1772 Friday SW
Modt and fair the caulkers empd caulking the ship & people empd fitting & arming.
May 30, 1772 Saturday variable
Light breezes ye wind variable Empd caulking ye sides Carpenters Empd repairing the boats.

May 31, 1772 Sunday Wterly
These 24 hours light breezes and cloudy.
June 1, 1772 Monday SE
Light breezes and fair weath ye people empd fitting ye awnings caulkers caulking the sides.
June 2, 1772 Tuesday Soerly
First and latter parts modt and fair middle part heavy rain with thunder and lightening the caulkers finished caulking ye sides the people Empd as above.
June 3, 1772 Wednesday variable
Light airs and variable ye carpenters empd painting ye pinnace at 5 PM ye *Polly* returned from carrying the surveying parties to ye Eastward.
June 4, 1772 Thursday vari.
Do. weath ye people necessarily empd.
June 5, 1772 Friday Soerly
Light airs and clear, at 1 PM fired 21 guns it being ye anniversary of the Kings Birth Day. Launched the pinnace.
June 6, 1772 Saturday var.
Light airs the wind var: at 2 PM His Excellency Governor Wentworth came onbd fired 13 guns ½ past 7 he went on shore saluted him with 13 guns more AM got all ye sails out of ye sail and store rooms & spread them ashore, in examining them found several of them eat by the rats.
June 7, 1772 Sunday var.
Light breezes & fair the wind variable, PM got all the sails made up and stowed them away in the sail room.
June 8, 1772 Monday var.
Do. weath empd scraping the sides Opened a cask of pork contg 154 pieces weigh 6 pieces and found them to be 13 pcs deficient.
June 9, 1772 Tuesday SE
First part light airs and clear middle and latter part fresh breezes and cloudy PM finished scraping ye sides & paid them with turpentine AM blacked the wails.
June 10, 1772 Wednesday ESE
Moderate breezes & fair the people empd cleaning the hold.
June 11, 1772 Thursday E
Do. weath people empd variously.
June 12, 1772 Friday ENE
Fresh gales and cloudy with some thunder and lightning People empd as before paid the lower mast with varnish pine.

June 13, 1772 Satuday WNW
Modt and fine fair weath empd as occasion Sail'd the *Polly* tender for Boston.
June 14, 1772 Sunday var.
Do weather.
June 15, 1772 Monday ENE
Fresh breezes and clear weath Empd twisting up yards for gaskets struck yards & topmasts.
June 16, 1772 Tuesday Eterly
Modt and clear weath got up yards and topmasts.
June 17, 1772 Wednesday var.
Dark cloudy weath with drizling rain Empd variously.
June 18, 1772 Thursday Eterly
Modt and cloudy with some rain Empd as occasion.
June 19, 1772 Friday var.
dark cloudy weath AM came in here the *Polly* tender from Boston.
June 20, 1772 Saturday Eterly
Cloudy with rain empd variously.
June 21, 1772 Sunday var.
Do weather AM up T.G. yards.
June 22, 1772 Monday Eterly
Dark cloudy weath with rain PM down T.G. yards.
June 23, 1772 Tuesday Eterly
Do weather with rain at times, empd variously
June 24, 1772 Wednesday WNW
PM dark cloudy weath AM fresh breezes and clear at 8 do. hawled the ship ashore & scrubb'd her bottom and boottoop'd with rozin and brimstones.
June 25, 1772 Thursday Eterly
Dark cloudy rainy weath at 3 PM hauled the ship off to the mooring Empd as occasion.
June 26, 1772 Friday var.
Do. weather Empd variously
June 27, 1772 Saturday Wterly
Modt and fair weath got up yards and topmasts & the T.G. yards across.
June 28, 1772 Sunday var.
Modt and fine fair weath.
June 29, 1772 Monday var.
Light airs and variable with very hot weath stay'd the masts and set the rigging fore and aft.

June 30, 1772 Tuesday Wterly
Light airs and variable with very hot weath bent the topsails mizon and jibb Empd getting all the provisions off and filling of water.
July 1, 1772 Wednesday var.
Light airs and cloudy with rain at times very hot weath AM read the articles of war and abstract to the ships company.
July 2, 1772 Thursday var.
Fresh breezes and cloudy weath.empd variously.
July 3, 1772 Friday Wterly
Light airs and variable Empd as occasion.
July 4, 1772 Saturday Soerly
Do. weath Empd cleaning the hold.
July 5, 1772 Sunday WNW
PM modt and cloudy AM fresh gales and clear weath.
July 6, 1772 Monday Soerly
PM fresh gales and clear weath AM light airs and variable.
July 7, 1772 Tuesday SW
Fresh gales and cloudy with rain at times Empd variously.
July 8, 1772 Wednesday SW b W
Do gales and clear weath Empd as occasion Opened a cask of pork short 2 pieces Do. a cask Beef short pieces,
July 9, 1772 Thursday WNW
Modt & fair weath Empd variously at Noon sail'd hence the *Polly* Tender for Boston.
July 10, 1772 Friday var.
PM light airs and cloudy with thunder and rain AM modt and clear weath empd as occasion.
July 11, 1772 Saturday var.
Light airs and fair weath Empd sounding the river.
July 12, 1772 Sunday Wterly
Do. weath.
July 13, 1772 Monday Soerly
Modt with thick fogg Empd filling water.
July 14, 1772 Tuesday var,
Fresh breezes and foggy with some rain AM returned the *Polly* Tender from Boston Recd from onbd of her 30 barrels of bread ? at 8 fired a gun and loosed ye yard arms of ye fore top sail as signal.
July 15, 1772 Wednesday var.
Modt with thick fogg empd filling of water.
July 16, 1772 Thursday Soerly
Modt and clear weath loosed sails to dry.

July 17, 1772 Friday Soerly, NW
Modt and foggy with rain AM fresh breezes & clear weath Empd getting our water onbd came in here the *Wentworth* mast ship from London six weeks out.

The cargo of the mast ship is one of the reasons for the British presence in New England. The ships carried large white pines from New England to the naval shipyards of England. These mast ships took about two months to unload English goods and complete the backbreaking task of snaking a full cargo of masts through the stern ports. Fluyts and snows were used as well as specially built ships that have been called super carriers of the day ranging from four hundred to an extreme of one thousand tons burthen. Mast ships had huge stern ports through which the great sticks were hoisted and stored. Convoyed and protected by the British navy these huge sticks were a strategic commodity critical to the fleet and even the empire.

July 18, 1772 Saturday var.
Modt and fair weath Empd as occasionally.

July 19, 1772 Sunday Soerly
Do. weath Empd unmooring ship found Bt Br buoy and rope gone

July 20, 1772 Monday var., NW
Isles of Sholes Church SSE
Modt and variable at 11 AM weighed & came to sail & went out at Noon the Isle of Shoals Church SSE hawled the ship between York ledge and the shore ? NE wind NW.

July 21, 1772 Tuesday NNW, SW, S, SSW
PM fresh gales and clear weath at 8 do. Wood Island WSW distance 2 leagues ENE at Noon anchored in Abenecook harbour Sheepcoat River in 5 fm at low water, soft bottom. The going in is a narrow entrance Eastward & westward sheltered from all winds as being land locked all round do. veered away and moored a cable each way anchors N and S of each other.

July 22, 1772 Wednesday SW
Fresh breezes and cloudy AM Empd unbending our sail came onbd Mr. Sproul and party deputy surveyor who had lost boats grapling and rope one measuring line of 75 fms and one hand lead & line & two oars. Supplied him with others as also 2 (Hhds) water casks.

*July 23, 1772 to Aug. 4, 1772

Aug. 5, 1772 Wednesday do.
First part fresh gales and squally, latter fresh breezes at 7 PM the boat returned in sounding Sheepscot River with ye raft one was drove out to sea the wind and a very strong tide being against her which obliged her to cut away the raft in all 11 casks.

*Aug. 6 1772 to Aug. 17, 1772

Aug. 18, 1772 Tuesday W
Moored in Townsend Harbour
Fresh breezes and hazey weath latter squally and clear weath Employed turning into Bay at ½ past 7 came to off Sqirrel Island and near to Townsend Gutt in 7 fms water rocky bottom with the stream anchor & cable and veered out a cable. At 8 AM were obliged to ship our cable by reason of the rapidcity of the tide and the violent squalls of wind, and being on a lee shore Empd turning into Townsend Harbour at ½ past 10 anchored in do. Harbour and moored a cable each way the So. Point of the Harbour SE b S dist. of shore about a cable length.

*Aug. 19, 1772 to Aug. 27, 1772

Aug. 28, 1772 Friday Soerly
Light airs and fair weath at 4 PM came in three merchant vessels and saluted with 11 guns each answered do. with 9 guns Empd making gaskets &c.
Aug. 29, 1772 Saturday do.
Light breezes and fair weath Empd as yesterday returned a surveying party.
Aug. 30, 1772 Sunday do.
Do. weath Empd. occasionally.
Aug. 31 1772 Monday do.
Light airs and calm weath PM received 5 casks of bread from onbd ye *Admiral* Tender.
Sept. 1, 1772 Tuesday var.
First part fair weath middle hazey, latter light airs and fair weath. AM punished Geo. Davis Seaman with 12 lashes for drunkeness, and mutinous expression.

*Sept. 2, 1772 to Oct. 1, 1772

Oct. 2, 1772 Friday var.
Light airs and cloudy PM came in from the survey Mr. Grant Deputy Surveyor lost out of his boat during ye summers survey 4 (water casks) Hhds a tent 8 hand leads and 8 lines also a depsea lead & line and a boat hook Fresh breezes & fair weath Empd variously.

*Oct. 3, 1772 to Oct. 14, 1772

Oct. 15, 1772 Thursday SW
Modt. breezes and fair weath AM arrived here ye *Jupiter*
Oct. 16, 1772 Friday Soerly, var.
Modt breezes & fair weath PM came in from the Survey Mr. Wright Deputy Surveyor lost out of his boat during ye summer survey 2 hand leads & 2 lines 3 oars, boat hook, 2 deepsea lines and 1 lead & also the boats mizon.

*Oct. 17, 1772 to Oct. 19, 1772

Oct. 20, 1772 Tuesday Soerly
First part modt & fair weath latter do. foggy with drizling rain AM arrived here the *Polly*, schooner.
Oct. 21, 1772 Wednesday Noerly.
Modt breezes and hazey with drizling rain AM sail'd hence ye *Polly* schooner Empd variously.

*Oct. 22, 1772 to Oct. 31, 1772

Nov. 1, 1772 Sunday var.
Light winds with calm and fair weath Read the articles of War to the ships company. At 8 PM arrived here the *Halifax* armed schooner.
Nov. 2, 1772 Monday var.
Moored in Townsend Harbour
Variable winds and fair weath Empd variously AM sailed hence the *Halifax*.
Nov. 3, 1772 Tuesday do.
Modt. breezes and fair weath Empd variously.
Nov. 4, 1772 Wednesday do.
Light winds and fair weath came in here his Majesty's surveying schooner *Diligence*.

Nov. 5, 1772 Thursday do.
Do. weath Latter part strong gales.
Nov. 6, 1772 Friday NW
Strong gales and clear at 1 PM fired 15 guns being the anniversary of Gun Powder treason AM sail'd hence his Majesty's schooner *Diligent.*
Nov. 7 1772 Saturday do.
Do. weath latter part light winds AM Empd hauling the ship ashore to clean.
Nov. 8, 1772 Sunday NE, N b W
Light winds and fair PM hauled ship and moored as before Arrived Mr. Blankswitz from the Survey out of whose boat were lost some boatswains stores.
Nov. 9, 1772 Monday N
Do weather Empd getting on board wood.
Nov. 10, 1772 Tuesday var.
Light winds and fair weath latter fresh gales and cloudy PM getting on board wood Sail'd henace the *Polly.*

*Nov. 11, 1772 to Nov. 18, 1772

Nov. 19, 1772 Thursday var.
Cuckold Rock NW 2 miles dist. Modt and cloudy at 6 AM weighed and came to sail at Noon the Cuckold Rocks NW quarter.
Nov. 20, 1772 Friday var., SE
At single anchor in Townsend Harbour
PM fresh gales and dark cloudy weath winds var. at 7 do. bore up for Townsend harbour at 5 anchored in Townsend harbour with Bt Br in 6 fms water soft bottom the south point at the harbour SE b S AM hard gales with heavy rain Empd taking soundings. Recd this day 7 half Hhds, 5 Hhds & 1 butt.
Nov. 21, 1772 Saturday SE, NW
Seguin Island NNE 4 leagues
PM hard gales at 4 do. weighed and came to sail at Noon Seguin Island NNE dist. 3 leagues.
Nov. 22, 1772 Sunday var.
At single anchor in Casco Bay
Modt & cloudy weather at ½ past 5 PM came too with Bt.Br under an island in Casco Bay Falmouth Church steeple WNW.
Nov. 23, 1772 Monday Noerly
Moored in Falmouth road
Modt & cloudy with rain at 7 AM weighed and came to sail

at 8 do. came to with the Bt Br in Falmouth Road in 4 fm water soft bottom Moored here with the stream anchor and cable.

Nov. 24, 1772 Tuesday do.
Modt and fair weath Empd variously.

Nov. 25, 1772 Wednesday do.
Do. Empd variously.

Nov. 26, 1772 Thursday NNE, NNW
Fresh breezes and fair weath AM weighed and came to sail.

Nov. 27, 1772 Friday NNW
At single anchor under Hogg Island in Casco Bay
Falmouth Church WNW
Do. Breezes at 5 PM anchored under Hogg Island in Casco Bay Falmouth Church Steeple WNW.

Nov. 28, 1772 Saturday NW
Nubble Point SW b W dist 4 leagues
Modt and cloudy at 4 AM weighed and came to sail at 8 do. abreast of Cape Elizabeth where we found a great sea at Noon the Nubble Point SW b W dist. 4 leagues.

Nov. 29, 1772 Sunday Wterly
Modt and clear weath at 3 PM abreast of Piscataqua River at 5 finding ye tide run very strong against us anchored the light N b W 1 mile at 8 AM weighed & run into Spruce Creek and moored her.

*Nov. 30, 1772 to Dec. 14, 1772

Dec. 15, 1772 Tuesday Soerly
Fresh breezes and clear weath at 8 AM fired a gun and made the signal to unmoor do. unmoored in order to go to town.

Dec. 16, 1772 Wednesday var., Wterly
Little wind inclinable to calm at 4 PM moored ship then not being wind enough AM fresh breezes and cloudy with snow at times,

Dec. 17, 1772 Thursday E b S, Wterly
PM hard gales and thick cloudy weath AM fresh breezes and fair at 8 loosed sails to dry at Noon furled do.

Dec. 18, 1772 Friday do.
Fresh breezes and fair weath PM arrived here the *Polly* schooner with provisions and officers stores from Boston. Empd receiving onbd do.

*Dec. 19, 1772 to Dec. 31, 1772

Jan. 1 1773 Friday W, NW
Moored in the Pool Piscataqua River
PM Mod and cloudy, Am fine clear W. with light breezes with light breezes. Empd.variously.
Jan. 2, 1773, Var:, NE PM Modt. and cloudy weath, AM fine clear weathr. Saturday Var.
Moored in the Pool Piscataqua River
Do Wr. Read the Articles of War to the Ships Company
Jan. 3, 1773 Sunday NE
Moored in the Pool Piscataqua River
First part Modt. And Cloudy with rain at times, latter fresh breezes and Cloudy.
Jan. 4, 1773 Monday Eterly
Moored in Pool of the Piscataqua River
Fine Clear Wr. AM empd bending Sails
Jan. 5, 1773 Tuesday WNW
Moored in Pool Piscataqua River
PM Fine Wr empd. Getting ready to go down to Spruce Creek
AM fresh breezes and cloudy - at 8 unmoored, at 9 came to Sail, ½ 10 came to in Spruce Creek.
Masters log
PM fine clear Weath. AM Empd getting reddy for going down to Spruce Creek. AM fresh breezes and cloudy at 8 unmoored at 9 came to sail ½ past 10 came too in Sprous (Spruce) Creek.
Jan. 6, 1773 Wednesday WSW
Moored in Spruce Creek Piscataqua River
PM Fresh breezes and Cloudy empd. Mooring Ship - AM Do. Wr empd new birthing her - the Bt. Br Bouy NW, Sheet Anchor to the SE acrofs the River.
Jan. 7 1773 Thursday W, WNW
Moored in Spruce Creek Piscataqua River
PM Do Wr Struck yards and Topmasts - empd unrigging do and unbending the Sails.
Jan. 8 1773 Friday W, WNW
Moored in Spruce Creek Piscataqua River
Do. Wr. Empd stripping the Ship and sounding the Cables - Fore & Maintopsail Buntlines and Clewlines much wore converted to Rounding the Cables.
Jan. 9, 1773 Saturday Var:
Moored in Spruce Creek Piscataqua River
Slight Aires. Empd occasionly: the fore and Maintopsail Halyards, & Fore Clue garnets much wore, converted for Rounding the

Cables.
Jan. 10, 1773 Sunday NE, ENE, NW
Moored in Spruce Creek Piscataqua River
Fresh breezes and Cloudy with rain at times AM Clear Wr.
Rounded the Bt. Br. 6 fms and cachled 4 Do. Rounded the Sheet Cable 6 fms. And cachled 4 fathoms.

*Jan. 11, 1773 to Mar. 9 1773

March 10, 1773 Wednesday NW
Moored in Spruce Creek Piscataqua River
Mod. And Cloudy - hove off the *Jupiter* Surveying Vessel - Emp. fitting her.
March 11, 1773 Thursday Var: NW
Moored in Spruce Creek Piscataqua River
Cold and Raw - Emp. About the Rigging - Sailed to the eastward the *Polly* Tender.

*March 12, 1773 to Mar. 22, 1773

March 23, 1773 Tuesday Var:
Moored in Spruce Creek Piscataqua River
Mod and fair - Empd Rigging the Topmasts
March 24, 1773 Wednesday Soerly, Werly
Moored in Spruce Creek Piscataqua River
Do. Weathr. Empd Rigging the Ship.
March 25, 1773 Thursday Var, NE
Moored in Spruce Creek Piscataqua River
PM Mod and Cloudy - AM hard gales and hazy - Empd as before
March 26, 1773 Friday NE to NNW
Moored in Spruce Creek Piscataqua River
PM Strong gales with heavy rain - AM Do. Gales & squally
The Bt Br Anchor came home which occasioned the ship ashore at low water - Emp getting the anchor carried out.
March 27, 1773 Saturday Noerly
Moored in Spruce Creek Piscataqua River
Fresh gales and squally with flying clouds - Empd new Mooring the ship.
March 28, 1773 Sunday Werly
Moored in Spruce Creek Piscataqua River
Fresh breezes and fair - Arrived the *Polly* Tender from the Southward.

March 29, 1773 Monday Var:
Moored in Spruce Creek Piscataqua River
Mod. And fair Empd occasionaly.

March 30, 1773 Tuesday Soerly
Moored in Spruce Creek Piscataqua River
Fresh breezes and cloudy - Empd drawing yarns

March 31, 1773 Wednesday Var:
Moored in Spruce Creek Piscataqua River
Light winds - Empd Variously

April 1, 1773 Thursday Noerly
Moored in Spruce Creek Piscataqua River
Dark Cloudy Wr. - got the Topsail yards and Rigged them.

April 2, 1773 Friday NE
Moored in Spruce Creek Piscataqua River
Fresh gales and Cloudy with frost and snow - AM
Sailed hence the *Jupiter* for Boston with the *Polly* Tender Empd as occasion.

April 3 1773 Saturday E
Moored in Spruce Creek Piscataqua River
Fresh gales with rain at times Empd Variously - Read the Articles of War and new Abstract of Parliament to the Ships Company.

April 4, 1773 Sunday Var:
Moored in Spruce Creek Piscataqua River
Mod. and fair

April 5, 1773 Monday Soerly
Moored in Spruce Creek Piscataqua River
Light winds and foggy - Empd Variously

April 6, 1773 Tuesday Var.
Moored in Spruce Creek Piscataqua River
PM Calm - AM light Winds - Empd as occasion

April 7, 1773 Wednesday SW
Moored in Spruce Creek Piscataqua River
Fresh wind and Cloudy, PM Arrived the *Polly* with Provisions from Boston.

*April 8 1773 to April 20, 1773

April 21, 1773 Wednesday Var:
Moored in Spruce Creek Piscataqua River
Do. Winds and Cloudy with Rain at times - Returned the *Jupiter* from Boston.

April 22, 1773 Thursday Esterly
Moored in Spruce Creek Piscataqua Creek
Mod. And hazy with Rain at times - Empd Recd Provisions from the *Jupiter*.

April 23, 1773 Friday Do.
Moored in Spruce Creek Piscataqua River
Fresh gales with Rain - Empd Variously

April 24, 1773 Saturday Noerly
Moored in spruce Creek Piscataqua River
Cold, dark, cloudy Wr.

April 25, 1773 Sunday Esterly
Moored in Spruce Creek Piscataqua River
Dark and Cloudy with show, Sleet, and Rain

April 26, 1773 Monday Do.
Moored in Spruce Creek Piscataqua River
Do. Weathr. With Rain - Empd Variously

April 27, 1773 Tuesday Var:
Moored in Spruce Creek Piscataqua River
Do. Weathr. - Sailed the *Jupiter* a Sounding

April 28, 1773 Wednesday Esterly
Moored in Spruce Creek Piscataqua River
Do. Weathr. - Empd Occasionaly

April 29, 1773 Thursday Variable
Moored in Spruce Creek Piscataqua River
Dark Cloudy Weathr. PM Thunder and Lightening - AM Sailed The Tender to take Soundings.

April 30, 1773 Friday Do.
Moored in Spruce Creek Piscataqua River
Do Weathr. in the evening Thunder lightening Empd. Variously

May 1, 1773 Saturday Do, Werly
Moored in Spruce Creek Piscataqua River
Mod and fair, in the evening lightning - Empd cleaning the Hold - Read the Articles of War &.

May 2, 1773 Sunday Werly
Moored in Spruce Creek Piscataqua River
Fresh gales and squally

May 3, 1773 Monday Var:
Moored in Spruce Creek Piscataqua River
Mod and fair - Empd Occasionaly

May 4 1773 Tuesday Soerly
Moored in Spruce Creek Piscataqua River
Do. Weathr. - Empd Variously

May 5, 1773 Wednesday Do.
Moored in Spruce Creek Piscataqua
Mod and hazy - Do. Empd
May 6, 1773 Thursday Soerly
Moored in Spruce Creek Piscataqua River
Mod and hazy PM Arrived the *Jupiter* AM Empd getting the *Polly* Tender ready for Boston to receive stores.
May 7, 1773 Friday NW, NE, SE
Moored in Spruce Creek Piscataqua River
Do Weathr. Do Empd AM Fresh winds & Cloudy - at 8 sailed the *Polly*.

*May 8, 1773 to May 16, 1773

May 17, 1773 Monday Var:
Moored in Spruce Creek Piscataqua River
Mod and hazy Empd Variously - at 8 AM Fired a Gun & lower the Foretop sail as a signal for Sailing.
May 18, 1773 Tuesday SW, NW, Var:
Moored in Spruce Creek Piscataqua River
Fresh winds and hazy - from 6 to 9 PM very hard gusts of wind With thunder and lightening.
Fresh breezes and hazy Weathr from 6 to 9 PM very hard gusts of wind with thunder and lighting.
May 19, 1773 Wednesday Werly
Moored in Spruce Creek Piscataqua River
Mod and fair Empd watering and setting up the Rigging Fore and Aft.
May 20, 1773 Thursday Soerly
Moored in Spruce Creek Piscataqua River
Thick fogg with drisling rain Empd as occasion - Sailed Hence the *Surveyor* Sloop to the Eastward with two parties.
May 21, 1773 Friday Do.
Moored in Spruce Creek Piscataqua River
Fresh breezes and hazy - Empd Variously
May 22, 1773 Saturday Do.
Moored in Spruce Creek Piscataqua River
Do. Weathr. Came in and Anchored his Majesty's Schooner *Halifax*
May 23, 1773 Sunday NNW
Moored in Spruce Creek Piscataqua River
Fresh gales and clear

May 24, 1773 Monday WSW
Moored in Spruce Creek Piscataqua River
Mod. And Clear - Sailed hence the *Halifax.*
May 25, 1773 Tuesday Soerly
Moored in Spruce Creek Piscataqua River
Thick Weathr with Rain Empd as occasion
May 26, 1773 Wednesday Var:
Moored in Spruce Creek Piscataqua River
Cloudy with Rain Empd Variously
May 27, 1773 Thursday Var:, NW
Moored in Spruce Creek Piscataqua River PM heavy rain -
AM Clear with fresh gales - Sailed the *Jupiter* with Parties.
May 28, 1773 Friday NNW
Moored in Spruce Creek Piscataqua River
Fresh gales and Clear - sent a Man to Quarters.
May 29, 1773 Saturday Var:
Moored in Spruce Creek Piscataqua River
Mod. And foggy - Empd as occasion
May 30, 1773 Sunday Var:
Moored in Spruce Creek Piscataqua River
Mod and hazy - at 1 PM fired 21 Guns being the anniversary Of King Charles the seconds Restoration.
May 31, 1773 Monday Easterly
Moored in Spruce Creek Piscataqua River
Thick fogg - Empd as occasion
June 1, 1773 Tuesday Var:
Moored in Spruce Creek Piscataqua River
Ditto Wr. Empd Variously - Read the Articles of War &c.
June 2, 1773 Wednesday Eterly
Moored in Spruce Creek Piscataqua River
Dark Weathr Empd getting Water on board - lost by a Boats over setting In a squall off the fort, one pr Pistols, one Musket, with two Cartorech Boxes.
June 3, 1773 Thursday Var:
Moored in Spruce Creek Piscataqua River
Light Airs empd getting ready for Sea - came onbd Capt. Holland With our Surveying Party.
June 4, 1773 Friday Var:, SSW
At Single Anchor off Kittery Point
PM light Airs and Cloudy - Empd warping out of Spruce Creek Fired 21 guns being His Majesty's Birth Day.
June 5, 1773 Saturday SSW, SW

At Single Anchor in Townsend Harbor.
Fresh gales and hazy Weathr. Empd turning out of the Harbor, at 2 PM the Fort Saluted, returned the Salute with 11 Guns - at 4 Got out, steered away NE within York Ledges - at 6 the Nubble W b N 1 ½ leagues. At 8 Wood Island N b E 3 leagues - at 12 fresh gales & hazy Wr. Brought to with Maintopsail to the Mast, with her head off, up SE b S, Of SE - in reefs Topsails - handed the Mizen topsail - at 4 bore away Course N b E, thick hazy wr: - at 6 Small Point ENE hauled out East. At 7 Sequin Island NE b E 1 mile. From this island to the Cuckold Rocks NE. At 9 abreast of the Cuckolds - ½ past 10 Anchored In Townsend Harbor in 3 ½ fms soft Bottom - Outer pt. SE ½ S.

June 6, 1773 Sunday SSW, Var:
At Single Anchor in Townsend Harbor
PM Fresh gales and thick hazy Weathr. AM Mod & clear fair Wr.

June 7, 1773 Monday Werly
At single anchor in Townsend Harbor
PM Mod and hazy Wr: Middle Calm - latter fresh gales And squally.

June 8, 1773 Tuesday SW
At Single Anchor in Townsend Harbor
PM Fresh gales and Squally - Middle Calm - AM Fresh gales And Cloudy Weather.

June 9, 1773 Wednesday NW, WNW, W, SW
Little Minan Harb. S ½ S Sanes Gut off Skutock Pt W b N
First part fresh gales and Squally - Middle Mod. & cloudy Latter, fresh gales and hazy - at Noon Sailed from Townsend Harbor And left the Sloop *Surveyor*, in st. Reefs Topsails - at 4 PM Monhegan S b E 2 mile - at 8 Mintinicus Rock NW b W 2 miles At 8 AM Mount Desert NE b N - at 4 Do ESE 2 leagues.

June 10, 1773 Thursday SW, S, SSE
Moored in Goldsborough Harbor
Fresh gales with very hard Squalls for the most part with some Rain - at ½ past 1 came to with the Bt Br in 2 ½ fms at low Water, soft bottom, veered away 1/3 of a cable - at 5 lower T.G. yds. At 4 AM veered away to the long service, at 8 let go the small Br: and veered to ½ of a cable - struck yards and topmasts.

June 11, 1773 Friday Werly
Moored in Goldsborough Harbor
PM Mod and Clear - AM Fresh gales with Rain and very Cold With some rain, hove up the small Br: anchor - at noon got up The topmasts and yards.

June 12, 1773 Saturday Noerly, Var:
Moored in Goldsborough Harbor
Mod and Cloudy - Empd shifting our Birth, the upper most No. in Town W b N Bluff Pt: SW 5 ½ Leagues - AM fresh gales and cloudy, - came in The Sloop *Surveyor.*

June 13, 1773 Sunday Soerly
Moored in Goldsborough Harbor
Cold Weather with some Rain - Empd. Occasionally

June 14, 1773 Monday Soerly, Var:
Moored in Goldsborough Harbor
PM fresh breezes and Cloudy with heavy rains - AM Fresh Breezes and Clear Weathr. - at 10 AM weighed and came to Sail – at Noon Little Minan Island E ? 2 mi. Light Winds and Variable: with some Rain - Sailed hence the Sloop *Surveyor* for the River St. Lawrence.

June 15, 1773 Tuesday Var:, SSW
At Single Anchor in Cranberry Island Harbor
Light Airs with some Rain - At 8 PM Lane Isld. N 2 ½ W - Little Minan ENE - The S-most Mount on Mt. Desert N b E - Outer Duck
Isld NW at 8 AM - At 10 working to Cranbury Isld Harbor; at Noon anchored in 12 fms hard bottom, between the Island & the ledge.

June 16, 1773 Wednesday Soerly
At Single Anchor in Cranbury Island Harbor
Slight airs with a thick fogg - Empd. Variously

June 17, 1773 Thursday Do.
At Single anchor in Cranbury Island Harbor
Do. Wr. Empd Sounding the Harbor with the Longboat.

June 18, 1773 Friday Var:, Soerly
Mount Desert Rock 15 degrees W dist: 2 ½ Leagues
Light Airs and Var: at 5 PM hove up the Anchor to right it, At 6 a breeze sprang up off the land, S b W - Long Isld W b N - Outer Duck Island NW - At Noon Ermost Hill of Mt Desert NW - So pt. Of outer Duck Isld. No 41 W - S. pt. Bachus Isld N b W - Mt. Desert Rock S 5 degrees W distant 2 ½ leagues.

June 19, 1773 Saturday SW b S, SSW, WSW, SW b W
Ditto N 37 degrees 23 miles
Mod and hazy - at 4 PM last point of Long Isld N b E 3 miles South most Pt of Isle au Holt W b S - South most Long Pt. E b N - Thick and foggy - Cleared up saw a Schooner in the NE quarter.

June 20, 1773 Sunday SW, SW b E, SW b W, SW

Outer Point of Isle Holt E ½ N distant 2 Leagues
Mod Wr. With a thick fogg, Empd sounding - at 8 the Eastmost Point of Seal Isld SSW, the Outer pt.. Of Isle Holt ENE - A fresh breeze Lost a Deep sea lead and line in sounding - latter part hard gales - at noon outer point of Isle Holt E ½ N 2 leagues.

June 21, 1773 Monday S b W, SW b S, SSW
Monhegan NW ½ N 12 leagues
Most part hard gales and thick fogg, at 1 PM Down T.G.sails & reefd top sails - at 6 lost a logg and three lines at 10 AM out Reefs of the topsails and up T. G. yards.

June 22, 1773 Tuesday SW b W, W, W b N, W, Calm
Ditto NE b N 7 or 8 Leagues
First part fresh breezes and clear, latter light Airs and Variable with Calm, at 2 PM saw the Land bearing from N to NW b W - at 9 Monhegan S point - N b W and W 3 miles & Seguin W ½ N at 4 AM Monhegan N b E 6 leagues.

June 23, 1773 Wednesday SW b W, NNW, W, SW b S
Agamenticus Hill NW & Cape Ann, SW 8 or 9 Leagues
Mod. And Clear Wr. At 4 PM Sequin Isld NNW 7 Leagues at 7 Squally with rain in reef Topgallant at 8 Seguin N b E 7 leagues AM fresh breezes & clear - at 4 Agasmenticus Hills W b N 11 or 1 2 leagues.

June 24, 1773 Thursday SW, W, Calm, Var:
William & Mary Fort WSW 2 mile.
PM Mod. And hazy Wr. at 6 Boon Isld. NNE - Winds var: some Thunder and lightening with rain from 6 to 10 Empd turning between ? Shoals& Duck Isld, 1/3 pt. 2 AM anchored in the ents: of Piscataqua River in 13 fm. Soft bottom Outer Sisters ESE, at 10 got under sail, turning into the River, lost a hand line & lead sounding line.

June 25, 1773 Friday Var:
Moored in Piscataqua River
Mod. And fair Wr. At 2 PM came to with the Bt. Br in 13 fms: - Light winds SSE - New Castle Church Steeple S b W - Moored with the Stream Anchor & cable.

*June 26, 1773 to July 3, 1773

July 4, 1773 Sunday Do.
Moored in Piscataqua River
Dark hazy Weathr: at 7 AM began to unmoored & hove, short on the best Bower.

July 5, 1773 Monday SW, SSW, SW
Seguin Isld NE
Weighed anchor and came to Sail, empd turning out, got out, Bear away, bring the Nubble NE b N or NNE and steer right for it, carries You within York Ledge - Nubble pt.W b S 2 leagues - Bald Head NNW 4 miles - Middle, thick fogg ½ leagues 10 AM it cleared up saw the Land with Small pt., and Seguin Isld: NE, under easy Sail - empd. Sounding.
July 6, 1773 Tuesday SW, Calm, Eterly
Monhegan NE b E
PM Fresh breezes and hazy, at 2 Seguin SW b W 4 mi. at 8 Damascove NE 5 or 6 mi.- Empd sounding having from 16 to 24 faths.Hard bottom, at 9 Calm anchored with the Stream anchor and cable at 8 AM Light Airs, weighed and came to sail, at Noon Monhegan NE b E - joined Compy with the *Jupiter* from the Parties.
July 7 1773 Wednesday Eterly, Soerly, Calm
Do. WNW 9 leagues
Mod. & fine. Empd. Sounding at 8 PM Monhegan Island NNW 7 or 8 leag. Calm - tried the Current, set to the Westward 2 ½ knots an hour
July 8, 1773 Thursday SW
At anchor under George Isld. Gt. Isld. WNW 4 miles
Dark cloudy Wr: came along side the *Jupiter* & took provisions for The parties, at 6 PM sailed hence the *Jupiter* - at 8 AM came to With the Stream anchor under Gorges Island 14 Fm. - the Isld WNW 4 miles.
July 9, 1773 Friday Calm
Ditto
Hazy and Calm - at Noon cleared up weighed & came to Sail.
July 10, 1773 Saturday Var:
At single anchor
Light airs and variable: - out reefs Topsails - empd Sounding standing To the Wtward, at 8 Pemaquid Pt. N b W 6 or 7 leagues stood to the So. Ward, at 11 brought to with the Maintops: to the mast, - Damascove W b S 4 leagues. Curr. To 2 knotts to the Westward.
July 11, 1773 Sunday Var:
Damascove W b S 4 leagues PM light airs and variable: at 2 weighed and came to sail Standing to the Wtward, at 3 Pemiquid Pt. N b W 6 or 7 leagues stood to the So. Ward, at 11 brot. To with the maintops:to the mast, - Damarcove W b S 4 leagues Currt to 2

knotts to the Westward.

July 12, 1773 Monday Do.

Fishermans Isld. SSW 2 miles

Fresh breezes and clear, empd Sounding - at 10 came to with The smal Br. Under Squirrel Isld in 12 fms. At 6 AM weighed, at 10 up with Fishermans Island, going thro the Narrow passage in 6 fms water - Fishermans Island SSW 2 miles.

July 13, 1773 Tuesday Var:

At single anchor, Pemiquid Point NE 2 miles

PM light airs. Empd Sounding in the Mouth of Damarcove the River - at 8 PM anchored with the stream anchor in 16 fms.

July 14, 1773 Wednesday Do.

At single Anchor under Bald Island, it bearing WSW near a mile. At 1 PM weighed and stood towards Broad Bay, sounding, at 6 PM And stood to the Westward, at 9 came to under Bald Isld. In 7 fms water Hard bottom within a mile of the Island bearing WSW.

July 15, 1773 Thursday Do.

At anchor in Booth Bay, Squirrel Isld W. 2 miles

At 5 AM weighed and stood to the Northward at 8 tacked & stood Towards Fisherman Isld - light Airs - at 11 going thru the narrow passage At Noon anchored in Booth Bay in 7 fm: water. Boats Empd Sounding the bay.

July 16, 1773 Friday Do.

At anchor in Booth Bay, Squirrel Isld W. 2 miles

Mod. And fine Weathr: Boats Empd. Sounding sound Damascove Isld and the Islands adjacent all these 24 hours.

July 17, 1773 Saturday Do.

At anchor in Booth Bay, Squirrel Isld Westward 2 miles.

Cloudy with rain all these 24 hours - Empd variously.

July 18, 1773 Sunday Noerly

At single anchor in Townsend Harbor Burnt Isld. SE 1 mile.

Mod and cloudy at 1 PM weighed and turned further into The Bay, sounding at the same time, at 3 PM anchored in Townsend Harbor in 5 fm water, Burnt Isld. SE 1 mile - Reverend Mr. Murrays House ENE.

July 19 1773 Monday Variable

At single anchor in Townsend Harbor Burnt Isld SE 1 mile.

Mod and Clear, at ½ past 12 weighed and ran up into the Western arm of the Harbor, came to with the Bt Br and moored with a cable each way in 4 fms water at low water - Tide rises and falls 15 feet - the finest bottom and one of the safest harbors in this World - So point of the Harbr. SW b S.

July 20, 1773 Tuesday Do.
At single anchor in Townsend Harbor Burnet Isld SE 1 mile
Do Wr. Empd Rounding the cables.
July 21 1773 Wednesday Do.
At single anchor in Townsend Harbor Burnt Isld SE I mile.
PM Empd. As above - AM Dryed and unbent the small sails.
July 22, 1773 Thursday Do.
At single anchor in Townsend Harbor Burnt Isld SE 1 mile.
Fine clear Wr: - Empd drying and unbending the sails.
July 23, 1773 Friday NW
Moored in Townsend Harbor
Ditto Wr. Fitted out the Pinnace to Sound Sheepscot River
July 24, 1773 Saturday Werly
Moored in Townsend Harbor
Do. Wr. Paid the lower Masts and greased the Topmasts.
July 25, 1773 Sunday Var:
Moored in Townsend Harbor
First part file of these 24 hours small rain - later fresh gales and clear.
July 26, 1773 Monday Noerly
Moored in Townsend Harbor
Do. Wr. AM paid the Ships sides with varnish of Pine
July 27, 1773 Tuesday NW b W
Moored in Townsend Harbor
Fine Weatr. People Empd Variously.
July 28, 1773 Wednesday
Moored in Townsend Harbor
Do. Wr. People Empd variously
July 28, 1773 Wednesday WSW
Moored in Townsend Harbor
Mod Wr. Fired at a Sloop for having a pendant hoisted.
July 29, 1773 Thursday SW
Moored in Townsend Harbor
Fresh breezes and cloudy Empd. Wooding and Watering.
July 30, 1773 Friday Serly
Moored in Townsend Harbor
Fresh breezes and clear Employed as above.
July 31, 1773 Saturday NW
Moored in Townsend Harbor
Mod and fair - Empd variously - The Lat of this Harbor
Obs: 43. 50 30 No.
Aug. 1, 1773 Sunday Soerly

Moored in Townsend Harbor

Aug. 2, 1773 Monday Var:

Moored in Townsend Harbor

Light breezes & hazy - Empd clearing ship - Read the Articles of War.

Aug. 3, 1773 Tuesday SE

Moored in Townsend Harbor

Slight breezes and cloudy with with rain - Empd occasionally

Aug. 4, 1773 Wednesday Soerly

Moored in Townsend Harbor

Do. Breezes and hazy Empd Variously

Aug. 5, 1773 Thursday SW

Moored in Townsend Harbor

Light breezes and fair - Empd watering

Aug. 6, 1773 Friday SW

Moored in Townsend Harbor

Fresh breezes and cloudy - AM arrived Mr. Sproule & party from Surveying - some stores lost - Fired two Swivels shotted to bring to a Sloop.

Aug. 7, 1773 Saturday Esterly

Moored in Townsend Harbor

Fresh breezes and squally with rain - Ret. The Penance from Sounding Sheepscot River.

*Aug. 8, 1773 to Aug. 15, 1773

Aug. 16, 1773 Monday WSW, NW

Moored in Townsend Harbor

Clear Wr. - Pinnace Empd. Among the outer Islands of this Harbor; laying down Naval Remarks &c.

Aug 17, 1773 Tuesday Var: Calm NW

Moored in Townsend Harbor

Light airs and calm Pinnace Empd as before.

Aug. 18, 1773 Wednesday Var:

Moored in Townsend Harbor

Fresh breezes and clear, Pinnace Empd. Out on Booth Bay taking Soundings and laying Naval Remarks.

Aug. 19, 1773 Thursday Do.

Moored in Townsend Harbor

Do. Weathr. Emp. Variously - Boat as before.

Aug. 20, 1773 Friday Do.

Moored in Townsend Harbor

Do. Weathr, Came in a Sloop from Tryal with Wine, bound to Salem Boat Empd. as before.

Aug. 21, 1773 Saturday Soerly, calm, NW
Moored in Townsend Harbor
Fresh breezes and clear, PM came Mr. Grant Deputy Surveyor with his Party - lost sounding Stores.

*Aug. 22, 1773 to Aug. 27, 1773

Aug. 28, 1773 Saturday Var.
Moored in Townsend Harbor
Mod. And cloudy Arrived here Mr. Blashonitz and party - lost out of His Boat sundry stores.

Aug. 29, 1773 Sunday Eterly, Soerly
Moored in Townsend Harbor
Do. Weather

Aug. 30, 1773 Monday Soerly., calm, Werly.
Moored in Townsend Harbor
Mod. And fair. Empd. Fitting out Mr: Grants and Blashonitz Parties To proceed to Portsmouth.

Aug. 31, 1773 Tuesday SW
Moored in Townsend Harbor
Do. Weathr. People Empd as yesterday.

Sept. 1, 1773 Wednesday SW
Moored in Townsend Harbor
Fresh breezes and thick hazy Weathr. AM sailed hence the two Surveying Parties to the Westward - Read the Articles of War.

Sept. 2, 1773 Thursday SW, Var: Soerly
Moored in Townsend Harbor
Dark cloudy Weathr. With lightning and rain

Sept. 3, 1773 Friday Var:
Moored in Townsend Harbor
Mod. And pleasant Weathr. Pinnace Empd. Sounding the Bay.

Sept. 4, 1773 Saturday SE
Moored in Townsend Harbor
Thick foggy Weathr. With rain - People Empd. Variously

Sept. 5, 1773 Sunday Var:
Moored in Townsend Harbor
Mod. And cloudy with small Rain.

Sept. 6, 1773 Monday SW
Moored in Townsend Harbor
Cloudy with Rain, at 4 PM arrived here the *Jupiter* from

Taking soundings and laying down Naval Remarks - lost sounding stores.
Sept. 7, 1773 Tuesday Var:
Moored in Townsend Harbor
Mod. And Cloudy Empd Variously
Sept. 8, 1773 Wednesday Do.
Moored in Townsend Harbor
Light airs and Variable Empd as above.
Sept. 9, 1773 Thursday Do.
Moored in Townsend Harbor
Fresh gales and squally
Sept. 10, 1773 Friday Eterly
Moored in Townsend Harbor
More Mod. With Rain - Sailed the *Jupiter* to the Wtward to Attend as Surveying Party empd from Cape Ann to Boston.

*Sept. 11, 1773 to Sept. 25. 1773

Sept. 26, 1773 Sunday Do.
Moored in Townsend Harbor
Do. Weathr. PM arrived the *Surveyor* Sloop, with Mr. Weights Deputy Surveyor from the River St. Lawrence.
Sept. 27, 1773 Monday Eterly
Moored in Townsend Harbor
Do. Weathr. Sailed the *Surveyor* Sloop with Mr. Wright for Piscataqua,With orders to lay down the soundings &c.

*Sept. 28, 1773 to Oct. 3, 1773

Oct. 4, 1773 Monday Wterly
Moored in Townsend Harbor
Mod. And fair AM sent the Pinnace to Sound Kennebec River.

*Oct. 5, 1773 to Oct. 18, 1773

Oct. 19, 1773 Tuesday NW
Moored in Townsend Harbor
Fresh breezes and clear Ret. The Pinnace from Sounding Kennebec.
Oct. 20, 1773 Wednesday NW b W
Moored in Townsend harbor
Weather much the same.

Oct. 21, 1773 Thursday Wterly
Moored in Townsend Harbor
These 24 hours variable Weathr. - empd. Occaionaly.
Oct. 22, 1773 Friday NW
Moored in Townsend Harbor
Fresh breezes and fair Wr. Came onbd. Mr. Malcom to inform Of a Brig. At the Whitchcasset having no Register.
Oct. 23, 1773 Saturday Noerly
Moored in Townsend Harbor
Mod. And fair Variously Empd,
Oct. 24, 1773 Sunday NE
Moored in Townsend Harbor
Thick hazy Weathr. With rain at times
Oct. 25, 1773 Monday Noerly
Moored in Townsend Harbor
Thick hazy Wr. Excercised the People at Great Guns and Small arms.
Oct. 26, 1773 Tuesday Noerly
Moored in Townsend Harbor
Thick hazy Weathr. Excercised the People at Great Guns and Small arms.
Oct. 27, 1773 Wednesday Var:
Moored in Townsend Harbor
Mod. And fair - AM sent the Pinnace to sound the adjacent Rivers.
Oct. 28, 1773 Thursday Do.
Moored in Townsend Harbor
Weathr. The same as yesterday, came into the second time Mr. Malcom Confirming that the Master had arrived from Falmouth with a Register for The above mentioned Brigg.
Oct. 29, 1773 Friday Do.
Moored in Townsend Harbor
Weather the same as yesterday - Empd. Occasionaly
Oct. 30, 1773 Saturday NW
Moored in Townsend Harbor
Mod. And fair, frosty Weathr. Sent Mr. Hogg to go and seize the Above mentioned Brigg.

*Oct. 31, 1773 to Nov. 18, 1773

Nov. 19, 1773 Friday Var:
Moored in Townsend Harbor
Mod. And fair Weathr. Pinnace returned from Sounding - AM

The *Jupiter* returned from Boston - People empd. About the Rigging.

*Nov. 20, 1773 to Dec. 9, 1773

Dec. 10, 1773 Friday NNW
Moored in Townsend Harbor
PM light airs and variable, at 4 AM thick cloudy Weathr. Fired a gun a signal to sail, Do. Weighed and came to sail, the Brigg *Brothers* and *Surveyor* Sloop in company at 6 abreast of Sequian Island Hard gales with thick Wr. Close reefed the topsails - hauled in for Casco Bay but could not get in, bore away with the Brig in company At ½ past 10 made Wood Island, strong gales, hauled in for Winter Harbor At Noon came to with the Bt. Br. In 5 fms she did not bring up, let Go the small Br. And brought up in 3 fms at low water - the ship Touched the Grossird but received no hurt.

Dec. 11, 1773 Saturday NNE, NE, ENE
In Winter Harbor
Hard gales and cloudy with rain - AM More Mod do. Heave ahead Found the Bt. Br. Cable parted, being cut or chafed by some rock or anchor about 7 or 8 fms from the anchor, got hold of the Buoy rope in weighing it, it broke this being a very unsafe harbor, empd warping the ship out, but there being a great sea, could make no haste of it.

Dec. 12, 1773 Sunday ENE, SSE, NE, NNE
Moored in Winter Harbor
Light breezes and cloudy, empd as before, at AM got the ship anchored In 3 fm at low water, at Noon got the ship into the safest part of this Harbor.

Dec. 13, 1773 Monday Noerly
Moored in Winter Harbor
Small Breezes and varible, empd. Unmooring & heaving short, At Noon the wind came to the Soward - moored ship again.

Dec. 14, 1773 Tuesday Wterly, calm
Moored in Winter Harbor
Mod. And cloudy, empd. Sweeping for the anchor, which we found.

Dec. 15, 1773 Wednesday Var:
Moored in Winter Harbor
Light airs and foggy, AM unmoored ship, and hove short on the Bt. Br.

Dec. 16, 1773 Thursday Eterly, Soerly
Moored in Winter Harbor
Fresh breezes and thick Weathr. PM Moored ship with the stream Anchor and cable - AM unmoored and warped out, at Noon foggy with Rain, Veered away the warps and dropped to where we came from, and anchored with the Bt. Bower.

Dec. 17, 1773 Friday Noerly, Esterly, Noerly
Moored in Winter Harbor
Very thick drizling Wr. At 3 fresh gales veered away and let go the small Br., and moored ship. AM unmoored and hove short on the Bt. Br.

Dec. 18, 1773 Saturday NNE, NE b N
Moored in Winter Harbor
PM dark cloudy Weathr. With rain - AM Do. Wr. At single anchor.

Dec. 19, 1773 Sunday NE, Var:
Moored in Winter Harbor
Do. Weathr. With some sleet and fresh gales, AM moored ship with the stream anchor and cable, 3 ½ fms at low water - Ward Isld E b N, The small Isld on the Wrd side of the Harbor NW b W.

Dec. 20, 1773 Monday NW
Moored in Winter Harbor
Hard frosty Wr. With a fresh gale and clear, empd. Cleaning the ship.

Dec. 21, 1773 Tuesday W b S, WNW, W
Moored in Winter Harbor
Hard gales and clear, at 4 PM our stream cable parted, AM Strong gales and clear, at Noon weighed, and was 2 hours before we Could loose the sails.

Dec. 22, 1773 Wednesday NW
At Anchor in Falmo. Harbor, Outer pt. Of small Hogg Isd SW, & Falmo Church W b N. Hard gales and flying clouds at 2 PM close reefed the topsails. Cape Elizabeth bearing NNW 2 miles, at 4 got up to Portland Point Empd working out Falmouth Harbor, at 5 came to with the Bt. Br. In 6 fms - Outer point of Small Hogg Island SW, Falm. Church W b N. At Noon thick hazy Wr. With snow.

Dec 23, 1773 Thursday Do.
At anchor in Falmo. Harbor, Outer Pt. Of Small Hogg Isld. SW, of Falmo. Church W b N PM Mod. And clear, AM hazy, with extreme cold Weathr., at 8 Fired 2 guns and made the signal for sailing, loosed sails, and out all Reefs - handed the topsails.

Dec 24, 1773 Friday Var:
Wood Island NNW dist. 4 miles
Mod. And cloudy with hard frost, at 4 AM weighed & came To sail, at 8 Cape Elizabeth WSW 2 miles, at noon Wood Island NNW 4 miles, got up Topgallt. Yards and set Topgallt. Sails.
Dec. 25, 1773 Saturday Var:
Moored in Spruce Creek Piscataqua River
Light airs and cloudy, at 2 PM Cape Porpores NW ½ league at 4 Boon Isld SbW 3 or 4 leags., half past the Nubble Pt. SW 2 W 2 leagues At 7 Do. Point NW 1 mile at 10 opened the Lighthouse, at 11 anchored In 8 fms water, Lighthouse N b W, at 7 weighed, at 11 got into Spruce Creek, empd. Mooring ship.

*Dec. 26, 1773 to Feb. 28, 1774

Mar. 1, 1774 Tuesday Var:
Moored in Spruce Creek Piscataqua River
Mod and fair began to unmoor, at Noon warped the ship further Out, Read the Articles of War &c.
Mar. 2, 1774 Wednesday Wterly
Moored in Spruce Creek Piscataqua River
PM Do and cloudy Weathr: with snow, sleet and Rain, attended with frost AM light airs and cloudy; Empd variously.
Mar. 3, 1774 Thursday Var:
Bald Head N b W and Boon Isld NE ½ N 4 or 5 miles
Light airs at 7 AM weighed and came to sail, at 8 the Fort NNW 1 mile, stood off E and E b N till Noon, Bald Head N ½ W - Boon Isld NE ½ N 4 or 5 mi. Meeting Island on the Isle of Shoals SW ½ S 2 or 3 mi at Noon.
Mar. 4, 1774 Friday Var:
Piscataqua Light NW b NE 3 miles
Light airs and clear, at 5 came to with the small Br: in 8 Fathoms in Piscataqua Entrance, Lighthouse N b W ½ mile, at 9 weighed & came to dropped out with the tide, at Noon the Lighthouse NW b N 3 miles.
Mar. 5, 1774 Saturday NE, NE b E, ENE
Small breezes, throughout went between York ledge and the land At 6 PM Nubble point N b W ½ W 2 mi. - at 7 Sequian SE 7 or 8 Leagues.
Mar. 6, 1774 Sunday Var:, S
Small breeze and hazy, at 3 bore away for Townsend Harbor Damarscove Isld E ½ N 3 miles, Cuckold Rocks West 1 cable

length, came to with the Small Br. In 3 ½ fms at low water - latter part fresh breezes.

Mar. 7, 1774 Monday ESE, NE

In Townsend Harbor

PM fresh gales with rain, AM more Mod and cloudy.

Mar. 8, 1774 Tuesday Var:

In Townsend Harbor

Light airs and variable, Empd Variously

Mar. 9, 1774 Wednesday SW, SSE

In Townsend Harbor

PM fresh gales and hazy, AM strong gales with heavy rain
Let go the Bt. Br. And veered away 1/3 of a cable.

Mar. 10, 1774 Thursday SSW, WNW, NNW, Var:, S

In Townsend Harbor

PM fresh gales and squally attended with rain, hove up The Bt Br and hove short, at 5 came to sail, So-most point of Damarcove ESE 2 mile, at 8 Sequin isle NW b W 4 Leagues - at Noon fresh breezes and clear.

Mar. 11, 1774 Friday S, SSW, S b W, SSW

Cape Sable NE b E 6 or 7 miles

Fresh gales and squally with some Rain, at 2 PM reefed Topsails, at ½ past 9 the boat lashed on ships side was carried Away by some very heavy seas - hove to and sounded no Ground with 70 fm - at 6 AM out reefs topsails & bore away at 8 saw The land bearing NE b E - at 11 Cape Sable NE b N, at Noon the Cape NE b E 6 or 7 miles.

Mar. 12, 1774 Saturday SW, SSW

Fresh breezes and hazy, at 2 PM Cape Negro N b W, at 6 Port Metone Isld NW 3 leagues under the two topsails and foresail - thick fogg with some rain - at 3 AM out sd reefs each topsail, At 5 with some rain - at 3 AM out sd reefs each topsail, at 5 bore Away, being thick - at 6 brought the ship to, at 7 bore away close Reefed topsails, at 9 brought to - thick fogg.

Mar. 13, 1774 Sunday SW, Var: Calm

Cape Sambro No. 5 or 6 Leags.

At 2 PM began to clear up, bore away and made sail, at 6 Sambro light N b E - at 10 Do. NNW - at Noon Cape Sambrough N 5 or 6 Leagues.

Mar. 14, 1774 Monday SW

PM Fresh breezes and cloudy at 4 Do. Mod. and fine. Cape Sambro SW 1 League, at 6 Do. anchored off the Kings Warf, Halifax yard, hard frost, Empd. heaving the ship to the wharf -

unbent the sails.
Mar. 15, 1774 Tuesday Wterly, Eterly
Alongside the wharf in Halifax Harbor
Fresh gales with some snow, Empd. unrigging the ship got the guns onshore.
Mar. 16, 1774 Wednesday Var:
Alongside the wharf in Halifax Harbor
Fresh breezes and cloudy, Empd. getting the ballast out.
Mar. 17, 1774 Thursday Noerly
Mod. and fair - Empd. as above.
Mar. 18, 1774 Friday Soerly, NW
Alongside the wharf in Halifax Harbor
Dark cloudy Weathr. with snow and sleet, attended with hard frost, A survey on Boatswains stores and slops clothing.
Mar. 19, 1774 Saturday NW
Alongside wharf in Halifax Harbor
Modt. and clear with hard frost, Empd. as before, Survey on Boatswains stores.
Mar. 20, 1774 Sunday Var:
Alongside wharf in Halifax Harbor
Dark hazy soft Weathr.
Mar. 21, 1774 Monday Werly
Alongside wharf in Halifax Harbor.
Clear with hard frost, A Survey on Pursers slops.
Mar. 22, 1774 Tuesday SSE, Var:
Alongside wharf in Halifax Harbor
PM Dark cloudy Weathr:, snow and strong gales.
Mar. 23, 1774 Wednesday Var:
Alongside wharf in Halifax Harbor
Mod. breezes and clear - sailed the Armed Schooner (no name).
Mar. 24, 1774 Thursday SW, Calm, Noerly
Alongside wharf in Halifax Harbor
PM Mod. and hazy, got the Ballast out, & lower y: ashore &c.
Mar. 25, 1774 Friday Wterly
Alongside wharf in Halifax Harbor
Fresh breezes and clear, with hard frost, Empd. about the Rigging.
Mar. 26, 1774 Saturday Do., Eterly, Noerly
Alongside wharf in Halifax Harbor
Do. breezes with frost and snow, arrived the *Kingsfisher* from Boston.
Mar. 27, 1774 Sunday Werly
Alongside wharf in Halifax Harbor

Mod. and clear with hard frost.
Mar. 28, 1774 Monday Var:
Alongside wharf in Halifax Harbor
PM Mod. and clear, AM thick snow & sleet, Empd. heaving the ship off.
Mar. 29, 1774 Tuesday Noerly, Var:, SSE
Alongside wharf in Halifax Harbor
PM Do. Weathr. Sailed hence His Majs Sloop *Kingsfisher*.
Mar. 30, 1774 Wednesday Var:
Alongside wharf in Halifax Harbor
Fresh gales with snow and sleet, AM more Modt. - Carpts Empd reparing the sheathing.
Mar. 31, 1774 Thursday Soerly, Wterly, Noerly
Alongside wharf in Halifax Harbor
PM Fine Weathr: Middle part fresh breezes with snow & rain, Empd. shifting the careening gear, and about the Rigging.
Apr. 1, 1774 Friday Noerly
Alongside wharf in Halifax Harbor
Fresh breezes and clear, Empd. as above Read the Articles of War.
Apr. 2, 1774 Saturday Var:
Alongside wharf in Halifax Harbor
Do. breezes with some snow and rain - Empd. getting the Ballast in.
Apr. 3, 1774 Sunday Do.
Alongside wharf in Halifax Harbor
PM Mod. and cloudy - middle & latter hard gales and squally.
Apr. 4, 1774 Monday NW, Wterly
Alongside wharf in Halifax Harbor
PM Fresh gales and clear, AM sleet & some snow, Empd. variously.
Apr, 5, 1774 Tuesday Wterly
Alongside wharf in Halifax Harbor
Mod. and cloudy Empd. Rigging the ship got all the Ballast in and storing away the ground gear - carpt. and caulkers Empd. below.
Apr. 6, 1774 Wednesday Do. Noerly
Alongside wharf in Halifax Harbor
Fresh gales with snow Empd. rigging the ship.
Apr. 7, 1774 Thursday Noerly
Alongside wharf in Halifax Harbor
Clear Weathr. with frost, Empd. as before - AM sailed hence the *Fowey*.

Apr. 8, 1774 Friday Do.
Alongside wharf in Halifax Harbor
Do. Weathr. Empd. as above - Retd. Boatswains stores.

*Apr. 9, 1774 to April 21, 1774

Apr. 22, 1774 Friday Do.
Alongside wharf in Halifax Harbor
Mod. and clear workmen as before, AM fresh gales at 6. cast off from the careening wharf, and dropped down abreast of the town took in gunners stores.
Apr. 23. 1774 Saturday NE, NNW, Var: Calm
Cape Negro NW b N 4 miles
Fresh gales and clear, weighed and came to sail, at 4 AM Cape Scarborough Lighthouse NNW 2 leagues, at 7 do. NE b E 7 leagues, at 2 AM the No. lights very bright, at 4 do. Cape Negro WNW - at Noon Cape Negro NW b N 4 miles.
Apr. 24, 1774 Sunday SSW, SW, WSW, SW, W
Cape Negro NW b N 4 miles
Cloudy Weathr. throughout, at 4 PM Cape Negro NW b N 6 leagues at 6 Do. reefed the topsails, and down topsail yards - at 8 AM out reefs topsails - got topgallt. yards up.
Apr. 25, 1774 Monday W b N, Var:, NW
Cape Negro
Fresh gales and hazy, at 5 PM Cape Negro NNE 2 miles at 7 NE b N 3 Leagues - Latter part fresh gales and clear.
Apr. 26, 1774 Tuesday NW, Var:
Cape Negro
Fresh gales and clear Wr. - lost a logg and three lines, hauling it in - crowded all sail.
Apr. 27, 1774 Wednesday ESE, SE, Var: NE b E
Cape Negro
Light airs and variable, middle fresh breezes and cloudy - saw Thatcher Isld. Lighthouse WSW 3 or 4 leagues - saw the Shoales N b E 3 or 4 leagues fired 3 guns as signal in fogg - fired 2 guns - thick fogg.
Apr. 28, 1774 Thursday Var:
Moored in Spruce Creek Piscataqua River
Fresh breezes and thick foggy weathr. - standing off and on, at 3 PM cleared up - saw the wr. shore 1 mi. distant 7 and 6 faths hard sand Empd turning up to Ordean Point, the Wt.most Pt. going into Piscataqua River, at 5 abreast of the Lighthouse, ½ past anchored

in Spruce Creek.

Apr. 29, 1774 Friday N, NEtrly

Moored in Spruce Creek Piscataqua River

Fresh gales with heavy rain, Empd. mooring ship, the lighthouse being SSE - Kittery Church E b S ½ S -New Castle Church S ½ W.

Apr. 30, 1774 Saturday NW

Moored in Spruce Creek Piscataqua River

Fresh gales - Empd rounding the Bt. Br. cable.

*May 1, 1774 to May 6, 1774

May 7, 1774 Saturday Wterly

Moored in Spruce Creek Piscataqua River

Do. Weathr. hauled the *Juniper* alongside to fix her.

May 8, 1774 Sunday Var:, Eterly

Moored in Spruce Creek Piscataqua River

PM Mod. and cloudy - AM fresh gales with rain.

May 9, 1774 Monday Var:

Moored in Spruce Creek Piscataqua

PM heavy Rains and hazy cold weathr.- AM cloudy.

May 10, 1774 Tuesday NW

Moored in Spruce Creek Piscataqua River

Fresh gales and clear, painters empd. painting - Rec. bread onbd.

May 11, 1774 Wednesday NE

Moored in Spruce Creek Piscataqua River

Dark cloudy Weathr. with rain, Empd. occasionaly

May 12, 1774 Thursday Var:

Moored in Spruce Creek Piscataqua River

Mod. and cloudy Empd. Rounding the small Br. cable the Jupiter fit for sea.

May 13, 1774 Friday NE

Moored in Spruce Creek Piscataqua River

Dark cloudy Weathr. with Rain Empd variously

May 14, 1774 Saturday Do.

Moored in Spruce Creek Piscataqua River

Heavy rains and thick Weathr. - Empd. getting Wood onboard.

May 15, 1774 Sunday NE, Noerly

Moored in Spruce Creek Piscataqua River

Cloudy Weathr. with rain - AM Sailed hence the *Jupiter*, Surveying vessel for Boston with stores and Provisions for the Parties.

May 16, 1774 Monday Var:

Moored in Spruce Creek Piscataqua River
Ditto Weathr. Empd variously.

May 17, 1774 Tuesday Wterly
Moored in Spruce Creek Piscataqua River
Cold raw Weathr: with rain, empd. as above.

May 18, 1774 Wednesday Var:
Moored in Spruce Creek Piscataqua River
Mod. and cloudy scraped the sides, and paid them with Varnish of Pine.

May 19, 1774 Thursday Do.
At single anchor in Piscataqua River, Lighthouse WSW 2 cable lengths. Mod. and fair at 8 AM began to unmoor ship, at 10 hove short, at 11 weighed and came to sail, at Noon light airs, came to with the Bt. Br. in 8 fath. water soft bottom Lighthouse WSW, two cables lengths.

May 20, 1774 Friday SW, calm, Soerly
Turning to Windward Piscataqua River
First part light airs and clear, at Noon fresh breezes and hazy, weighed and came to sail - Empd. turning to windward.

May 21, 1774 Saturday Soerly, Var: SE
Piscataqua River
Fresh breezes and cloudy, reefed the topsails, So. Mt Shoales NE b E, Oedorn Hill S b E thick Weathr. - latter Mod. and clear.

May 22, 1774 Sunday So., NW b W, W
Working into Boston Harbor:
Fresh breezes and cloudy with thunder, and lightning, at 8 PM small breezes and clear, Thatchers Isld. NNE 3 miles, at 1 AM Boston light WSW 5 or 6 Leagues at 8 came onbd a Pilot & took charge of the ship.

May 23, 1774 Monday WNW, NW, Wterly
Moored in Boston Harbor
Fresh breezes and clear, at 3 PM weighed and came to sail, and turned up to Boston, at 7 abreast of the Fort, fired 15 guns to salute the Admiral, at 9 came too off the Town, found here four of His Majestys ships, the *Captain*, *Admiral Montague*, *Lively*, *Mercury* Tender, and *St. John* Schooner - AM moored ship.

May 24, 1774 Tuesday Wterly
Moored in Boston Harbor
Fresh breezes and cloudy, came in his Majs Schooner *Magdalen*.

May 25, 1774 Wednesday Noerly
Moored in Boston Harbor
Dark cloudy Weathr. with rain, came into Nantasket Road His

Majestys Ship *Tartar.*

May 26, 1774 Thursday Eterly

Moored in Boston Harbor

Do. Weathr Empd. variously.

May 27, 1774 Friday Noerly

Moored in Boston Harbor

Fresh breezes and hazy with rain Exercised small arms.

May 28, 1774 Saturday Do., Calm, Soerly

Moored in Boston Harbor

Modt. and clear- at 11 began to unmoor.

May 29, 1774 Sunday Soerly, Calm. Var:

Moored in Boston Harbor

Fresh breezes and clear, at 4 PM weighed, and came to sail - at 6 came to near Charlestown Ferry and Moored ship, Charlestown Church WNW - AM all the ships and Schooners got under way to proceed to their stations.

May 30, 1774 Monday Var:

Moored in Boston Harbor

Light airs and variable, fired 13 guns it being the Restoration of King Charles the second.

May 31, 1774 Tuesday Do.

Moored in Boston Harbor

Mod. airs cloudy with some rain.

June 1, 1774 Wednesday Var: NW

Moored in Boston Harbor

Do. Weathr. with some thunder and lightning, unmoored ship in order to go further up the Ferry - Read the Articles of War to the ships company and officers. Empd. making flags for the Surveyers boats.

June 2, 1774 Thursday NW

Moored in Boston Harbor

First and latter parts fresh gales and clear Wr. Middle part light airs - AM Empd. mooring ship, nr. Fort point SE, Charlestown Church NW b W in 3 fms water - Recd. fresh Beef - cooper as before.

June 3, 1774 Friday Noerly, Soerly

Moored in Boston Harbor

Fresh breezes and cloudy with thunder and Rain.

June 4, 1774 Saturday Var:

Moored in Boston Harbor

Mod. and fair, fired 21 guns being the Kings Birth Day.

June 5, 1774 Sunday Do.

Moored in Boston Harbor
Fine pleasant Weathr. Recd fresh Beef.
June 6, 1774 Monday Werly
Moored in Boston Harbor
Mod. and fair Weathr, fitted out Mr. Wherterd Dep. Surveyors Boat with line &c.
June 7, 1774 Tuesday WSW
Moored in Boston Harbor
Fresh gales and hazy fitted out the *Jupiter* with stores & Provis: &c: for the Survey. at Noon she sailed for Portsmouth.
June 8, 1774 Wednesday Var:
Moored in Boston Harbor
PM fresh gales and cloudy with some Rain - middle light airs.
June 9, 1774 Thursday NE
Moored in Boston Harbor
PM fresh gales and cloudy - AM arrived his Majestys Schooner *Halifax*.
June 10, 1774 Friday WSW
Moored in Boston Harbor
Do. gales and hazy, sailed hence His Majestys Schooner *St. Johns*.
June 11. 1774 Saturday SW
Moored in Boston Harbor
Fresh gales and hazy, came in the *Wentworth* Mast ship, a ship and Brigg with troops.
June 12, 1774 Sunday SW, Soerly
Moored in Boston Harbor
PM Do. gales and cloudy, latter part Mod. with rain.
June 13, 1774 Monday Soerly
Moored in Boston Harbor
Fresh breezes and cold hazy Weathr. - AM thick fogg.
June 14, 1774 Tuesday Soerly, NW
Moored in Boston Harbor
PM hazy Weathr. at 11 AM the Kings own Regiment landed at the wharf.
June 15, 1774 Wednesday Var:
Moored in Boston Harbor
Mod. and clear Weathr. - arrived 3 transports with the 43 Regiment.
June 16, 1774 Thursday Wterly
Moored in Boston Harbor
Fresh gales and squally - Arrived His Majestys Sloop *Savage*.

June 17, 1774 Friday Do.
Moored in Boston Harbor
Mod. breezes and cloudy with Rain - Empd. variously.
June 18, 1774 Saturday Do., Noerly
Moored in Boston Harbor
PM cloudy with Rain - AM clear Weathr. - loosed sails to day
June 19, 1774 Sunday Var:
Moored in Boston Harbor
Light airs and fine weather.
June 20, 1774 Monday Werly
Moored in Boston Harbor
Mod. breezes and fair, PM arrived his Majestys Schooner *St. Lawrence.*

*June 21, 1774 to June 28, 1774

June 29, 1774 Wednesday Do.
Moored in Boston Harbor
Fine pleasant Weathr. sailed hence the *Wentworth* and two more Transports.
June 30, 1774 Thursday Wterly
Moored in Boston Harbor
Ditto Weather Empd. Variously
July 1, 1774 Friday Soerly
Moored in Boston Harbor
Light airs and variable, came in his Majestys ship *Preston,* Vice Admiral Graves 9 weeks Passage, Saluted the Admiral with 15 guns - Read the Articles of War &c.
July 2, 1774 Saturday Wterly
Moored in Boston Harbor
Fresh breezes and cloudy Empd variously.
July 3, 1774 Sunday Var:
Moored in Boston Harbor
Mod. breezes and cloudy - Empd fitting out the *Jupiter.*
July 4, 1774 Monday Do.
Moored in Boston Harbor
Ditto weather Empd variously.
July 5, 1774 Tuesday Werly
Moored in Boston Harbor
Fresh breezes and squally with rain.
July 6, 1774 Wednesday Var:
Moored in Boston Harbor

Light airs and variable, unbent the sails, except the mizon topsail and jibb.

July 7, 1774 Thursday Do., WNW

Moored in Boston Harbor

PM cloudy Weathr. with rain - AM pleasant Wr. - Sailed His Majts. ship *Captain*, Rear Admiral Montagu for England.

July 8, 1774 Friday Noerly

Moored in Boston Harbor

Fine pleasant Weathr. Empd. variously.

July 9, 1774 Saturday Wterly

Moored in Boston Harbor

PM fine clear Weathr. AM cloudy Sailed hence the *Jupiter* Surveying Sloop with a party.

*July 10, 1774 to July 18, 1774

July 19, 1774 Tuesday Noerly

Moored in Boston Harbor

Fine pleasant Weathr. came in the Sloop *Surveyor* Tender, from the Surveying Parties - Empd. fitting out tender.

July 20, 1774 Wednesday Var:

Moored in Boston Harbor

Pleasant Weathr. Empd. fitting out the Tender.

July 21, 1774 Thursday Wterly

Moored in Boston Harbor

Do. Weather Empd as yesterday.

July 22, 1774 Friday Do.

Moored in Boston Harbor

Do. Weather Empd. as above.

July 23, 1774 Saturday Do.

Moored in Boston Harbor

Strong gales and clear - AM lost two water cask by the Boats sinking alongside - Recd. Guard from the *Preston.*

July 24, 1774 Sunday Do.

Moored in Boston Harbor

Light winds and clear, latter part some rain - Ret: the guard the *Lively.*

July 25, 1774 Monday Do.

Moored in Boston Harbor

First part rain, latter pleasant Weathr. - Sailed the sloop *Surveyor.*

July 26, 1774 Tuesday Var: Noerly

Moored in Boston Harbor

Pleasant Weathr: Recd. the guard from the *Preston.*

While in areas of potential strife between the British Naval forces and colonists, guards from a larger ship were placed aboard smaller vessels for security and to prevent piracy and unauthorized boarding. They were placed in the afternoon and returned to their ships the next morning.

*July 27, 1774 to Aug. 5, 1774

Aug. 6 1774 Saturday Noerly
Moored in Boston Harbor
Fresh breezes and fair, AM arrived his Majestys Ship *Scarborough* from England and the Transports from Halifax with the 59 Regiment.
Aug. 7, 1774 Sunday Eterly
Moored in Boston Harbor
Mod. and fair AM arrived the *Tamer* from Halifax - Recd: the guard from the *Preston.*
Aug. 8, 1774 Monday Var:
Moored in Boston Harbor
Do. Weathr. AM Retd: the guard to the *Lively.*
Aug. 9, 1774 Tuesday Do.
Moored in Boston Harbor
PM Mod. and fair - AM fresh breezes and foggy.
Aug. 10, 1774 Wednesday Eterly, Calm
Moored in Boston Harbor
Thick fogg - AM Recd. the guard from the *Preston.*
Aug. 11, 1774 Thursday Var:
Moored in Boston Harbor
Mod. and fair - Retd: the guard to the *Scarborough.*
Aug. 12, 1774 Friday Wterly
Moored in Boston Harbor
PM fresh breezes and cloudy AM Mod. and fair.
Aug. 13, 1774 Saturday Var:
Moored in Boston Harbor
Fresh breezes and fair - arrived the Sloop *Surveyor* from the parties.
Aug. 14, 1774 Sunday Do.
Moored in Boston Harbor
Mod. airs fair AM Recd. the guard from the *Preston.*
Aug. 15, 1774 Monday Do.

Moored in Boston Harbor
Do. Weathr. AM Retd: the guard to the *Scarborough.*
Aug. 16, 1774 Tuesday Do.
Moored in Boston Harbor
Do. Weathr. Empd. variously.
Aug. 17, 1774 Wednesday Do.
Moored in Boston Harbor
Cloudy and fresh breezes Empd fitting out the *Surveyor* Sloop.
Aug. 18, 1774 Thursday Do.
Moored in Boston Harbor
PM Dark cloudy Weathr. with rain, Recd. the guard from the *Preston.*
Aug. 19, 1774 Friday Do.
Mod. and fair AM Sailed the Sloop *Surveyor,* with stores for the Parties. Retd. the guard to the *Scarborough.*

*Aug. 20, 1774 to Aug. 24, 1774

Aug. 25, 1774 Thursday Do.
Moored in Boston Harbor
Mod. and fair AM arrived an express from Majestys *Wheeler* and the Special Deputy Surveyor Empd. to the Westward of Cape Codd, that the *Jupiter* Sloop was lost with all the provisions and stores and some men drowned.

*Aug. 26, 1774 to Sept. 3, 1774

Sept. 4, 1774 Sunday Var:
Moored in Boston Harbor
PM Mod. breezes and fair Weathr., at 3 came onboard an officer from the *Preston* with a Party to assist in unmooring and remooring the ship to the part of the town, bent the topsails and Mizon, unmoored and hove short; the wind dying away and a strong flood tide against us could not proceed, at 7 the officer and people returned to the *Preston*, at 6 AM weighed and came to sail with a breeze at NE at 9 abreast of the So. the Admirals long boat to lay on the Middle Bank, and endeavored to place this ship in such a situation as to lay barely afloat at low water, but found the channel too small,
Sept. 5, 1774 Monday Eterly
Moored in Boston Harbor
Sept. 6 1774 Tuesday Do.

Moored in Boston Harbor
PM Fresh breezes and thick fogg, with rain, moored ship abreast of Winnisimit Ferry - AM Mod. and fair, dryd sails and unbent them - Sailed hence Transports to Quebec for troops.

Sept. 7, 1774 Wednesday Var:
Moored in Boston Harbor
Modt. breezes and cloudy Empd. occasionaly.

Sept. 8, 1774 Thursday Soerly
Moored in Boston Harbor
Fresh breezes and cloudy Empd. occasionaly.

Sept. 9, 1774 Friday Var:. Wterly
Moored in Boston Harbor
Mod. and cloudy, PM loaded the guns and swivels fore and aft.

Sept. 10, 1774 Saturday Noerly
Moored in Boston Harbor
Mod. and cloudy with some rain AM fresh gales and squally, at 11 sent the Pinnace to the opposite side, Winnisimit Ferry to bring over the 59th: Regiment in company with the rest of the Boats of the Fleet.

Sept. 11, 1774 Sunday Wterly
Moored in Boston Harbor
Mod. breezes and fair - the Boats of the Fleet Empd. bringing over the 59 Regiment - AM light breezes and fair.

Sept. 12, 1774 Monday Swerly
Moored in Boston Harbor
Do. Weathr. Excercised great guns and small arms - Recd. the guard.

Sept. 13, 1774 Tuesday Do., Wterly
Moored in Boston Harbor
Mod. and fair, AM fresh gales and squally. Retd. the guard.

Sept. 14, 1774 Wednesday Do., Noerly
Moored in Boston Harbor
PM Modt. breezes and Rain, AM Squally and clear.

Sept. 15, 1774 Thursday Var:
Moored in Boston Harbor
Modt. and fair - Recd. the guard from the *Preston*.

Sept. 16, 1774 Friday Do.
Moored in Boston Harbor
Do. Weathr. at 8 AM came in the Sloop *Surveyor,* Expressed by her in taking soundings several hunchions (stanchions?) being laid down to take Intersections.

Sept. 17, 1774 Saturday Do.

Moored in Boston Harbor
Modt. breezes and fair Empd. occasionaly.
Sept. 18, 1774 Sunday Do., Soerly
Moored in Boston Harbor
Do. Weathr. Received the guard from the *Preston*
Sept. 19, 1774 Monday Var:, Noerly
Moored in Boston Harbor
Do. Weathr. Excercised great guns and small arms.
Sept. 20, 1774 Tuesday Var:
Moored in Boston Harbor
Modt. and cloudy at 11 PM sent an armed Boat to Hancock Wharf to prevent any attempt to carry ammunition, stores, &c from the Town.
Sept. 21. 1774 Wednesday Var:
Moored in Boston Harbor
Do. Weathr. Recd. the guard from the *Preston.*
Sept. 22, 1774 Thursday Do.
Moored in Boston Harbor
Fresh breezes and cloudy - Retd: the guard to the *Lively.*
Sept. 23, 1774 Friday Eterly
Moored in Boston Harbor
Modt. and fair - Empd. fitting the Tender for Sea, at 1 PM fired 17 guns being the anniversary of His Majesty' Coronation.
Sept. 24, 1774 Saturday Noerly
Moored in Boston Harbor
Fresh breezes and fair, at 2 PM Sailed hence the Tender for the Parties - AM Recd. the guard.
Sept. 25, 1774 Sunday Var:
Moored in Boston Harbor
Modt. breezes and fair - AM Retd: the guard to the *Lively.*
Sept. 26, 1774 Monday Calm, Var:
Moored in Boston Harbor
Light airs and fair - Exercised the People at small arms.
Sept. 27, 1774 Tuesday Werly
Moored in Boston Harbor
Calm and fair Weathr. - AM Recd: the guard from the *Preston.*
Sept. 28, 1774 Wednesday Var:
Moored in Boston Harbor
Modt. breezes and fair - Empd. blacking the yards &c - Retd. the guard.
Sept. 29, 1774 Thursday Do.
Moored in Boston Harbor

Modt. and cloudy Empd. as yesterday.
Sept. 30, 1774 Friday SWterly
Moored in Boston Harbor
Do. Weathr. Empd. blacking the Rigging &c. Recd. the guard.
Oct. 1, 1774 Saturday SW, Wterly
Moored in Boston Harbor
PM fresh breezes and rain, Paid the ships sides and wales - AM cloudy and fresh gales Retd: the guard.
Oct. 2, 1774 Sunday Var:
Moored in Boston Harbor
Fresh gales and thick Weathr. with Rain Read the Articles of War.
Oct. 3, 1774 Monday Var:
Moored in Boston Harbor
Modt. and cloudy AM Recd. the guard - Excerised the People at great guns and small arms, fired 6 shott at a mark.
Oct. 4, 1774 Tuesday Do.
Moored in Boston Harbor
Modt. and fair - AM Retd: the guard to the *Lively*
Oct. 5, 1774 Wednesday Do.
Moored in Boston Harbor
Fresh breezes and fair Empd. occasionaly
Oct. 6, 1774 Thursday Do.
Moored in Boston Harbor
Do. Weathr. AM Recd. the guard from the *Preston* - Cleaned between decks.
Oct. 7, 1774 Friday Do.
Moored in Boston Harbor
Modt. and fair Weathr. Empd. variously Retd. the guard.
Oct. 8, 1774 Saturday Do.
Moored in Boston Harbor
Do. Weather Empd. variously.
Oct. 9, 1774 Sunday Do.
Moored in Boston Harbor
Do. Weathr. with Rain - Recd. the guard.
Oct. 10, 1774 Monday Noerly, Var:
Moored in Boston Harbor
Fresh breezes and fair weathr. Exercised at great guns & small arms.
Oct. 11, 1774 Tuesday Var:
Moored in Boston Harbor
Fresh breezes and fair Weathr.
Oct. 12, 1774 Wednesday NW

Moored in Boston Harbor
Modt. breezes and fair - AM arrived the *Rose* Frigate from N.F.land with part of the 65 Regiment Recd. the guard.

Oct. 13, 1774 Thursday Var:
Moored in Boston Harbor
Do. Breezes and cloudy Retd: the guard.

Oct. 14, 1774 Friday Do.
Moored in Boston Harbor
Do. Weathr. for the most part.

Oct. 15, 1774 Saturday Soerly
Moored in Boston Harbor
Fresh breezes and thick Weathr. with rain - AM Recd. the guard.

Oct. 16, 1774 Sunday Do., Var:
Moored in Boston Harbor
Modt. breezes and fair, Retd. the guard to the *Lively.*

Oct. 17, 1774 Monday Var:
Moored in Boston Harbor
Modt. and cloudy, Exercised at great guns and small arms.

Oct. 18, 1774 Tuesday Do.
Moored in Boston Harbor
Do. with drizling rain, AM Recd. the guard from the *Preston.*

Oct. 19, 1774 Wednesday Do.
Moored in Boston Harbor
Fresh gales and squally, Retd: the guard to the *Lively.*

Oct. 20, 1774 Thursday Do.
Moored in Boston Harbor
Modt. and fair - AM our Signal out onbd. the Admiral- answered do.

Oct. 21, 1774 Friday Do.
Moored in Boston Harbor
Light breezes and cloudy, Recd. the guard from the *Preston.*

Oct. 22, 1774 Saturday Eterly
Moored in Boston Harbor
Modt. breezes and cloudy, Retd: the guard to the *Lively.*

Oct. 23, 1774 Sunday Do., Calm
Moored in Boston Harbor
Light breezes and cloudy with some Rain - AM calm & foggy.

Oct. 24, 1774 Monday Var:
Moored in Boston Harbor
Modt. and cloudy, at 8 AM Excerised people at great guns and small arms - Recd. the guard.

Oct. 25, 1774 Tuesday Var:

Moored in Boston Harbor
Modt. and fair, Returned the guard to the *Lively.*
Oct. 26, 1774 Wednesday Do.
Moored in Boston Harbor
Do. Weathr. at 1 PM fired 17 guns being his Majestys assesion.
Oct. 27, 1774 Thursday Eterly
Moored in Boston Harbor
Do. Weathr. PM Sailed hence the *Rose* Frigate - Recd. the guard.
Oct. 28, 1774 Friday Do.
Moored in Boston Harbor
Fresh gales and squally - AM thick fogg with Rain, Retd: the guard.
Oct. 29, 1775 Saturday Soerly
Moored in Boston Harbor
Modt. and cloudy.
Oct. 30, 1774 Sunday Soerly
Moored in Boston Harbor
Do. Weathr. arrived the Transports from Quebec, Recd. the guard.
Oct. 31, 1774 Monday Var:
Moored in Boston Harbor
Do. Weathr. AM Retd. the guard to the Lively - Exercised the People at great guns and small arms.
Nov. 1, 1774 Tuesday Var:
Moored in Boston Harbor
Modt. and fair Read the Articles of &c.
Nov. 2, 1774 Wednesday Eterly
Moored in Boston Harbor
Cloudy - Empd. watering - AM Recd. the guard.
Nov. 3, 1774 Thursday Var:
Moored in Boston Harbor
Modt. and fair Empd. cleaning between Decks - Retd: the guard.
Nov. 4, 1774 Friday Do.
Moored in Boston Harbor
Ditto Weather
Nov. 5, 1774 Saturday Do.
Moored in Boston Harbor
Fresh breezes and thick hazy Weathr. Sailed hence the *Deligent* Armed Schooner for Halifax - Recd. the guard from the *Preston.*
Nov. 6, 1774 Sunday Eterly
Moored in Boston Harbor
Hazy with rain and fresh gales, came up the *Tartar*, Retd, the guard.

Nov. 7, 1774 Monday Do.
Moored in Boston Harbor
Fresh gales and thick hazy Weathr. - Arrived the *Hope* Schooner
Modt. and cloudy with rain - AM clear - Recd. the guard from the *Preston.*
Nov. 8, 1774 Tuesday Var:
Moored in Boston Harbor
Modt. and cloudy with rain - AM clear - Recd. the guard from the *Preston.*
Nov. 9, 1774 Wednesday Wterly
Moored in Boston Harbor
Modt. and fair, AM Retd. the guard to the *Lively.*
Nov. 10, 1774 Thursday Var:
Moored in Boston Harbor
Fine pleasant Weather.
Nov. 11, 1774 Friday Do.
Moored in Boston Harbor
Modt. breezes and fair Weather.
Nov. 12, 1774 Saturday SWerly
Moored in Boston Harbor
Fresh breezes and clear, AM Recd. the guard.
Nov. 13, 1774 Sunday SW, N
Moored in Boston Harbor
Light Winds and clear , latter hazy, AM Retd. the guard.
Arrived the Duputy surveyor Tender, lost by her sundry stores

*Nov. 14, 1774 to Nov. 23, 1774

Nov. 24, 1774 Thursday Noerly
Moored in Boston Harbor
Modt. and fair, Middle part rain at times, PM Sailed hence the Sloop *Surveyor* to the Etward - Recd. the guard.

*Nov. 25, 1774 Dec. 2, 1774

Dec. 3, 1774 Saturday Noerly
Moored in Boston Harbor
Do. Weathr. AM Fresh breezes and rain, arrived his Majestys Ship *Scarborough* from England.
Dec. 4, 1774 Sunday Var:
Moored in Boston Harbor
Modt. and fair AM Recd. orders to fit for sea - Empd getting

the yards and topmasts up.

Dec. 5, 1774 Monday No, NE
Moored in Boston Harbor
Do. Weathr. Empd. about the Rigging, & getting water - Recd Provisions.

Dec. 6, 1774 Tuesday Noerly
Moored in Boston Harbor
Fresh breezes with hard frost. Empd watering the ship.

Dec. 7, 1774 Wednesday Do.
Moored in Boston Harbor
PM hard frost, and clear Weathr. AM Modt. and cloudy.

Dec. 8, 1774 Thursday Var:
Moored in Boston Harbor
Squally with some Rain, Sailed hence His Majestys Ship *Tartar*. Came onbd Mr. James Symnons from the *Preston* as Boatswain in the room of Mr. Wm. Bray.

Dec. 9, 1774 Friday Soerly
Moored in Boston Harbor
Fresh breezes with some Rain - Empd occasionaly.

Dec. 10, 1774 Saturday NW
Moored in Boston Harbor
cloudy Weathr. with snow - AM Modt. and clear.

Dec. 11, 1774 Sunday Eterly
Moored in Boston Harbor
Hard frost and clear Weathr.

Dec. 12, 1774 Monday Soerly
Moored in Boston Harbor
Modt. breezes and soft Weathr. Empd variously

Dec. 13, 1774 Tuesday Var:
Moored in Boston Harbor
Slight airs and variable Empd. getting Wood & Water onbd. AM came onboard a Party of Marines from the *Preston*.

Dec. 14, 1774 Wednesday Do.
Moored in Boston Harbor
Light breezes and cloudy AM unmoored ship, at Noon weighed and dropped down abreast of the *Preston*.

Dec. 15, 1774 Thursday Soerly, Wresly
Moored in Boston Harbor
Light airs & Ver: AM fresh gales & clear - came onbd Mr. Joseph Pluoknet as Carpt. in the room of Mr. Hayood Snook appointed to the *Scarborough*.

Dec. 16, 1774 Friday WNW

At anchor in Boston Harbor
Fresh breezes and clear - Empd. variously - came onbd a Party of Marines.

Dec. 17, 1774 Saturday NW
Thatchers Isld SSW 3 leagues
Moored off the Fort, Piscataqua River
At 1 am weighed (Boston Harbor) and came to sail, at 1/3 past 3 abreast of Boston light, at noon Thatcher's Isle SSW 3 leagues Pigeon Hill SW b W 4 leagues PM ½ pt 3 Iles of Shoals NE b N at 4 do. Isle ENE, at 8 SE calm Piscataqua light bearing N b W, at 9 a light breeze Sprung up at Wt at 11 anchd within the fort of Piscataqua

Dec. 18, 1774 Sunday Var:, Calm, W, Var:
Moored off Fort, Piscataqua River
PM light breezes and cloudy, ½ past 3 Isles of Shoals NE b N, at 4 Do. Isles, ENE, at 8 SE, calm, Piscataqua light bearing N b W, at 9 a light breeze sprung up at W at 11anchd: within the fort of Piscataqua - AM fresh breezes and cloudy.

Dec. 19, 1774 Monday Do., SSW, SW
Moored off Fort, Piscataqua River
Dark cloudy Weathr: with Rain - at 11 AM came in His Majestys Ship *Scarborough* and anchored by us - Recd, fresh Beef.

Dec. 20, 1774 Tuesday Var:
Moored off Fort, Piscataqua River
PM Fresh gales with rain, Middle and latter strong gales with hard frost, - Veered away a whole cable, Fort So: half a cable length.

*Dec. 21, 1774 to Dec. 25, 1774

Dec. 26, 1774 Monday NNE, NE
Moored off Fort, Piscataqua River
PM light airs with sleet and dark cloudy Wr. AM heavy rains, at 2 found the ship tailed near the shore men warping hawser to the *Scarborough*, hove her further out, and let go the hn: Br: anchor.

Dec. 27, 1774 Tuesday Var:
Moored off Fort, Piscataqua River
PM Do. Weathr. AM Modt. and cloudy.

*Dec. 28, 1774 to Jan 3, 1775
Disposition of the Squadron Under Admiral Samuel Graves

List of the North American Squadron on the 1st of January 1775

Ship	Guns	Men	Commander	Station
Preston	50	300	Vice Adml Graves Capt Jno Robinson	Boston Harbour
Somerset	68	520	Edwd LeCras	"
Boyne	70	520	Brodk Hartwell	"
Asia	64	480	Geo Vanderput	"
Mercury	20	130	Jno Macartney	"
Glasgow	20	130	Wm Maltby	" (disabled by running on the rocks10th Decr)
Diana Schoonr	6	30	Lt Thos Graves	" (just purchased intended for an Armed Schooner)
Rose	20	130	Capt Jas Wallace	at Rhode Island
Swan Sloop	16	100	Capt Jas Amsouth	"
Hope Schr	6	30	Lt Geo Dawson	"
Kingfisher Sloop	16	100	Capt Jas Montague	at New York
Magdalene Schr	6	30	Lt Henry Colins	at Philadelphia
Fowey	20	130	Capt Geo. Montagu	at Virginia
Cruizer Sloop	8	60	Tyrn Howe	at North Carolina
Tamer Sloop	14	100	Edwd Thornborough	at South Carolina
Savage Sloop	8	60	Edwd Bromedge	on coast of Et Florida & at the Bahamas Islands
St John Schr	6	30	Lt Wm Grant	"
Lively	20	130	Capt Thos Bishop	at Salem & Marblehead
Scarborough	20	130	Andrew Barkley	In Piscataqua river in New Hampshire Province
Canceaux	8	45	Lt Henry Mowat	"
Gaspee Brigg	6	30	Lt Wm Hunter	from Casco Bay to the Entrance of the Bay of Fundy
Halifax Schr	6	30	Lt Josh Nunn	"
Diligent Schr	6	30	Lt John Knight	at Windsor in the Bay of Fundy
Tartar	28	160	Capt Edwd Meadows	at Halifax in Nova Scotia

Graves's Conduct, I, 40,41, Mass HS Transcripts

Jan. 4, 1775 Wednesday Var:
Moored off Fort, Piscataqua River
Modt. with hard frost, AM Empd. bending sails - AM unmoored ship, at Noon came onbd a Pilot from Portsm. to carry the ship up to the Pool.

Jan. 5 1775 Thursday Var:, WNW
PM light airs and var. At 2 weighed and came to sail 1/2 past anchored in the entrance of Spruce Creek in 15 fm water soft bottom secured the stream anchor and cable out to steady the ship. Trettary Church NNE & New Castle Church S by W. AM fresh gales cloudy at 10 unmoored and came to sail at 11 the ship refused stays and sailed ashore with the assistance of the *Scarborough* boat carried the stream anchor out. at noon hove her off

Jan. 6 1775 Friday Nerly
PM fresh gales & clear weathr. bent two 5 inch hawsers and one mile of 3 inch rope to the stream cable and veered away the ship in the tide at 5 minutes before we could get an anchor out to heave

her out the tide fell and the ship struck . Emp at getting the top mast and yard down and the booms & lower yards over to shore the ship up as there is 10 feet difference from the in to out side of the ship cut all the lashings & propping of the boom getting the guns provisions & ballast out fired 6 guns a signal for assistance from the *Scarborough*. AM fresh gales and clear weathr. with hard frost.

Jan. 7 1775 Saturday Nerly/Easterly

Fresh breezes, with hard frost Emp getting ballast out at 1/2 past 3 got the ship off found she made water Do. hauled her into the Pool & steadied her between four arms. Emp getting proper fasts? out the best bower to the NE With the anchor 2/3 of a cable one whole cable to the SE fast to the rocks the bridle cable to the WNW to the port of the wharfe one inch hawser to the SW to a post of 14 fathom distant from the wharfe lower proper mast.

Jan. 8 1775 Sunday

Mod breezes & clear weathr with very hard frost. Emp clearing the deck & hoisting the guns in.

Vice Admiral Samuel Graves to Philip Stephens

Sir Preston Boston January 8th 1775

In a Letter dated the 19th of December, and sent by the Sloop *Phoenix* from Salem, I acquainted you with the Arrival of his Majesty's Ship *Somerset* on that day from Plymouth. This Ship with the *Boyne* and *Asia* are now moored before the Town of Boston, and had I have the pleasure to say their Companies are in general very healthy. The *Somerset* was so leaky at Sea that two hand pumps were continually at Work, and it is the constant Employment at present of one hand pump to Keep her free.

In consequence of a Letter from Governor [John] Wentworth of New Hampshire, which I received by express on Friday Evening the 16th December, a Copy of which is enclosed. I ordered the *Canceaux* and *Scarborough* to sail immediately for Piscataqua, And as the Governor had represented the Custom House and Province Treasuries to be in Danger I put a Subaltern Officer and twenty Marines on board the *Canceaux* who sailed that Night, and the *Scarborough* on Sunday Morning, through the Weather was very severe. I gave Captain [Andrew] Barkley Orders to afford the Governor, upon his requisition , every aid and assistance in his power, and to do his utmost to protect the King's Servants and Stores with his Majesty's Ships under his command.

On the 24th following I received Letters from the Governor, Captain Barkley, and Lieu [Henry] Mowat, Copies of the two first are enclosed. You will perceive by those Letters that the sudden and unexpected appearance of the King's Ships in the River prevented a great Number of Cannon being carried off, and all further riotous proceeding at Portsmouth.

I transmit a copy of a Letter from Governor Wentworth. I declined complying with his Excellency's Request for the Sloop of War and the Marines therein mentioned, and acquainted him that having a great extent of Coast to guard I could not conveniently spare so large a part of his Majesty's Squadron to be at one place. More especially as I was of opinion the *Scarborough* and *Canceaux* were fully capable of protecting the Treasuries, and of affording Refuge to his Majesty's Servants should the at any time consider themselves to be in Danger.

On the 18th instant I received a letter from Captain [James] Wallace of his Majesty's Ship *Rose* with a copy of his letter to Governor [James] Wanton on the riotous behavior of the Mob at Rhode Island. Copies of both letters are enclosed. Though I was highly pleased with the Spirit of Captain Wallace showed on that occasion, I could not avoid expressing to him my satisfaction that the Mob declined putting their tarring and feathering Scheme into execution being apprehensive his waiting so long for their Approach was not strictly justifiable, and may have been attended with fatal consequences.

General [Thomas] Gage having requested that the Supernumerary Marines on board the Squadron might be landed at Boston to be disciplined this Winter in a manner to enable them to act on Shore with the rest of the Kings Troops, and it being our opinion that whilst they re on shore they should be on the same footing with the rest of the Soldiers in regard to their pay and provisions, as they are all employed on the same Service; I have in Compliance with the requisition disembarked all the Supernumerary Marines and ordered them to be discharged from their Discharged respective Ships; And by desire of Major [John] Pitcairn have lent them three subaltern Officers and three Sergeants, part of the Compliment of the Ships lately arrived from England.

On the 20th of December I received by express from Captain Wallace an account that the *William and Ann* Ordnance Transport from Plymouth, laden with five hundred Barrels of Gunpowder, bound to New York, had put into Rhode Island the

19th in great Distress, her Rudder lost, and her mainmast disabled; as the powder is consigned to the commanding Officer of Artillery in America for the use of the Army, the General and Colonel [Samuel] Cleaveland have give directions concerning it; In the meantime the Transport is assisted and protected by the *Rose*, who by being at Rhode Island has most certainly prevented that powder from being seized and carried to Providence.

The *Halifax* Schooner is so very leaky and out of Repair, and is in such continual want to patching to make her swim, that she is totally unfit for any Service but to be at Anchor, which I have directed her to do this Winter, and in the Spring intended to have her surveyed; she is a very bad low vessel, and so extremely wet and uncomfortable to the Sea Men that no consideration will keep them belonging to her.

The *Hope* is in very little better Condition, and must go to England when the Season will allow me to venture her, therefore as there is an absolute necessity for good armed Schooners capable of performing real Service to the Crown, and one is at this time particularly wanted to guard one of the Channels at Rhode Island to prevent the unlawful Importation of Gunpowder Arms and Ammunition &c which from very good Intelligence I am told will be attempted in large Quantities at that place I have taken upon me to purchase the *Diana* Schooner of 120 tons, about eight Months old, so exceedingly well built that she is allowed to be the best Vessel of the Kind that has been yet in the Kings Service, her first cost is 750 pounds Sterling and as I have thought it best for his Majesty's Service that she should be an established armed Schooner, I have directed the necessary alterations to be made in her Hull, and for her to be fitted in all respects like other vessels of her Class; She will have the *St. Lawrence's* Guns. On this occasion I have appointed Lieut. Thomas Graves of his Majesty's Ship *Lively* to command the *Diana* Schooner, and Mr. William Lechinere of the *Preston* to be Lieutenant of the *Lively*. The *Diana* will soon be ready for Sea, and I shall send her to Rhode Island.

As I am extremely desirous of carrying on the King's Service with all possible frugality, I shall defer taking up the two Schooners their Lordships have directed me to hire for guarding the Harbour until the Weather being less severe than at present will admit of Vessels navigating: The Schooners then will be of great use, but at present only an unnecessary Charge.

In consequent of their lordships permission signified to me in your Letter of the 14th of October to purchase a small Sloop to supply the place of the late *Jupiter* employed on the Survey under the direction of Captain [Samuel] Holland, I caused the Sloop *Spinckes* [*Sphynx*] of 46 Tons Burthen to be purchased for two hundred and twenty pounds Sterling and delivered to Lieut. Mowat of the *Canceaux* for the above Service. I am sorry I am obliged to add that after having fitted and stored her property for the Service she was intended, in going round to Piscataqua after *Canceaux*, she ran ashore about Cape Anne; I have sent a Sloop with a Number of hands to endeavor to save the Vessel, if that shall be impossible, to bring away the Stores.

I omitted in a former Letter to acquaint you that a Vessel being to depart from this Harbour in Ballast to New York, I procured her to go to Piscataqua and take in Captain Holland, his instruments Servants and Baggage, and carry them to Perth Amboy, as he desired, for 50 pounds Sterling, instead of hiring a ship on purpose, which must otherwise have been dine at a much greater Expense.

The Weather has been lately so severe that we have not been able to get the *Glasgow* cleared for the Carpenters, neither is it possible till that is done and she is hawl'd ashore to ascertain the damage she had received; In the mean time her Sails and Rigging and all her other Stores are put in some Store house on Noodle's Island, which I have caused to be hired at the rate of 430 pounds per Annum for that purpose, and which shall be discharged when ever the *Glasgow* can received her Stores again.

The *Lively* got round to Salem to 30th of December. The *Swan* arrived here from New York the 18th and sailed again for Rhode Island the 6th instant. The *Hope* Schooner sailed for the same place on Christmas Day.

On the 24th of December I received your letter of the 2d of November concerning the Sloop *John* David Fenton Master, and in obedience to their Lordships Directions I have given Orders to endeavor to intercept the said Sloop which I find upon Inquiry is, as well as the Master well known.

I have lately heard from the Captains of all his Majesty's Ships to the Southward of Boston, and think it proper to transmit a Copy of the *Tamers* Defects for their Lordships Information. I transmit also the State and Condition and Disposition of his Majesty's Squadron under my Command, with the State of the Hospital.

I am &c

Sam Graves

Jan. 9 1775 Monday
Do weathr. Emp unbending all the sails. PM came into the river his Majestys schooner *Halifax*.
Jan. 10 1775 Tuesday
PM Light airs & var. AM Dark cloudy Weather with some sleet & rain at noon fresh gales with Rain & soft weather. Emp variously.
Jan. 11 1775 Wednesday
Fresh gales with rain at 6 AM light airs & varble soft weathr. sailed hence his Majestys Schooner *Halifax* to the eastward.
Jan. 12, 1775 Thursday
Mod. & cloudy. Emp variously
Jan. 13, 1775 Friday
PM Mod & cloudy weathr with some snow AM fresh gales & clear weathr Emp on occasion.
Jan. 14, 1775 Saturday
Dark Cloudy weathr. with some rain Emp on occasion.
Jan. 15, 1775 Sunday
Do. Weathr. Emp variously

Vice Admiral Samuel Graves to Philip Stephens

Sir *Preston* Boston 15th January 1775

Since my last Dispatch dated the 8th instant two Courts Martial have been held: upon Captain [William] Maltby, and the Gunner of his Majestys Ship *Glasgow*, I transmit Copies of the sentences and will send the originals by the first conveyance of a King's Ship. The Court having dismissed Captain Maltby from the Command of the *Glasgow*, I have appointed Mr. Tyringham Howe Commander of the *Cruizer* to succeed him; and Lieutenant Francis Parry of the *Preston* to command the *Cruizer*. I have also removed Lieut. John Graves of the *Somerset* into the *Preston* and appoint Mr. William Fulk Greville to be fourth Lieutenant of the *Somerset*.

On the 12th instant I received Letters from Captain [Andrew] Barkley of the *Scarborough*, and Lieutenant [Henry] Mowat of the *Canceaux* acquainting me that in getting the *Canceaux* near the Town of Portsmouth at the desire of Governor [John] Wentworth the Pilot ignorantly anchored her at high water in a spot where she had not room to live afloat, and where she was benipped four and twenty hours. Captain Barkley sent every assistance in his power from the *Scarborough*, and hired a light Sloop to go along side, and take out her Stores, but the Weather being extremely cold, and the wind down the River, the Sloop could not reach the *Canceaux* till the next morning, when the Tide being somewhat higher than usual, upon heaving their Iron Ballast overboard, she got off. Lieutt Mowat acquaints me that the Ship makes little or no water, and that he believes the only damage she has sustained is losing a part of her false keel, and that part below the Iron Work on her Rudder a little shattered; therefore as no immediate inconvenience attends this accident, the *Canceaux* shall continue before the Town of Portsmouth until the Spring affords a proper opportunity to examine and repair her bottom.

Captain Barkley writes me that the people in general are at present pretty quiet; and that it is reported the Principal Inhabitants of Portsmouth will soon have a Meeting to consult upon the returning the Guns and Gunpowder carried off by the mob. It is however certain that those who committed the late outrage are skulking about there Country, and are only prevented by the King's Ships in the River from being as insolent & troublesome as ever.

I am &c. Sam Graves

*Jan. 16, 1775 to Feb. 15, 1775

Journal of His Majesty's Brig *Gaspee*, Lieut. William Hunter, Commanding

Moor's in Falmouth Harbor Casco Bay

Fair Weare with a frost PM Four of our People Vizt Joseph Cox, James Craven, James Varner and John Lutey took the Boat from alongside, we fired at them, but having no boat to pursue them they got on shore and Deserted we afterwards heard one of them (John Lutey) was shot.

Feb 16, 1775 Thursday SW

Fresh Breezes & raw cold weathr Emp as occasion came in here from Boston a small Schooner belong Capt. Mowat came in her Mr. Alexander Aiken as Boatswain. in the room of Mr. James Simmons appointed. to his Majestys sloop *Kingfisher*

*Feb. 17, 1775 to Feb. 26, 1775

COURT MARTIAL OF LIEUTENANT WILLIAM HUNTER AND MASTER MALTIS LUCULLUS RYALL

At a court marital assembled and held Onboard His Majesty's Ship *Somerset* at Boston in New England the 27th day of February 1775

Present

Edward Le Cras Esqr Senior Captain of His Majesty's Ships and Vessels at Boston, President. Captain Brodk Hartwell

Captain Geo. Vandeput

John Marcartney Jno. Robinson

Who being all duly Sworn

At Court in pursuance of an Order from Samuel Graves Esqr Vice Admiral of the Blue and Commander in Chief of His Majesty's Ships and Vessels employed and to be employed in the River St. Lawrence &ca proceeded to try Lieut William Hunter Commander, and Mr. Maltis Lucullus Ryall Master of his Majesty's Brig *Gaspee* fore the death of John Lutey Seaman, late belonging to the said Brig and the Court having heard all the evidence and carefully examined into every Circumstance attending the desertion of the four Seamen with the Brig's Boat; and very naturally weighed and considered the

Whole are of opinion that it being proved to the Court, the four Seamen entered in the Act of Desertion with the King's Boat at Falmouth Harbour in Casco Bay on the 13th of February 1775, Lieutenant Hunter in doing his duty behaved like a good officer by Firing at them on tier refusing to return according to his Orders; and that Mr Maltis Lucullus Ryall the Master of the said Brig is justified in obeying the Lieutenant's Order to fire likewise; The Court do therefore acquit the said Lieutenant William Hunter and Mr. Maltis Lucullus Ryall of the Murder of the said John Lutey, and they are hereby acquitted accordingly.

E. Le Cras Geo: V'andeput

J. Robinson

B. Hartrwell John Marcartney

G. Gefferina, appointed to execute the Office of Deputy Judge Advocate

A True Copy G. Gefferina

[Endorsed] Sentence of a Court martial. In Vice Adml Grave's Letter/dated 4h March 1775.

Feb. 28, 1775 Tuesday Serly

Do. weathr Emp as before

March 1, 1775 Wednesday Werly, NE

PM mod. & clear weathr mid & latter Part dark cloudy weathr including rain Punish Pat V Burns with 12 Lashes for neglect

of Duty Read the Articles of War to the Ships Company
March 2, 1775 Thursday Werly
PM dark cloudy weathr with haze sleet & snow AM fine pleasant weathr emp overhauling the rigging

*March 3, 1775 to March 20 1775

Narrative of Vice Admiral Samuel Graves

[Boston] 21st [March, 1775]

The *Spinkes* [*Sphynx*] Sloop (formerly Tender to the *Canceaux* on the Survey) sailed for Piscataqua with the Admirals Order to Captain [Andrew] Barkley to send the *Canceaux* to Halifax to be hove down and have the damage she received by running aground repaired, and Lieut. [Henry] Mowat her Commander had Orders, when the Ship should be completed again to proceed on the Survey as usual under the direction of Captain [Samuel] Holland.

*March 22, 1775 to March 27, 1775

March 28, 1775 Tuesday Noerly, NW
Fresh gales & clear fair weathr Punished Robert Thomas with 12 lashes for behaving with contempt to his Officer
March 29, 1775 Wednesday NW, SW
Strong gales & squally emp as occasionally AM sailed hence our Tender on a cruise
March 30, 1775 Thursday NW
Fresh gales & clear frosty weathr

Vice Admiral Samuel Graves to General Thomas Gage

Sir Boston 30th of March 1775

At present I can only endeavour to protect Captain [Thomas] Courson's Ship and the vessel with Rigging from Bristol, about which Your Excellency is pleased to inform me there are great disturbances at Falmouth; The *Canceaux* is the only ship I can spare, the rest in this Neighborhood being employed at places where, I trust your excellency is satisfied, their presence is indispensably necessary; And although the *Canceaux* is under Orders to go the Halifax, to repair some damage We suspect She received laying aground at Piscataqua last January, I have notwithstanding ordered Captain [Andrew] Barkely to send her away with all possible Expedition, and to direct Lieutenant [Henry]

Mowat to assist the New Ship till she can go to Piscataqua, or Salem; at either of which Places She can fit and compleat under the Protection of the Kings Ship there. While the *Canceaux* remains at Falmouth I hope her presence will be some Check to the common disturbers, and I shall very readily station some other Vessel at that place whenever it is in my power. I am with great Respect, and Regard Sir Sam Graves

March 31, 1775 Friday Varbl, SSW
PM weathr mod. hazey got down the flagg staves & up Top Gallant Masts Emp Reeving the running Rigging
April 1, 1775 Saturday NNW, NE
PM mod & hazey. AM up Top-gallant yard, emp about the rigging
April 2, 1775 Sunday NE
PM mod. & hazy emp. about the rigging & getting onboard the iron ballast AM bending the sails, & getting ready for sea
April 3, 1775 Monday NNW
PM Fresh Breezes & cloudy emp as before discharged went away in the long boat all the Marines on board the *Preston* Tender for Boston
April 4, 1775 Tuesday W, Varbl
PM Do. weathr emp getting on board Provisions, AM unmoored at 9 weighed and came to sail. the wind dying away could not stem the tide, anchor with bower 10 fathoms water
April 5, 1775 Wednesday WNW, Varbl, WSW, NE
Mod and hazey, at 3 PM weighed & came to sail, at 3 anchor with he Br. Br. in 20 fathoms water off the entrance of Spruce Creek at 5 moored ship, at 12 squally let go the small Br. Anchor - Lighthouse SE b E Kittery Meeting house NNE
April 6, 1775 Thursday NW b N, Werly, NW b W
Fresh airs & middle part light Aires & hazey with sleet & snow AM fresh breezes & fair. hove up the small Br. emp watering the ship
April 7, 1775 Friday Werly
PM mod & cloudy emp watering & cleaning stowing the hold AM fresh breezes & squaly at 1 1/2 past 8 weighed and came o sail, at 9 abreast of the light house, at Noon the Nubble S b W Boon Island south and the Eastern part of Wells Bay NNE 7 miles
April 8, 1775 Saturday Var, NNW, Var
Moored in Falmouth Harbor Casco Bay
Light airs & variable 1/2 past 2 PM Wood Island NW, at 5 Cape Elizabeth weathr distance 1 mile, fired a gun a signal

for the *Spincks* Tender 1 1/2 past fired another, at 7 calm, at 8 came to with the Stream anchor in 7 fathoms water at 12 light airs at 2 AM fresh breezes being up a lee shore were obliged to slip the stream cable, 1/2 past made sail at about. 3 came to under Flagg Island with the Br. Br. in 6 fm, at 10 weighed at No on anchored close to the town (of Falmouth - appears only in ADM 52/ 1637.).

April 9, 1775 Sunday NW
Moored in Falmouth Harbor Casco Bay
PM mod and clear, Emp mooring ship in 4 fm at low water Meeting House steeple with Townhouse NW.

April 10, 1775 Monday Var.
Moored in Falmouth Harbor Casco Bay
Do. weathr. at 11 PM fired a Great Gun loaded with grape at some boats that were approaching the ship, and would not answer when hailed. AM exercised great guns & small arms & fired 12 shot at a mark, sent the *Spinckes* Tender out for the stream anchor & cable.

April 11, 1775 Tuesday Eserly
Moored in Falmouth Harbor Casco Bay
Light airs and hazy at 4 PM fired a great gun & made a signal for the *Spinckes* Tender, at 5 she returned - Recd on board the stream anchor and cable.

April 12, 1775 Wednesday Do.
Moored in Falmt Harbor Casco Bay
Mod and Hazy sent 8 men to assist the *Minerva* Merchant (mast) Ship - AM fresh gales with rain and sleet.

April 13, 1775 Thursday Do., WNW
Moored in Falmt Harbor Casco Bay
Strong gales and squally with rain sleet and snow, at 6 PM struck yards & topmast at 8 AM mod and cloudy - up Topmasts & yards loosed sails to dry.

*April 14, 1775 to April 23, 1775

April 24, 1775 Monday Varbl
PM Do. Weathr. AM light airs and thick drizling rain. Emp occasionaly - Unmoored & hauled the ship nearer the town & claped a spring on the cable

April 25, 1775 Tuesday SW
Fresh breezes and cloudy. PM came in here his Majestys schooner *Diana* & the *Neptune* schooner belonging to

General Gage with an officer and party on board belonging to the 46th Regiment. Cloudy & hazy Weathr.

April 26, 1775 Wednesday Soerly, NW

First and middle part hazy Thick Weathr. PM sailed hence the two schooners for Boston. Fresh gales & clear Weathr. AM clear

April 27, 1775 Thursday NW, SW

PM fine clear Weathr. AM fresh gales and cloudy, Emp variously

April 28, 1775 Friday Varbl

Mod & cloudy Emp variously

April 29, 1775 Saturday Soerly

Fresh breezes & var. Emp variously - loosed sails to dry

Brunswick April the 29th 1775

Lieutenant Henry Mowat, R.N., to Edward Parry

Sir- *Canceaux* Falmouth April 29 1775

I am just this moment informed that you are interrupted in your occupation by the misled people of the Place where you are; I therefore think it incumbent on me as a Servant under the Crown, to warn those Infatuated people of the Consequences that will issue from the detaining, or interfering with you, or any other of his Majesties Loyal subjects in their lawful avocations, & I do by the same Authority authorize you to made known to me, without loss of time your present Situation, & the names of those that have presumed to molest you. Should a Reply to this letter not appear by the time that I have a Right to expect it, I shall Naturally Suppose that it has been interrupted, & you may depend, as soon as I know that to be the case, that assistance Shall soon release you, or any other Subject whose treatment may furnish me with a just cause of Complaint. My best Compliments to Mr. Barnard I hope he is not in the same predicament with yourself please to acquaint him that I Received his letter, & that I have been in hourly expectation of Seeing him for some days past I also hope to have the Pleasure of Seeing you very Soon, I am Sir

Your most Obedient Humble Servant H: Mowat

April 30, 1775 Sunday Do.

PM mod & clear AM fresh gales & cloudy

May 1, 1775 Monday Do., varbl

PM fresh gales and cloudy with Rain. Am thick misty Weathr. with Rain Emp variously

May 2, 1775 Tuesday Varbl

Mod breezes with thick misty Weathr. and heavy Rains

Some of the Principal Inhabitants of Falmouth to Lieutenant Henry Mowat, R.N.

To Henry Mowat Esqr Captain of His Majesty's Ship *Canceaux*.

The Memorial of Us the Subscribers, for themselves and many other faithful Subjects in the County of Cumberland.

Showeth That since the Arrival of His Majesty's Ship under your command, we have been relieved by your Spirited Conduct from those Anxieties natural to Persons who are obnoxious to the Enemies of our happy Constitution; and by your courteous and kind behavior to all the Friends of Government, flattered Ourselves with the pleasing Prospect of a continuance of your Protection; but those agreeable Sensations are entirely vanished, and we are reduced to the last degree of despair, by your information, that when Captain Coulsins's ship will be ready for Sea, you are immediately to leave this place - and consequently us, a prey to the Sons of rapine and lawless Violence. We therefore intreat that in your goodness you will remain with us till we can make known our deplorable Situation to General [Thomas] Gage, which we shall do without delay. We further intreat you will be so obliging to represent our dangerous Situation to Admiral [Samuel] Graves - and as we are now deprived of sending a Petition to his Excellency by land and having no effectual Method of conveyance by Water, we beg you will suffer an Officer, and a few men from your Ship tp proceed for that purpose.

18 names with occupations

Falmouth 2d May 1775

May 3, 1775 Wednesday Do.

Do. breezes with thick misty Weathr. and heavy Rains.

May 4, 1775 Thursday Varbl, Eterly

PM thick fogg. - AM fresh Breezes and cloudy with Rain, emp variously

Lieutenant Henry Mowat R.N. to Vice Admiral Samuel Graves

Canceaux, Falmouth, Casco Bay

4th May 1775

Sir, Since my Letter to you of the 24th Ult: by Ensign Hill, the greater part of the people in this part of the Country have been constantly under Arms, threatening destruction to the Persons and Properties of those who refuse to join with them; in the Town of

Brunswick near Kennebec River, two hundred of them into Custody and all the Masts in the River belonging to him, which they hourly threaten to destroy: they also laid hold of Five of the principle Friends to Government, one of which they buried Alive, and put the rest in Jail; as soon as they had finished this, they resolved to embark on board of two sloops in order to repaired to Falmouth, board, and burn the *Canceaux*, and the two Vessels she had in Charge, this Resolution was made know here, the Night before last, upon Which their Association of the Town assembled, disapproved of the plan, and refused assistance, excepting Major [Enoch] Freeman and the lower class;- this Man I have mentioned in my former Letters as a leading Instrument of Sedition in these parts, and it is a great pity he should be left so long among them. Since I was made acquainted with this History I have dared them to put their Plan in execution through the Sip is not manned equal to my wishes, yet the few Hands that I have picked up since I have been here, gives me a fairer prospect of the safety of those Vessels I have in charge. The new Ship is now almost in a condition to go to sea, which she would have been some time ago, had the Smiths and Carpenters been suffered to work the laborers to a Man refuse to load, and as yet Mr. [Thomas] Coulson has not been able to procure any Seamen, although he has used every means, not only here, but at Marblehead and Salem, to which place he sent the Master of his Sloop for that purpose -

The Friends of Government of this Town, have represented their situation in General [Thomas] Gage, and they have also requested me to spare them an Officer and a few Hands to go in a Vessel to Boston, which they have hired for that purpose; a Copy of which application I herewith enclosed: indeed I am happy in this opportunity myself, as I am still without a reply to the letters that I wrote to Captain [Andrew] Barkley; though I can now have put poor hopes of your sparing any Marines, if there is any truth I can now have but poor hopes of your sparing any Marines, if there is any truth in the reports that circulate here.

Mr. [William] Tyng the Sheriffe of this Country carries the Petition to the General, and at the same time means to pay his respects to you: this Gentleman is well acquainted with the dispositions of the People in this part of the Country and not less so with the Seditious and Rebellious Principles that are daily practiced hereabouts, by which he had suffered not a little. With this I transmit the State and Condition of the Armed ship under my Command.

I am Sir

[&c.] H. Mowatt

May 5, 1775 Friday Werly
Moored in Falmouth Harbor, Casco Bay
Varbl Weathr. - at noon saw a number of people under arms in the town, hove the spring on the cables broadside to the Town.

May 6, 1775 Saturday Soerly
Moored in Falmouth Harbor, Casco Bay
Fresh gales with some rain. Country people under arms - kept the crew under arms day and night.

May 7, 1775 Sunday Eterly
Dark cloudy weathr. with Rain & fresh gales - veered off the spring

May 8, 1775 Monday E, NW
PM fresh gales with rain AM fresh gales breezes and clear Dryed sails

May 9, 1775 Tuesday Soerly
Moored in Falmouth Harbour, Casco Bay
Fresh breezes & clear Weathr. AM Capt. Mowat & Doctor Baillie went on shore to walk, and were intercepted and made Prisoners by some Armed men. At 2 PM hove taught the Spring, the ships Broadside to the town, fired 2 Guns as Signals at 9 came on board the Captain and Doctor.

May 10, 1775 Wednesday Do.
Moored in Falmouth Harbor, Casco Bay
Fresh Breezes & clear weathr at 7 PM hove tight the Spring, the Ships broad side to the Town, fired 2 guns as signals - at 9 came on bd. the Captain and Doctor - AM Exercise at small Arms - a shot was fired from the shore & entered the ships side - kept under arms all night.

Edward Parry to Lieutanant Henry Mowat, Commander of His Majesty's Ship *Canceaux*

George Town May 10, 1775

Sir I am very much obliged to you for your kind letter of the 29th ult. P Lambert, which was intercepted and demanded with my other letters &c at Brunswick by Samuel Thompson of that place and broke open, copies of which have been industriously circulated thro the Country bay the different Committee men &c., several parts thereof being misconstrued or misunderstood by the illiterate - I should have answered your letter sooner but did not know how to procure any safe conveyance - On the 4th inst. Thompson

attended by a number of Armed Men to the
Amount of Forty or upwards insisted on my being his Prisoner, and to go with him; or give Bail Bond with two Securities in the Penal Sum of 2000 pounds payable to the Provincial Congress, the condition of the Bond compelled to be given, is that I should not nor no one for or under me remove my Masts, Plank &c now here, nor write to any Officer of the Army or Navy for protection, or against the Country - I prefer'd giving the Bond rather than to risk myself with him - A State of my Case has been sent to the Congress; who I hope will think it reasonable to release me; but such is the unfortunate Temper of the Times, that I am Apprehensive I shall be unable to proceed with my Business and fulfill my Engagement for Halifax Yard for the present and I think it will be extremely hazardous for some time to attempt it, unless affairs take a Sudden Turn

I am with Great Respect Sir [7c.]

Edw Parry

Mr [John] Bernard is also under Bond, and in the same Situation. There are some Reports spread here of an attempt to Surprize the *Canceaux*

May 11, 1775 Thursday Do.
Moored in Falmouth Harbor, Casco Bay
Fresh Breezes & clear Weathr. the town full of Armed Men threat'ning destruction to the Ship, and Plundering the Town - came onbd. the Collector and Minister for Protection.
(The Rev.John Wiswell and George Lyde Collector of Customs)

May 12, 1775 Friday Do.
Moored in Falmouth Harbor, Casco Bay
Fresh gales & hazy Weathr Emp as before, watching the motion of the Rebels - Fired several shot at different craft to bring them to heard that the Rebels began to Disperse

May 13, 1775 Saturday Do.
Moored in Falmouth Harbor, Casco Bay
Do. Weathr. heard that the rebels began to disperse - fired 3 shots at 2 sloops to bring them to, but they got off.

May 14, 1775 Sunday Do.
Fresh gales & hazy Weathr. Emp watching the motions of the Rebels.

May 15, 1775 Monday Soerly, SEerly
Moored in Falmouth Harbor Casco Bay
PM Do. weathr AM mod & Variable, unmoored, & got under sail,

as did the ship [the merchant ship *Minerva* & sloop and a convoy & *Spinckes* [*Sphynx*] Tender Fired 2 three Prs. as signals to Do.- ½ past 1 P.M. Anchd under Hog Isld.

Journal of His Majesty's Ship *Canceaux*, Henry Mowat, Commanding
Moored in Falmouth Harbor Casco Bay
AM Modt and Variable, unmoored, and got under sail as did the Ship (*Minerva*) and Sloop under convoy, and *Spinckes* [*Sphynx*] Tender Fired two three Prs as Signals to Do - ½ past 1 PM Anchd under Hogs Isld.

May 16, 1775 Tuesday Varb.
Light airs & var. 1 1/2 past 1 PM anchored under Hogg Island in 3 fathoms water at 5 weighed & came to sail in Co. as before - at 8 the cape West 2 miles.
May 17, 1775 Wednesday SSW, SW, NW, Varb.
At single anchor off Piscataqua
Light breezes & varb. at 4 PM fired two shots & brought to Brig from Biddeford - Fired guns occasionally as signals to tack at 3 AM fired 3 guns as signal to anchor - came to in 9 fm soft bottom, the ship in Co. refused stays and sailed onshore - Emp getting warps to get the ship off - came two Boats from the *Scarborough* to assist - at 11 got her off, and she went into the Harbor.
Initial: Wm Hogg
May 18 1775 Thursday Var:, Serly
Moored in Piscataqua River
Light airs and Varb:, at 2 PM weighed and came to sail at 1/2 past. anchored in Piscataqua Harbor in 10 fm hard bottom - the light house is 2 cable length Kittery Church. steeple N b W found here his Majestys ship *Scarborough* & Moored ship with stream anchor and cable.
May 19, 1775 Friday Var,. NE
Moored in Piscataqua River
Light airs and variable at 3 unmoored ship and hove short - AM fresh gales and clear weathr employed variously at 10 sighted the anchor.
May 20, 1775 Saturday Var., ENE
Moored in Piscataqua River
PM fresh breezes and clear weath winds varb. emp getting wood and water on board.
May 21, 1775 Sunday SSE

Moored in Piscataqua River
Fresh breezes and clear weathr. AM sighted the anchor and let it go.

May 22, 1775 Monday ENE
Moored in Piscataqua River
PM fresh gales & hazy AM gales & cloudy with rain, steadies the ship with the stream anchor and cable.

May 23, 1775 Tuesday ENE
Fresh gales & cloudy with drisling rain. Emp variously Emp drying sails

May 24, 1775 Wednesday Var.
Moored in Piscataqua River
Light airs and variable - emp drying sails

May 25, 1775 Thursday Var., ENE
Moored in Piscataqua River
The first & middle part clear weathr. the latter thick fogg emp variously

Vice Admiral Samuel Graves to Captain Andrew Barkley, H.M.S. *Scarborough,* Piscataqua

Sir *Preston* Boston 25 May 1775

I have received your Letters to the 10, 18, & 19 of May with their Inclosures, when three hundred men; were assembled to prevent it; but, suppose with the loss of Men you had effected it, the Consequences would have been destruction to every other Mast marked for the King: and I will do not at present see the use of the Governors acquainting you with a proceeding of the Rebels detrimental to his Majestys Interest, when he at the same time had no request to make concerning it, and did not think it advisable for you to attempt the preventing the Masts being carried higher up the River. I very much approve and commend Lieutenant [Henry] Mowat intrepid and Officerlike Conduct at Falmouth; the Behavior of Mr Hogg also deserves great Commendations; That Transaction ought to be a caution to all Officers not to trust themselves in the Hands of Rebels, who carry on War like no other People upon Earth. It was quite right to dispatch the *Canceaux* to Halifax, as you was not apprized of the *Tartar* being there expressly for the purpose of guarding that Arsenal. The *St. Lawrence* and *Halifax* armed Schooners lately purchased are also at Halifax fitting out. The Account of the Hay being burnt was brought here by the *Centurion* Sloop I have great pleasure in expressing my entire Approbation of your Proceedings since you have been at

Piscataqua and am satisfied you will on ever occasion exert yourself for the good of the Kings Service.

Herewith you will receive an Order to seize all Provisions &c. Sam Graves

May 26, 1775 Friday Soerly
Moored in Piscataqua River
PM thick fogg AM cloudy weathr. emp variously
May 27, 1775 Saturday Varbl
Moored in Piscataqua River
Mod & hazy weathr winds varb emp variously
May 28, 1775 Sunday Varb..
The light house NW 1/2 mile in Piscataqua River
Light airs & varb. AM fired a gun & made signal for sailing at 11 AM weighed and came to sail at noon the lighthouse a quarter of a mile met here his Majestys Ship *Scarborough*
May 29, 1775 Monday Varb., Calm., Varb
In Piscataqua River
Light airs & varb with hazy weathr at 4 PM calm - at 6 a small breeze to the Soward bore up for Piscataqua, at 9 anchored near the *Scarborough*. brought in with us a sloop from Long Island with provisions - AM cloudy & hazy fired 15 guns at being the anniversary of King Charles the 2nd Restoration as did the *Scarborough*.
May 30, 1775 Tuesday NE
In Piscataqua River Single anchor light house SSE 1/4 mile
Light breezes and cloudy - AM fresh gales and cloudy with rain Emp Variously
May 31, 1775 Wednesday NE, varb,
At Single Anchor Piscataqua River
Undersail Light house N b W 1mile
Fresh breezes and hazy weathr. with rain AM light airs & hazy weathr. At 8 weighed and came to sail in company the *Spincks* tender & two provision sloops, ½ past 9 came onbd the *Scarboroughs* Boat with Orders to stand off and on Little Harbor saw a great No. of Armed People at the No point of Ditto, supposed they had been taking way some Old Cannon that lay there - at 11 the *Spinckes* was ordered to Boston with the Provision vessels - at noon all the Men disappeared - standing off and on.
At 3 PM came onbd Orders from the *Scarborough* [to] return to the Harbor - at 5 Anchored there in 9 fms water - Saw a number of

people on Battery Hill. the *Scarboroughs* boat came on board & ordered us to stand off and on Little Harbor, - & ? at the North Point of Little Harbor a great number of armed men to the amount of 5 or 600 supposed they had been taken away 10 cannon that lay there at 11 the *Spinkes* Tender was ordered for Boston. Taking under her convoy the two provision sloops at Noon all the men disappeared at Noon the lighthouse N by 1 mile. At 9 hove up and went near the *Scarborough*, and moored with the Stream Anchor and Cable -

Journal of His Majesty's Ship *Canceaux*, Henry Mowat, Commanding
At Single Anchor Piscataqua River
AM Light Airs and hazy - at 8 AM weighed and came to sail in Co with the *Spinckes* [*Sphynx*] Tender, and two Provisions Sloops, ½ past 9 came onbd the *Scarboroughs* Boat with Orders to stand off and on Little Harbor, - saw a great No of Armed People at the No point, supposed they had been taking away some Old Cannon that lay there - at 11 the *Spinckes* was ordered to Boston with the Provision Vessels - at Noon all the Men disappeared - standing of and on.

At 3 PM came onbd Orders from the *Scarborough* [to] return to the Harbor - at 5 anchored there in 9 fms water - saw a No of People on Battery Hill, at 9 hove up and went near the *Scarborough*, and moored with the Stream Anchor and Cable -

June 1, 1775 Thursday Varb, Calm, Werly
At Single anchor Piscataqua River
Light airs and variable - at 3 PM came onboard. orders from the *Scarborough* her boat with orders to go into the harbor & anchor at 5 anchored there in 9 fm. water the fort SW by S 2 cable length Do. saw a great number of armed men over on Kittery side 9 (Battery Hill) where there had been a fort supposed mounting of cannon at 9 hove up & went nearer to the *Scarborough* & moored with the stream anchor & cable AM fresh breezes loosed sails to dry at 10 unmoored ship at Noon single anchor & furled sails. People at work on Battery Hill.
June 2, 1775 Friday Werly
Moored in Piscataqua Harbor
Fresh breezes & clear weathr - at 3 PM moored ship - about 3 Am as *Scarborough's* boat and ours were rowing guard, the former was fired on from the western part of Great Island, one man was

wounded and several shot went thro' the Boat - AM sailed hence several Brigg & sloops moored ship with the stream anchor & cable at 3AM as the *Scarborough* & our boats were rowing guard the former as fired upon from the western part of Great Island several shot through the boat & one man wounded. 1/2 past the *Scarborough* fired three guns over Newcastle town.

June 3, 1775 Saturday Var.

Under sail

Mod Breezes and fine clear weather At noon unmoored and hove short in order to get under way Do. weighed & came to sail

June 4, 1775 Sunday Serly

Moored off Spruce Creek

Do. weather at 1 PM anchored with the small bower in 7 fathoms water at the entrance of Spruce Creek - Moored ship with stream anchor & cable - fired 21 guns being the Kings Birth Day in loading one of the guns a second time, it went off and carried away the Boatswains hand, at 1/2 after 2 his arm was cut off below the shoulder.

After the first discharge of the cannon in this salute water was to be sponged down the barrel to extinguish any burning or smoldering debris, cartridge paper or felt wadding. Apparently this did not happen and when the cannon was loaded again the paper cartridge was exposed to smoldering debris and exploded taking off the hand of the Boatswain standing and working the cannon at the muzzle. There was a surgeon's mate aboard who performed the amputation with the aid of his attendants, usually in the cockpit where there was candle light if need be. Using saws and knives heated to reduce the pain of amputation and tourniquets to stop the flow of blood from the wound. Due to the damage and the possibility of gangre as well as massive infection it was decided to remove the limb just below the shoulder and the operation took probably less than a minute. To reduce the pain, rum was given to the seaman to bring on stupor as well as laudanum and opium. The stump of the amputated arm was sealed by searing steel of cauterization then covered with tar. Shock and infection were killers of those with major wounds.

June 5, 1775 Monday Serly

Moored in Piscataqua River Lighthouse SSE

Ditto Weathr. at 6 PM began to unmoor, at 9 hove short, at 10 weighed & dropped down along side of the *Scarborough* off the

fort William & Mary.
June 6, 1775 Tuesday Serly
Moored in Piscataqua River Lighthouse SSE
Do. weathr. PM moored ship - Lighthouse SSE New Castle Meeting Steeple SW b W AM emp variously
June 7, 1775 Wednesday Serly, varb.
PM do. Weathr. AM Thunder and Lightening attended with rain arrived here the *Spincks* Tender from Boston
June 8, 1775 Thursday Varb
Moored as before Piscataqua River
PM thunder with rain winds variable - AM mod and hazy loosed sails to dry emp as occasion at noon handed sails
June 9, 1775 Friday Var.
Moored as before Piscataqua River
Fresh Breezes & variable Emp on occasion
June 10, 1775 Saturday Soery
Moored as before Piscataqua River
PM Moderate & clear weather AM fresh breezes & hazy weather. unmoored ship at noon hove short
June 11, 1775 Sunday SSE, SSW, SW
Cape Sable N: 70 E 39 leagues
Fresh breeze and clear wt. latter hazy - at 1 PM weigh came to sail emp warping out of the harbor
at 4 the Isle of Shoals SSW 4 miles
at 5 set the MS
at 6 fresh gales and clear weathr. in the 1 & 2d reefed T sails
at 9 the Isle Shoals W1/2 for 7 or 8 leagues
at 4 AM gales cloudy weathr
at 6 raining weathr.
at 10 emp reef Top sails
at 12 Hazy weather lat observed 42.67 - 42.41.62 - 62-39
June 12, 1775 Monday SW b S, NNW
Cape Sable N 27 E 10 leagues
PM First part fresh gales and thick foggy weathr - Middle clear the latter mod and Do Weathr. - Lat: Obs: 42:58 No.-
at 1 fresh gales & thick foggy weather
at 4 do. weathr
at 12 fresh breezes & clear weather
at 8 Do. weathr
at 12 Do. weathr Lat observe 41.50
June 13 , 1775 Tuesday N b W, Werly, SW
Cape Negro NN 2 -N5 Leagues

Cape Sambrough N 50 E 36 leagues
Fresh breezes and clear weathr this most part,
at 5 PM hazey weathr fired 4 shot and brought too a sloop from Newfoundland in ballast
at 8 light airs
at 12 fine clear weathr.
at 4 AM saw the land bearing NE b E 6 or 7 leagues which proved to be Cape Negro - Cape Negro NW b N 5 leagues
at 10 AM fired 2 shot, an brought too a schooner belonging to New York from the River St. Lawrence
at 12 slight breezes & clear Cape Negro NW b N 5 leagues
Lat: 0bserved 42:23 No.

June 14, 1775 Wednesday Werly, WSW
Cape Sambro (Sambrough) Lighthouse N b W 2 miles
Mod and clear Weathr all sail set at 8 saw the high land L. house at midd night down studding sails at 10 AM Sambrose Light house NNE 6 or 7 leagues.
Fresh gales and clear at 5 AM fired 2 shot, and brought to a schooner from Yarmouth - at 10 Sambro light NNE
at 1 all sail sett clear weathr
at 7 Do. weathr high land of Lehaver N b E 8 leag
at 12 Down studding sails
at 3 saw the high land of Lehave bear NNE
fired two shot at & brought too a schooner from Yarmouth bound for Halifax
at 10 Sambro light house NNE 6
at 12 Fresh gales & cloudy wear. the lighthouse N b W dist. 2 miles

June 15, 1775 Thursday WSW, W, NW, NE
At the dock in Halifax harbor along side of the careening wharf
Fresh gales and squally - hauled down all the studding sails at 3 PM anchored of the Kings yard in Halifax Harbor found there his Majestys ship, *Tartar*, and the *Halifax* of St. Lawrence armed schooners - middle & latter part strong gales with heavy rains extreme cold

June 16, 1775 Friday NNE
At the dock in Halifax harbor along side of the careening wharf
Strong gales with heavy rains very cold weathr. - PM transported the ship alongside the Careening wharf -Emp occasionaly

June 17, 1775 Saturday Soerly
At the Dock in Halifax Harbor along side of the careening warfe
Fresh gales and cold Weathr: with Rain - AM more mod airs

secured the quay side emp variously aired all the spare sails

June 18, 1775 Sunday Varb

At the Dock yard in Halifax harbor a long side of the careening wharf Mod and fine Weathr. with flying clouds Emp unbending sails.

June 19, 1775 Monday Varb

At the Dock Yard in Halifax Harbor a long side of the careening warfe

Mod breezes and Varb: - Emp unrigging the ship & Came in here a transport from Boston

June 20, 1775 Tuesday Varb

At the Dock Yard in Halifax Harbor a long side of the careening wharf.

PM fair Wear: AM cloudy with some rain - Emp getting the guns out

June 21, 1775 Wednesday Varb

At the Dock Yard in Halifax Harbor a long side of the careening warfe

PM cloudy with some rain - AM fine Weathr: Emp getting the anchor on shore and cleaning the hold

June 22, 1775 Thursday Noerly

At the Dock in Halifax Harbor a long side of the careening warfe

PM cloudy with rain - emp getting the Ballast out AM fair Weathr - came on board the Caulkers emp caulking recd 260 pound fresh beef

June 23, 1775 Friday Var

At the dock Yard in Halifax Harbor a long side of the careening wharf

Mod and fair Weathr. Emp getting out the Ballast caulkers emp as before

June 24, 1775 Saturday Nerly

At the Dock Yard in Halifax Harbor a long side of the careening wharf

Do. Weathr. People as before caulkers as before

June 25, 1775 Sunday Noerly

At the Dock Yard in Halifax Harbor a long side of the careening wharf

Cloudy weathr. caulkers Emp as before

June 26, 1775 Monday Noerly

Alongside the careening wharf Halifax Harbor

PM fresh gales and hazy with rain Middle part hard gales with thick Weathr: and rains - AM light airs and cloudy People Emp getting the ballast out caulkers emp as before

June 27, 1775 Tuesday Eterly

Alongside the careening wharf Halifax Harbor

Mod. and fine Weathr: People Emp hauling the ballast out caulkers as before

June 28, 1775 Wednesday Eterly

Alongside the careening wharf Halifax Harbor

Fresh breezes and hazy weathr: Emp as before

June 29, 1775 Thursday Noerly, Soerly

Alongside the careening wharf Halifax Harbor

PM fresh breezes and thick foggy weathr - middle & latter Part fresh gales and heavy rains - People Emp overhauling the rigging - a survey on Boatswains stores - got all the Ballast out, got the main yard ashore, and the top off.

June 30, 1775 Friday SE

Alongside the careening wharf Halifax Harbor

PM cloudy with rains - AM strong gales and heavy rains. Emp overhauling the Rigging

H: Mowat. W: Hogg Alexr Aikin

July 1, 1775 Saturday Soerly

Alongside the careening wharf Halifax Harbor

PM more mod. Getting the out rigging on board and already to hove down

July 2, 1775 Sunday Soerly

Alongside the careening wharf Halifax Harbor

Fresh Breezes & raw cold weathr. all the yard People emp variously

July 3, 1775 Monday Soerly

Along side the careening wharf Halifax Harbor

Fresh Breezes & cloudy with rain Emp overhauling & fixing the rigging

July 4, 1775 Tuesday Soerly, Var.

Along side the careening wharf Halifax Harbor

Mod & hazey weathr Fresh Breezes & cloudy with rain at Noon fair weathr PM hove down Keel out found some of her false Keel gone & her main Keel much Bruised 2 hours righted ship compleat & payed her bottom

July 5, 1775 Wednesday Var.

Along side careening wharf Halifax Harbor

Mod & fine weathr PM emp winding ship & shifting all the

careening gear AM hove the ship keel out three hours down at 4 righted ship & compleated her bottom

July 6, 1775 Thursday Nerly

Along side careening wharf Halifax Harbor

Mod & fine weathr caulkers emp caulking PM emp getting all the careening gear a shore & getting the spars on board to get the foremast out AM took foremast out & sailed hence Majestys schooner *St. Lawrence* for Boston Peoples emp getting up spares to take foremast

July 7, 1775 Friday Soerly

Along side careening wharf Halifax Harbor

Do. weathr Caulkers as before People emp returning the Condemmed Stores & getting onboard Ballast

July 8, 1775 Saturday Werly

Along side careening wharf Halifax Harbor

Do. Weathr emp getting Ballast on board

July 9, 1775 Sunday Soerly

Along side careening wharf Halifax Harbor

Fine Pleasant weathr at 11 PM was alarmed with the dock bell ringing for fire found it was in one of the cabbins of the boathouse but by early assistance it was put out.

July 10, 1775 Monday Soerly

Along side careening warfe Halifax Harbor

Fresh Breezes with raw cold weathr. emp getting on board Ballast.

July 11, 1775 Tuesday Varb.

Along side careening wharf Halifax Harbor

Mod & fine warm weathr. emp as before. Painters employed Painting

July 12, 1775 Wednesday Varb.

Along side careening wharf Halifax Harbor. Pleasant weathr emp about rigging Painters emp Painting the ship Joiners & shipwrights and Painters as before.

July 13, 1775 Thursday Var.

Along side careening wharf Halifax Harbor

PM pleasant Clear weathr at 6 got the foremast in employed in unraveling the gear and taking the spars down AM thick hazey weathr. with drisling rain

July 14, 1775 Friday Noerly

At the careening wharf in Halifax

Mod & cloudy with drizling rain at times Got in all the Ballast and the casks of water which contains 14 Butts & 31 ? AM emp rigging the ship the Painters as before.

July 15, 1775 Saturday Noerly
At the careening wharf in Halifax
PM dark Cloudy weathr. with some small rain AM cloudy emp rigging the ship Carpenters Joiners painters as before.

July 16, 1775 Sunday Soerly
At the careening wharf in Halifax
Fine clear weathr, Got the sheet cable in carpenters Joiners as before

July 17, 1775 Monday Soerly
At the careening wharf in Halifax
Do. weathr employed as before carpenters joiners as before

July 18, 1775 Tuesday Var.
At the careening wharf in Halifax
Mod & fine weathr emp as before Carpenters, Joiners Painters as before

July 19, 1775 Wednesday Var.
At the careening wharf in Halifax
Do. weathr emp as before Carpenters, Joiners Painters as before

July 20, 1775 Thursday Noerly
At the careening wharf in Halifax
Do. weathr emp as before Carpenters, Joiners, Painters as before

July 21, 1775 Friday Westerly
At the careening wharf in Halifax
Do. weathr emp variously Got on board the cables carpenters, joiners, painters as before. Carpenters are finished

July 22, 1775 Saturday Soerly
At the careening wharf in Halifax
Do. weathr emp variouly taking out Boatswains & carpenters stores

July 23, 1775 Sunday Soerly
At the careening wharf in Halifax
Do. weathr. emp as before AM bent sails

July 24, 1775 Monday Soerly
At the careening wharf, in Halifax
Do. weathr. emp getting Boatswains & carpenters stores onboard

July 25, 1776 Tuesday Werly
At the careening wharf in Halifax
Do. weathr. emp getting wood & water in

July 26, 1775 Wednesday Werly
At the careening wharf in Halifax
Do. weathr. emp as before Got onboard all the Gunns Came in here his Majestys sloop *Hinchingbrook*

July 27, 1775 Thursday Soerly
At the careening wharf in Halifax. Mod & cloudy with rain
July 28, 1775 Friday Varb
At Halifax single anchor
PM rainy weathr AM cloudy & fair weathr holed on side of Bootopped
July 29, 1775 Saturday Werly
At Halifax single anchor
Fair weath at 3 PM hauled of from the wharf & anchored between the Town & Kings Yard at 4 heeled ship & bootoped AM got on board the Powder & with Gunners stores
July 30, 1775 Sunday Serly
Single anchor Church steeple WSW
Do. weathr at 4 AM made the signal for sailing at 6 came on board the Master attendant to carry her down and turned down abreast of the town the church Steeple WSW 1 cable from the shore
July 31, 1775 Monday Soerly
Undersail the Major Beach SSW a cable length
PM med & fair middle part calm AM fresh Breezes & cloudy Wear at 8 do. weighed & came to sail emp turning down to ye the Beech at Noon came to in 10 fm water soft bottom the Beech Point SW 8 cables length
August 1, 1775 Tuesday SW, Var.
Beach Point 7&1/2 miles
PM fresh breezes and hazey Weathr middle thick fogg with some rain AM mod and clear Weathr at 10 weigh and came to sail at noon came too in 17 fm water soft bottom the Beach Point S b E near 1/2 a mile dist.
August 2, 1775 Wednesday Soerly, Varb
Somboro Light House WNW 3 Leagues
Slight airs and variable Emp variously at 4 AM weighted and came to sail with a light airs Noerly from 5 till ten all Round the Compass at 6 saw a top sail vessel in the offing made sail and gave chase Lighthouse NNW 20 leagues
August 3, 1775 Thursday So.
Cape Sambrose 1/2 league
P.M Spoke the Chace she proved to be the *Elizabeth* belonging to Newberry from haver de gras in Ballast. She had no Provision on board Spaired her Bread Pork & Rum 5 of her men enter'd on board* Mode & clear wear lattd obsd 43:39 N.
Mod. breezes & cloudy still in chase draw up with ye chase all sail out at 6 PM Cape Samborough NW b N distant 8 or 9 leagues

rainy weathr fired as shot at ye chase but she took no notice of it we made her to be a brigg at 3 AM spoke the chase she Proved to be the *Elisabeth* belonging to Newberry from Haver de grace in ballast she had no Provisions on board spared her Bread Pork and Rum 5 of her men entered on board
(* These five seamen were impressed into English naval service from the ship *Elizabeth*)
Master's Log
Remarks on Thursday the 3d of Augt 1775
[P.M.] Spoke the Chase she proved to be the *Elizabeth* belonging to Newberry from haver de gras in Ballast She had no Provision on board Spared her Bread Pork & Rum 5 of her Men enter'd on board Mode & Clear Wear Lattd obsd 43 39 N.
[The *Canceaux* had cleared Halifax the previous day and began the chase around noon, identifying her quarry as a brig. The five were impressed from the *Elizabeth.]*

August 4, 1775 Friday Werly
Do Cape N28 E Dist 13 Leagues
Fresh Breezes & clear weathr Fresh gales & squally with rain in 1 & 2 reef of top sails Down T.G. handed topsails Set topsails light breezes & clear Fresh gales handed fore top sail Saw a sail in ye ESE Made sail gave chase at 7 fresh gales and squally in ? & 2 keep topsail down top gallant yard at 11 handled the Top sail at 6 am got up Top sail at 9 added sail and gave chase at 10 AM fired a shot at and brought her too spoke the chase she proved a schooner from Halifax bound for Boston Fresh breezes & clear weathr out all reefs T:S:

August 5, 1775 Saturday Werly
Cape Sable So 79 W 25 Leagues
PM fresh breezes and clear Weathr. 1/2 past 1 saw the land bearing the east seen from NW to NE and the land proved Lehave R. dist off shore two miles in 1st. part Til ? the entrance of Schoodic Harbor NNW 2 leagues at 8 in the PM T.S middle and Later part light breezes and clear weathr. Latt obsd 43:33 S

August 6, 1775 Sunday W, NE
Cape Sable No 38 W 19 Leagues
At 1 Mod. and clear Weathr
at 4 fresh breezes and hazy
at 7 down the top gallant yards
At 11 Do. Weathr
at Noon Light Breezes
at 4 AM fine clear Weathr.

at 6 up top gallant yards and set studding sails fore & aft
At 11 light breezes weathr Latt observed ? 40N
At 12 found the ship 13 miles to ye Southward of her reckoning corrected it accordingly

August 7, 1775 Monday — Estery

Cape Ann W Dist 46 Leagues
At 1 fresh breezes & clear weathr all sail set
At 6 cloudy weath
At 12 do. weath
At 2 dark cloudy weath with drisling rain
At 6 fresh gales with rain down studding sails fore and aft
At 10 close reefed the fore & mizen topsails down
At 11 top gallant yards Fresh breezes and clear Weath all sails set
at mid Night Dark cloudy with drizling rain
at 6 AM fresh gales with rain downed studding sails fore and aft
at 10 close reefed the fore aft mizen topsails and down top gallant yards

August 8, 1775 Tuesday — S, WSW

Cape Anne NW by N 11 Leagues
At 1 fresh gales with Drisling rain
At 3 cloudy weathr a Great swell lost a logg
At 4 Served limes & leeks to ye ships company
At 6 1st & 2d reef M:T:S in reef four mizen
At 10 out 2d Reefs topsail
At 4 Mod & fair weath up top gallant yds
At 6 out reefs topsails set studding sails fore & aft
At 12 Mod & clear weath
Fresh gales with drizling rain at 4 PM cloudy weathr. a great swell lost a log & served limes & leeks to the ships company
at 4 mod and fair weathr up top sails gall yards out reefs top sails and set studding sails

The leeks and limes served the ships company on this day were a means to prevent the incidence of scurvy among the ships company.

August 9, 1775 Wednesday — SSW

At single Anchor along warfe WSW 1/4 mile Boston harbor
At 1 fresh breezes & clear weathr
At 5 saw Pidgeon Hill bearing NW b W dist 10 leagues
At 6 Fresh gales & cloudy Pidgeon Hill No.
At 8 Saw the light house but no light in it

At 10 anchored in 17 fm water the Brewers
At 12 WSW 3 or 4 leagues
At 4 drisling rain
At 5 weighed came to sail empd turning in to Boston Harbor at 11 saluted Admiral Graves with 15 guns Vice Admiral of the White in His Majestys Ship *Preston* as also the *Symmetry, Boyne, Lively, Scorpion, Kingfisher & Fowey* At ½ past 11 anchored near the *Preston* off long wharfe Fresh breezes and cloudy weathr at 4 pm saw Pidgoen Hill bearing NW bW dist 9 or 10 leagues do. fresh gales and cloudy weathr at 8 saw Boston light house at 10 anchored in 17 fms water the great Brewers WSW 4 leagues at 5 AM weighed and came to sail in to Boston Harbor at 11 saluted Admiral Graves with 15 guns of the whole in his Majestys Ship *Preston* and also the *Sumerside, Boyen, Lively, Scorpion, King Fisher* At 1/2 past 11 anchored in 4 fms

August 10, 1775 Thursday Eerly
Moored in Boston Harbor
Fresh breezes and cloudy with rain at times empd watering

August 11, 1775 Friday Var.
Moored in Boston Harbor
Light airs and cloudy with rain at times

August 12, 1775 Saturday Var
Moored in Boston Harbor
Mod. & cloudy with some Thunder lightening & rain

August 13, 1775 Sunday Var
Moored in Boston Harbor
Light airs and var Sailed hence his Majestys Sloop *Kingfisher*

August 14, 1775 Monday Var.
Moored in Boston Harbor
Do. weathr. AM the signal on board the flagg to excercise Great Guns and small arms Do. Excercised small arms and fired 6 shots of ye Great guns at a mark

August 15, 1775 Tuesday Var.
Moored in Boston harbor
Light airs & var very hot weathr loosed sails to dry at noon handed sails Do.

August 16, 1775 Wednesday Werly
Moored in Boston Harbor
Fresh breezes and hazy weat. Got on board some Provisions empd variously Several guns fired from ye rebel lines to Boston Neck came in his Majestys Sloop *Falcon*

August 17, 1775 Thursday Soerly

Do. Breezes & weathr emp variously & getting ready for sea

Vice Admiral Samuel Graves to Philip Stephens, Secretary of the British Admiralty

Sir   Preston Boston 17 August 1775

In my last Letter July 29 by Col. James I acquainted you that the *Falcon* was ordered to convoy the *Russia Merchant* Transport twenty leagues to the Eastward of Cape Cod; Captain [John] Linzee accordingly sailed the 30th with Directions to cruize between Cape Ann and the Isle of Shoals to intercept Supplies of Ammunition and Provisions coming to the Rebels.

On the 10th instant the *Falcon* anchored at Nantasket, and I received a Letter from Captain Linzee, (a copy of which is inclosed) giving an Account of an unsuccessful attempt to take a large Schooner in Cape Ann Harbor and to destroy the Town, and that he was obliged to come away with the Loss of two Boats, his master Gunner, Sixteen Seamen and seven Marines taken Prisoners, and his Lieutenant wounded. It is so difficult to procure British Seamen that the loss becomes considerable. At present they cannot be replaced with Europeans and experience shows Americans are not to be trusted.

In a former Letter I mentioned the Rebels having burnt the Wooden part of Boston Light House. The Governor ordered it be repaired immediately; Materials and Artifcers are accordingly sent down, and at his request I ordered Lieut. Coulthurst and a Party of Marines from the *Preston* and *Boyne* for their Guard. The *Preston's* long boat also staid with them, and Captain [Thomas] Bishop of the *Lively* at Nantasket had directions to give them all the assistance in his power, and to settle Signals to be made in case of danger. They had exceeded a week on this Duty and were to have relieved on the 31st when to my great astonishment, I was informed they had been all cut off just after Day Light. The inclosed Account from the Midshipmen who commanded the Long Boat will shew more particularly how this affair happended. As the Light house Island with 30 men was judged capable of being defended against 1000, it was extremely unfortunate the Party of Marines made so little resistance, for in less than half an hour a great Reinforcement arrived: but I am sorry to say it appears to me the Party were intent only of escaping, although the marine Officer was at the Reduction of Belle Isle and accounted a brave and experienced Officer.

Captain [John] Robinson of the *Preston* happened the night

of the 30th to have the Boats, secreted in a Wood near the Water Side; this Scheme failed, but he arrived tome enough to chase the Whale Boats across the lighthouse Channel to Hull Beach, from whence he brought away two of them and Lieut. Colthursts Body. Seven Artificers having got away from the Rebels, after being landed on the Main were brought off in one of the Boats, with Captain Robinson; Two more escaped in the Long Boat. But two wounded Marines out of the whole Party were not taken, one of whom is since dead of his wounds.

The *Merlin* anchored the 2nd instant in the Lighthouse Channel from a Cruize.

On the 5th his Majestys ship *Fowey* arrived from Virginia and brought fifty two men for the Squadron, many of them very indifferent. I ordered Captain [George] Montagu to place his Ship between Charles Town and Boston, but I shall send her to Halifax as soon as I can put another in her place.

On the 6th. His Majestys Sloop *Kingfisher* arrived with a Vessel having on board 20 head of Cattle seized in the Sound on the restraining Act. They have been since condemned in the Admiralty Court at Boston. By Captain George Montague I received a letter from Lord Dunmore Governor of Virginia exhibiting complaints of a very serious nature against Captain [John] Macartney of his Majestys ship *Mercury* and referring me to Captain Montague for Particulars. I inclose also Captain Montagu's upon my requiring him to inform me of such Facts relative to Captain Macartneys Misconduct as had come to his knowledge. Conceiving it therefore unsafe to the Command of his Majestys Ship any longer with Captain Macartney I ordered the *Kingfisher* to Virginia, and have sent Lieut [Alexander] Graeme in her with directions to put Captain in Arrest, and to bring the *Mercury* forthwith to Boston. The *Kingfisher* accordingly sailed from hence the 14th instant.

A Tender belonging to the *Rose* came in the 6th instant, and I received from Captain [James] Wallace a Parcel of Rebel Letters taken from two men who came lately from Philadelphia and were going in a Boat to Providence. I transmit Copies of three of them, the rest are chiefly written on domestick & trading subjects.

The *Merlin* sailed the 8th with a transport carrying a part of the poor of Boston, and returned again the 16th with the transport having landed them at Marblehead.

The *Canceaux* arrived from Halifax the 9th and sailed again the 17th. With the *Spinckes* Tender laden with provisions for the

Scarborough at Piscataqua.

On the 112th I determined to send the *Somerset* to Halifax to stop her Leaks, and accordingly have given Captain [Edward] Lecras orders to that Purpose, and respecting the Security of the yard and Stores while he remains there, and to return as soon as possible to Boston; but not to leave Halifax unless a 20 Gun ship at least is in the harbour. He now waits only for a Wind to put to sea directly.

The Governor expressing his Uneasiness for the Safety of a number of Transports sent to Gardiners and Fishers Islands for Cattle and other live Stock, I sent Captain [Thomas] Bishop in the *Lively* to cruize for them from Cape Cod to the Isle of Shoals. He returned the 15th with the whole Convoy, which has brought the Garrison a very good supply of cattle and Sheep.

On the 11th instant I received a letter from Lieu [John] Knight. Late Commander of his Majestys Schooner *Diligent*, but now a prisoner at Cambridge. I inclose a Copy of his Letter, to which I can only say that Mr. Knight must have been totally unacquainted with the disposition of the people at Mechias, and the fate of the *Margaretta*, and apprehending no danger, had put in there as usual; but as I now of no good service that could call him to Mechias, until his release and an enquiry is made into his conduct, no true Judgement can be formed. In the mean time the Rebels having possession of the *Diligent* not only deprives the Squadron of her assistance, but will I fear for some time hinder the publication of such of Mr Des Barres Draughts as wait only for the Soundings.

I have appointed the Honorable Mr [John] Tollemache to be Captain of the *Scorpion* by Commission dated 29th July, and Mr James Drew of the *Preston* Lieutenant in his room. This sloop is nearly ready for Sea and I intend to send her to relieve the *Cruizer* at North Carolina, and that both the *Cruizer* and *Tamer* shall forthwith come to Boston. I am &c

Sam Graves

August 18, 1775 Friday Var.

Single anchor in Nantasket Road

Light airs and variable at 4 PM unmoored and at 5 came to sail under our convey ye *Spinks* sloop at 8 anchored in ye Narrows near Nexes Middle thunder & lightening with heavy rains at 8 AM weighed & came to sail *Spinks* Sloop in company empd turning through the narrows at Noon Anchored in Nantasket Road where we found his Majestys Ship *Lively* & *Marlin* Sloop

August 19, 1775 Saturday Var

Light airs and variable until 4 AM small Breezes at No. weighed & came to sail as did the Sloop *Spinks* at 8 the light house NW 3 miles at Noon the lighthouse Nb W 2 leagues emp turning to Windward wind Easterly

August 20, 1775 Sunday Var

Under sail at Noon Thatcher Island NNW 3 miles

PM light airs & varb emp turning to windward at 4 the Lighthouse SW dist 4 Leagues at 6 Marblehead Church steeple NW b N ½ N ½ Past 1/2 way rock No. 1 cable length dist: Point of Cape Ann Harbor NE b E dist: 4 leagues from 6 till 10 thick fogg at noon Thatchers Island NNW 3 Miles

August 21, 1775 Monday Soerly

At single Anchor in Piscataqua harbor Light House S and steeple SWbS Slight Breezes and hazey all sail out fore & aft at 4 PM made the Isle of Shoals bearing N b E at 8 Do. Islands ENE at 11 anchored in the Entrance of Piscataqua Harbor Adams Point WSW 1/2 a mile 8 fm water at 7 weighed & came to sail 1/2 past 8 came to with the small Bower anchor in 10 fm water. lighthouse South New Castle Church steeple SW b S found here his Majestys Ship *Scarborough* with a ship and schooner she had taken

August 22, 1775 Tuesday Var

At single anchor in Piscataqua Harbor

Light airs and variable very warm weathr Emp watering

August 23, 1775 Wednesday Var

At single anchor in Piscataqua Harbor

Do. Weathr employed serving the cables

August 24, 1775 Thursday Var

At single anchor in Piscataqua River

Do. Weathr employed as before at 9 the *Scarborough* got under sail 1/2 past she came too again and anchored having little winds

August 25, 1775 Friday Eterly

Under sail Boston Light house WNW 4 miles

Small breezes and variable at 1 PM came to sail as did the *Scarborough* and *Spinks* Tender with a ship and schooner at 4 the Isle Shoals E NE 1 1/2 leagues at 6 took ye *Spinks* and governor Wentworth barge in tow at 4 am Thatchers Island NW 4 leagues at Noon Boston Light House WNW 3 or 4 miles the *Scarborough* made sail already with ye sloop & ship in tow

August 26, 1775 Saturday Eterly, S

At single anchor in Boston harbor near the long warfe

Mod. hazey wear. at 1/2 past 2 abreast of the fort at 4 PM anchored in 8 1/2 fm at low water soft Bottom of Long wharf with the small bower veered to 1/3 of a cable found here his Majestys ship *Preston* Adml Graves *Falcon* Sloop with a number of transports with the *Scarborough.* AM came in his Majestys Sloop *Hunter* from England Emp watering

August 27, 1775 Sunday Var

At single anchor in Boston Harbor near the long wharf

Mod & cloudy weathr with some thunder lightening and rain all this day there is a continual fire from the lines at Charles Town on the Rebels and the rebels at them came in here his Majestys Sloop *Savage*

August 28, 1775 Monday Var

At single anchor in Boston harbor near the long wharfe

First & middle part light airs and var. with heavy rains thunder and lightening AM Cleared up loosed sails to dry at noon handed them Sailed hence his Majestys ship *Scarborough*

August 29, 1775 Tuesday NNE

At single anchor in Boston harbor near the long wharf

PM light Breezes & cloudy AM fresh gales & cloudy with heavy rains emp as occasion

August 30, 1775 Wednesday NE

At single anchor in Boston harbor near the long wharfe

Mod. Breezes with heavy rains AM fresh Breezes with heavy rains Sail'd hence his Majestys Sloop *Savage*

August 31, 1775 Thursday NE

At single anchor in Boston harbor near the long wharf

Thick hazey rainy weathr for this 24 hours Emp variously

Sept 1, 1775 Friday NNE

Moored in Boston harbor

Thick Hazey cold rainy weathr all this 24 hours

Sept 2, 1775 Saturday NE

Moored in Boston harbor

Fresh gales and thick rainy weathr firing from the lines at each other arrived here the *Halifax* schooner

Sept 3. 1775 Sunday ESE

Moored in Boston harbor

Do weathr came in here two transports from Quebec with Provisions and stock

Sept 4, 1775 Monday Eterly

Moored in Boston harbor

Do. Weathr. Employed variously

Sept. 5. 1775 Tuesday Eterly, WNW
Moored in Boston Harbor
PM Mod and hazey foggy weathr. AM small breezes and fine weathr Sailed hence his Majestys Sloop *Falcon* with two transports Aired all the sail
Sept. 6, 1775 Wednesday Westy
Moored in Boston harbor
Fresh breezes and clear weathr Emp as occasion
Sept 7, 1775 Thursday Westy
Moored in Boston harbor
Mod and fine clear weathr sailed hence the *Halifax* schooner with 4 transports
Sept 8, 1775 Friday Var
Moored in Boston harbor
Mod and fine clear weathr PM came in here his Majestys sloop *Viper* from England 10 weeks out
Sept. 9, 1775 Saturday Var
Moored in Boston Harbor
Do. weathr Employed variously
Sept. 10, 1775 Sunday Soerly
Moored in Boston Harbor
Do. weathr AM came in here two of his Majestys schooners the *St. Lawrence* and *Hope* with several sloops and schooners with fresh stock
Sept. 11, 1775 Monday Soerly
Moored in Boston Harbor
PM light breezes and fine weathr AM fresh gales and clear weathr some flying showers of rain
Sept. 12, 1775 Tuesday Norely, var
Moored in Boston Harbor
PM Fresh gales and clear weathr AM mod and fine weathr Emp variously

Vice Admiral Samuel Graves to Samuel Holland
Sir *Preston* at Boston 12 Sepr 1775

Your letter of the 27th of July, delivered to me this day, confirms my opinion that we are risquing the Loss of all your Drawings, Plans, Instruments &c. and perhaps the Liberty if not the Lives of all concerned by continuing to prosecute the businesss of the Survey you are employ's on: I have therefore ordered Captain Vandput to receive on board the *Asia* all your Instruments, Plans, Drawings, Charts &c for their Security, in order that the publik may not lose the Benefit of your Labours purchased at so econsiderable an Expense.

It is impossible for me to spare the *Canceaux,* but Captain Vaneput is ordered upon your Requisition to give you every Assistance he can in getting your things on board, & also to receive such of the Gentlemen and People employed on the Survey as may prefer being secure in the Kings Ship to remaining among the Rebels. It is of very great consequence to send the above mention'd valuables immediately on board the *Asia*. You may assure yourself that affairs are growing worse, and that hostilities will not continue to be carried to partially as at present.

When all your Matters are safe on board the *Asia* they can be removed at leizure; and I shall gladly suit your convenience in that or any thing in my Power. I am &c

Sam Graves

Captain Samuel Holland, the Surveyor General, was working and living in the vicinity of Perth Amboy at the mouth of the Raritan River. Holland probably was aboard the survey vessel Diligent, Lt. John Knight, Commander. The art work used for the cover of the atlas for New York portion of Atlantic Neptune depicts a scene at the lower end of Manhattan Island – the unnamed ship depicted on the artwork is a full rigged ship and therefore is probably not the Diligance. The hull appears to be that of the Canceaux. Additionally the ship depicted on the cover art of the Annapolis Royal portion of the Atlantic Neptune Atlas also appears to be the Canceaux. While the rigging of both ship depictions is that of a sloop of war, the detail shown on the stern windows and quarter windows matches closely that shown on the plans of Canceaux held by the National Maritime Museum in Greenwhich, England. Additonal elements of the scenes shown include crews in the ships boats rowing out to undertake the survey and the ships company aboard the vessel anchored in Annapolis Royal. Other ships are depicted.

Sept 13, 1775 Wednesday Soerly
Moored in Boston Harbor
Mod and clear weathr Emp variously at 8 AM a signal on board of the *Boyne* for a Court Martial

Sept 14, 1775 Thursday Soerly
Moored in Boston Harbor
Mod & cloudy weathr very hot emp variously AM sailed hence his

Majestys Sloop *Viper*
Sept 15, 1775 Friday Soerly
Moored in Boston Harbor
Fresh Breezes & cloudy with very hot weathr. emp as occasion
Sept 16, 1775 Saturday Var
Moored in Boston Harbor
PM fresh gales with rain AM Mod & very hot sultry weathr found the stream anchor come home unmoored ship & new moored her with the two Bowers between ye *Preston* & Long wharf loosed sails to dry at Noon handed them
Sept. 17, 1775 Sunday Var
Moored in Boston Harbor
PM a smart cannonade from the Lines at Boston Neck on the Rebels and the Rebels on them in which the rebels hove their shot four hundred Yards within our lines Mod & hot sultry weathr winds variable
Sept 18, 1775 Monday Werly
Moored in Boston harbor
Fresh Breezes & cloudy weathr PM a smart cannonade of some of the lines at Boston Neck on the Rebels & the rebels on them in which the rebels have shot four hundred yards within our lines
Sept. 19, 1775 Tuesday Noerly
Moored in Boston harbor
Mod & fair weathr. AM sailed hence his Majestys Brigg *Balton* firing from the lines as before
Sept. 20, 1775 Wednesday Noerly
Moored in Boston harbor
Dark cloudy weathr Recd. three small mortars on board with a number of shells AM sailed hence his Majestys schooner *Hope* with Governor Wentworth
Sept 21, 1775 Thursday Esterly
Moored in Boston harbor
Dark Drizling weathr emp variously
Sept 22, 1775 Friday
Cold raw cloudy weathr fired 21 guns it being the anniversary of his Majestys Coronation as did all the ships & Castle William
Sept. 23, 1775 Saturday Var
Moored in Boston harbor
Fresh Breezes & cloudy weathr with some rain Emp as occasion firing as usual from the lines when one of the rebels shot carried away Capt Pollards leg of the 59th Regiment
Sept. 24, 1775 Monday Noerly

Moored in Boston Harbor
PM Cloudy with some rain latter clear dryed sails

Sept. 25, 1775 Monday Westy
Moored in Boston harbor
Fresh Breezes & dry weathr emp adjusting & fitting out of the *Spitfire* armed sloop

Sept 26, 1775 Tuesday Soerly
PM cloudy weathr came in here his Majestys schooner *Hope* with her tender having Governor Wentworth on Board & two transports from Quebeck with stock & provisions AM cloudy with some small rain came in here his Majestys ship *Cerberes* from England

Sept. 27, 1775 Wednesday SW
Moored in Boston Harbor
Fresh gales with rain at times came in several transports from different ports with stock and provisions at 10 AM hard gales struck Top gallant masts at noon do. gales

Sept. 28, 1775 Thursday Wesly
Moored in Boston Harbor
PM fresh gales with some rain AM more mod. Loosed sails to dry and got up top gallant masts and yards

Sept 29, 1775 Friday Wesly
Moored in Boston harbor
Mod breezes and cloudy Employed variously.

Narrative of Vice Admiral Samuel Graves

Boston 29 [September]

The *Cerberus* was ordered to man a scow, stationed at Roxbury Neck, which before was done by the *Preston* and *Fowey*; and the latter Ship went down the Harbour to sail in a few days for Halifax.

The *Hope* Schooner, after many Caulkings and Patchings the last year, was grown so crazy and leaky that it was necessary to lay her ashore to be repaired, which was now done, but the Admiral, being unwilling the Crew should remain idle, ordered the whole (except a few to look after the *Hope*) to go aboard the *Symmetry* an armed Transport, which had been some time fitting for the intended expedition under Lieutenant [Henry] Mowat; and such of the *Hope* Stores as her Commander thought necessary the Admiral directed him to take into the *Canceaux*.

Sept 30, 1775 Saturday Eerly
Moored in Boston Harbor

Fresh breezes & cloudy weathr Came in here his Majestys store ship *Adventure* with some other vessels with provisions

Oct. 1, 1775 Sunday Soerly

Moored in Boston Harbor

Fresh breezes and dark cloudy weathr AM came in here his Majestys ship *Mercury*

A List of Seamen and Marines, sent on board His Majestys Armed Ship *Canceaux*, *Symmetry*, and *Spitfire*, borne on the *Canceaux* Books for Vituals by ordered Vice Admiral Graves.

Note: SHIPS MUSTER - These documents from PRO are hand written on a Royal Navy preprinted sheets (book pages) and include in column format the following headings:

Bounty paid	*Information shown on Ships Muster sheets:*
No	*(Number of listed individuals)*
Entry	*(date shown)*
Year	*(year shown)*
Appearance	*(day and month)*
Whence and whether Preft of not.	*(Location)*
Place and Country where born	
Age at Time of Entry on this ship	
No. and Letter of Tickets	
MENS NAMES	*(name)*
	(rating or rank of listed name)

D., D.D. or R. - the letters imply discharged or rejected
Time of Discharge
Year
Whither or for what Reafon
Stragling
Neglect
Slop Cloaths supplied by Navy
Venereals
Truffes
Cloaths in Sick Quarters
Dead Mens Cloaths
Beds
Tobacco
Wages remitted from Abroad
Two Months Advance

Neceffaries supplied Marines on shore
To whom tge Tickets were delivered
When Muffered Month Days

Where and When Preft or not.

Hope **Schooner**
Geo: Dawson, Lieut.
Alex: Hawthorn, Ab
Jn: Higgins, Ab
Joseph Rofs, Ab
Jn: Murray, Ab
James Perry, Ab
Geo: Dawson, Lieut.
Abraham Rose, Master
Alex: Machay, Gunner
Samuel Jones, Boatswain
James Graves, Quarter Master
Andr. Kickman, do.
Magnus Brown, Ab
Peter Sutherbut, Ab
Henry Currey, Ab
Wm: Bennett, Ab
Nich: Burt, Ab
Sam: Chapman, Ab
Sam: Foster, Ab
Edw: Molland, Ab
John Shean, Ab
Jn: Hirbin, Ab
Edw: Waters, Ab
Thos: Vincent, Ab
Jerimiah, Hunt, Ab
Rob: Thompson, Ab
Ja: Forrester, Ab
James Shaw, Ab
Wm: George, Ab
Richman Fowler, Ab
Marshall Taylor, Ab
Jn: Croft, Ab
Ja: M. Goul, Ab
Jn: Branby, Ab
Wm: Saunderson, Ab
Wm: Hays, Ab

Thos: Dodds, Ab
Jn: Dewrybanks, Ab
Robt: Lofthouse, Ab
Jn: Mell, Ab

Where and when Preft or not.
Boston:
Gurtaris Lagie, Lieut.
Jn: Elphinston, Midshipman
Nich: Duverne, Midshipman
Walter Arab, Ab
Ja: Sheppard, Ab
Thos: Barrel, Ab
Sam: Hall, Ab
Rob: Wallace, Ab
Wm: Franklin, Ab
Edwd: Bryan, Ab
Matth: Powell, Ab
Jos. Weldale, Ab
Thos: Dennis, Ab
Ant. Pendar, Ab
Wm: Sherward, Ab
Wm: Symmons, Ab
Ph. Bumpstead, Ab
Thos: Reynolds, Ab
Jn: Young, Ab

Captain Forster of the Royal Marines commanded 100 men
Lieutenant Grant was the artillery officer
Lieutenant Frasier, junior officer under Mowat lead landing parties totaling 30 seamen and marines.

The expedition had expended all of it ammunition, and suffered from the concussion of the naval guns during the long siege. The Master of the Halifax died of smallpox a few weeks after the Falmouth affair and the crew was quarantined by Admiral Graves as a precautionary measure (see entry for November 8, 1775

Oct. 2, 1775 Monday Noerly
Moored in Boston Harbor
Fresh breezes with raw cold weathr AM Do. Weathr Emp variously came down from the Back of ye town his Majestys ship

Fowey Fresh breezes with raw cold weathr with some rain Employed fitting out the Armed transports the *Symmetry* and *Spitfire* sloop

Oct. 3, 1775 Tuesday Soerly

Moored in Boston Harbor

Mod breezes cloudy weathr with some rain emp fitting out & getting ready the armed transports *Symmetry* & *Spitfire* sloop Supplying them with stores of all kinds out of ye *Canceaux* by orders. Fresh breezes and cloudy weathr do. Emp variously came down from the back of Town his Majestys ship *Fowey*

Oct. 4, 1775 Wednesday Noerly

Moored in Boston Harbor

Mod breezes and cold weathr AM sailed hence his Majestys ship *Fowey* with a transport Empd as before supplied the *Symmetry* transport with 11 ton of water casks *Spitfire* sloop with 9 tons of water casks

Oct. 5 1775 Thursday E

Moored in Boston Harbor

Dark cloudy weathr with rain PM Came in here his Majestys Sloop *Raven* from England 11 weeks out Emp as before

A list of Seamen and Marines, sent on board His Majestys Armed Ship *Canceaux*, *Symmetry*, and *Spitfire*, bornes on the *Canceaux* Books for Vituals by order Vice Admiral Graves
Where and when Preft or not.

Boston:
George Atkins, Midshipman
Adventure Store Ship:
Jn: Pringle, Surgeon
Dennis Bond, Ab
Jn: Nixon, Quarter Master
Jn: Steele, Ab
Sam: Croaker, Ab
In: Moody, Ab
Jn: Gorsier, Ab
Jn: Buck, Ab
Rob: Steele, Ab
Dennis Bond, Ab
Thos: Smith, Ab
Jn: Lofton, Ab
Wm: Shaw, Ab
Jn: Spencer, Ab

In: McKensey, Ab
Jn: Human, Ab
Jn: Hawkins, Ab
Manuel Condut, Ab
Rich: Barrey, Ab

Oct. 6, 1775 Friday var
Moored in Boston Harbor
Dark cloudy weathr this morning there was a brisk cannoning from Boston neck on the rebels and the rebels on them a Corporal of the 63 Reg' killed - Do Wear PM Employed Embarking troops on board of the *Symmetry* [*Symmetry*] and *Spitfire* armed vessels

A List of Seamen and others, sent on board His Majestys Armed Ship *Canceaux*, *Symmetry*, and *Spitfire*, borne on the *Canceaux* Books for Vituals by order Vice Admiral Graves.
Where and When Preft or not.
Nath: Shields, Midshipman
Geo: Tuckey, Ab
Wm: Batson, Ab
Ben: Lewis, Ab
Jn: Simpson, Ab
Joab Merden, Ab
Scipio Woodbridge, Ab
Sam: Mash, Ab

Master's Log
Do [Moored in Boston Harbour]
This morning there was a brisk cannonading from Boston Neck to the Rebels and the Rebels on them a Corporal of the 63 Regt Killed - Do Wear PM Employed Embarking troops on board of the *Symmetry* and *Spitfire* armed vessels.

Narrative of Vice Admiral Samuel Graves
[Boston] 6 [October]
Lieutenant [Henry] Mowats little Squadron being now ready the Admiral ordered on Officer and seven men to be lent to the *Canceaux* from the *Scarborough* and ten from the *Boyne*. The *Symmetry* and *Spitfire* requiring a great deal of Carpenters Work to be done to them to receive the Mortar Shells and other Artillery Stores, and these being obtained with much difficulty at different periods notwithstanding the Admiral made several applications for

them in person to the General, much more time was consumed in this Equipment than if the Business had received that ready assistance from all concerned which such an undertaking might expect and required: and the taking Artillery Stores quietly off by night, to prevent our intentions being discovered, occasioned also additional delay. As to the Naval Stores and provisions wanted, they had been early supplied from the men of war.

Vice Admiral Samuel Graves to Lieutenant Henry Mowat, H.M. Armed Vessel *Canceaux*

Whearas the four New England Governments are in open an avowed Rebellion against his Majesty, and they have been daring enough to make Seizures of several of his Majestys Ships and vessels, and to send the Crews to Prison, and have also fired upon killed and wounded many of the Kings Subjects serving on board his Majesty's Ships; And whereas there is undoubted Intelligence of their fortifying their Sea Ports, and of the determination to cut off and destroy his Majesty's Subjects serving in his Fleet and Army whenever it is in their Power.

And whereas I have caused the *Symmetry* Transport and *Spitfire* Sloop to be armed and fitted in the best manner the Situation of our Affairs would admit in order to proceed along the Coast, and lay waste burn and destroy such Seaport Towns as are accessible to his Majesty's Ships; And whereas from your having been employed on the Survey of the Coast to the Eastward of this Harbor, you cannot but be qualified to carry on this Service from your knowledge of all the harbors, bays, creeks, Shoals, and having full confidence in your integrity, Loyalty and Naval Experience, and in particular for your late spirited and judicious Conducy at Falmouth, I have thought proper that you should command on this Expedition: You are therefore hereby required and directed to take the *Symmetry* and *Spitfire* under your Command together with his Majestys Schooner *Halifax*, and proceed with them as soon as possible to Cape Ann Harbour, that Town having fired in the month of August last upon his Majestys Sloop *Falcon*, wounded her People and taken many Prisoners; you are to burn destroy and lay waste the said Town together with all Vessels and Craft in the Harbor that cannot with ease be brought away. Having performed this Service you are to take the advantage of Wind and Weather, or any other favorable Circumstances, to fall upon and destroy any other Towns or places within the Limits aforesaid, and all Vessels or craft to seize and destroy.

My Design is to chastize Marblehead, Salem, Newbury Port, Cape Ann harbor, Portsmouth, Ipswich, Saco, Falmouth in Casco Bay and particulary Mechias where the *Margueritta* was taken, the Officer commanding her killed and the People made Prisoners, and where the *Diligent* Schooner was seized and the Officers and Crew carried Prisoners up the Country, and where preparations I am informed are now making to invade the Province of Nova Scotia.

You aware to go to all or to as many of the above named Places as you can, and make the most vigorous efforts to burn the Towns, and destroy the Shipping in the harbors. And as the Number of marines you carry in the Vessels are too few to land and maintain any Post, you are to be careful not to risqué their Lives or the Lives of any of your People by attempting where there is not great probability of Success, bur to content yourself with falling upon the Rebels, doing what you can with Expedition and coming away before they can assemble to cut off your retreat, and never risque your ships aground or where you cannot put to sea at all times of Tide, Wind permitting.

You are to bestow your whole attention to annoying the Rebels and the Security of your own vessels; to observe in all your operations the strictest discipline, not to suffer plundering upon any Account, as I will make an Example of whoever shall presume to be guilty of it.

Whenever you can distinguish the persons or property of those who have taken no part in the rebellion and have given proofs of their
Attachment to the Constitution by effusing to concur in the unwarrantable measures that have been adopted to subvert it, you are to protect and defend them in the utmost of your power.

I leave entirely to your own discretion where to go and when to return, relying upon your Zeal for his Majesty's Service and the good of your Country for the steady and effectual Execution of these Orders.

Given under my Hand on board his His Ship *Preston* at Boston the 6. Of October 1775 Sam. Graves
By Command of the Admiral
G. Gefferina

Bomb vessels or bombs were specially armed and reinforced vessels that carried heavy sea mortars on the main deck positioned on special cribbing between the stem and the main mast.

Oct. 7, 1775 Saturday var

At single anchor Castle William SE Governor Island ENE 1/2 mile Dull weathr PM Employed Embarking troops on board of the *Symmetry* and *Spitfire* Armed vessels. AM light airs and variable at 9 weighed and came to sail as did the two above mentioned vessels at 11 anchored in 3 1/4 fm low water Castle William SE Governors Island ENE

A List of seamen and Marines Sent onboard His Majestys Armed Ship *Canceaux*, *Symmetry* and *Spitfire* Armed Transports, Borne on the *Canceaux's* Books for Vituals by Order of Vice Admiral Graves.

Whence and whether Prest or not.

Boston

Wm: Foster, Capt:
Ja: Lamb, Lieut.
Wm. Huff, Serjt.
Geo Dixon, Corpl.
Dan Saway, Drum:
Jn: Poe, Private
Edw: Bray, Private
Hen: Burns, Private
Wm: Sandland, Private
Hen: Ronley, Private
Wm: Rowlin, Private
Jn: Morrison, Private
Rich: Burn, Private
Simon M. Garty, Private
Jn: Grimmes, Private
Thos: Crowder, Private
Jn: Alsop, Private
Fra: Ireland, Private
Rich: Fannon, Private
Jn: Fox, Private
Wm: Osburn, Private
Jer: Bowlin, Private
Thos: Grace, Private
Ja: Morris, Private
Chas: Richardson, Private
Thos: Ferret, Private

Thos: Fagg, Private
Alex: James, Private
Jn: Carringcrof, Private
Wm: Townsend, Private
Ja: Blaney, Private
Jos: May, Private
Rich: Mitchel, Private
Wm: Reid, Private
Edw: Handfield, Captain
Jn: M: Clintack, Lieut.
Geo: Ridley, Serj.
Ferguchen McKensey, Corpl.
James Styles, Drummer
Rich: Davies, Private
Jn: Walker, Private
Geo: Chriswell, Private
Thos. Kettle, Private
Nath: Prebble, Private
Thos: Barron, Private
Jn: Smith, Private
Alex: Fraser, Private
Wm: Nealer, Private
Ja: Vollum, Private
Henry Smith, Private
Ja: Anderson, Private
Wm: Bell, Private
Geo: Black, Private
Wm: Williams, Private
Wm: Gordon, Private
Wm: McDonald, Private
Chas: Bagnall, Private
Wm: Wilson, Private
Wm: Firr, Private
Duncan Fraser, Private
Wm: Sill, Private
Jn: Dixon, Private
Matth: Kell, Private
Geo: Mower, Private
Cornelian Calahan, Private
Geo: Newman, Private
Ja: Robinson, Private
Wm: Baxter, Private

James Bristol, Private
Wm: Grimshaw, Private
Wm: Neale, Private
Wm: Juiet, Private
Ar: Miller, Private
Jn: Nickelson, Private
Duncan Smith, Private
Rob: Budge, Private
Thos: Kelly, Private
Wm: Gillard, Private
Jos: Rushworth, Private
Dav: Hill, Private
Jn: Morton, Private
Manuel Solomon, Private
Wm: Milford, Private
Jacob Fulman, Private
Sam: Hunyley, Private
John Gillaspie, Marine
Sam: Lycett, Lieut.
Jn: Hamilton, Serj.
Rob: Watkins, Corpl.
Ja: Sutherland, Private
James Bull (1) Private
James Bull (2) Private
Jn: Single, Private
Gab: McEnny, Private
Wm: Atkins, Private
Ja: Male, Private
Rich: Waldrum, Private
Jn: Burn, Private
Hen: Rider, Ab

Where and When Preft or not.

H.M.S. *Boyne*
Jn: Holebrook, Ab
Jn: Rentfree, Ab
Tim: Rourke, Ab
Matth: Pitts, Ab
Jos. Dallison, Ab
Thos: Disturnal, Ab
Rob: Armstrong, Ab - Rejected 18 October
Ja: Lamb, Ab - Rejected 18 October

Wm: Ellis, Ab
Ja: Mossis, Ab
Wm: Hayman, Private
Jn: Wilson, Private
Fra: Billey, Private
Rob: Bragg, Private
Josh: Bradley, Private
Rich: Pennington, Private
Wm: Grant, Lieut.
And: Goldey, Private
Ja Smith, Private

Men reassigned to Expedition from *Halifax* Schooner and subsequently discharged on 9th October 1775
Wm: Griffith, Lieut.
Ja: Bennett, Serj.
Rich: Lovering, Corpl.
Devereux Goodwin, Private
In: Stancomb, Private
Geo: McBarth, Private
Noah Wilber, Private
Dan: Feddeman, Private
Geo: Frankland, Private
Thos: Gull, Private
Jos: Priestly, Private
Rob: Mugford, Private
Josh: Maddin, Private
Ja: Mc Dermot, Private
Jn: Stevens, Private
Jn: Holland, Private
Matth: Vennell, Private
Thos Bell, Private

Oct. 8, 1775 Sunday E, SE
At single anchor Castle William SE Governors Island ENE 1/2 mile
Light airs and dark cloudy Weathr with heavy rains from two in the morning till 6 fresh gales the remainder little Winds with rain
Oct. 9, 1775 Monday WSW, NW
Cape Cod SE b S 3 leagues
at 1 light winds & fair
at 8 PM weighd in company and came to sail the *Symmetry* &

Spitfire as did the other vessels Light House WNW Point Alderon SW b W 15 Fm water
at 10 hove too lighthouse WNW Pt. Adenton SW b W 15 leagues
at 11 Fresh wind
at 1 AM made sail the great Brewster WSW
at 3 hove too in single reef the topsails
at 6 made sail
at 8 fresh gales squally close reef'd Top sails handed the mizen TS
at 9 wore ship
at 10 handed main sail Cape Ann NNW 7 or 8 leag.

Cape Ann NNW 7 or 5 Leagues Do
bore up for Cape Cod the *Halifax* Schooner joined company

at 12 Cape Cod SE b S 3 leagues latt obsd 42:14 N
Master's Log
Cape Code SE b S 3 Leagues
At 1 AM made Sail the great Brewster WSW at 3 hove too do Double reeft the Top sails at 6 fresh gales and Squally close Reefed the Topsails handed the Mizen TS [illegible] Ann NNW 7 or 8 Leagues do fore up for Cap Cod the [illegible] Schooner joined company at 4 PM come too under the Beach of Cape Cod Harbour in 18 fm Water Saw a Schooner under the Et Shore at anchor Sent the *Halifax* and *Spitfire* after her at 7 Saw the flashes of [several] guns between them at 10 the above vessels Joind us and Run the Schooner ashore

Vice Admiral Samuel Graves to Philip Stephens

Sir *Preston* Boston 9 October 1775

A small Sloop from Bermuda anchored here the 28, and I received by the hands of a trusty Negroe a Letter from Governor [George] Bruere. I enclose a copy of it.

You may perceive that the Rebels of the Continent are indefatigable in spreading their poison, and that even Bermudas and the Bahama Islands abound with men under their influence, who though liable to be crushed with a single blow are yet daring enough to be guilty of Robbery and Rebellion. Governor Bruere does not mention it, but I am informed 40 pieces Cannon are in Store at Bermuda besides a number of fine Ordnance in the Forts round the Island, and that here is reason to apprehend the Rebels will endeavour to carry them off. I have therefore acquainted Governor Bruere what I will send a ship for the preservation of the Kings Stores, and the Support of this Majestys Government there, the moment it is in my power, which shall accordingly do.

The *Halifax* anchored at Nantasket for the first inst and Lieut Grame arrived from Virginia in the *Mercury*, with Captain Macarteny under an Arrest in consequence of a Complaint against him by Lord Dunmore Governor of Virginia, of which Complaint I acquainted you in my Letter August 17 and transmitted Copies of Lord Dunmore's accusation, of my Answer, and of Captain George Montagu's Answer upon my requiring him to inform me of such facts relative to Captain Macartney's misconduct as had come to his knowledge. I now inclose a Copy of Another Letter to me from Lord Dunmore, two from Captain Macartney and my Answers; these contain the whole of this business that I am acquatined with: It is a present impossible to his Lordship to come here to prosecute his charge. The accusuation is so controvertible that if a Court Martial was ordered to sit, in all likehood from want of evidence no satisfactory Judgement could be given, and above all the Service at this Juncture not admitting of long trials, I have granted Captain Macartney's request to send him to England, there to be disposed of as their Lordships may think best. My letter to Lord Dunmore on receiving his Lordships accusation against Captain Marcartney fully shewed the opinion I entertained of that Gentleman's abilities as an Officer; farther in justice to him I desire to represent that the Account of Proceedings, met my entire approbation. I shall continue Lieutenant Grame acting by my order in the *Mercury*, and to discharge Captain Macarteny until I am honored with their Lordships Commands.

His Majesty's Sloop *Raven* arrived the 4th instant after a long and tedious passage from Plymouth; by Captain [John] Stanhope I received their Lordships Orders and your Letters agreeable to the inclosed list.

Finding that forbearing to punish the people of the four New England Governments, for their many rebellious and piratical acts, only encouraged them to go greater lengths, I determined to observe a difficult conduct, and if possible destroy some of their Towns and Shipping. To this end I sent General Gage a Letter dated Sepr 1st a Copy of which and of his Answer is inclosed: many difficulties occurred in the procuring and equipping the *Symmetry* Transport and *Spitfire* Sloop with proper Stores for the Expedition, and, the weak State of the Garrison hardly allowing any Draughts to be made, General Gage could spare but One hundred Men, commanded by Captain Lieut. Forster of Marines with a subaltern Officer. The Command of the whole consisting of the vessels as pr Margin: with a Shadow of success. I have ordered Mr. Mowat to protect the person and property of his Majesty's loyal Subjects wherever they can be distinguished; and he sailed Yesterday the 8th *Canceaux* armed ship

Halliffax armed Schr

Symmetry armed Transt

Spitfire armed Sloop

I have given to Lieut. [Henry] Mowat of the *Canceaux* armed ship, soley from his being well acquainted with the Pilotage of the Coast, where his operations are to carried on. I have ordered him to take advantage of Wind and Weather and enter any of the Harbours to the Estward of Boston, and if possible first to go to Cape Anne where the Rebels thought proper to fire upon the *Falcon* and were they took several of her Officers and Crew, and sent them prisoners in the Country; Lieut. Mowats Orders are to burn and lay waste the Towns and destroy the Shipping in harbors when they cannot with Ease be taken away. This flying Squadron lay ready to depart when the coinciding exactly *Raven* arrived. Their Lordships Orders by her with what was then doing gave me great pleasure; The few little advantages the Rebels have had over us have given them confidence, and there is no doubt of his Majesty's Ships being fired upon and opposed in every place where the Rebels can do it with impunity or with a Shadow of success. I have ordered Mr. Mowat to protect the person and property of his Majesty's loyal Subjects wherever they can be distinguished; And he sailed Yesterday the 8th instant from Nantasket.

On the 5th instant the *Nautilus* returned with three Brigs, two of them Captain Collins had taken, and according to his Orders carried them to Rhode Island, from whence Captain (James) Wallace sent them to Boston; I inclose a copy of Captain Wallace's Letter.

The *Fowey* sail yesterday for Halifax. The *Nautilus* is to cruize a few days in the Bay, where a Rebel Schooner last Saturday chaced and fired four shot at one of the transports coming in from Newfoundland.

General Gage being ordered to England takes his passage in the *Pallas* Transport. I have appointed the *Mercury* to convoy his Excellency over St. George's Bank and I expect he will sail tomorrow.

I have ordered the *Raven* to lie in Nantaket, and the *Scarborough* to come up to be caulked, which she is in great want of.

Inclosed is the state and condition and disposition of his Majesty's Squadron under my command and a state of the Hospital. I am Sir &c Sam Graves

Disposition of Ships Under the Command of Vice Admiral Samuel Graves

Rate	Ships	Commanders	Disposition
4	Preston	V. A. Graves	Moor'd before the Town
		Jno Robinson	
3	Boyne	Bk Hartwell	Off Castle Island
6	Scarbro	Aw Barkley	at Nantasket
5	Cerberus	Jno Symons	betwn Chas Town & Boston
6	Mercury	Lt. Graeme p order	
Slo	Raven	Capt Jno Stanhope	Moor'd before the Town
Store sp	Adventure	Lt. Jno Hallum	Do
Schr	Hope	Geo Dawson	haul'd ashore caulk'd
6	Rose	Capt Js Wallace	At Rhode Island
"	Glasgow	Tyrm Howe	Do
Slo.	Swan	Js Ayscough	Ordered to Boston
Brig	Bolton	Lt. Thos Graves	Do
3	Asia	Capt Geo Vandeput	New York
Slo.	Viper	Saml Graves	On his Passage to Do
"	Otter	Matw Squire	At Virginia
"	Kingsfisher	Jas Montagu	Do
"	Cruizer	Fras Parry	No Carolina, Order'd to Boston
"	Scorpion	Hble Tollemache	Do
"	Tamar	Capt Ed Thornbro	At So Carolina, Order' to Boston
Schr	St. Lawrence	Lt. Jno Graves (1st)	At St. Augustine
"	St John	Wm Grant	At the Bahama Islands
Slo.	Falcon	Capt Jno Linzee	Expected to arrive I in about a Week From new Providence with Two Transports with Ordce Stores
6	Lively with Transports sent for fuel	Thos Bishop	At Penobscot Bay
"	Tartar	Ed Medows	Bay of Fundy with Transports getting forage & fuel
Slo.	Merlin	W. C. Burnaby	Do.
"	Senegal	Wm Dudingston	Do.
	Somerset	Ed LeCras	At Halifax
Schr.	Hinchingbrook	Lt. Alexr Ellis	Do.
Slo	Savage	Capt Hu. Bromedge	Gone to Newfoundland
"	Hunter	Thos Mackenzie	Do Quebec
Brig.	Gaspee	Lt. Wm Hubter	At Montreal
6	Fowey	Capt Geo. Montague	Gone to Halifax to Careen
Slo.	Nautilus	Jno Collins	Cruizing Boston Bay
Ard Ship	Canceaux	Lt Hy Mowat	On an expedition along the Eastern Coast against the Rebels
Schr	Halifax	Jno De la Touche	Do

Preston Boston 9th Octr 1775

Oct. 10, 1775 Tuesday NW
Single anchor Cape Cod harbor
at 1 Fresh gales and clear weathr
at 3 came to under the Beach at ye entrance C. Cod Harbor 18 fm
at 6 saw a schooner to leeward sent ye *Halifax & Spitfire* to bring her away saw the flashes of several guns between them at 7 saw the flashes of swivels guns between them at 10 the above vessels joined us and run the schooner ashore at 8 AM up top gall yards
at 11 the *Halifax & Spitfire* anchored near us
at 12 single anchor in Cape Cod Harbor
at 1 mod.
at 9 up top gallant yds
at 12 single anchor in Cape Cod Harbor

A List of Prisoners taken out of the Vessels that were burnt and those taken and carried for Boston by H. M. Armed Ship *Canceaux* during the expedition Commanded by Lieut. Henry Mowat on the Coast of New England:
Whence and whether Preft or not.

At Sea:
Eber. Simmons
Sam: Thompson
Eleazer Thompson
Chas. Stuart
Jon. Read

Oct. 11, 1775 Wednesday SW b W, WSW
Halbut SW 4 miles
at 1 weighed came to sail
at 2 fresh breezes fair
at 4 the Race Point N 1.2 W Dist 2 miles
at 7 abreast of do. 2 miles
at 12 saw sail to ye NE
at 1 AM half Rock at about 8 miles ½ past tacked saw a sail in NE
at 2 saw 1/2 way rock bearing W 2 miles
at 3 mod and cloudy
at 4 hove too with the head sails to the mast
at 6 made sail
at 8 Cape Ann Light House NE b N 3 miles
at 9 set studding sails saw a schooner to ye eastward standing in

under the Cape Ann made the *Halifax* signal to chase to ye NE at 10 she brought too the chase she Proved a schooner with salt all the people had quited her Halbut Point SW ab 4 miles

Master's Log

Cape Elisabeth wood Island NW½ W 3 or 4 leagus

At 1 Am saw a Sail in the NE qr at 2 Saw ½ way rock bearg Wt 2 miles at 3 modr and cloudy Tke at 4 hove too with the head Sails to the mast at 5 Made Sail at 8 Cape Ann Light House NW b N 3 miles at 9 sitt Studding Sails Saw a Schooner to the Eterd Standing under the Cape made the *Halifax* Sigl to Chace to the NE at 10 She brought too the chace She Proved a schooner with Salt all her people had Quite her Halbut Point SW 4 miles in company as before fresh breezes and fair Wear at 4 [P.M.] in the 2d Reefs Topsails at Boer Island WNW 3 or 4 Leagus at 9 fresh breezes with thunder and Lightning all Round ship head to the Soerd

Oct. 12, 1775 Thursday N, NW b W

Cape Elizabeth Wood Island NW 1/2 3 or 4 Leagues

at 1 Fresh breezes and fair weat

at 2 in studding sails

at 4 in single reef topsails

at 6 Boon Island WNW 4 miles

at 9 light winds

at 10 fresh Breezes with thunder and lightening under F:S: very heavy claps of thunder and lightening all round company

at 2 Head to ye So' ward

at 3 wore ship set ye fore & main topsail

at 5 ½ past in fore topsail

at 6 Wood Island W?S Cape Elizabeth NW about 4 leagues

at 10 wore ship and let a reef out of ye Topsails

at 12 Cape Elizabeth & Wood Island NW b W 8 leagues

12 [Noon] Cape Elizabeth & Wood Island NW b W 3 leags Fresh Breezes & hazey ½ past [8] Made Sail *Symmetry* brough too a Sloop wt Wood from New Medows.

A List of Prisoners taken out of the Vessels that were burnt and those taken and carried for Boston by H.M. Armed Ship *Canceaux* during the Expedition commanded by Lieut. Henry Mowet on the Coast of Maine:

Whence and Whether Preft or not.

At Sea:

Jas. Macfarlan

Job: Nicholson

Hen. Nicholson
Zach: Ingersol
Jno Ingram
Caleb Drinkwater
Jon: Drinkwater
Ja: Freeman

Oct. 13, 1775 Friday NW
at 1 fresh breezes & hazey
at 3 passed ship Wood Island NW b W 3 or 4 miles
at 5 Strong gales and squally weathr
at 6 PM Cape Elizabeth N b W 2 miles
at 7 Main topsail to ye mast Cape Elizabeth N b W ½ past
at 9 Made sail *Symmetry* brought too a sloop with wood from New Meadows & cloud reef topsails
at 12 main topsail to ye masthead to ye Northward
at 2 cape Elizabeth NNE
at 3 Wore ship fresh gales closed reef mizen TS
at 7 ½ past handed T:S:
at 9 Cape Elizabeth WNW Siquin Island NE b E
at 10 Small Point N b W 3 miles Set ye Mizen T:S:
at 11 *Halifax* chased to ye SW
at 12 Seguin W b N 2 miles
Remarks Friday 13 Octr 1775
10 [A. M.] *Halifax* Chaced to the SW Strong Gales & cloudy 3 [P. M.] Came too with the best bower 18 fm Mud bottom in townsend Booth bay So Part to Dama[ri]scover Island S b W Cukolds SW b W Pt Squirrel Isld about ½ a Mile N b E handed Sails wore to a Cable came in & Achored wh Us the *Symmetry Spitfire* a sloop & a Schooner Prizes
Oct. 14, 1775 Saturday NW
at single anchor in Townsend Harbor Booth Bay
at 1 Strong gales and cloudy weathr
at 3 came too with the best bower 18 fm mud bottom in Townsend Boothbay S. Port of Dammariscove Island
at 7 Cuckold SW b W Pt. Squirrel Island about ½ mile NE Point of Rocks SW b W about 1/2 mile handed sails veerd to 1/2 a cable came in & anchored with us the *Symmetry Spitfire* and a sloop & at 2 more mod.
at 8 strong gales
at 12 fresh gales & cloudy weat
Master's Log

At Single anchor in Townsend Harbor Booth Bay
At 4 AM wore ship Fresh gales Closed Reeft the Topsail at 8 handed the Top Sails Cape Elisabeth NNW seguine Island NE b E Small Point N b W 3 miles - hove away for booth bay Strong gales and cloudy Wear at 3 PM anchord at the bottom of Townsend Harbour booth bay So part of Dammiscove Island S b W about ½ a mile veered to ½ a cable the *Symmetry*, *Spitfire* and Sloop and Schooner anchored Signal at 12 moor

Oct. 15, 1775 Sunday Werly, var

at single anchor in Townsend harbor at Noon weighed and came to sail at 1 Fresh gales and cloudy weathr Emp unloading the sloops deck load of wood on board of different vessels at 8 Do. weathr

at 12 thick hazey weathr at 4 do. weathr at 11 made *Spitfire* signal to weigh sent two boats armed to Damariscove Is for stock at 12 weigh & came and came to sail as did the *Symmetry* and two prizes.

Master's Log

Portland Point the So head of going into Falmouth
At 10 [AM] made the *Spitfire* Signal to weigh Send two Boats Manned and Armed to Dammiscove Island for Stock at Noon Light airs and varible weighd and came to Sail as did the *Symmentry* and two Prizes at 3 was 5 whail Boats with 10 men in Each making toward Dammiscove to putt off our boats but the *Spitfire* got between them and the Island when they thought best to return back at 5 the Boats returned with Stock at 6 anchord in 22 fm water Cuckold Point SW b ½ S So Point of Dammescove Island S ½ E small breezes with Drizling rain

Vice Admiral Samuel Graves to Captain John Symons, H.M.S. *Cerberus*

You are hereby required and directed to proceed to Sea in his Majesty's Ship under your command with all convenient Dispatch and cruize upon the Coast of the Provinces of Massachusetts Bay and New Hampshire between Casco Bay and Cape Anne to protect his Majesty's faithful Subjects trading according to Law, and to distress and annoy the Rebels by all means in your Power according to the Orders of yesterday, You are to observe if any Fortifications are erecting, and having got what Intelligence you can of the Rebels proceedings act accordingly, as you shall think best for the King's Service. If you anchor at the Isle of Shoals you will probably pick up Refreshments for your people and intelligence of what is doing a Portsmouth in New Hampshire.

And whereas Lieutt Mowat in the *Canceaux* armed Ship commands a small Expedition along the coast within the limits of your Station and whereon he is particulary employ'd from his thorough knowledge of the Coast and harbors: In case of your meeting the expedition you are to give Lieutt Mowat any assistance he may want, but not take the Command, unless your interposition becomes absolutely necessary for the preservation or success of the whole, but by cruising in the Offing cover the Expedition from unexpected Attacks of the Rebels by Sea. If nothing occasions your returning sooner you are to cruize a Month from this day and then return to Boston.

Given under my Hand on board his Majestys
By Command of the Admiral Ship *Preston* at
Boston the 15th October
G. Gefferina 1755
Saml Graves

Oct. 16, 1775 Monday WNW, NW
Portland Point the S. Head of grassy is to Falmouth Harbor W b N 3 miles PM Light airs and cloudy weathr at 3 saw 5 whale Boats with 10 men in each making toward Dammariscove to cutoff our boats but the *Spitfire* got between them and the Island when they thought best to return back at 5 the Boats returned with stock at 6 anchored in 22 fm water cuckold Point SW b 1/2 S. Point of Dammariscove Island S 1/2 E at 12 small breezes with Drizling rain at 3 AM made the signal to weigh at 4 weighed and came to sail the afore said vessels in company at 6 the *Halifax* joined us at Sequine W b N at 9 Sequine W b N 1/2 miles at noon fresh breezes and fair weathr.

Master's Log
Hog Island Ledge
at 3 AM made the Signal to weigh at 4 weighd and come to sail the afore said vessils in Company at 6 the *Halifax* Joind us at 8 Siguine WSW at 9 Siguine W b N ½ N½ mile at Noon fresh breezes and fair Wear at 1 PM fresh breezes and clear Wear Employed running into Falmouth harbor at 3 came to in hog island road in 7 fm as did the *Symmentry*, *Halifax* and *Spitfire* with the two Prizes

Lieutenant Henry Mowat, R.N., to the People of Falmouth

Canceaux Falmouth 16th October 1775

After so many premeditated Attacks on the legal Prerogatives of the best of Sovereigns After the repeated Instances you have experienced in Britian's long forbearance of the Rod of Correction; and the Merciful and Paternal extension of her Hands to embrace you, again and again, have been regarded as vain and nugatory. And in place of dutiful and grateful returns to your King and Parent state; you have been guilty of the most impardonable Rebellion, supported by the Ambition of a set of designing men, whose insidious crews have cruelly imposed in the credulity of their fellow creatures, and not at least have brought the whole into the same Dilemma; which leads me to feel not a little over the innocent of them, in particular on the present occasion, having it in orders to execute a just Punishment on the Town of Falmouth: in the name of which authority I previously warn you to remove without delay the human Species out of the said town; for which purpose I give you the time of two hours, at the period of which, a Red pendant will be hoisted at the main topgallant Masthead with gun: but should your imprudence lead you to show the least resistance, you will in that case free me of that Humanity, so strongly pointed out in my orders as well as my own Inclination. I also observe that all those who did upon a former occasion fly to the King's Ship under my Command for Protection, that the same door is now open and ready to receive them. The Officer who will deliver this letter I expect to return unmolested. I am &ca

H. Mowat

Canceaux complement 40 men to 28th April 1771 then 45 & Warrant 29th April then 55 men
Began wages & sea vitualling from former Books 1st Oct. 1775.

No.	Entry Year	Appearance	Where	Mens Names	Quality	Time of Discharge	Year	What reason
1	1st Oct 1775	Oct 1st	Books	Henry Mowatt	Comd.	2d June	1776	Superseded
49				David Bailley	Surgeon	29th Mar.	"	Do.
70				David Garrett	Guners Mte	6 Jun	"	Albany Sloop per orders
76				Henry Johnston	2d mate	6 Jun	1776	Adm Shuldham " "
89				Jacob Gulp	ab	9th Decm	1773	St. Law. per orders
119				John Scott	2d mte	2 Jun	1776	Albany Sloop per orders
128				Francis Maynard	Capt.	6 Dec	1776	SB 2b1
131				Wm. Hogg (1)	Master	2 Jun	1776	Superseded
134				Frances B. Mowatt	Mid	18 Oct	1779	Convert per orders
					clerk	1 Aug.	1776	
					Mid	1 May	1777	
152				Bateman Baker	Mid	5 Dec	1775	St. Law.
156				Michael Everitt	ab	2 Jun	1776	Albany Sloop per orders
180				Michael Daily	ab	3 April	1778	Hasfare
186				Geo. Cumberland	Mid	2 Jun	1778	Albany sloop
187				John Lilly	Corpl	2 Jun	1778	Do
194				Henry Black	ab	25 Apl	1778	St. Law
196				Geo. Marsden	ab	2 Jun	1778	Albany Sloop

199		Mark Wentworth	ab	2 Jun	1778	Albany Sloop
201	Halifax	Geofery L. Pierce	ab	8 Nov	1777	Tritore
203	Halifax	Michael Grace	ab	23 Oct	1780	Danoce
210		Wm. Hogg (2)	ab	2 Jun	1776	Albany Sloop
		Widows Man	ab			
214		John Bicquitt	ab	5 Dec	1775	St. Law.
215		Richd Shehane	ab	5 Dec	1775	"
219		George Davies	ab	5 Dec	1775	"
223		Joseph Blucknet	Corpl	10 Jan	1776	Superseded
224		John Larken	Mid	5 Dec	1775	St. Law
226		Alexr Aikin	Boatsn	10 Jan	1776	Superseded
228		Stephn Webster	ab	5 Dec	1775	St Law
229		Thos Walden	ab	5 Dec	1775	"
230		Patk Foy	ab	6 Jun	1776	Albany Sloop
		Wm Lupton	ab	3 Dec	1775	St. Law
		Francis Rourke	ab	31 Mar	1777	SB
				3 Jun	1776	Bo: Ml
		John Robinson	ab	6 Dec	1775	St Law.
		Jn. Wilson	ab	25 Aprl	1776	"
235		Christn Stevenson	ab	5 Dec	1775	"
		Solomen Hughs	ab	1 Feb	1776	Tryale Schooner
		Wm. Havilsck	ab	6 Dec	1775	St. Law
		Wm. Strong	ab	6 Dec	1775	"
		John Atkins	ab	1 Feb	1778	Tryale Schooner
240		Michael Davidale	ab	23 Apr	1776	unserviceable
241		Richd Ireland	ab	23 Apr	1776	unserviecable
243		Richd Martin	ab	8 Oct	1782	
			Mate	3 Jun	1778	
			Boatm	7 July	1780	
		Jan Leshi	ab	5 Dec	1775	SLw
		William Peakes	ab	10 July	1783	?
			Gunner mte	1 Jun	1786	
		Thos Halls	Gunner	4 June	1778	Superseded
		Charles Bandel	Mid	27 July	1782	Prifent: ?
			clerk	12 May	1777	
			Mid	4 Sept	1781	
		Joshua Smith	ab	31 Mar	1779	Prisoner with the Rebels
		Eben Hunt	ab	20 Jun	1779	Viper Sloop
		Jon. Murray	ab	1 Feb	1776	Tryale Schooner
		Alexdr Anderson	ab Rejected	31 May	1780	Quebeck
		Samuel Lamb	ab	1 Feb	1776	Tayale Schooner
		John Crosby	ab Rejected	1 Feb	1776	Tayale Schooner
		Ezra Fluent	ab	1 Feb	1776	Tayle Schooner
		Alexdr. Hawthorn	ab	1 Feb	1776	Tayale Schooner
		Joseph Prep (Refs)	ab	1 Feb	1776	Tayale Schooner
		Patk Dunn	ab	1 Feb	1776	Tayale Schooner
		Henry Rider		1 Feb	1776	Tayale Schooner
		Robt Reney	ab	2 June	1776	Albany Sloop
		Juba Wipwalt	Capt D.D.	25 Apr	1776	Haslar
		Francis Maymart	ab	25 Apr	1776	S Sp W
		Limd Stoopolad	ab	2 Jun	1776	Albany Sloop

The above lists officers and crew aboard the Canceaux receiving wages and provisions or food supplies aboard ship. The date of the name on the list is October 1, 1775 and names are carried over from the prior list for the vessel. The list gives the name, the rating of each person aboard, the date of discharge and the reason and place of discharge. The key thought here is that the handwritten lists were continually updated with information from 1775 to 1783. As it begins 1 October 1775, those listed were aboard ship during the bombardment of Falmouth on October 18, 1775. It is interesting to note that among the complement of the Canceaux was Frances B. Mowat, perhaps a relative of the commander Lt. Henry Mowatt.

Oct. 17, 1775 Tuesday Werly

At single anchor Hog Island ledge NNW 1/4 miles in 5 fm water At 4 PM fresh breezes and clear Weathr Employed turning into Falmouth harbor at 3 came to in Hog Island road in 7 fm as did the *Symmetry, Halifax* and *Spitfire* wait 1 hr. a peoples AM emp coming out ? to warp the ship ahead at noon warped close end Hog Island ledge at noon Mod. and clear.

Master's Log

At single anchor with a spring on the cable of Entrance of the Town of Falmouth

AM Employed carring out warps to warpe the ship ahead at Noon warped close under Hog Island ledge at Noon Mod and clear At 1 PM fresh breezes and cler wear at 2 made the sigl to weigh ½ Past weighd and came to sail do made the Sigl a line ahead one cables lenth at 3 do come too aline ahead abreast of the Town of Falmouth at 5 do our boat went on shor with an officer in her with a letter to the People of this Town ½ Past the boat returned ½ past 5. 3 of the Towns People came on board in a shore boat ½ Past [6] they went on Shorr at 8 the same men cam on board agin with some Small arms with the deliverd up at 3 ¼ aft 8 they wint on Shor again do Ligh[t] airs and vareable at 12 fine clear wear

Oct. 18, 1775 Wednesday Var

At single anchor with a spring on the cable the entrance of the Town of Falmouth from the NNW to the WSW

At 1 PM fresh breezes and clear weathr at 2 made the signal to weigh 1/4 past weigh and came to sail do made the signal a line ahead one cable length at 3 do came too abreast of the Town of Falmouth at 6 do our boat went on shore with an officer in his employee with a letter to the People of this Town 1/2 past the boat returned at 1/2 past 5. 3 of the Towns People came on board in a shore Boat 1/2 past they waited on shore at 8 the same man came on board again with some small arms which they delivered up at 3 1/4 after 8 they went on shore again do light airs and variable at 12 fine clear weathr at 4 AM do. weathr Employed getting everything ready to engage the town at 8 do the same three men came on board again 1/2 past they went on shore again at 9 light airs in 35 minutes after 9 made the signal to engage 40 minutes after 9 a smart fire began from the *Canceaux*, *Symmetry, Halifax*, and *Spitfire*. *Halifax* and *Spitfire* which was helped up by all at 10 several Houses was on fire the fire broke out with great violence in 1 or 3 houses of the south most part of the town at 11 fire broke out in different part of the town at Noon the fire began to be general both in the town and vessels but being calm the fire did not spread as was had ? at 1 PM small breezes from the So 1/2 past the town House and the English church began to burn a brisk fire was kept up by all the squadron at 2 fresh breezes and hazy weathr burning several detached houses to toward the thinest part of the town that could not be set on fire from the shipping at 3 Do a Lieut with thirty seamen and marines went on shore to set them on fire.

Master's Log

At single anchor with a spring on the cable entrance of the Town of Falmouth from the NNW to the WSW at 4 AM do Wear Employed getting Everything reddy to Engage the Town at 8 do the same three men came on board again ½ Past they went on shor again at 9 Light airs and fair 35 minutes [after] 9 made the signal to Engage 40 minuets after 9 a Smart fire begun from the *Canceaux, Symmentry, Halifax,* and *Spitfire* which was keeped up by all at 10 several Houses was on fire the fire broke out with great violence in two or 3 houses of the Southmost Part of the Town at Noon the fire began to be general both in the Town and vessels but being clam the fire did not spread as wished for at 1 PM Small breezes from the Soerd ½ Past the Town House and the English Church began to burn a brisk fire was keeped up by all the squadron at 2 fresh breezis and hazey Wear being several detached houses to toward the Soermost Part of the Town that could not be set on fire from the shipping at 3 do the Lieut with thirty Seamen and Marines went on shor to set them on fire when on that piece of duty they war attacked and fired upon by Numbers but by the alertness of that brisk officer keeped them off and Performed the duty they war Sent upon at 4 they came on board without the loss of a man and only on[e] slightly wounded at 5 ceased firing as most of the Houses and all the vessels at and about the town were destroyed to the number 13 sail two of which got off which we took possession most Part was Loaded to and from the West Indes ½ Past made the Sigl to get under sail as we being the last ship that got under was as the rest got under way some time before Pr Sigl we was fired upon by Numbers from both sids of the water being little wind it was some time before we got out of reach of ther Musquetry which did us no dammished at 8 anchor'd in Hog Island road in 10 fm, water as did all the rest of the Squadron at 10 dark cloudy Wear with rain.

A list of Prisoners taken out of the vessels that were burnt and those taken and carried for Boston by H.M. Armed Ship *Canceaux* during the expedition commanded by Lieut. Henry Mowat on the coast of New England:
Whence and whether Prest or not.

At Falmouth:
Dan: Woodbridge
Jn: Hodges
Tim: Morgan
Alex: Saunderson
Wm: Smith
Ja: Murphy
Neal Obrien
Ebonizer Turnham

Oct. 19, 1775 Thursday Var
At single anchor in Hog Island road
At 1 pm Small breezes from the So'rd half past the town house & English Church began to burn a brisk fire was kept up all the squadron at 2 Do. Fresh breezes & hazey weathr being several detached houses toward: the southern most part of the town that could not be set on fire from ye shipping at 3 the Lieut. with 90 seamen & marines went on shore to set them on fire when on that piece of duty they were attacked & fired upon by numbers but by the alarms of that brisk officer kept them off and performed the duty they were sent upon at 4 they came on board without the loss of one man & only one slightly wounded at 5 ceased firing as most of the houses & all the vessels at about the wharf to ye number of thirteen sail 2 of which were got off were consumed by ye fire the most part loaded to & from the West. Indies ½ past made the signal to get under sail and we bring the last that got under was as the rest got under way some time before the signal was fired upon by musketry from both sides being but little wind it was some time before we could get out of the reach of their musketry which did us no hurt at 8 anchored in Hogg Island Road in 10 fm water as did all the rest of our vessels at 10 dark cloudy weathr with rain. At 8 AM fresh breezes of rain at 10 do. Sighted our anchor & went farther up Hogg Island Road as did all the rest in company the *Symmetry*, *Halifax*, *Spitfire*, with two schooners & two sloops

prizes the fire still continues raging in the town.
To the Number 13 sail two which got off which we took top sails - must port were Loaded to and from the West Indies 1/2 past made the signal to get undersail as we being the last ship that got under way as the rest got underway some time before we was fired upon by Numbers from both sides of the water being little wind it was some time before we got out of reach of the musketry which did us no damage at 8 anchored in Hog Island road in 1 fm water aside all the rest of the Squadron at 10 dark cloudy Weathr with rain at 8 AM fresh breezes and rain at 11 Sighted the anchor and went first then up do. road as did all the rest of the vessels in company the *Symmetry*, *Halifax*, *Spitfire* with two schooners and two sloop prizes the fire still continues to gain in the Town.
Master's Log
At 8 AM fresh Breezes & rain at 10 do Sighted our anchor & went farther up Hogg Island Road as did all the rest in Company the *Symmetry*, *Halifax*, *Spitfire*, with two Schooners & two Sloops Prizes the fire still continues raging in the Town [P.M.] Fresh breezes with thick rainy wear.
(None of these prizes was listed by Admiral Graves, or his successor, Admiral Molyneux Shuldham. The *Canceaux* log states that the two sloops were missing in heavy gales off Cape Ann on October 25, but indicates that the two schooners, the one taken by the *Halifax* on October 11, and the other salvaged from Falmouth harbor, safely reached Nantucket road)

Lieutenant Henry Mowat, R.N., to Vice Admiral Samuel Graves
Canceaux in Casco Bay 19th
October 1775.
Sir, The fluctuating state of the winds and weather since my departure from Boston, have occasioned the delay of this letter, as will appear in the following part of it. The morning after leaving the harbour, the *Canceaux* with the other Vessels, were brought too off the entrance of Cape Ann harbour, with an intention of going in the moment that the day appeared; but to my no small morification a strong gale from the Northward reduced the Vessels under their low Sails, so much so, that the *Symmetry* and *Spitfire* went almost broadside to Leeward: finding myself in this situation, I judged it expeditent to secure a Harbour, and accordingly directed the course for Cape Cod; where we anchr'd in the evening of that day. The next morning the wind shifting to the Southward of the West, we got under Sail, and at day break the following morning, we were

close in with Cape Ann upon viewing the Town, Mr Grant the Artillery Officer, gave it as his opinion, that the houses stood too scattered to expect success, with the Ordnance and Stores of his department, and in particular from the small number of Carcases, and the uncertainty of their goodness. On considering the ill consequences of a disappointment in the first attempt of this expedition, and the advantage of encouragement it would afford the rebels, I though it most prudent to make a choice of an object, where the certainty was more secure; though it was not without reluctance I passed over this port, as your orders directed me there first, as well as the favorable opportunity of attempting Squam at the same time, which I certainly should have done, had the number of troops been sufficient to have landed. The proceeding morning the wind carried us off Cape Elizabeth, where we again were saluted with a second Northwester, which obliged us to take shelter in the evening of that day, under Squirrel Island in Townsend-bay, here we were detained a part of two days, and in the evening of the third, anchored at Hog Island road in Casco-bay: At four in the afternoon of the day following, the Vessels were all placed before the town of Falmouth without the least resistance: finding the people so disposed, I wrote them a letter (a copy of which I transmit with this) and sent Mr Fraser the Acting Lieutenant on shore to deliver it, which he did, and heard it read in the town house before a large number of the inhabitants; upon it being read, there was a profound silence, and it was desired to be read a second time, after which, the Chairman with many of the principle people, in particular those who had never joined in any part of the Rebellion, lamented and judged by the stile of the letter, that the punishment was very severe, and more so still, as the time limited was so very short, and that too with the night approaching. Mr Fraser seeing a general distress increase, among the women and children in the streets, he gave to understand, that if they had a proposal to make to me, he would be the bearer to it, at the same time he could not take upon him to say that it would be received: Upon which they observed that upon his going on board if the boat did not return again in a few minutes, a Committee in the name of the Town would wait upon me, which they did; by name - Brigadier [Jedediah] Pribble, Doctor [Nathaniel] coffin, and Mr. Pagan merchant, deputed to know the nature of the chastisement, and to request that a longer time might be allowed them, as it was then just upon Sundown. I replied that from the nature of their crime they had not the least right to expect any lenity, and that the power in me vested, authorized me to distinguish those only who I was certain had never aided or assisted in their rebellions proceedings but notwithstanding that, the known humanity of the British nation encouraged me, to take so far upon me, that on condition that the people of Falmouth in general would in the course of the time that I had given them, deliver up all their Arms and Ammunition with such of themselves as I should make choice of, that I would in that case put off destroying the Town until the determination of the Commanders in Chief of the King's forces at Boston should be known, To this the committee replied, that they would make my demand known to the people immediately, but that it would be impossible to accomplish it, without certain time being granted for the purpose of Assemblying them: I observed, that if it was not in their power to do it completely this night, they surely could be a part, and therefore the town expected a longer time, so many of their Arms must be delivered onboard the *Canceaux* before Eight o'Clock with the Five Guns that I knew to on carriages in the Town. also the rest of the arms with Brigadier Pribble and such other as I could make choice of, to be forthcoming in the morning: at the same time considering this and every other indulgence void, upon the least hostile appearance of any kind whatsoever. The Committee declared that the guns on Carriages were removed out of the town on the first appearance of the shipping but that they would do, their utmost in bringing off as many arms as could be brought together in so short a time; on this promise I suffered them to go on shore, and before the hour of Eight they returned with Ten stand only - redelivering them as a pledge of the faith of the Town in general, that nothing hostile should be offered, and that if my demand was not fully complied with at nine the next morning (which they beseeched me to grant them as it would be impossible to clear the town of the women and children before that hour in case of noncompliance). This request I agreed to, and desired a Committee to be with me half an hour before the time limited, to which they were punctual; when they declared that to their no small astonishment, they found that no part of the Inhabitants assembled in the morning, and that the whole town was then the greatest confusion, with many women and children still remaining in it; as to themselves, they had only t6o implore time to go on shore and get out of the way on which they took leave to the ship with women and children still in the town, I made it forty minutes after nine before the Signal was hoisted, which was done wit a gun, at the same time the cannonade began from all the vessels and continued till six, by that time the body of the town was in one flame, which would have been the case much sooner, has the Wind favored in the forenoon as it did in the evening, and altho' a regular cannonade was kept up all the time, numbers of armed men were employed extinguishing the fire before it became general which made it absolutely necessary for some men to be landed, in order to set fire to the vessels, wharfs, storehouses, as well as to may parts of the town that escaped from the shells and carcases, notwithstanding they were executed with the greatest dexterity to the no small credit of Mr Grant the artillery Officer, who employed his people, not only onboard, but on shore also, with a certain number of seamen from each of the vessels, and a party of marines, all under the command of Mr Fraser whose spirited conduct, and activity in the execution of that duty, does him every credit that could be expected from such a service, and indeed every man that was with him. And with equal justice I can say, that all the officers and men on this command, she'd the greatest readiness, and acted with the greatest composure and harmony in their respective duties; and with n o less satisfaction I acquaint you, Sir, that notwithstanding the vast numbers of armed men that assembled in , and near the town on the occasion; Falmouth, with the Blockhouse and battery, the principle wharfs and storehouse, with eleven sail of vessels, at and near this town, several of which with cargos all made into ashes, including a fine distillery, four vessels taken, all without the loss of one person, and only two slightly wounded, Mr. Larkin Midshipman of the *Canceaux* and one Marine. At the same time I am sorry to say, that had we not been situated close to the town, we should without a doubt have found great difficulty in accomplishing this piece of service , as we soon experienced the insufficiency of the artillery stores, not only in goodness, but in quantity; the particulars of which shall at more convenient opportunity be laid before you sir, which I am sorry to observe will not reflect great credit on the ordnance store at Boston: and with equal concern I observe, that the want of a sufficient number of troops, had prevented an effectual sweep being made of all the arms and ammunition not only belonging to the town of Falmouth but also of many islands and Villages in Casco-bay, which I am very certain could have been completely done with five hundred men - as well as numbers of cattle and other fresh provisions equally useful, and not less distressing to this part of the country.

Our Carcases excepting a few belonging to the Howitzers

are all expended, and these are rendered useless by the carriages being disabled which happened early in the Bombardment. The Spitfire Sloop is also much shattered, so that I shall be under the necessity of repairing to Nantasket to have those wants supplied before I can attempt any other place. The troops are also in great distresss for want of necessary, arms of them having embarked without a second shirt, from which cause they are rendered incapable of their duty, and are falling sick very fast. My intention was to dispatch the *Halifax* immediately with this letter, but having four vessels to man and take of I consider it most prudent to keep our small force together till we are nearer. I have the honor to have with the highest respect Sir [&c] H. Mowat

Oct. 20, 1775 Friday

At single anchor in Do. [Hog Island] Road

Fresh breezes with thick rainy weathr AM weathr. very cold the fire still continues Employed variously.

At single anchor in Do. [Hog Island] Road

AM do Wear very cold the fire Still continues employed variously ½ past 4 PM came on board a flagg of treus from the Town of Falmouth ½ Past they returned on Shor the fire Still continues in the Town

Oct. 21, 1775 Saturday

At single anchor in do. Road

Fresh gales with thick rainy weathr ½ past 4 PM came on board a flagg of truce from the town of Falmouth ½ past she returned on shore the fire still continues in the town

Do weathr at half past 4 PM came on board a flagg delegation from the Town of Falmouth 1/2 past they returned in shore the fire still continuous in the Town

Oct. 22, 1775 Sunday

At Single anchor in Do. Road

PM do weathr at 1 strong gales at 2 struck the lower yards and Top gallant mast do. veered away a whole cable at 3 struck the Top masts AM more mod. PM fresh gales and thick rainy weathr at two strong gusts struck top gallant mast and lower the lower yards Do. Veered to a whole cable at 9 struck the topmast AM mod.

Oct. 23, 1775 Monday Var.

P.M. mod and thick hazey weathr PM yard and top masts AM small breezes and variable Loosed sails to air Employed getting off stock.

Fresh gales & thick rainy weather at 1 strong gales at 2 down the lower yards & top gallant mast veer away a whole cable at 3 struck top mast AM more moderate

Oct. 24, 1775 Tuesday Soerly, Var., calm

Portland points N b W 1/2 W 2 Cables length

At 1 Mod breezes & thick foggy weath emp getting stock off

At 1 thick hazey weathr with small rain

At 3 small rain

At 5 fired a gun made a signal for sailing

At 10 weighed & came to sail light airs & variable the boats a head towing the ship off shore

At 12 Portland Point N b W ½ W 2 cables length

Thick cloudy weathr Emp getting off stock Middle parts thick weathr rain AM light airs and variable at 8 fired a gun made the signal for sailing at 11 weighed & came too sail at Noon boats ahead towing the ship off shore

Portland point N b W ½ W

AM light airs & variable at 8 fired a gun made the signal for sailing at 11 weig'd and came too sail at Noon boats ahead towing the ship off shore - [P.M.] Towing off shore with *Symmetry Halifax & Spitfire* - two schooners & two Sloops Prizes at 4 C. Elizabeth W b N ½ N 1 mile at 6 Wood Island NW b W 3 Leagues do in 1st & 2nd Rft Top Sails Fresh Gales & Clear at 12 Close Rfd Tsls HFT Sail

Oct. 25. 1775 Wednesday WNW, So, W b N

Cape Cod SE b S 6 leagues

At 1 Light airs with rain emp towing the ship of shore Small breezes from ye westward stood out to sea as did the *Symmetry, Halifax, Spitfire*, two schooners & two sloops prizes

At 4 Cape Elizabeth W b N dist 1 mile at wood Island NW b W 3 leagues

At 7 took in 1 & 2 reefs topsails

At 9 handed the mizen topsail

At 12 Fresh gales & clear weathr close reefd T:S & F:T:S:

At 3 Heard the report of several muskets to westward

At 4 Made the signal to shorten sail Do. Handed the M:T:S:

At 7 Fresh gales & clear weathr saw the land bearing NW b W 5 leagues which was Pidgeon Hill near C. Ann the two sloop Prizes were missing lay too under the Mizen & fore stay sail hauled the fore & main sail on board and stood to ye SW

At 11 Strong gales

At 12 Saw a man of war to ye Southward standing to ye Northward

Latt Obsd 42:46 S

Towing off shore with *Symmetry Halifax & Spitfire* two Schooners & two sloop prizes at 4 C. Elizabeth W b N & N 1 mile at 6 Wood Island NW b W 3 leagues Do. In ? & 2nd Reef of sails 10 11 ? TS. Fresh gales & clear at 12 clear Reefd. Sails HF T Sail at 3 am heard the report of several muskets to wind ward made the signal to shorten sail at 7 Saw Pigeon Hill NW b W five leagues the two sloop prizes was missing lay too under the mizzen & fore stay sail hauled fore & main Jack on board stood by Weathr stormy gales saw a ship of war to south standing to ye Northward.

Master's Log

At Single Anchor Entce Cape Codd Harbor

At 3 AM heard the report of Several Musquets to windward made the Signal to shorten sail at 7 Saw Pidgoen Hill NW b W five Leagues - the two Sloop Prizes was missing lay too under the Mizzen & fore stay sail hauld Fore & Main Tack on board stood to the SW Strong Gales Saw a Ship of War to Sd standing to the Northd Strong Gales & Clear ½ past Do to bear away for Cape Cod harbor at 3 Race point SE b E 6 miles at 4 made signal to anchor ½ past anchor'd 20 fm to the Sd of the Beach of the harbor in Company *Symmetry Halifax & Spitfire* & two Schooner Prizes

Oct. 26, 1775 Thursday NW b W, WNW

At Single Anchor Entrance Cape Codd harbor

At 1 Strong gales & clear weathr

at ½ past noon made a Signal for all cruises

at ½ past 1 PM made the signal to bear away for Cape Cod Harbor & bare away one of the schooners prizes had split all her sails Saw a man of war standing to ye Northward

At 3 the Race Point of Cape Cod SE b E 5 or 6 miles

At 4 made ye signal to anchor ½ past anchored in 20 fm water soft bottom the So. Side of ye long Sandy beach the westernmost Point W b N the Eernmost N in company the *Symmetry, Halifax, Spitfire* & two Schooner Prizes

AM fresh gales & clear weathr

Do. to bear away for Cape Cod Harbor at 3 Race point SE b E 6 miles at 4 made Signal to anchor off pass anchored 20 fm to ye South of the Beach of the Harbor W. part W b NW.Do. No in Company *Halifax, Symmetry & Spitfire* & two schooner prizes AM Fresh gales & clear weathr.

Oct. 27, 1775 Friday Westerly, Var

At anchor in C. Codd Harbor

Fresh gales & clear weathr Emp variously AM more mod & cloudy weathr

At 9 made Signal to weigh and came to sail and went farther up ye Harbor anchored in 6 fm water soft Bottom as did all the rest of the Squadron This day some of the shore people came off with fish to sell sent ye boat on shore for water

Oct. 28, 1775 Saturday Var. , NE

Do.

PM hazy with cloudy weathr at 6 Do. Boat returned with water AM thick weathr & rain with fresh gales veer'd to 1/2 a cable

Oct. 29, 1775 Sunday NE, NNW

At single anchor in Cape Cod

PM Fresh gales & thick rainy weather AM thick & cloudy weathr do gales loosed sails to air very cold weather

Oct. 30, 1775 Monday Nowerly, Do.

Fresh breezes & cloudy weathr at 3 pm handed sails AM Small breezes & cloudy weathr.

Fresh wind & cloudy at 9 PM handled sails AM lighter winds & cloudy

Oct. 31, 1775 Tuesday Var, NE, var.

Sandy Pt of Harbor NE b E 4 leagues Race pt N b E

Mod breezes & cloudy weathr

at 4 PM made signal for sailing ½ past weigh'd & came to sail as did all the rest Emp turning out of Cape Cod Harbor

at 9 light airs & Var fired two guns A Signal to anchor do.

Anchored in 17 fm water soft bottom West Point of the Sandy Beach W b N dist of the beach 1 mile

at 6 AM small breezes at NE made Signal to sail

at 7 weighd & came to sail

At Noon the Race Pt. N b E the sandy point

Sailed from NE b E Do. 4 leagues

Nov. 1, 1775 Wednesday N, Wtly, NW

C. Cod SW b W & W 3 leagues

At 1 Fine pleasant weathr

At 7 Slight airs & var. the westernmost land on the So. Shore

At 9 NW ½ W the outermost land of Cape Cod NE b N Cape Cod

At 10 Beach ? Fresh gales clear weathr close reefed T:S:

At 11 ? Mizen T:S: NW part of Cape Cod SW b E 1 league

At 12 Do, weathr Halifax Tkd & stood to ye westward

At 4 Do. Weathr

At 8 fired two guns made ye signal to wear, Wore

At 9 Ship *Symmetry*, *Spitfire* & two Prize schooners in sight

At 10 Sett ye Fore & Main:T:S Saw ye land to ye So 1 cable

At 11 land C. Codd NW 6 10 leagues *Symmetry*, *Halifax*, *Spitfire* &

two Prize schooners in sight
At 12 Cape Codd NNW Pt. SW b W ½ W 3 league
Light winds & fair at 7 PM C. Cod beach E b N at N Fresh Gales & Clear close reef top sail handle my T. Sail 7 AM fired two Guns made Signal to wear. Tack *Symmetry Spitfire* & two schooners on light airs - 10 ? F & M T. Sails. Saw land to ye South Halifax in sight.

Captain John Symons, R.N., to the People of Falmouth

Falmouth, Nov 1, 1775

Captain John Symons, commander of his Majesty's Ship *Cerberus* HEREBY causeth it to be signified and make known to all persons whatever in the town of Falmouth, as well as the country adjacent. That if after this public notice , any violence shall be committed, or offered to any of the officers of the crown, or other peaceably disposed subjects or his majesty - Or it any body of men shall be raised and armed in the said town and country adjacent, or any military works erected otherwise than by the order of his Majesty, or those acting under his authority, of it any attempts shall be made to seize or destroy any public magazines or arms, ammunition or other stores, it will be indispensably my duty to proceed with the most vigorous efforts against the said town, as in open rebellion against the King. And if after this signification thee town shall persist in the rebellious acts above-mentioned, they may depend on my proceeding accordingly.

And I do hereby also make known, That if any officers of the colonies, belonging to the crown, or any of his Majesty's subjects whatever, who may be compelled by the violences of the people to seek an asylum, that they may repair on board his Majesty's ship *Cerberus*, where they will receive every protection in my power. John Symon

GOD save the KING

Nov. 2, 1775 Thursday NW, N, NNE
Coahapoint Road SW b W 4 miles
At 1 Fresh breezes & clear weathr
At 3 Wore ship
At 5 K'd
At 8 wore ship Cape Cod SW b S 3 miles
At 9 K'd
At 12 light airs & fair weathr
At 2 out reefs topsails up top gallant yds.

At 7 Halifax parted company
At 8 Do. Weathr Scituate Pt. SW ? leagues
At 10 at noon Boston lighthouse W b N
At 11 Cape NNE Caliafet Rocks SW b W 10 miles
Fresh winds & Clear hove occasionally ? at 6 PM Cape Cod SW b S at 3 miles Mid Mod & fair at 1 AM ordered Reefs up Top Gallant. Yards at 7 Halifax parted company at 9 Situate Pt. NW 3 leagues at Noon Boston Lighthouse W b N

Narrative of Vice Admiral Samuel Graves
Lieut Mowat in the *Canceaux* with the *Symmetry, Spitfire* and *Halifax* came back from their expedition having destroyed the Town of Falmouth in Casco Bay, and destroyed and taken all the Vessels in the Harbour. In that Town were collected great Quantites of Melasses, Rum, Salt, Ammunition; it was the chief place of Trade in the whole Province of Main, and contained several very valuable Distillerys.

Nov. 3, 1775 Friday Var
Moored in Nantasket Road
At 1 small breezes & hazey weath lay too
At 2 bore away
At 3 Past by his Majestys ship *Mercury* at anchor 2 mile
At 4 without the lighthouse ½ past made the signal to anchor
At 5 anchor with ye best bower in 5 fm soft bottom in Nantasket Road found here his Majestys sloop *Raven*
At 8 Veered away & moored ship
At 12 Fresh gales & thick rainy weathr
At 7 Struck top gallant mast & lowered ye lower yards down
At 8 hard gales & do. Weathr
At 10 came in & passed by to town his Majestys sloop *Viper* with a Brigg & schooner
At 12 Do. Gales with heavy rains
Small breezes and hazy weathr at 4 PM Past by his Majestys ship *Mercury* at anchor two miles from the light house 1/2 Past made the signal to anchor at 5 came too with the best Br. in 5 fm water soft Bottom in Nantasket road veered away and moored ship found here his Majestys Sloop *Raven* AM fresh gales with rain struck Top Gallant. and Lowered the Lower yards down came in and passed by his Majestys Sloop *Viper* at Noon hard gales with rain
Nov. 4, 1775 Saturday SE, NW, Werly, Do.

PM fresh gales and thick rainy Weathr at 2 Came in and anchored here his Majestys ship *Mercury* passed by a schooner to town.
Middle part mod. & cloudy weathr
at 10 sailed hence his Majestys ship *Mercury* Emp watering the ship
AM fresh breezes and cold cloudy weathr
Nov. 5, 1775 Sunday NW, Var
Single Anchor Nichsesmati Island W b S two cables length
PM fresh gales and cloudy weathr.
Middle Part mod and clear weathr
AM light airs and varible
at 7 weighd and came to sail as did the *Symmetry*, *Spitfire* and two prize schooners
at 10 anchored Neckses Mate Island W b S two cables lengths Do. anchored in 6 fm water Dark Cloudy weathr drizling rain
Nov. 6, 1775 Monday Var, Early
At Single anchor
Light airs and Drizling
at 5 PM weighed and came to sail got the Boats ahead to tow the ship
at 9 anchored with ye B. Br. in 5 fm water abreast of ye Town of Boston found riding here his Majestys ship *Preston* Admiral Graves the *Swan, Nautilus, Falcon, & Viper* sloops and the *Halifax* schooner with a Number of transports
Nov. 7, 1775 Tuesday Eerly
At Single anchor in Boston harbor
Fresh gales and Dark cloudy weathr with some rain Employed in getting Provisions on board AM heavy rains Employed variously came in here his Majestys schooner *Hinchingbroke* from Halifax
Nov. 8, 1775 Wednesday Eerly
At single anchor in Boston harbor
PM fresh breezes with heavy rains Employed variously came in here several transports and victuallers from England and Ireland
AM sailed hence his Majestys sloop *Swan.*

Vice Admiral Samuel Graves to Philip Stevens
Sir *Preston* Boston Novr 8, 1775
The small Squadron under the Command of Lieut. Mowat mentioned in my Letter October 9 returned to Boston the 2d instant. I transmit a copy of Lieut. Mowats Account in his Expedition, and am extremely concerned the badness of his Vessels and Stores prevented his doing more than destroying the

Town of Falmouth. This however is a severe stroke to the rebels Falmouth having long been a principle Magazine of all kinds of Merchandize, from whence, besides supplying the scattered villages in the Province of New Hampshire and Massachusets Bay, large quantities of Goods were usually transported in small vessels to Newbury Port and from thence by land to the Rebel Army round Boston. This is our first Essay we shall in little time be better provided, and you may be assured we shall not allow the Rebels to remain quiet.
The Master of the *Halifax* having died on board of the small Pox, and many of the Schooners Crew having never had that Disorder, I have ordered her to anchor at a distance from the ships, and to have no Communication with them while any Infection remains....

Nov. 9, 1775 Thursday Eerly
At single anchor in Boston Harbor
Mod breezes and thick cloudy weathr with rain Employed getting on board Provisions from ye *Trident* victualler viz Bread 6400 lb, Beef 4 Punchons, Pork 4 Punchons, Brandy 4 Punchons, Butter 2 firkins, Pease
AM do. Weathr constant firing of great guns and small arms at the NW Part of the Town from 11 to 1 o'clock from the *Scarborough* Bunker Hill and ye North Battery at the Rebels, and they at us.

Journal Kept on board the Ordnance Transport *Charming Nancy* Thursday 9 Novr [1775] Rainy Morng but moon light between 12 & 1, the watch on Deck saw another sail bearing towards us, on which we was all order'd to our Quarters in Order to receive them in Case of an Attack, but after Viewing us for some time they stood off on which our men was order'd between Decks & to be ready with their on the shortest Notice we lay too for fear of Running too near shore & this morning at 7 got under Sail in order if possible to get into Boston before Night about ½ past 8, a Pilot came on board who was sent by Admiral Graves the Night before, at 11 came to anchor (on Account of having no Wind in Nantastic [Nantasket] road in 7 fathom, and about 7 Miles from Boston was informed by the Pilot that Genl Gage was gone for England about a Month Ago in *Pallas*, and the Genl Howe was commander in Chief, One of the Ships which we saw Yesterday Evening was the *Phoenix* & the other the *Juno* An Ordance Storeship which came to an Anchor last night in Nantastic Road, as likewise the *King George* Victuallar & *Whitby* came to and anchored in the above place Yesterday the above ships came from St Helens with us under the Convoy of the *Phoenix* at ½ past 12. The Wind coming to the Eastward Weigh'd Anchor in Compy with the Williamson, but was met by a Cutter from one of the Men of War who informed us that there was about 40 Whale boats waiting behind the Hills with 400 Rebels to attack us; on which we all got under Arms in Order for the attack and lay too for the *Mercury* frigate whom we saw coming in after us, but when we came around the Boats all dispersed and only saw a few Straggling boats, about 4 PM came to Anchor in Boston Harbour as we were sailing in some of the Sailors saw at the top Mast head, twenty one sail of Ships coming in to Nanteskets Bay at 5 Capt Stephelir went on shore in Order to wait on Colo Cleveland who is Commandant of the Royal Artillery rain's the whole day & in the Evening a violent hard gale of Wind which continued all Night, found riding here and at Nantaskets Bay H.M Ships the *Preston* 50 Guns Admiral [Samuel] Graves & Capt Robertson [John Robertson] the *Boyne* 70 Guns Capt Hartwick [Broderick Hartwell], *Phoenix* [*Phoenix*], [Hyde] Parker [jr.] 40 Guns, *Scarborough* 20 guns Capt Barclay [Andrew Barclay] *Mercury* Liet Hutt 20 Guns, *Norless* [*Nautilus*] Sloop [John] Colins, *Swan* do Ascough [James Ayscough]: *Raven* Do Capt [John] Stanhope *Falcon* Do Lindsay [James Linzee], *Cancer* [*Canceaux*] Do Mowat [Henry Mowat], *Emp of Russia* [*Empress of Russia*] Lt Bowmaster, *Symmetry* Lt [George] Dawson, *Adventurer* Lieu _____ & the *Viper* [Samuel] Graves, the time we was at Anchor at Nantaskets Bay we heard the Report of several pieces of Cannon which contd for some Hours, we was at a loss to know what the occasion of so much firing, but on enquiry, when we came into the harbour was informed that our forces had Intelligence of about 20 head of Cattle belonging to the Rebels was grazing on 1 of the Islands near Boston on which Liet Col. Clarke of the 43 Regt with six Companys of light Infantry and 2 small pieces of Cannon went to take them, on our Peoples landing the fired on us with several pieces of Cannon & small Arms, which we returned, & soon made them disperse, on which we took 15 head of fine Cattle (the other 5 could not be caught) put them into our Boats and came Of[f] very Quietly 9 of the Enemy supposed to be killed at the above affair.

Nov. 10, 1775 Friday Esterly
At Single anchor in Boston Harbor
Fresh breezes with heavy rain Emp variously came in here several

transports with fuel & provisions from London

Nov. 11, 1775 Saturday Esterly, WNW

At single anchor in Boston Harbor

PM fresh breezes with rain

Middle part fresh gales thick rainy weathr Struck Top gallant mast and lower the lower yards AM more mod. weathr up yards and top gallant masts at 11 weighd & came to sail

Nov. 12, 1775 Sunday Westerly, NW b N

Single anchor in Nantasket Road. Fresh gales and clear weathr at 2 PM anchored in Nantasket Road found here his Majestys Ships *Phoenix & Lively*, the *Swan* and *Raven* Sloops with several transports AM hard gales and clear weathr at 8 Do. sailed hence his Majestys sloop *Swan* her tender and one transport.

Vice Admiral Samuel Graves to Major General William Howe

Sir Boston Sunday 3 o'Clock 12 Novr 1775

I have sent Mr. Mowat Ordrs to put to Sea immediately to look for the Brig *Nancy*, and have given directions to set her on fire if found in Cape Anne harbour and who cannot be cut out; if she is not there Lieutt Mowat is to cruize for her and bring her in, but I am inclined to think that she stood to Sea the late thick Weather, and the strong Northerly winds since have prevented her getting in. I am &c Sam. Graves

Narrative of Vice Admiral Samuel Graves

[Boston] 12 [November]

…the General expressing particular Fears for the *Nancy* Brig with Ordnance Stores, then the only missing ship of the forementioned Convoy, the Admiral directed the *Canceaux* that had fallen down to Nantasket, to sail forthwith in Quest of her, and (as various Reports had been circulated of the Rebels being acquainted with the particulars of her Cargo and endeavoring to intercept her) to look particularly into Cape Ann harbour, and, if she should be there and could not be cut out, to set her on Fire, but if not arrived to cruize for and conduct her to Boston. It happened that the *Canceaux* had not Water sufficient go to sea with, and the Weather was too bad at the time to take any aboard, so that she was unavoidably obliged to tarry until it became more moderate. Indeed the last Week had been so tempestuous that it was impossible for any Ship, all things considered, to keep her station in the Bay.

Nov. 13, 1775 Monday NW b N
Single anchor in Nantasket Road
Hard gales and squaly at 8 PM let go the small bower anchor underfoot AM People Emp working up junk
Nov. 14, 1775 Tuesday NW b N, WNW
Single anchor in Nantasket Road
The 1st part strong gales and squaly the middle mod & latter little winds and fair weathr.
PM Employed as occasion
at 1 AM hove up the small Br and hove in to 1/2 a cable on ye Best Br at day light sent and got the *Prestons* long boat to water the ship at noon received on Board 13 Punchons and 12 Barrels of water Employed stowing them away got up top.gallant yards (in original log there is a note: "is a mistake in copying" as the entry is out of sequence)
Nov. 15, 1775 Wednesday W b N, SE b E, ESE
Single anchor in Nantasket Road
At 1 PM weighd and came to sail
At 2 came too with ye best bower in 9 fm the flood tide making strong ½ past 3 weighed and came to sail turning down to wards the lighthouse at 1/2 past 4 came too with ye Best Bower. In 7 fm Point Alderton SE 1/2 at Lighthouse NE outer Ragged Rocks NE b E The George Island W b S light breezes & cloudy weathr
at 12 fresh breezes & hazey weathr
at mid. Night veered to 2/3 of a cable
at 4 fresh gales and squaly with rain
at 8 hard gales and squaly with constant rain
At 9 began to heave to 1/3 of a cable the sea running high the pall of ye windlass upset which obliged us to cut the best bower cable Put a Buey on the cable the lighthouse NE b E Point Alderton SE Georges Island SW b S Cable much rubbed
At 10 came too in ? Road with the small bower long Island NW b W Island SW b W Georges Island NE b E
Nov. 16, 1775 Thursday SE b E, NW, var, NNW, Do.
The first and middle part strong gales & squally with sleet & rain
At 1 PM bent a new cable to ye sheet anchor and let it go under foot for a best bower
At 7 the wind coming round to ye NW down yards & topmasts got the lower yards fore & aft. Blowing very hard veered to 1/3 of a cable on the best Br. Lower topsail yards fore and aft got the spare anchor up and out of the hold slackened up and bent a cable to it. Carpenters emp securing the ship by getting every thing snug

as possible

at 8 AM sent on board of the *Empress of Russia* and got her long boat to weigh the two small Br. anchors

at 10 AM came along side with ye anchor got it onboard emp heaving in ye cable shifted the best bower to ye small bower cable unbent ye small bower cable & converted it to a short cable. The carpenter emp examining the windlas found the iron work & palls much damaged It was bent and pulled much away. Employed repairing it

Nov. 17, 1775 Friday NW b N, Do.

Fresh gales & clear weathr AM Carpenter Emp repairing the windlass AM do. gales got up yards and top masts

at Noon do gales close reefed the Top Sails begun to heave ahead as the windlas was repaired.

Nov. 18, 1775 Saturday NW to NNE

Under sail the Base Point of Cape Cod S b E 5 miles

At 1 fresh gales & squally weathr

At 2 weighed & came to sail ½ past running past the lighthouse

At 5 ½ past half way rock NW b W ½ W the entrance of Cape Ann Harbor NNE ¾ E Cape Ann E Point NE ½ E

At 9 Strong gales & squally lowered the topsails Normas Wor N 2 leagues

At 10 under foresail & mizen

At 12 wore ship Do. Gales with hard frost

At 5 Wore ship do. Weathr

At 6 Pidgeon Hill N b W Normans Rock N b W

At 10 strong gales & squally with a heavy sea bore away

At 10 set ye fore top sail

At 11 saw Monument land S b W 4 or 5 leagues Scituate Pt. W b N 10 leagues Monument land SW b W

At 12 Race Point of Cape Cod ESE 4 or 5 miles Saw three sail in Cape Cod Harbor

Fresh gales and squaly Weathr at 4 PM weigh and came to sail at 8 strong gales handled the Top sails Normans Bow No 2 leagues under the fore sail and Mizen at 10 Do. Bow NNE 3 Leagues at Med. night hard frost at 6 AM Pidgeon Hill N 1/2 W at 8 do. Strong gales with a heavy sea do bore away set the fore and main top sail at 10 saw the Monument Land SW b W the Base Point of Cap Cod ESE 4 or 5 miles Saw three sail in Cape Cod harbor.

Nov. 19, 1775 Sunday NW, Var

Single anchor in Cap Cod Harbor

At 1 Strong gales and cloudy weathr SW Point of the Cape Beach

NE b N one mile Employed turning in to Cape Cod Harbor
1/2 past 3 came too with the best Br. in 9 fms soft bottom ye eastern most point of the beach found here his Majestys Ship *Tarter & Mercury* with the *Baltick Merchant* Transport from England with the artillery troops on board put in here by stress of weathr

At 2 fresh gales & clear weathr with hard frost

At 8 more mod heeling ship to scrub her

At 10 light airs & var weighed and came to sail his Majestys ship *Tartar*

At 12 Sailed hence his Majestys ship *Mercury* Single anchor in Cape Cod Harbor

Vice Admiral Samuel Graves to Major General William Howe

Sir *Preston* Boston 19 Novr 1775

Captain Parker informs me that when lieutt Mowat received his Order last Sunday night [November 12] the *Canceaux* had not sufficient Water in to go to Sea with, and that he was unavoidable obliged to remain until the Weather was more moderate to take it on board. I hope the Ordnance Brig and all other bound here will get in safe, but it was impossible for any ship to keep her Station in the Bay last Week all things considered. The *Hinchinbrook* came up last Friday Night; Lieutt [Alexander] Ellis assures me that since the first day that he sailed from Boston, when he chaced a Pyrate into Salem, he did not see an Enemy. I have ordered him out again with the *Nautilus*. The Lively shall follow as soon as possible; I hourly expect the *Fowey* and *Tartar*; the former being a clean Ship shall relieve the *Mercury,* which is in great want of being repaired and cleaned. I do assure your Excellency I am equally anxious for the Safety of these Vessels we expect to arrive, and every precaution shall be used to prevent their falling into the Hands of the Rebels. I am &c Saml Graves

Nov 20, 1775 Monday NW

The Race Point of Cape Cod N b E 2 leagues

Mod and fine weathr Emp hoisting the best bower cable up and putting the 3 cable that was down in the hold Clear undermost in the Bs Br For a spare cable

At 10 AM weighed and came to sail as did the *Baltick Merchant* Transport

At 11 standing to the SW at noon the Monument land W ½ N the Race Point of Cape N b W his Majestys ships *Tartar* and *Mercury* in sight 3 sail more in the NW quarter

Nov. 21, 1775 Tuesday Werly

Normans Bow NNW Scituate Point SW dist 4 Leagues
At 1 working to windward and tacking occasionally
At 2 slight air and var.
At 4 Do. Weathr the pitch of Cape Cod N b E reefed top gallant
At 5 moderate breezes & fine weathr Race Point E b S 3 leagues
At 1 do weather
At 5 Do. Weathr fired a gun & made a signal to tack
At 7 Numan Row NW b N Scitate Point SW
At 9 Do, weathr fired a gun at a Brigg to windward
At 10 Out 1 reef top sails
At 11 Minument Land S b W Numans Row NNW dist 6 leagues
At 12 Scituate Point SW 4 leagues the transport in company 11 sail in sight in the NW quarter

Nov. 22 1775 Wednesday NNW

Boston lighthouse W 3 Leagues
At 1 light airs and varble
At 3 Numans Row NW b N dist 6 leagues
At 5 Cape Ann N ½ E the entrance of Boston Harbor W ½ N at 6 Reef top sails tack
At 7 light breezes and cloudy weathr
At 9 Fresh breezes and Squaly
At 10 Thick sleet close reef'd the top sails
At 12 Do weathr made the signal to tack fired 1 gun
At 2 thick snow made the signal to tack fired 1 gun
At 4 fresh gales & squaly, made the signal gun to tack handed the top sails more moderate sett the top sails
At 8 Fresh gales & squaly Boston light house W b N dist 5 leagues saw his Majestys ships *Tartar* and *Mercury* with 6 sail of transport
At 9 The *Mercury* bore away, passed by a ship of war standing to the East ward
At 11 Fresh gales & squaly bore away & made the signal for our convoy to follow the *Tartar* Boston light house Westward 3 leagues

Light airs and varb at 6 PM Cape Ann N 1/2 E the entrance of Boston harbor is W 1/2 N in ? B TS. Th at 10 fresh gales and squaly weathr sleet and some rain close reef Top sails at 12 made the signal and Tack at 8 thick snow made the signal and TH at 5 AM made the signal and Th handed the Topsails at 8 the Light House W b N 5 Leagues Saw his Majestys ship *Tartar* and *Mercury* with 3 sail of Transport at 10 bore way the *Mercury* Noon fresh gales and squaly fired a gun and made the signal for our convoy to follow the *Tartar* in to Boston bore away Boston Light House W 3 Leagues

Nov. 23, 1775 Thursday NW, WNW

St. Parnt of the Beach SW 1/2 mile

At 1 PM fresh gales and squaly Middle ½ part Saw a sail to ye Eastward made sail and gave chase

at 3 ½ past showed our colours found it to be his Majestys ship *Cerberus*

At 4 Do. Weathr Cape Cod SE b S Monument Land SW b W

At 6 The W most Point of the Beach ESE

At 8 Anchor on the best bower in 11fm with muddy bottom wear to a whole cable the Westmost part of the beach W by N the Et ward of NW b W

At 10 Truro Church E ½ So dist off shore 1 ½ mile

At 12 Do. Weathr

At 4 Do. Weathr

at 8 fresh breezes & squaly

9 Weigh and came to sail

At 11 anchor with the best bower in Cape Cod Harbor in 7 fm water muddy bottom

At 12 Found here his Majestys ship *Mercury* and 4 sail of transports.

Cape Cod S E b S monument Land SW b W the Westmost Part of the Beach Land ESE at 8 anchor in 11 fm Soft bottom veered to a whole cable Westernmost Part of the Beach W b N at 8 AM fresh; gales and squaly weigh and came to sail Employed working to windward TH occasionally at Noon Anchored in Cape Cod Harbor in 11 FM water muddy Bottom red House at lower head of the Harbor NW Truro Church ESE ? Et point of the Beach 1/2 a mile found here his Majestys ship *Mercury* with 4 sail transports and a schoor.

Nov. 24, 1775 Friday NW, SSW, S

Single anchor in Cape Cod

1st part fresh breezes and cloudy weathr the Middle and latter moderate and fine weathr AM got on board a long boat of water and shingle ballast aired the Studding Sails

Nov. 25, 1775 Saturday NW

Race Point of Cape Cod N b S 1/2 Dist 3 leagues monument Land W b S 4 Leagues

At 1 Light airs and veriable

at 2 PM weigh and came to sail from 3 till 6 working out 1/2 past

anchor with the best Bower in 18 fm water muddy bottom the Northern most part of the Beach W b N South most part Is N b S dist off shore 1/2 a mile
At 5 bore away for Cape Cod Harbor
at 6 AM anchor with the best bower in 18 fathm muddy bottom the Westmost part of the beach W b N dist off the shore ½ mile
At 12 do. Slight airs and variable
At 4 do. Weathr
At 5 weigh and came to sail at 8 Do. Weathr
At 12 Mod breezes & fine Race Point NE b E ½ E 3 leagues Monument Land W b S 4 leagues
Nov. 26, 1775 Sunday S b E, SE, ESE, W
Cape Cod Table Land South 7 miles
At 1 light & varible at 1 saw several small schooners in shore hoisted out our boats and sent after them found two small schooners loaded with oysters & no men on board them, put a petty officer & 4 men on board each. At 5 Plymouth light house WSW½ W Scituate Point NNW ½ W At 6 Race Point E b S close reefed the top sails At 8 haul up the fore sail, standing under easy sail, sent on board the schooner swivells 3, Musquets 8, Pistols 11, cartrages ½ pounder 72 cases of wood 4 pounder 6, boathooks ½ pr 2, round shott 72, grapeshott, swords 6 cartooch boxes 10, belts with frogs 10 powder horns 2 ramming irons 4, musquett shot 16 pounds, flints for 12, pistol shot 11, flints for 6 musquetoon 2
At 2 fresh gales & squaly, hand the top sail, struck the top gallant masts At 3 Found the ship labour much and found she made at the rate of 8 inches pr hour gott the guns off the quarter into the hold to ease the ship At 5 hard gales with snow, thunder & lightening, haul up ye courses
At 7 Light winds and variable
At 8 Seven sail in sight & a vessel on fire in the NW quarter sett the courses fore and main top sail
At 10 Cape Cod Table Land So sett the Mizen top sail
At 12 Moderate and cloudy. The hull of the vessel still burning Light airs and var. at one PM saw several small schooners in shore hoisted the boat out and went after them found 2 small schooners loaded with oysters no men onboard Put an Petty officer and 4 men on board of each of them sent on board of them both swivels and small arms with ammunition at mid night fresh gales and squaly weathr. handled the Fore and mizen Topsail and handled the main T.S. stricken Topgallant masts found the ship labors much struck the 4 sails lash guns in the hold to ease their ship found the ship

makes 8 inches in an hour at 5:6:7 AM hard gales with snow sleet Thunder & Lightening at 8 Light winds and variable *Swan* sail in sight saw a ship on fire in WSW 2 miles set the courses Cape Cod Table Land So.

Nov. 27, 1775 Monday Var, No, NNW, NW, No

Cape Cod W Table land N b S dist 3 leagues

At one taken with a snow storm, bore away before the wind, clew up all the sails, handed the top sails & main sail, reefed the fore sail set the fore sail and mizen, saw a ship of war to leeward under her courses, Strong gales & squaly, saw the table lands off Cape Cod bearing S b W Reef the main sail and sett it

At 8 Do. Weather a heavy sea, found the ship made one foot of water per hour gott 4 of the main deck Gunns into the hold

At 10 more moderate

At 12 Fresh breezes and cloudy

At 4 Moderate breezes & cloudy more out reef courses & sett the top sails get up top gallant masts and yards

At 6 Light airs inclinable to calm

At 8 Do. Weathr the high land of Cape Cod SW b W 7 leagues out reefs T:S:

At 11 Fresh breezes inclinable to snow, Cape Cod W ½ S the W most part of the Table Land

At 12 SW b W ½ W 3 leagues a ship of war & a sloop in in the NE quarter One ship in the ES quarter

Fresh breezes and cloudy weathr at on PM taking with a snow storm bore away before the wind clew up all the sail handed the Topsails do set the fore sail

at 8 saw a man of war and is ours

at 4 strong gales and squaly do. saw the Table land of Cape Cod being S b W Reefed the main sail and set it

at 5 AM mod and cloudy wore our Reefs and Set. the T.S.

at 8 up T.G. made a yard at noon fresh breeze and variable no snow

Nov. 28, 1775 Tuesday Var, NW, NNE, SE,

Do. Table land SW b W 6 or 7 Leagues

At 1 Light breezes & varble dark cloudy weathr close reefed the top sails

At 3 Cape Codd W ½ S distances 5 leages, gott the guns up out of ye hold

At 4 Fresh breezes and squaly with dark cloudy weathr

At 6 Do. Weathr

At 12 Tack moderate breezes and cloudy

At 4 Do. Weathr saw a ship to the SW gave chase fired 2 guns to bring
At 5 Spoke his Majestys sloop *Nautilus* on a cruise
At 9 Light airs & cloudy The table Lands of Cape Codd SW b W 6 or 7 leagues
At 10 4 sail in sight 2 in the NW quarter & 2 in the S East
Light breezes with dark cloudy weathr. close reef Topsails Cape Cod N 1/2 S dist 5 Leagues got the guns up out of the hold at 4 fresh breezes and squally weat at Mid night mod and cloudy weathr at 4 saw a sail to the southward of us gave chase fired 2 shot at 5 spoke his Majestys sloop *Nautilus* upon ? at 8 light airs and cloudy the Table of Cape Cod WSW 1/2 W at Noon
Nov. 29, 1775 Wednesday S, SE, SW b S, WSW
Nerimas Bow N 1/2 W halfway Rock NW 1/2 W 3 leagues
At 1 Light breezes and cloudy
At 4 Do W Cape Codd WSW 2 miles So part of the Table Land SSE
At 6 Fresh breezes & cloudy Race point South 2 miles
At 7 Tack
At 11 Anchor with the stream anchor in 18 fm muddy bottom; found the ship drive into hole water cutt away the hawsers about 15 fm from the inner end,
at 12 bore away reef the fore sail and gett mizen
at 4 Hard gales and squaly with rain
at 7 ½ past more sett main sail & main top sail clew reef
at 9 Sett fore and mizen top sail
at 10 Numans N b W 5 or 6 leagues Out 3 reefs Fresh gales & squaly
at 11 Cape Ann light house NE The entrance of Cape Ann harbor N b E Numans N ½ W half way rock NW ½ W 2 or 3 leagues
PM light breezes and cloudy weathr at 4 Cape Cod WSW dist 2 miles Part of the Table Land SSE at 11 anchored with the stream anchor in 18 fm fresh gales found the ship drove into shallow water cut away the Hawser 15 fm from the clinch at 1 AM reef ? Fr at 2 hard gales Post 7 wore set up Main sail & close reef M T.S. at 10 at 10 Nermans rock N b W 5 or 6 Leagues out 3 Reefs Top Sail at Noon fresh gales Cape Ann Light house is N 2 Leagues Cape Ann Harbor N b E
Nov. 30, 1775 Thursday W, WSW, W
Thachers Island NW b W 3 Leagues
At 1 Fresh breezes & cloudy brought too spoke his Majestys ship
At 4 Moderate and fair

At 6 Scituate Point SW b W 3 leagues Monument SW b S
At 7 Close reef the top sails, and landed mizen sail
At 9 Wore handed the top sails Fresh gales and cloudy weathr
At 12 Do. Weathr
At 7 Sett the topsails Fresh breezes and squaly Weath gave chase to a schooner in the NE quarter Fired 2 guns shott to bring schooners too
at 10 spoke a schooner from Annapolis Royal bound for Boston, with Bullocks & hay, show our colours to his Majestys schooner *Henshenbrook* At 11 Gave chase to a schooner in the NE quarter
At 12 Fresh breezes & clear Thatcher Island NW b W 3 leagues
PM fresh breezes and cloudy weathr at 1 brought too and spoke his Majestys ship *Fowy* at 2 bore away after her at 6 ? water Point SW b W 3 Leagues monument Land SW b S close Br T.S at 3 wore handled the T.S. at 4 AM wore at 7 set of T.S. at 10 fired 2 shots at and brought to a schooner from Annapolis Royal bound to Boston with stock and hay on board at 11 gave chase in the NE Qr.
Dec. 1, 1775 Friday W, W b N
Monument Land W b S Race Point E b N Dist. 5 miles
At 1 Fresh breezes and cloudy
At 3 Tack spoke his Majestys ship *Nautilus*
At 4 Pigeon hill WSW ¾ W Thatchers Island SW b W ½ W
At 6 Fresh gales and squaly carry away the main top yard in the sling
At 8 unbent the sail and got the yard down & got up another in its place
At 9 handed the fore and mizen top sails
At 12 Do weathr
At 5 Do weathr Wore sounded in 12 fm water
At 6 Sett the top sails
At 8 Fresh gales & squaly his Majesty ship *Fowey* to Windward
At 10 Cape Codd SSE bore away as did his majesty ship *Fowey*
At 11 Do. Gales Monument land W b S Race Point E b n 4 or 5 miles
At 12 His Majestys ship *Fowey* in Company
PM fresh breezes and cloudy weathr at 4 spoke his Majestys sloop *Nautilus* Pidgon WSW middle Part fresh gales and squaly carried away the main Top sail yard in the slings Emp getting up another at 5 am sounded 12 fm water on a fishing bank at 7 wore at 8 saw his Majestys ship *Fowy* to windward at 10 Cape Cod SSE bore away as did his Majestys ship *Fowey* do. in company
Dec. 2, 1775 Saturday WNW, SW

Truro Church E 1/2 N off the Beach 1/2 a mile
First part fresh gales & cloudy the middle fresh breezes Latter light airs
AM at one running in for Cape Cod harbor
At 2 anchor under the Beach with ye Bt. Br. in 17 fm water muddy bottom as did his Majestys ship *Fowey* & veer to a shallow cable at 4 his Majestys schooner *Henshenbrook* came in & anchored ye Kenmechi on ye beach NW the NE part of ye beach N the SW part of N W b N the church E ½ N dist. Off the shore ½ mile
At noon sail hence his Majestys schooner *Henshonbrook* received. on board 4 cask of water unbent the old main top sail and bent a new one.
PM fresh gales & cloudy weathr AM light airs running in for Cape Cod Harbor at 2 PM anchored under the bank beach with the Bower in 17 fm water Muddy Bottom as did his Majestys ship *Fowey* cleared to a whole cable at 4 his Majestys schooner *Henchingbrook* come in and anchored on the Beach NW the NS part of the beach Near the SW part of do. W b N Truro Church site N dist. off shore 1/2 a mile AM at noon sailed hence the *Hinchingbrook* got some fresh water on board
Dec. 3, 1775 Sunday SSW, SW
Georges Island W 1/2 N Light House NS b N 1/4 mile
At 1 Mod & cloudy
At 2 weigh & came to sail as did his Majestys ship *Fowey*
At 4 Fresh breezes & cloudy, Monument Land SW b W ½ W Scituate Point NW b W ½ mile
At 6 Race Point ENE ½ E 6 or 7 miles, close reef the top sails and handed Do.
At 8 Reef the fore sail, under the fore stay sail and mizen
At 12 Fresh gales & cloudy Sound in 30 fm muddy bottom at 4 Do. Weathr
At 7 sett the courses and main top sail
At 8 Running along shore to the Northward Squaly with drizly rain
At 10 Boston Light house WNW ½ W 2 leagues sett the fore and mizen top sails
At 11 Anchord in the light house channel with the best bower in 5 fm bottom of sand and mudd veer to ½ a cable, Point Altenry SSE
At 12 Granger Island N ½ N The light house NE b N
PM mod breezes and cloudy weathr at 2 weigh and came to sail as did the *Fowey* at 4 the monument Land SW b W 1/2 W Sciutate Point NW b W Race Point EWNE 1/2 E dist 6 or 7 miles close reefed of Top sails at 8 AM squaly with drizling rain at 10 Boston

light house WNW 1/2 W dist 2 leagues at 11 anchored in the Light House Channel with the B.B. in 5 fm water mixture with sand and mud old race Point ? SSE ? cinyhawsed rocks SE b E ?

Disposition of Ships Under the Command of Vice Admiral Samuel Graves
3d December 1775

Names	**Guns**	**Commanders**	**Complement**	**Station**
Preston	50	Capt. John Robinson	300	Off the Town In Boston Harbour
Boyne	70	Hartwell	500	Kingroad
"				
Scarborough	20	Barkley	130	In Charles River
"				
Cerberus	28	Symons	160	Off the Town
"				
Tartar	28	Medows	160	Off the Town
"				
Mercury	20	Graeme	130	At Nantasket
"				
Falson Sloop	14	Linzee	100	Gallows Creek
"				
Adventure Storeship	8	lt. Hallum	40	Off the Town
"				
Hope Schooner	6	Dawson	30	Condemned by Survey"
Hinchinbrook	6	Ellis	30	off the Town
"				
Halifax Schr	6	Dela Touche	30	Off Winnisimmet
"				
Rose	20	Captn Wallace 130		At Rhode Island
Glasgow	20	Howe	130	At Rhode Island
Swan	16	Ayscough	100	At Rhode Island
Bolton Brig	6	Lieut Thos Graves		At Rhode Island
Phoenix	44	Captn Parker	250	On her passage to New York
Asia	64	Vandeput	500	At New York
Viper	10	Saml Graves	80	On her passage to New York
Otter	16	Squire	100	At Virginia
Kingfisher	16	Jas Montagu	100	At Virginia
Raven	114	Stanhope	100	On her passage to Virginia
Cruizer	8	Parry	60	At N Carolina ordered to Boston
Scorpion	14	Capt Tollemache	100	On passage to N C
Tamar	16	Thornborough	100	At S Carolina ordered to Boston
St Lawrence Schr	6	Lt John Graves	30	On passage to St. *Augustine*
St. John Schr	6	Wm Grant	30	At Bahama Islands
Roebuck	44	Captn Hamond	250	At Halifax
Somerset	64	Commodore LeCras	500	At Halifax
Senegal	14	Capt: Dudingstone	100	Do to Victual
Savage	8	Bromedge	60	At Halifax just arrived from NF
Merlin	16	Barnaby	100	Annapolis [Royal].
Lizard	20	Hamilton	130	At Quebec
Hunter	10	Mackenzie	130	At Quebec
Gaspee Brig	6	Lt Hunter	30	At Quebec

Lively	20	Capt Bishop	130	Cruizing bet. C. Anne C. Cod
Fowey	20	Geo. Montagu	130	"
Nautilus	16	Collins	100	"
Canceaux	6	Lieut. Mowat	45	"

Dec. 4, 1775 Monday SSW, NW b N, W

Normans Rose N b E dist 3 miles

At 1 Fresh Breezes & cloudy

At 3 Weigh & came to sail at ½ past running out of the light house Channel, Moderate breezes & cloudy Boston Light House W ¾ S

At 5 Saw a ship to leeward, fired several gunns at a schooner in the shore

At 6 Light airs shorten sail Cape Ann NE b N Halfway Rock N ½ E 2 leagues

At 10 Wore Numans N ½ E 4 or 5 miles sound in 30 fm muddy bottom

At 11 Handed fore and mizen top sails

At 12 Fresh gales and clear

At 3 Wore

At 4 Do. Weathr

At 6 Do. Weathr wore stood in close off Manchester harbor to see if the schooner the ship fired at last night was in shore, East Point of Cape Ann harbor NE b E

At 9 halfway Rock WSW distance off shore on mile

At 11 Fresh gales & squaly half way Rock WSW Numans W N b e 3 miles

PM mod breezes & cloudy weathr at 3 weigh and came to sail at 6 saw a ship to Leeward fired several guns at a schooner in shore at 8 halfway rock N 1/2 E 2 leagues

at 12 handed the Fore & miz Topsail Fresh gales and clear weathr at 8 wore ship

at 9 the East point of Cape Ann Harbor NE b E halfway rock WSW dist. off shore one mile

Dec. 5, 1775 Tuesday NW, W, SW

Single anchor in Nantasket Road

The first part fresh gales, the middle fresh breezes with sharp frost, latter moderate and variable, PM between 1 and 4 standing along shore to ye Windward

At 4 Boston Light house SW by W the Rocks called the Graves, NW b N one league

Between 5 & 6 working up the light house Channel, at ½ past 6 anchor in Nantasket Road, with the Best Bower in 7 fm water

muddy Bottom & veered to ½ a cable the house on Gorges Island ENE the East part of Pittoch Island S b E Long Island head NW b N found riding here his Majestys ship *Mercury*
AM emp. Watering Sailed hence his Majestys ship *Boyne* Read the Articles of War and abstract of the last act of parliament to the ships Company & Muster Documents PM fresh gales AM Mod and cloudy weathr at 4 Boston Light house SW b W the graves NW b N dist. one League between 5 and 6 working up the Light house channel at 1/2 past 6 anchored in Nantasket Road with Best Bower in 7 fm water muddy bottom veered to 1/2 a cable the House on Georges Island ENE found here his Majestys ship *Mercury* AM Emp watering sailed hence his Majestys ship *Boyne* Read the articles of war to the ship company

Dec. 6, 1775 Wednesday SW
Single anchor Nantasket Road
Fresh breezes throughout, and cloudy weathr
PM employed watering making Points & gasketts & etc. At 6 came in here and anchored his Majestys sloop *Nautilus*, employed as above
Fresh breezes and cloudy weathr PM Emp watering making Points and gaskets came in and anchored here his Majestys sloop *Nautilus* AM Employed as before

Dec. 7, 1775 Thursday Werly
Do.
Moderate breezes & cloudy, throughout PM compleating our watering
AM employed in sundry jobs about the Rigging
At noon came in & run up the Harbor his Majestys ship *Fowey* with a New England Privateer of 10 guns Recd from his Majestys ship *Preston* 10 men
Throughout fresh breezes and cloudy weathr PM completed our water AM
Employed about the riggin came in and run up the Harbor his Majestys ship *Fowey* with a New England and Perat (pirate) Brig of 10 guns received from his Majestys ship *Preston* 10 men

Dec. 8, 1775 Friday S, SSE, var,
The first and latter moderate & variable, the middle fresh breezes with drizling rain PM at one came in & anchord here his Majestys ship *Lively*. AM recd on board 2 chord of Wood. At 11 sail hence his Majestys ship *Lively* AM recd on board 2 chords of Wood
At 11 sailed hence his Majestys ships *Lively* & *Nautilus* at noon weighed and came to sail

The first and light mod the middle fresh gales with drizling rain PM came in and anchored here his Majestys ship *Lively*. AM received on board 2 chord of wood at 11 sailed hence his Majestys ship *Lively* and *Nautilus* sloop at Noon weighed and came to sail

Dec. 9, 1775 Saturday E, N

Light House channel Nantasket Road

The first part light airs, middle strong gales & squaly with Rain, snow & sleet

The latter more moderate, at ½ past noon the boats a head towing us through between Georges Island and Gallops, At 1 towing us between Gorges and the Beach. At 2 towing us through the light house channel, at ½ past made fast a hawser to the Buoy of the small Bower we left behind at 4 weighed Do. and anchored with the small Br in 5 fm water muddy bottom and veerd to 1/3 of a cable the light house N b E the S. end of Georges Island W ½ N found riding here his Majestys ships *Lively* and *Nautilus* The carpenter employed unstocking the former small Br put down in the hold At 6 looking like bad weather weigh and run in for Nantasket at 7 anchor with the Best Br in Nantasket Road in 5 fm water muddy bottom and veerd to ½ a cable at 9 came in here and anchored his majesty ships *Lively* and *Nautilus* found riding here his Majestys ship *Mercury*. Long Island Head NW the Et part of Pittochs Island S b E the House on Georges Island NE b E Dist. Off the shore 3 cables length.

The first part light airs intermixed with clouds the Middle strong gales & squaly with rains snow and sleet the Later mod gales and cloudy 1/2 past Noon the boats ahead towing us out between Georges and Gallop Islands at 4 anchored in 5 fm water muddy Bottom and veered to 1/3 of a cable Lighthouse N b E South most end of Georges Island W 1/2 N *Lively* and *Nautilus* at anchor here at 6 looking bad weathr weighed and run into Nantasket road at 7 came too with the Best Br muddy bottom veered to 1/2 a cable the houses on Georges Island AM aired the Topsails

Lieutenant Henry Mowat, R.N., to Vice Admiral Samuel Graves

Sir Since I was with you last, I have been informed of Fluent the Mate of the *Newbury* Brig (who I mentioned on a former occasion) that he knows a vast number of Vessels belonging to New England now trading from different places particularly from the Dutch, and French West India Islands to a port in North Carolina, situated nine or Ten leagues to the Westward of Cape Hatteras, by name Beacon Island, which lies a little way in the inside of Oricock Bar; he was there Seven Months ago, and he declares that there is no port in the continent so famous for smuggling; giving for reason, that no Kings vessels ever have been over this Bar, nor is there any Customhouse authority near it; he has been at this place eight voyages, and Says that the Pilots for the Bar have orders from all the Trading people near it, not to make known to any Kings Vessel the depth of Water in the Bar, and to persist should they fall in with any, that there is not water sufficient for them, at the same time, this man declares that there are at full Tides 15 or 16 feet, and that he has seen larger ships than the *Canceaux* Pass. I though it incumbant on me to lay this information before you, and am

[&c] H. Mowat

Canceaux Nantasket 9th December 1775

Dec. 10, 1775 Sunday N Var.

The first part fresh breezes & cloudy middle & latter light breezes & variable

PM At 2 came down & anchor his Majestys schooner *Hinshenbrook* Recd on board a long boat load of water People employed variously Fresh breezes and cloudy PM came down and anchored here his Majestys schooner *Hinchingbrook* got on board water

Dec. 11, 1775 Monday Var, S, SE, ESE, SSE

The first part light airs & variable the middle and latter strong gales with several gusts of wind with rain. People employed making points & such AM at noon found the ship arrived veered to a whole cable lett go the small Br and veerd to 1/3 At 8 struck lower yard & top gallant mast. At 11 the wind shifted suddenly from the SW to the NW struck the top mast & veerd to ½ a cable on small bower

First part Mod and var. the middle and later part strong gales and squaly found the ship ? Iseve veered to a whole cable Let go the small bower veered to 1/3 at 11 the wind shifted suddenly from the SW to NW struck yards and topmasts veered to 1/3 cable on the small bower

Dec. 12, 1775 Tuesday NW

Fresh gales & squaly throughout with severe frost AM at 11 weighed the small Br and hove into ½ a cable on the best bower Fresh gales and squaly with snow and hard frost at 11 AM weigh the small bower and hove into 1/2 a cable on B.Br.

Intelligence Received from Sion Martindale

[H.M.S. *Fowey*, December 12, 1775]

That a Brig laden with Ordnance Stores from Boston was taken the 28th or 29th of November last, by a Schooner of Six 3 pounders commanded by a Captain Manley, and carried into Cape Ann Harbor;- That part of her Cargo was conveyed to the Head Quarters of the Rebel Army at Cambridge on the Saturday following: - That an Express had arrived at Cambridge from Montreal that Governor Carleton had destroyed the Ammunition and Provisions at that place, And retreated to Three Rivers, a (Place so called) and that a Colonel (thought to be) Harris with one thousand Canadians were endeavoring to cut off his retreat to Quebec.

That there is a Schooner of four Carriage guns and ten Swivels having 50 men on board to sail from Plymouth the 5th or 6th instant on a Cruize for Ten days only, and that she has black Sides, Tallowed bottom, two Topsails and oars on her Quarters, commanded by one Coit, that her Colours are a Green Pine Tree in a White Field, with the Motto, "Appeal to Heaven," that the Signal to know each other was to hoist the Colours at the Fore topmast head, And lower the Main Sail half down. - Beverly has fitted out three Schooners two are of four Carriage Guns each Swivels and Men not known, the third is the Schooner above mentioned commanded by Manley.

Dec. 13, 1775 Wednesday WNW

Normans House N b E 1/2 E 5 miles half way rock NW b W 1/2 N 1 1/2 mile

The first part moderate gales, the middle & latter moderate breezes & clear PM at 6 up yards and top mast, stay ? & sett up the rigging. AM at 2 his Majestys ship *Lively* made the signal to weigh fired gun. At 3 weighed and came to sail at 4 Running down the light house Channel, the *Nautilus & Hinchenbrook* in company. At 5 the light SW b W 2 leagues; between 5 and 8 standing alone ? to the Northward at 8 the halfway Rock N b W Dist. ½ a mile, between 11 working to windward into Marblehead at 11 the harbor open, saw no vessels Wore and stood out to sea after the Lively. At noon Nurmans Rock N b E ½ E dist 5 miles the halfway Rock NW b W ½ W dist 1 ½ mile

Mod breezes and clear frosty weathr at 6 pm up yard and top mast and set the riggen up at 2 AM the Lively made the signal to weigh at 3 weigh and come to sail at 4 running close the Light house channel *Nautilus* and *Hinchenbrook* in company at 5 the light SW b W dist 2 leagues at 8 1/2 way rock N b W 1/2 a mile at 11 working to windward toward Marblehead

Dec. 14, 1775 Thursday WNW, W b N, WSW, SW, W b S

Table land of Cape Cod S 1/2 E Cape Cod SW 1/2 S 49 or 10 miles

At 1 Moderate Breezes & fine weathr Parted Company with ye ships

At 2 The ships company employed fishing

At 4 Do. Weathr halfway Rock NW 5 or 6 Miles Numan N b E ½ 4 leagues light breezes and cloudy weathr

At 9 Do. Weathr sett the fore sail & handed Fore & mizen top Sail sounded 45 fm

At 12 Fresh gales & cloudy founded in 40 fm muddy bottom

At 2 Wore, handed main top sail sounded in 30 fm Do. Bottom

At 4 Fresh gales 7 squaly sounded in 10 fm hard bottom

At 7 Wore sounded in 30 fm soft bottom sett the main sail

At 9 Do. Weathr with showers of rain

At 10 More moderate, sett the top sails saw the land of Cape Codd bearing SSW Found the ship make a great deal of water, the carpenter on examination found ¼ water to come in at ye Bows under the knee of the head, the table Land SW ½ S 9 or 10 miles

At 4 PM mod breezes and cloudy weathr People Emp fishing Normans Bow N b S 1/2 E 4 leagues at 9 handed the Fore. Top mizen Top Sail. sounded 4 fm muddy bottom at Midnight fresh gales and cloudy weathr at 2 AM wore ship Handed M: T:.S: sounded 3 fm muddy Bottom at 4 sounded 18 fm at 7 wore ship at 8 showers of rain at 10 more mod set up TS saw the land of Cape Cod bearing SSW at 11 found the ship making a great fall of water the carpenter examining found the water to run in at the Bows of the ship supposed to be under the knees of the head out of 3 & 2 reefs TS at Noon mod gales and cloudy

Dec. 15, 1775 Friday W, W b N

Cape Cod S b W 4 leagues

At 1 Fresh breezes & cloudy standing in shore, the back of Cape Codd

At 2 tacked ye pitch of Cape Codd SW 5 or 6 miles Race Point SW

At 4 Moderate breezes cloudy

At 5 Race point SW b S 11 leagues

At 6 Do. Weathr

At 7 Close reefed the topsails

At 8 Do. Weathr with drizling rain

At 12 Do weathr sounded in 45 fm hard ground

At 3 sound 50 fm Do. Ground
At 4 Do weathr
At 5 Tack
At 6 Spoke his Majestys sloop *Nautilus*, his Majestys ship *Lively* in sight in the NW Quarter out all reefs & got top Gallant yards up
At 8 Do. Weathr
At 11 Cape Codd S b W ½ W 5 leagues
At 12 Do. Cape S b W 3 or 4 leagues Mod breezes and fine weathr
Fresh breezes and cloudy weathr at 2 PM Cape Cod SW 5 miles at 5 the Race Point SW b S 4 leagues at 8 drizling rain at Midnight sounded 45 fm 3 sounded 50 fm hard ground at 6 spoke his Majestys sloop *Nautilus* the *Lively* in sight out all reef TS get up Top Gallant yards at Noon Mod and fine weathr

Dec. 16, 1775 Saturday WNW, NNW, NE, Var

Single anchor Cape Cod Harbor Red House on the Head of the harbor NW b W 1/2 W 2 miles

Mod breezes & fine weathr throughout PM at one running in for ye Race Apoint at 2 the East part of the Table Land SE ¼ S the land about Scituate Point NW b W ½ W the Cape S b E ½ E 2 leagues At 3 the Race Point & ye W part of the Beach in one bearing SE ½ S at 4 running along ye shore in 26 fm about ½ mile from the beach when you bring ye houses open N ye high land They bear N with West part of the Beach & steer ESE the Race point seen in at NW ½ N source E when you bring the E part of the Beach & ye Westerly most hill but one in one steer WNW but you must give the E point of the beach a birth of half a Mile. At 5 Do. Point NNW At 6 anchor in Cape Codd harbor with the Best Bower in 9 fm water muddy & veerd to 1/3 of a cable the bearing of the Red House is the bottom of the Harbor NW b W ½ W the Point if the beach S bW ½ W 1 mile AM found the wooded end & the ? Of the Head very open the carpenter employed stopping the leak, Dry all the sails

Throughout Mod and fine weathr at 1 PM running in for the Race Point at 2 the east point of the table land at E 1/4 S the land about Sictuate land NW b W 1/2 W the Cape S b E 1/2 E 2 leagues at 3 the race Point and the W part of the Beach in an bearing of SE 1/2 S at 4 running along the shore in 26 fm about 1/2 a mile from the Beach when you bring the house open with the high land they bear North the W part of the Beach East Steer ESE Race Point sheet in at NW 1/2 W course E when you bring the East part of the Beach and the West hill in one at 6 anchored in Cap Cod Harbor in 9 fm water mud and sandy bottom veered to 1/3 of a cable the Red

House in the head of the harbor NW b W 1/2 W an found the wooded end of the howses of the head open the carpenter Emp stopping the leak People Emp variously

Dec. 17, 1775 Sunday E, var., S,

Cape Cod bearing as before

This first part light breezes Var. the Middle & later Fresh breezes & hazey with hail & rain and drizling rain PM the carpenter employed as before the ships company emp making points and gasketts Excercised great guns & small arms AM at 9 weigh & run farther N Ward at ½ past anchor in 10 fm muddy bottom veered to ½ a cable the w most sand hill & the monument in one bearing W the Red house NW ½ W the NE Point of the Beach SE ½ S dist ½ mile at 1/2 past anchor in 10 fathom water muddy bottom veered to ½ a cable Western most sand hills & the monument on a bearing westerly the red house NEW the NE pt of the beach SE 1/2 S Distance 1/2 a mile

Dec. 18, 1775 Monday S, WNW

The first & Middle part Moderate breezes with thick hazing weather & Drizling rain the latter fresh breezes & cloudy Recd a long boat load of water Carpenter & people emp as before.

AM the darken skys Employed as before. The people making points & gaskets & got here on board a long boat load of water

Dec. 19, 1775 Tuesday WNW, NW, NNW

The first Middle part, Mod breezes the latter fresh breezes and squally PM the carpenter repairing the Bows People Emp variously At at 8 loosed the top sails and hove short found it blon hard veerd to a whole cable & handed ye sails.

Carpenter emp making repairs about the rigging at 9 AM loosed topsails & veered short found it blew hard veered away to a whole cable & handed the top sails

Dec. 20, 1775 Wednesday NNW, NW

Strong gales & squaly throughout with frost & snow PM at 1 let go the small Br anchored under foot AM at noon employed clearing the decks of snow

Throughout Strong gales & squally the middle & latter thick snow with frost AM at one let go the small BR anchor under fort AM at North Emp cleaning the decks of the snow

Dec. 21, 1775 Thursday NW b N

Throughout fresh gales & squally weathr with severe frost the middle Snow

Dec. 22, 1775 Friday NW b N

Gales with part cloudy weathr throughout with severe frost the

latter snow
Throughout fresh breezes with dark cloudy weathr severe frost the latter Snow

Dec. 23, 1775 Saturday N, NNE, NE

The first part mod breezes with dark clouds weather the middle & latter. fresh gales and cloudy with frost the latter fresh gales & cloudy with frost at 3 PM weigh the small Br at 4 weigh & cam to land stood a little farther to the Eastern at ½ past anchored with the Best Br in 8 fm with muddy Bottom veered to ½ a cable, the Red house in the bottom of the harbor NW ½ W the east point of the Beach S ½ E 1/ a mile Recd on board a chord of wood AM at 4 veered to a whole cable came to sail bower out to weigh & came to sail stood a little farther to the E at 1/2 past anchored with mud in 8 fm water muddy bottom veered to 1/2 cable the bearings the Red House in the bottom of the harbor NW 1/2 W the east pt of the beach S 1/2 dist 1/2 a mile Rec' on board a chord of wood at 10 AM veered to whole cable

Dec. 24, 1775 Sunday NE, ENE

The first part & middle part Fresh breezes & Squally with dark cloudy weather latter strong gales with snow & rain AM struck yards & top gallant mast

Dec. 25, 1775 Monday ENE, N, NW

The first & middle parts strong gales & squally with rain & snow the latter Mod gales & var with a sharp frost at 5 PM veered to 1/2 cable on the best bower AM at day light saw a large ship riding between the race point & the SW part of the beach sent the boat to her assistance but it blowing hard could not get on board At 8 pm up lower yards at 10 Do. ship made the signal for a pilot a whale boat made an attempt but could not get on board at 11 weigh & came to sail run out into the bay & stood off and on shore in order to show the ship the way in at noon anchored with the Bt Br in 18 fm water to ye S of ye Beach muddy bottom Veered to a whole cable Truro Church ESE ½ E
At the Southward of the beach muddy bottom veered to a whole cable SE 1/2 E the part of the beach NNW the ship part of Do. WNW dist of the beach shore 1 mile

Dec. 26, 1775 Tuesday NW NNW, NE

The first part mod gales the middle & latter strong gales & squally with a severe frost AM at one came in and anchored here his Majestys ship *Niger* from England

Dec. 27, 1775 Wednesday N, NW, W

Through out fresh breezes cloudy with sharp frost AM at 7

weighed and came to sail at 8 working to wind out into the bay at 10 the Race Pt N b W dist 3 mile at 11 squally with a heavy sea from WNW bore away at noon anchored in Cape Cod harbor with the Bs.Br. in 9 fm water muddy bottom & veered to a whole cable his Majestys ship *Niger* weighed & run into the harbor the bearing the red house in the bottom of the harbor NW The NE Point of the Beach S ½ E dist. 1 mile

Dec. 28, 1775 Thursday WSW, Var, NNW

The first part Fresh Gales & squally the middle & latter Mod breezes & fine weathr AM Dry'd all the sails & washed between Decks Finished the top gallant masts

Dec. 29, 1775 Friday NNW, NW, N

Throughout Mod breezes & fine weathr AM at 2 saw a brigg in the bay sent our boat with an Officer to pilot her in, at 4 anchored here a brig with Ordnance stores & on board at 9 saw a vessel off the SW part of the beach sent a boat with an Officer to pilot her in AM at one the *Lord Heynd* packet boat came in and anchored from Falmouth at 8 weighed and came to sail a 9 standing to the NNW at 1/2 past 10 the SW part of the beach bore ESE ½ E Monument land NSW Scituate Point NW b N Race Point NE b E ½ E dist 4 miles. Then in 26 Fathoms water muddy bottom. At Noon Scituate Point NW b W Cape Codd E. dist 4 leagues

Dec. 30, 1775 Saturday NW, NE b E, NE, S

Cape cod SSE 4 leagues Scituate Point W
at 1 Light breezes and cloudy
at 2 Scituate Church NW be W 5 leagues Plymouth Light house
at 4 Tacked Plymouth Light house SSW Cape Codd ESE dist 6 leagues
at 6 moderate breezes and cloudy, the monument land SW ½ W
at 8 Do. weathr Monument land WSW ½ W
at 9 Race Oiunt NE b N Dist. ½ a mile
at 2 Anchor in Cape Codd Harbor in Bbr in 10 fm muddy Bottom & veered to ½ a cable found Riding here his Majestys Ship *Niger* & 9 Brigg, the Red house in the Bottom of the harbor NW b W ½E
at 4 the NE part of the Beach SW dist. ¾ a mile
at 8 Fresh breezes and cloudy weathr
at 9 Weigh & came to sail as did his Majestys ship *Niger* with her convoy & run out of the harbor. Part company with the *Niger*, at ½ past ran a schooner under ye Cape gave chase ye Race Point E ¼ of a mile
at 11 found the schooner gott away from us Cape Cod SSE 3 or 4 leagues. Scituate point West. The *Niger* and her convoy in sight

bearing W b S

PM light airs and cloudy Weathr at 4 Plymouth Light House SSW Cape Cod ESE dist. 6 leagues at 10 the Race Point NE b N dist 1/2 a mile at ll working into cape Cod Harbor at 2 anchored in Cap Cod harbor in 20 fm water muddy Bottom veered to 1/2 a cable found here his Majestys ship *Niger* and *Astor* Brigg the Red House in the bottom of the bay NW b W 1/2 W part of the Beach SW 3/4 of a mile at 9 AM weighed and came to sail as did his Majestys ship *Niger* and convoy at 10 parted company with the *Niger* 1/2 past saw a schooner under the Cape gave chase the Race Point E dist 1.4 mile at Noon fresh breezes and squally found the chase got away from us the *Niger* and convoy in sight

Dec. 31, 1775 Sunday E b N, S, var.

Cape Cod Race Point NE 4 miles

at 1 fresh breezes & squaly tacked

at 2 Saw a sail to windward shorten sail & clear reefed the top sails

at 3 make the signal fired a gun to come under our stern

at 4 Do. weathr the ship close up with us, made sail, the Race Point E b S 2 miles

at 5 working to windward between the Race Point & SW part of the Beach fired a gun and made the signal to prepare to anchor ½ part fired 2 guns a signal to anchor

at 6 anchored with the B. Br. In 25 fm water muddy bottom veered to a whole cable, the Race Point N b W ½ W 2 ½ miles the SW part of the Beach SE b E Dist. ¾ of a mile

at 12 Fresh gales & squaly with rain

at 4 More moderate with rain

at 6 Thick hazy weathr

At 8 Light airs & variable Drizling rain clear up a little saw nothing of the ships

at 9 weighed and came to sail

at 10 Race Point N 3 miles

at 12 Light airs & hazy Race point NE 3 or 4 miles in 29 fm muddy bottom

PM fresh breezes and squally at 1 Kd ? at 2 close reefs the Topsails at 4 the Race Point E b S 2 miles at 5 working to windward between the Race Point and SW part of the Beach fired a gun and made the signal to anchor at 6 anchored with the Br Br in 25 fm water muddy Bottom veered to a whole cable the Race Point N b W 2 1/2 miles the SW Part of the Beach SE b E dist off shore 3/4 of a mile at mid might fresh gales and squally with rain at 8 light airs and variable with drizling rain at 10 weigh and came to sail in 29 fm water muddy bottom

Jan. 1, 1776 Monday SSW, WNW, NNW

Truro Church ESE 1/2 E SW part of Beach W

The first part fresh breezes later a thick fogg middle & latter fresh gales & squaly with rain, sleet and snow PM at one bore away at 2 saw the SW part of the beach at 3 anchored in the Cape Codd harbor with the B.Br in 18 fm muddy bottom Veered to a whole cable. Truro Church ESE ½ E

AM struck lower yards & top gallant masts

PM fresh breezes with thick fogg the latter part fresh gales and squally with rain sleet and snow at 1 PM bore away at 2 saw the W Part of the Beach bearing ENE 1/4 a mile 1/2 part running in for the Harbor at 5 anchored in Cape Cod harbor with BB in 18 fm muddy veered to a whole cable struck the lower yards and Top Gallants

Jan. 2, 1776 Tuesday NW , Var

The first part fresh gales, with clear frost, middle gales, latter moderate and fine

AM at 6 up lower Yards & top gallant mast at 8 saw a sloop in the Bay at 11 weighed and came to sail At noon working to windward tacked occasionally by the SW part of the Beach & the Race Point in one bearing NW ½ N dist. Off the beach ½ a mile

Jan. 3, 1776 Wednesday SW, SSW, Var, SW

Moderate breezes & fine throughout PM at 4 ye Race point NE 4 miles, stand after the sloop att 8 fired 2 guns to bring her too at 9 spoke to her from Annapolis Royale bound to Boston, Scituate Point WSW 4 or 5 miles at 10 saw Boston light house standing in for it the sloop in company. AM at 1 anchored off the light house with the BB in 6 fm hard ground and veered to ½ a cable as did the sloop. At 4 his Majestys schooner *Halifax* passed by. The lighthouse NNW ½ W 3 miles

At 5 weighed & came to sail at 6 working up the harbor at 7 anchor with the B.Br in 54 fm water in Nantacket Road. Veered to ½ a cable. The house on Gorges Island NNE ½ E The SW part of Pottocks island S by W Long island head NW ½ N found riding here his Majestys ships *Renown*, *Niger*, *Scarborough*, *Mercury*, *Nautilus* Sloop, *Hinshionbrook* Schooner with several transports.

Jan 4, 1776 Thursday SW, var.

First & middle parts, light airs & fine weathr the lattr strong breezes with dark cloudy weathr PM Recd on board 2 long boat loads of water, people employd in Sundry jobs, about the rigging &c AM recd on board two long boat loads of water, people employd as above, came in and run up the harbour his Majesty's schooner *Halifax.*

Jan. 5, 1776 Friday varble

Moderate breezes & variable throughout, PM at 4 weighed & came to sail, at ½ past towing through between Georges Island and Gallops, at 6 running up Koings Road, east of Ron & past the castle, AM 8 anchored off Long wharf, with the Bt Br in 5 fms muddy bottom, veerd away & moord a cable each way, the Br to ye S, E and small to the w in 5 ½ d ground, Castle William SSE ye North Battery NNE Long Wharf, W ½ S distant 3 cables length found riding here his Majesty's ships *Preston*, Vice Admiral Graves Flag on board the *Chatham* with Rear Adm. Shouldham's Flagg on Board *Falcon* Sloop, *Adventure* store ship, & *Halifax* schooner.

Jan. 6, 1776 Saturday SW, var., NW

The first part fresh breezes, & clowdy, Middle moderate with rain, lattr strong gales & squally AM at 9 struck yds & top gallant mast.

Jan. 7, 1776 Sunday calm, varble, do.

The first part fresh gales & squaly, middle do. lattr light airs & variable.

AM at 11 unmoored and unmoord & hove short, on the Bt Br at noon weighed & employd wharping up the harbour.

Jan. 8, 1776 Monday varble

Light airs, & variable throughout, PM employed warping up the harbour, at 4 anchored with the BtBr anchor a little to the Southward of the No. Battery in 3 ½ fms muddy bottom, veerd to 1/3 of a cable, securd her by making two hawsers fast to the shore, AM at 10 veerd away on the small bower & hauled along side the wharf, at Noon employed securing her with hawser.

Jan. 9, 1776 Tuesday varble, S, WSW

The first part modt breezes, the middle fresh breezes, the lattr strong gales & variable, with rain, PM, the carpenters employed over hauling the ship & found her very bad, recd on board 453 fresh beef for the use of the ships company.

Jan. 10, 1776 Wednesday W, WNW, NW

Fresh breezes & varbl throughout, with sharp frost, PM carpenters employd repairing the boats, came on board Mr. John Reed carpenter in the room of Mr. Plucknett, appointd to another ship.

*Jan. 11, 1776 to Jan. 18, 1776

Jan. 19, 1776 Friday Werly

Fresh gales with strong frost Employed variously & deleverd 6 four pounders to the *Hope* brigg per order and 4 three pounders to the deposit ?, sailed hence his Majesty's sloop *Falcon*.

Narrative of Vice Admiral Samuel Graves

[Boston] 1776 Janry 5.

Lieutenant [Christopher] Mason, who now commanded the *Nautilus* by Order, received directions of the accustomed kind to proceed to Sea and cruize in Boston Bay and about Cape Anne and Marblehead; to be careful not to be blown of; in bad Weather to achor off Cat Island, in Cape Cod Harbour, Nautasket Road, or any other place he should think best, and put to Sea again as soon as Weather would permit, to sink, burn and destroy the rebels, assist and protect all Vessels coming to Boston, and see them safe within the Lighthouse: and to remain on this service till further Order.

The *Renown* was ordered to continue in Nantasket Road for the protection of every thing below, and in particular of George Island whereon was a Well of the best Water in the whole Harbour and form which all the ships in Nantasket were supplied. And the *Canseaux* armed Ship was ordered to be surveyed, her Captain having reported her unfit to keep at Sea.

Narrative of Vice Admiral Samuel Graves

[Boston, January] 18

His Majesty's Ship *Centurion* of 50 Guns, captain [Richard] Brathwaite, now arrived from England with a War Complement of 350 men. And the *Nautilus* went on a Cruize. Rear Admiral Shuldham wrote to the Admiral to desire Lieutt [Henry] Mowat whose Ship, the *Canceaux* had a Survey been reported unserviceable) might be left in America, as being well acquainted with the Coast, But, as the Lieutenant was very desirous of returning to England, having many years Accounts to settle, and the detaining him longer in America would be much to his own Prejudice; and his knowledge of the coast extended only from Boston Harbour Eastward to the River St Lawrence, and Mr Graves knew full well that Operations of his Majs Forces must be far to the Southward to be of Real Service: He acquainted the Rear Admiral therewith, and continued his Orders for the *Canceaux* to sail for England on Company with the *Preston*.

Disposition of the Fleet upon the Admirals [Graves] Quitting the Command of it on 27 Jan 1776

Name	Guns	Commanders	Complement	Station
Preston	50	Vice Adml Graves Capt John Robinson Rear Adml Shuldham	350	Before the Town In Boston
Chatham	50	Capt John Raynor	350	Before the Town in Boston
Renown	50	Banks	350	In Nantasket
Centurion	50	Brathwaite	350	Do
Lively	20	Bisshop	150	Before the Town in Boston
Nautilus	16	Llieutt. Mason	110	Cruizing in the Bay
Adventure Storeship	8	Hallum	40	Off Longwharf Boston
Canceaux A Ship	6*	Mowat	45	Do ordered to England
Halifax	6	Quarme	30	Cruizing in the Bay
Diligent	6	Dodd	30	New Vessels fitting out Boston
Tryal Adv. Boat	2	Browne	20	"
Dispatch Schr	6	Goodridge	30	"
Niger	32	Talbot	180	In Cape Cod harbour
Rose	20	Wallace	150	At New York - Rhode Island
Glasgow	20	Howe	150	"
Swan	16	Ayscough	110	"
Bolton Brig	6	Sneyd	30	"
Hope Brig	8	Dawson	30	Cruizing in the Bay
Phoenix	44	Parker	250	At New York
Asia	64	Vandeput	500	"
Viper	10	Saml Graves	80	On her Passage to New York
Liverpool	20	Bellew	130	Supposed to be at Virginia
Otter	16	Squire	100	At Virginia
Kingsfisher	16	Jas Montagu	100	"
Roebuck	44	Hammond	250	On her passage to Virginia
Raven	14	Stanhope	110	Do. Georgia
Cruizer	8	Parry	60	At N Carolina ordered to Bos.
Scoprion	14	Tollemache	100	On pass. To N. Carolina
Tamer	16	Thornborough	100	At N Carolina ordered to Bos.
Mercury	20	Graeme	130	With Maj. Genl Clinton south
Falcon	14	Linzee	110	On passage to Cape Fear
Scarborough	20	Barkley	150	On passage to Savannah Georg
Hinchinbrook Schr	6	Lt. Ellis	30	"
St Lawrence Schr	6	Jno Graves	30	At St Augustine
St John Schr	6	Wm Grant	36	Bahama Islands
Cerberus	28	C Symons	150	At Halifax
Savage	8	Bromedge	60	"
Senegal	14	Duddingstone	110	At Liverpool
Merlin	16	Burnaby	110	At Annapolis [Royal]
Lizard	20	Hamilton	150	At Quebec
Hunter	10	Mackenzie	80	"
Fowey	20	Geo. Montagu	150	Off Bakers Island nr. Salem

- This list is in error as period references state on two occasions that the number of guns was 21

[Northwest of] Long Island [Boston harbor]

Master's Log

The commander in chief representing Captain Mowat's Services and Usefulness on that coast, and at the same time to request from them, that he might therefore be returned to America without loss of time in a Ship fit to do Justice to his experience of the Station, - Collections and Proceedings of the Maine Hist. Soc., 2nd series

Jan. 20, 1776 Saturday Wterly
Do. weathr AM shifted to the other side of the wharf to make room for the *Lively*, caulkers employed as before, saild his Majesty's ship *Mercury*, with some transports.
Jan. 21, 1776 Sunday Soerly
Light wnds & clear strong frost, AM transporting the ship & placing her about her length from the wharf, AM our signal for a petty officer.
Jan. 22, 1776 Monday NW
Fresh winds, & cloudy, Middle part snow, latttr fair weathr, employd variously, caulkers employd.
Jan. 23, 1776 Tuesday Werly
Moderate and fair, caulkers as before.
Jan. 24, 1776 Wednesday do.
Light winds, with calms, caulkers as before, AM sent our boat to the assistance of a brigg drifting up.

*Jan. 25, 1776 to Jan 30, 1776

Jan. 31, 1776 Wednesday SW
Fresh winds, with snow middle rain, lattr light airs, and fair, AM transported the ship to Handcocks Wharf.
Feb. 1, 1776 Thursday do.
Light winds & hazey Moord with the small Br. off Handcocks Wharf, at 10 weighed & came to sail, at Noon came too, to the NW of Long Island in 6 fms The *Preston* & 6 merchant ships lying here.
Feb. 2, 1776 Friday Soerly
Fresh breezes and cloudy at 8 AM weighed and came to sail as did the Preston and the 3 merchants ships ½ past anchored in Nontasket Road where we found his Majesty's ship viz *Renown, Centaur* and *Hope* armed brigg with a number of transports at Noon the Admiral made the signal to weight do. weighed and came to sail left the above mentioned vessels in the Rhoad.
Feb. 3, 1776 Saturday NNW
At Noon saild from Nantaicolt Road Moderate & clear, weath the light house W b N 2 leagues little winds.
East Point of Cape Ann N about 4 leagues Boston Light House WSW 7 leagues.
Took my departure from Boston Light House in the latitude 42:19 N Longitude by computation 71:11 W from Greenwich Dark cloudy weathr with hard frost hove overboard condemned

provisions: bread, beef, pork, peas, butter, Keepd on board for the use of boatswain per order.
Squally, with snow
Thick snow with hard frost in companion with ye *Preston*, and three merchant ships.

Feb. 4, 1776 Sunday NNW
Fresh breezes with thick snow, & hard frost.
Do. weathr.
Cloudy with hard frost.
Do. weathr
Clear weathr
Sett steering sails parted company two ships bound to the West Indies.

Feb. 5, 1776 Monday W, N, W
Fresh breezes with thick snow
Fresh gales, & squally with snow Handed ye mizon top Sail in the first, & 2d reefs topsails.
Down top gallant with Yards & close reefd maintop sail
Do weath last sight of the *Preston* & merchant ships
Out 3d & 2d reefs Main top sail
Saw the merchant ships ahead 3 or 4 leagues
Fresh gales and squaly with ran.

Feb. 6, 1776 Tuesday NNW
Fresh gales, & squally with show, sett the mizen top sail.
Hand do top sail.
Lost sight of the *Preston* and merchant ship.
Do. weathr
Do weathr close reefd the main top sail
Do. weathr hard squalls close reefed the foretop sail
Our 3d reef top sails

Feb. 7, 1776 Wednesday WNW, var.
Thick fogg, and snow
Squally handed the top sails
Sett main top stay sail, and mizon

Feb. 8, 1776 Thursday NW, var, N
Fresh gales, and squally cloudy weathr
Sett the fore, & main top sails double reefd.
Do weathr
Squally with snow and hard frost
Fresh gales & cloudy weath with hard frost.

Feb. 9, 1776 Friday NW, varb, Wterly
Fresh breezes, & fine clear weathr, out 1st R topsails

½ past hove too & sound'd no gound at 75 fathoms, made sail in 1st reef top sails
Light airs with rain Out reef top sails & up top gallant yards
Fresh breezes and cloudy.

Feb. 10, 1776 Saturday NW, NNW
Cloudy, with rain
In the first reef top sails
Moderate and cloudy weathr
Thick snow
Cold raw squally weathr.

Feb. 11, 1776 Sunday varble, SE b S, SSW, S b E, WSW
Fresh breezes and cloudy weathr
Squally with rain
½ past down studding sail and driver
In the 1st reef top sails
Dark rainy weathr
Do weathr
Close reef the topsails
Out 3d reef top sails
Do weathr.

Feb. 12, 1776 Monday N b W,
Fresh gales, & cloudy weathr
Strong gales, & squally weathr
close reefd the top sails
Do. weathr
Hard squalls, with rain a great sea from the westward
Drizling rain
Dark cloudy weathr with drizling rain out ye 1st & 2nd reefs Mizon Topsail, and 3d reef the fore top sail.

Feb. 13, 1776 Tuesday
Fresh gales and cloudy weathr
Close reefd the top saills
Fresh gales squally with rain and hail
Strong gales and Do weathr
Do weathr with a great sea from the westward
gott down the mizzen sail and cross jack yard & top mast
Do. gales & flying clouds
Lattd Obs 46.22 N

Feb. 14, 1776 Wednesday W b N, varble, S b W, N b W
Fresh gales and cloudy weathr
Do. gales
Do. gales

More moderate
Dark cloudy weathr with a great sea
Hard squalls with rain handed the top sails and set the main sail
Hard squalls handed the main sail, under the fore sail
Sett the main top sail close reefd
Strong gales and hazey weathr.

Feb. 15, 1776 Thursday W, NNW, NW

Strong gales squally with a great sea from the westward
Lost a logg and three lines
Hard squalls
Handed the main top sail
Do Weathr
Do Weathr
Drizling rain
Sett the fore and main top sail
Squally with rain

Feb. 16, 1776 Friday W, NW, NW b W, NW

Hard gales & squally with rain sleet and snow
Squally with drizling rain
Hard squalls, with rain, lightening in the SE Quarter
Do weathr handed the fore top sail
Handed the main top sail
Sett the Main top sail
Hard gales and squaly with heavy showers

Feb. 17, 1776 Saturday N b W, N, N b W, W, SSE, SW, WSW

Strong gales and squally with rain and hail
Do weathr
Heavy rains
Thick squally weathr with rain, handed ye fore top sails
Sett the main sail Do weathr handed the main sail washd over board the head of the companion and logg board
Strong gales and thick weather.

Feb. 18. 1776 Sunday W b S, WNW

Fresh gales & hazey with rain
Handed the main top sail
Sett the fore top sail
Handed the top sails
Squally with rain
Hard squalls with rain handed ye M.T. sail under the fore sail
Do. gales
Very strong gales and squally
Do. gales with a very great sea

Feb. 19, 1776 Monday WNW, NW, WNW, W b N, W
Strong gales and squally weathr.
do weathr lowered down the mizon yard do. struck
Hard gales and squally with rain
Modt and cloudy weathr set the fore and M: T.G. out all reefs T.S.
Do weathr sway up the T.G. mt: a large swell from ye NW
found the bitts of the heel of the bowsprit block inward.
getting the jibb boom and sprit sail yard Carpenter employed
fixed the heel.
Latd by Obn 48.0 D No.
Feb. 20, 1776 Tuesday W b N, WSW, SW, W b N,
85 fm green sand
Fresh breezes and cloudy weath carpenters employed
securing the heel of the bowsprit.
2d reeft topsail
Fresh gales and drizling rain
Modt and fine weath
Out the reefs top sails
Up the main top gallant yd and set steering sails
got up the mizon top mast and yard
Modt and cloudy weath Employed bending the cables
Latd by obs 48. 55
Feb. 21, 1776 Wednesday SW, WSW
Fresh breezes and cloudy weathr 80 fm fine sand
Close reeft the top sails 70 fm
Fresh gales and thick hazey weathr 65 fm & 55 fm gray sand, 58 fm mud
Fresh weathr
Feb. 22, 1776 Thursday WSW, var., NNW, WSW
Fresh gales and hazey weathr out reefs top sails
Saw the land from the E b S to NE b N which proved to be the Lands End and about Monts bay
Bearing and dist. at Noon Portland N b E 4 leagues by the compass.
Feb. 23, 1776 Friday W b S, W
Strong gales and squally clewed up the top sail
Set the last reef top sails Point Peneral WNE
Do. gales saw the Isle of Wight
The Needle Point ENE ½ past 5 got in through the Needles at ½ past eight anchored in Canes Road.in 10 fm water
clear weather
Cloud : weath weighed and came to sail at 8 anchored at Speethead

where we found his Majesty's *Resolution* with the Red flag at the fore top sail head viz Admiral Doughlafo with a number more of his Majesty's ships of war.

Feb. 24, 1776 Saturday

Remarks at Speethead the *Canceaux*

Fresh gales and squally weathr AM struck yards and top masts, the Admiral made the signal for all boats received on board 249 lb fresh beef, moored ship with a cable each way 3 fm at low water githeeher NW Haspatalltown N b W struck yards and top masts.

*Feb. 25, 1776 to Mar. 8, 1776

Mar. 9. 1776 Saturday Soerly

Fresh gales and squally with rain came on board the Pilot to carry us into the harbour Employed in unmooring the ship.

Mar. 10, 1776 Sunday var.

Fresh gales and squally weathr at 1 PM take up small beer at 2 up same yards and topgallant yard and weighed and came to sail at 4 got into Portsmouth Harbor and a long side of the wharf AM fresh breezes and clear weathr: loosed sails to dry Employed unbending the sails struck yards and top masts

Mar. 11, 1776 Monday Noerly

Mod: fine clear weathr Employed in unrigging the top mast got a lighter along side to take the cables rigging and ye masts of the out ward bound man of war sailing to the westward.

Mar. 12, 1776 Tuesday Wterly

Mod. and fair weather Employd variously.

Mar. 13, 1776 Wednesday var.

Do weathr Employd clearing the ship for the dock.

Mar. 14, 1776 Thursday var.

Do weathr the latter parts modertly Employed variously

Mar. 15, 1776 Friday var.

Light winds and clear weathr Employd clearing the ship for ye dock.

Mar. 16, 1776 Saturday SW

Do var Empd getting out ballast 38 tons.

Mar. 17 1776 Sunday var

Slight winds and cloudy Employed clearing the ship

Mar. 18, 1776 Monday do

Do and clear AM hauled along side of the shear hulks got out bowsprit, got into dock.

Mar. 19, 1776 Tuesday Wterly

Mod and clear Employed stripping the lower mast.
Mar. 20, 1776 Wednesday Eterly
Do weathr 10 AM Frances Roake Seaman fell from the main mast head much hurt and sent to hospital Empld variously.
Mar. 21, 1776 Thursday do
Do weathr Employed variously
Mar. 22, 1776 Friday do
Do
Mar. 23, 1776 Saturday
Light winds and fair Employd variously hauled al. the shear hulk Recd fresh beef.
Mar. 24, 1776 Sunday
Do weathr later part cloudy Empd variously came in his majesty ship *Centaur* recd fresh beef.
Mar. 25, 1776 Monday
Fresh winds and hazey weathr rain AM lifted the mast head along side *Lanceston* and made fast.
Mar. 26, 1776 Tuesday
PM fresh do. and cloudy got for and main shrouds over head AM clear and employed variously.
Mar. 27, 1776 Wednesday
Do weathr the latter part fair PM Delvered iron hoops 32 doz 11 do staves butts, 8 punchons nine Hhds 40 gal casks five barrels 13 bread 6 punchans of beer
Mar. 28, 1776 Thursday
Do weathr Employd variously AM turning in dead eyes in shrouds.
Mar. 29, 1776 Friday
Do weathr employed variously AM recd one firken of butter and one bagg of bread
Mar. 30, 1776 Saturday
Employed about the rigging &c AM recd 14 fresh beef.
Mar. 31, 1776 Sunday
Fresh winds and cloudy Employed as before AM recd 410 bags bread.
April 1, 1776 Monday do
Light do and fair Employd as above.
April 2, 1776 Tuesday
Do weathr employed do,
April 3, 1776 Wednesday
Do weathr employed getting the top sail yards across
April 4, 1776 Thursday
Fresh wind and cloudy employed getting in the ground tier and

stowing the hold.
April 5, 1776 Friday
Light breezes and clear Employed getting ballast for the ground floor and moving it.
April 6, 1776 Saturday
Light breezes and cloudy Empd serving the mast head and yards Recd fresh beef and sundry other provisions viz bread 358 lbs, Rum 4169 gallons beef 874 pices Pork 1234 pieces suet 102 lbs pease 24 bushels 4 gallon oatmeal 56 bushels 5 gallon vinegar 67 gallon flour, butter 4 firkins 348 & 522 lbs oyle 58 gallons.
April 7, 1776 Sunday
light breezes and hazey weathr employed variously
April 8, 1776 Monday
PM modt and hazey AM fresh breezes Empd about ye rigging
April 9, 1776 Tuesday
PM fresh breezes and squally AM more modt and clear empd storeing the hoald recd on board 16 guns.
April 10, 1776 Wednesday
Mod gales and fair weathr Employd about the rigging
April 11, 1776 Thursday
Mod and clear latter part cloudy Empd do and taking in water and stowing it away.
April 12, 1776 Friday
Do weather employed getting on board and lashing the booms
April 13, 1776 Saturday
Mod and clear employed in getting on board carpenters and boatswains stores and stowing them away.
April 14, 1776 Sunday
Mod and cloudy employed in bending sails
April 15, 1776 Monday
PM cloudy set sails latter part misty AM getting in our guns.
April 16, 1776 Tuesday
Mod and cloudy PM transported to single moorings AM misty with rain Commisioner paying the ships company.
April 17, 1776 Wednesday
PM fresh winds and misty later part cloudy Empd variously
April 18, 1776 Thursday
PM light winds and cloudy middle part misty with rain at 8 AM made a signal for going out of the harbour
April 19, 1776 Friday
PM fresh winds and cloudy moord ship gelkecher N b W ½ W

South Sea Castle E b N
April 20, 1776 Saturday
Mod and fair Employed variously AM light winds and clear
April 21, 1776 Sunday
Do employed working up junk AM load sails to dry Recd one man from the *Resolution* set sail Recd 8 men fro m the ?
April 22, 1776 Monday
Do weathr Employed variously AM cleaned hawse
April 23, 1776 Tuesday Noerly
Paid Bounty
AM loosed T.G. and moored inclining to calm at Noon weighed and turning to windward.

END OF VOYAGE OF *CANCEAUX*

Bibliography

Albion, R.G. Forests and Sea Power (Cambridge, Mass. 1926)

Malone, J.J. Pine Trees and Politics (London, 1964)

Rowe, W.H. The Maritime History of Maine (New York, 1948)

Barry, W.D. Tate House Crown of the Maine Mast Trade (Portland, Me, 1982)

Manning, S.F. New England Masts and the Kings Broad Arrow (Kennebunk, Me. 1979)

Lever, Darcy The Young Sea Officers Sheet Anchor (London, 1819)

Lower, A.R. G reat Britian's Woodyard (Montreal, 1973)

Coggins, J. Ships and Seamen of the American Revolution (Harrisburg, PA. 1969)

Yerxa, D.A. The Burning of Falmouth, 1775 A Case Study in British Imperial Pacification (Portland, Me. 1975)

Evans, G.N.D.Uncommon Obdurate: The several Public Careers of J.F.W. DesBarres (Toronto, 1969)

Leamon, J.S. Revolution Downeast (Amherst, Mass. 1993)

Williamson, W. D. The History of the State of Maine (Howell, Me. 1832)

Clark, W.M. Naval Documents of the American Revolution Vols I, II, III (Washington, D.C. 1964)

Chapelle, H. The History of American Sailing Ships (Washington, D.C. 1935)

Chapelle, H The History of the American Sailing Navy (Washington, D.C. 1949)

Millar, J. F. American Ships of the Colonial & Revolutionary Periods (New York, 1978)

Longridge, C.N. The Anatomy of NELSON'S SHIPS (London, 1955)

Stevens, Henry N. Catalogue of the Henry Newton Stevens collection of the Atlantic Neptune, together with a concise biographical description of every chart, view and leaf of text contined therein, as also of certain other states observed elsewhere. (London, 1937)

Des Barres, Joseph F. W. The Atlantic Neptune; published for the use of the Royal Navy of Great Britain, by Joseph F.W. Des Barre, under the directions of the Right Honble, the Lords Commissioners of the Admiralty, London, 1780. (London, 1780)

J.J. Colledge, "Ships of the Royal Navy: An Historical Index" (New York: Augustus M. Kelly, 1969), 1:105
Grace S. Machemer, "Headquartered at Piscataqual: Samuel Holland's Coastal and Inland Surveys 1770-1774" Historical New Hampshire Volume 57, Nos. 1&2
http://members.shaw.ca/caren.secord/location/NewBrunswick/Gl impses/XCIX.html
http://mercator.cogs.nscc.ns.ca/9-27958-o.html
http://www/bluepete.com/Hist/BiosNS/1800-67/DesBarres.htm
http://collections,ic.gc/westpei/samuelholland.htm
http://mercator.cogs.nscc.ns.ca/neptune.html

ABOUT THE AUTHOR

ANDREW J. WAHLL, a native of Columbus, Ohio, graduated from Ohio State University with a BS and MA in Geography. Although a geographer/cartographer by profession his main interest is history. Mr. Wahll recently retired from the National Geographic Society where he worked for 25 years. While at NGS he was a major contributor to the first historical atlas of North America and latter to the *Making of America,* a 17 supplement map series covering all regions of North America, which was a highlight in his career. Due to his interest in history he has written *Braddock Road Chronicles 1755* in 1999, *Sabino Popham Colony Reader 1602-2000* in 2000. Andrew J. Wahll lives in Derwood, MD with his wife Maruja, a multi-media artist who has illustrates his works.

www.ingramcontent.com/pod-product-compliance
Lightning Source LLC
LaVergne TN
LVHW020520100826
845148LV00010B/1300
9780788423499